THE NEW NATURAL

A SURVEY OF BRITISH NAT

THE ISLES OF SCILLY

THE NEW NATURALIST LIBRARY

THE ISLES
OF SCILLY

ROSEMARY PARSLOW

Collins

This edition published in 2007 by Collins,
an imprint of HarperCollins Publishers

HarperCollins Publishers
77–85 Fulham Palace Road
London w6 8jb
www.collins.co.uk

First published 2007

A cip catalogue record for this book is available
from the British Library.

Lines from *The West Wind* reproduced with kind
permission from The Society of Authors as the Literary
Representative of the Estate of John Masefield

Set in ff Nexus by
Rowland Phototypesetting Ltd
Bury St Edmunds, Suffolk

Printed in China by Imago
Reprographics by Saxon Photolitho, Norwich

Hardback
isbn-13 978-0-00-220150-6
isbn-10 0-00-220150-X

Paperback
isbn-13 978-0-00-220151-3
isbn-10 0-00-220151-8

Contents

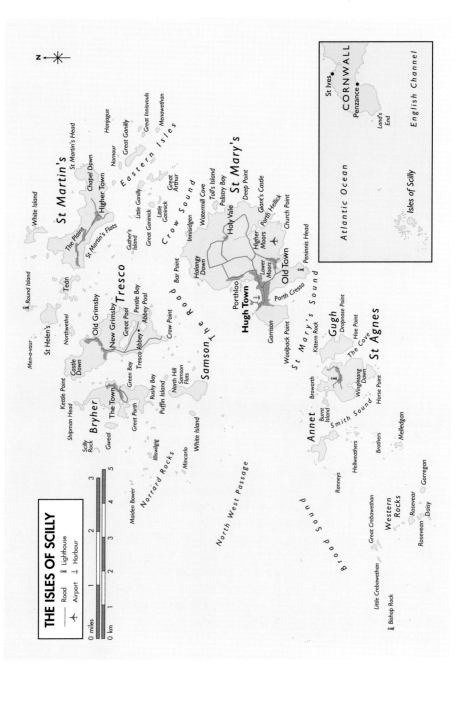

THE ISLES OF SCILLY

— Road   ☒ Lighthouse
✈ Airport   ⚓ Harbour

0 miles 1 2 3

0 km 1 2 3 4 5

☒ Bishop Rock

Little Crebawethan

Great Crebawethan

Western Rocks

Rosevear

Rosevean

Daisy

Garregan

Melledgan

Ranneys

Hellweathers

Brothers

Burnt Island

Annet

Broward

Smith Sound

Horse Point

Wingletang Down

The Cove

St Agnes

Gugh

Kitterm Rock

Hoe Point

Dropnose Point

Periglis

St Mary's Sound

Woolpack Point

Garrison

Porth Cressa

Porthloo

Hugh Town

Old Town

Peninnis Head

Church Point

Porth Hellick

Giant's Castle

Lower Moors

Higher Moors

Holy Vale

St Mary's

Deep Point

Pelistry Bay

Toll's Island

Watermill Cove

Innisidgen

Halangy Down

Bar Point

Crow Point

Abbey Pool

Tresco Abbey

Pentle Bay

Great Pool

New Grimsby

Old Grimsby

Tresco

North Hill

Samson Flats

White Island

Puffin Island

Rushy Bay

Great Porth

Gweal

The Town

Bryher

Green Bay

Kettle Point

Shipman Head

Castle Down

St Helen's

Northwethel

Teän

Men-a-vaur

Round Island

White Island

St Martin's

The Plains

St Martin's Flats

Chapel Down

Higher Town

St Martin's Head

Narrour

Great Ganilly

Great Innisvouls

Menawethan

Hanjague

Eastern Isles

Little Ganilly

Great Ganinick

Little Ganinick

Guther's Island

Great Arthur

Crow Sound

St Mary's Road

Samson

Norrard Rocks

Illiswilgig

Mincarlo

Maiden Bower

Scilly Rock

North West Passage

Broad Sound

Inset map:

Atlantic Ocean

CORNWALL

St Ives

Penzance

Land's End

English Channel

Isles of Scilly

N

Editors' Preface

EARLIER VOLUMES OF the New Naturalist library have concerned the natural history of the islands of northern Britain – the Highlands and Islands (1964), Shetland (1980), Orkney (1985) and the Hebrides (1990). Here, in the Isles of Scilly, a group of islands at the extreme southwest of Britain presents a totally different aspect of island natural history.

Any account of the natural history of the Isles of Scilly has to comprehend an unusually wide variety of life and environments. In this striking archipelago of inhabited and uninhabited islands, southwest of Land's End and on the fringes of the Atlantic, marine and terrestrial natural history are intimately connected. The oceanic climate, with mild summers and winters and stormy weather, exerts a strong influence, resulting in a flora and fauna unique in Britain. Added to this is the effect of thousands of years of human occupation, governed by changing economic conditions and isolation from the mainland, a history which has produced, for example, an extraordinary mix of native, introduced and cultivated plants.

The author, Rosemary Parslow, has an unrivalled knowledge of the natural history of the Isles of Scilly, gained over nearly fifty years of active involvement in observation and survey. Her studies have included the marine life and the life of terrestrial environments, including both fauna and flora. With such a range of practical experience, she is in an excellent position to give a synthesis which covers the variety of natural history of the islands, as well as issues of conservation and future development. Such a synthesis will be welcomed by Scillonians and by the many visitors to the islands, as well as by those with wider interests in the British fauna and flora.

Author's Foreword and Acknowledgements

HOWEVER OFTEN YOU go to Scilly it is still a magical experience as the islands slowly emerge out of the line of clouds on the horizon, to resolve into a mass of shapes and colours against the sea and sky. Whether you go there by boat, stealing up gradually on the islands, or by air, flying in low over the coastline of St Mary's to land with a rush on the small airfield – like one of the plovers that feed there on the short turf – it brings a thrill of excitement every time.

I first went to Scilly in 1958, to stay at the St Agnes Bird Observatory that had started up the previous year. It was an 'un-manned' observatory, run by a committee of enthusiastics, organising self-catering holidays for groups of bird-ringers to operate it as a ringing station over the spring and autumn migrations. The first year had been based in tents at Lower Town Farm, but by the time of my visit they were renting the empty farmhouse. Like many similar establishments they ran on a small budget and lots of commitment; the living conditions were very basic, but the surroundings idyllic. That first visit was the start of a lifetime love affair with Scilly, which has influenced my whole adult life and has led to writing this account of the natural history of the islands.

Those early visits were made when I was working as a very junior scientific assistant at the British Museum (Natural History) in South Kensington. At that time collecting specimens was still an important element of the work, in order to build up the Museum's taxonomic collections. So staff holidays often became unpaid collecting trips, and mine were frequently timed to go to Scilly at the best times for 'shore collecting', to collect marine invertebrates. These were when the equinoctial spring tides occur, around Easter and again in autumn, when the most extensive areas of shore are exposed. This was in the days before cheap wet suits and underwater photography meant that marine biologists were no longer constrained by tides. At that time it was boulder-turning and wading and following the tide down to the lowest level accessible, laden with heavy collecting gear. Most of the collecting I did was to order: specific groups of animals were targeted because these were ones where information on their distribution and status was needed, as well as adding representative specimens to the Museum collections. This resulted in a series of Isles of Scilly collections in the 1960s and '70s, mostly shore fishes, sponges, worms, and other invertebrates, especially echinoderms, my specialist group.

Even after I had left the Museum, a colleague would send a small milk churn packed with collecting paraphernalia to the island of St Agnes to await my arrival for the family holiday, and then we would return it with the carefully preserved and labelled specimens packed inside. This system usually worked very well, but in the early days there were some hiccups – like the time the churn was nearly dispatched to Sicily due to a misunderstanding with the carriers, or the year it was put back on the launch by a puzzled islander because he did not know anyone who used milk churns on the island!

This first-hand experience – firstly the shore collecting, then the species records when collecting specimens became unfashionable, my involvement with the bird observatory, and then starting listing plants – was fortuitous in that it gave me a unique opportunity to study, photograph and get to appreciate the wildlife, scenery and history of these enchanting islands. I have been fortunate in that I was also to spend many weeks over the succeeding years on Scilly, usually based on St Agnes, and later St Mary's.

Since those early days I have visited the islands at least once every year (except for a break of a couple of years in the late 1960s), have had several prolonged stays, and have been there in every month of the year and probably most kinds of weather. This has probably been the best way of getting to know as much as possible about the islands without being resident there. At various times I have been employed to survey and produce reports on a number of subjects from bats to plants. In 2002 I was commissioned to write a Management Plan for the land leased by the Isles of Scilly Wildlife Trust. This gave me a further opportunity to spend a longer time on the islands, getting to know them, their habitats and the people whose job it is to manage those habitats (Parslow, 2002).

Due to the climate and the geographical position of the islands there are some species, particularly plants, which are not usually easy for the holiday visitor to see. Certainly if you want to see some of the plants which flower in the middle of winter, such as some of the introduced aliens, German ivy *Delairea odorata* and some of the *Aeoniums*, then a visit at Christmas or New Year is essential. This is also a good time to find the tiny least adder's-tongue fern *Ophioglossum lusitanicum*, a great rarity found in Britain only on the Channel Isles and on St Agnes in Scilly. Every month has its specialities, so there is always something to look out for at any time of the year. If your interests are more ornithological then everyone will recommend the spring and autumn migrations for the 'falls' of unusual migrants. In summer there are breeding seabirds, and a boat trip can take you out to see puffins, shags, guillemots, fulmars and other seabirds among the uninhabited islands – and there are also grey seals hauled out among the distant rocks. Even in winter there are peregrine and raven to look out for, and sometimes in cold weather large numbers of woodcock seem to fall out of the sky. For the other natural history groups, lichens, insects, fish or seaweeds, there are nearly always things to do and things to see!

It is not possible to write about the flora and fauna of the Isles of Scilly without considering all the other aspects that go to make them so unique. Their geography, geology and climate are intimately bound up with the history of the people of the islands, the way they have used the land, and present-day management. Over the next few chapters we will consider many of these aspects of the islands, as well as the major habitats found in Scilly – the heathlands, coastland, cultivated fields and wetlands. Each of the islands has its own unique character and special plants and animals – from St Mary's and the inhabited smaller 'off-islands' to those uninhabited islands and rocks which are home to the rest of the islands' wildlife. Then there are those people who have been important in the study of the island flora and fauna, the story of the rise in popularity of the islands for birdwatchers, the effect climate has had in shaping the flora and the escapes from cultivation which have now become established as part of the landscape. The sum of all these is what makes up the fabric of these unique and beautiful islands, the Isles of Scilly.

ACKNOWLEDGEMENTS

Compiling this book has taken a long time; it represents several decades of involvement with the Isles of Scilly, and it would never have been written without the help and encouragement of many people. There are too many individuals to mention everyone, but I hope that they will understand that I am hugely grateful to them all. The real generosity of those naturalists who allowed me free access to their work and who commented on sections of the text has made it possible for me to include many aspects of flora and fauna about which I know very little.

The artwork in this book has been selected from a huge volume of material I have been offered; unfortunately I could only use a small selection. Many of the photographers and artists also helped in other ways, with information and comments. For permission to use their material I would like to acknowledge Andrew Cooper, Paul Gainey, Sandra Gibson & Frank Gibson (Gibson Collection), Martin Goodey, Richard Green, Mark Groves, Alma Hathway, Ren Hathway, David Holyoak, Chris Hopkin, David Mawer, Paul Sterry, Bryan Thomas, Ian Wallace, the Isles of Scilly Museum (for Hilda Quick woodcuts) and the Cornwall Archaeological Unit and Jeanette Ratcliffe. I consulted libraries at the Cornish Studies Library, Redruth, the Natural History Museum, London, and English Nature (now Natural England), Truro.

I am very grateful to the many people in the Isles of Scilly who have helped in so many ways, although space does not allow me to mention them all. In particular I thank Martin Goodey, Anne and Mike Gurr, Ren Hathway and Jo Wrigley, Wendy Hick, Francis and Carol Hicks, Johann Hicks, Lesley and David Knight, Jim Liddon, Julie Love, Amanda Martin (IoS Museum), Cyril Nicholas, Steve and Julia Ottery (and the Museum Flower Ladies), Adrian and Mandy Pearce, Penny Rodgers.

Specific help and comments on individual chapters and topics were generously given by Jon Akeroyd, J. F. Archibald, Ian Bennallick, Sarnia Butcher, Adrian Colston, Bryan Edwards, Bob Emmett, Chris Haes, Steve Hopkin, Julia MacKenzie, Rosalind Murphy, John Ounstead, Helen Parslow, John Parslow, Mark Phillips, Peter Robinson, Katherine Sawyer, Sylva Swaby, Andrew Tompsett, Stella Turk, Steve Westcott and Will Wagstaff. Keith Hyatt not only read all the first draft text but found lots of useful snippets of information as only he can; Ian Beavis freely allowed use of all his material on Aculeate Hymenoptera and other groups; Jeremy Clitherow and Alison Forrester (English Nature) gave me access to many unpublished reports and other scientific information; David Mawer (IoSWT) has been a constant source of information on all aspects of natural history in the islands. The *Isles of Scilly Bird & Natural History Review* published by the ISBG has also been a rich source of recent information.

I must also acknowledge the team at HarperCollins, especially Richard West, who read the first draft, Helen Brocklehurst and Julia Koppitz, and above all Hugh Brazier, for many improvements to the text.

To my son Jonathan (Martin) Parslow and daughters Annette and Helen, who shared the early visits to Scilly and still love Scilly as much as I do, I dedicate this book.

CHAPTER 1

An Introduction

It's a warm wind, the west wind, full of birds' cries;
I never hear the west wind but tears are in my eyes.
For it comes from the west lands, the old brown hills,
And April's in the west wind, and daffodils.

John Masefield, *The West Wind*

ALTHOUGH MASEFIELD probably did not have the Isles of Scilly in mind when he wrote those lines, they often remind me of the islands. In the early days of the year the low hills are brown with dead bracken stems and heather and there are daffodils and narcissus everywhere (Fig. 1). Seabirds wheel and call and often the climate is quite mild and balmy.

The rocks and islands that form the Isles of Scilly are located about 45 kilometres (28 miles) southwest of Land's End. Mysterious, romantic and beautiful, they have long exercised the imagination of storytellers and historians, and legends abound that the Isles were once the lost islands of Lyonnesse or the undersea land of Atlantis. Or they may have been the islands known to the Greeks and Romans as the Cassiterides, the Tin islands, although there is little evidence of there having ever been any significant tin-mining on the islands.

The hills in Scilly are not high: most are under 45 metres, and the highest point is near Telegraph on St Mary's, 49 metres above chart datum. The Isles of Scilly archipelago forms a roughly oval-shaped ring of islands in shallow seas of fewer than 13 metres in depth, except for the deep channels of St Mary's Sound between St Agnes and St Mary's, Smith Sound between St Agnes and Annet, and the deep waters towards the Western Rocks. Among the main group of islands are extensive sand flats the sea barely covers, with less than three

FIG 1. February on St Agnes, with daffodils flowering among the dead bracken. (Rosemary Parslow)

metres depth of water over much of the area at high tide, and with wide sand spits and shallows. At low water St Martin's may be inaccessible by launch.

When you fly into the islands you first see the low-lying islands of the Eastern Isles looking green and brown with vegetated patches and rock (Fig. 2). Often the sand spits in the turquoise sea over the sand flats are revealed before you descend over the neat fields and cultivated land of St Mary's to land on the airfield (Fig. 3). From the air the huge number of tiny islands and the many reefs and rocks under the water show how easily so many hundreds of ships have been wrecked in Scilly over the centuries (over 621 known wrecks have been recorded) (Larn & Larn, 1995). Even today, with depth gauges, GPS and radar, as well as more accurate charts, ships and other craft still get into trouble among the islands every year.

The inscription on an eighteenth-century map based on Captain Greenville Collins' *Great Britain's Coasting Pilot* survey (Fig. 4) refers to one of the most notorious Scilly shipwrecks, in addition to several other features of the islands:

The Iſands of Scilly are very fruitfull abounding in Corn & Pasture, here are plenty of Conies, Crains, Swans, Herons, Ducks, & other Wild Fowl, theſe Islands were Conquer'd by Athelstana Saxon King, & have ever since been Counted part of

FIG 2. The Eastern Isles: the view from Great Arthur towards Little Ganilly and St Martin's. (Rosemary Parslow)

FIG 3. A patchwork of bulb fields, St Mary's, February 2004. (Rosemary Parslow)

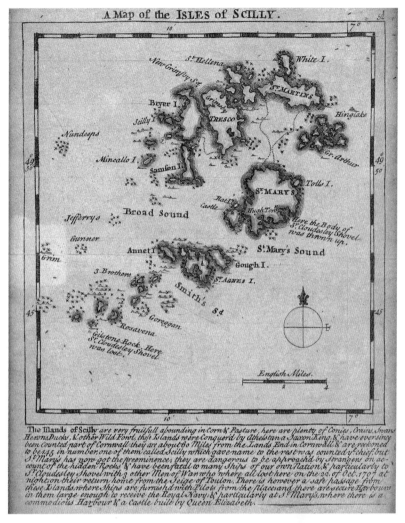

FIG 4. Eighteenth-century map of the Isles of Scilly, probably based on the *Great Britain's Coasting Pilot* survey by Captain Greenville Collins, first published in 1693.

Cornwall: they are about 60 miles from the Lands End in Cornwall & are reckoned to be 145 in number; one of them called Scilly which gave name to the rest was counted ye chief, but St Mary's has now got the preeminence; they are dangerous to be approach'd by strangers on account of the hidden Rocks & have been fatal to many Ships of our own Nation, & particularly to Sr. Cloudsley Shovel with 3 other Men of War who where

all lost here on the 22. of Oct. 1707 at night, on their return home from the Siege of
Toulon. There is however a safe passage from these Islands, where Ships are furnish'd
with Pilots from the Place; and there are secure Harbours in them large enough to
receive the Royal Navy: & particularly at St Mary's, where there is a commodious
Harbour & a Castle built by Queen Elizabeth.

Although there is an island called Scilly Rock off the west coast of Bryher that
is reputed to have given its name to the group, this is probably not so. In the
Middle Ages the name for all the islands was variously Sullia or Sullya, becoming
Silli later. The current spelling as 'Scilly' is a more recent form to prevent
confusion with the word 'silly' (Thomas, 1985). The islands are usually referred
to as the Isles of Scilly or Scilly, never the Scilly Isles!

There are five islands that are now inhabited, plus some forty or so uninhabited (by people, that is – rather arrogantly we ignore the other inhabitants)
and large enough to have vegetation on them, and then a further 150 or so rocks
and islets. The figure cannot be definite as every stage of the tide changes one's
perspective as land is alternately exposed and hidden by the sea. From the
isolated Bishop Rock with its tall lighthouse in the southwest of the group (Fig. 5)
to Hanjague, east of the Eastern Isles, is 17.5 kilometres, and the archipelago

FIG 5. The Western Rocks and the Bishop Rock, the westernmost point of the Isles of
Scilly, with resident grey seals. (David Mawer)

extends some 13km from north to south. The islands have a total land area of about 1,641 hectares or 16km², more of course at low tide when more land is uncovered (Table 1). Situated on latitude 49° 56′ N and longitude 6° 18′ W, the islands are on the same latitude as Newfoundland, but the climate under the warming influence of the Gulf Stream is very different. Although the islands are part of Watsonian vice-county 1 (West Cornwall) for recording purposes, they are often treated as vice-county 1b for convenience. All the islands fall within four 10km grid squares, with most of the land being contained within just three, the fourth square being mostly water.

TABLE 1. The Isles of Scilly: areas of the principal islands. Areas are all in hectares at MHWS. (Figures from Isles of Scilly Wildlife Trust)

ISLAND	AREA (HA)	ISLAND	AREA (HA)
St Mary's	649.29	Nornour	1.64
Toll's Island	2.88	Menawethan	2.81
Newford Island	0.85	Great Innisvouls	1.82
Taylor's Island	0.49	Little Innisvouls	0.98
St Mary's total	**653.52**	Ragged Island	0.97
		Great Ganinick	1.82
St Martin's	223.05	Little Ganinick	1.15
White Island	15.25	Guther's	0.47
St Martin's total	**238.30**	Hanjague	0.30
Tresco	**297.66**	**St Helen's group**	
		Teän	16.13
St Agnes	106.29	Round Island	4.09
Gugh	37.34	St Helen's	18.85
Burnt Island	1.09	Men-a-vaur	0.55
St Agnes total	**144.72**	Northwethel	4.63
		Foreman's Island	0.37
Bryher	129.32		
Shipman Head	4.61	**Samson group**	
Bryher total	**133.93**	Samson	36.33
		White Island	1.30
		Puffin Island	0.75
Eastern Isles		Green Island	0.05
Great Ganilly	13.83		
Little Ganilly	2.71		
Great, Middle & Little Arthur	7.75	**Annet**	22.40

TABLE 1. – *cont.*

ISLAND	AREA (HA)	ISLAND	AREA (HA)
Western Rocks		**Norrard Rocks**	
Melledgan	0.96	Mincarlo	1.82
Little Crebawethan	0.14	Illiswilgig	0.90
Great Crebawethan	0.51	Seal Rock	0.20
Rosevear	2.17	Castle Bryher	0.39
Rosevean	0.63	Scilly Rock	1.98
Daisy	0.57	Maiden Bower	0.66
Gorregan	1.57	Gweal	5.82

Isles of Scilly total area at MHWS = 1,641ha

Total area at LAT (lowest astronomical tide) = 3,065ha

Number of islands (includes rocks and stacks) of any size at MHWS = 818

Number of islands at MLWS = 3,825

Number > 0.03 ha at MHWS = 203

Number > 0.09ha (so possibly with some vegetation) = 101

CLIMATE

The climate of the Isles of Scilly is characterised as oceanic, with mild wet winters, mild sunny summers, frequent strong winds and gales, and also sea fogs. A major influence on the climate is the North Atlantic Drift, an arm of the Gulf Stream. Compared with the Cornish mainland Scilly has milder winters (February mean 7.3°C) and cooler summers. The average monthly mean temperature is 11.7°C (National Meteorological Library). With most days in the year having a temperature usually above 5°C, many plants can grow in Scilly that cannot survive on the mainland. This also includes winter annuals that grow throughout winter and flower very early in spring. As many plants on the islands are frost-sensitive the occasional bad winter can cause a considerable amount of damage. Fortunately snow and frost are much less frequent than on the adjacent mainland. Snowfalls are relatively infrequent; frosts are occasional and usually neither very hard nor long-lasting.

The rare occasions when there have been more severe frosts have had a devastating effect on the vegetation, especially the 'exotic' plants. Winter 1987/8 was one such occasion, with almost all the evergreen *Pittosporum* hedges being either killed outright or cut to the ground. Hottentot fig *Carpobrotus edulis* is one species that can be susceptible to both frost and salt water, but as the stands are usually dense there is nearly always a piece of the plant protected enough to survive and grow again. Rainfall is low compared with Cornwall, 825mm per year on average; some of the rain clouds appear to pass over the low islands without precipitation. The islands are prone to sea fogs and this increases the general humidity, which is reflected in the rich lichen flora – also an indicator of the clean air and lack of industrial pollutants.

As the former Duchy Land Steward wrote, 'the weather in Scilly is character-istically unpredictable' (Pontin, 1999). Gales and strong winds over force 8 are a frequent feature, and not just in winter: gales can happen throughout the year. Visitors can sometimes find themselves marooned on the island they are staying on for several days when the boats stop plying due to rough seas. Some of us have considered this a bonus at times!

THE SCILLONIANS

The Isles of Scilly have had almost 4,000 years of continuous occupation since the arrival of Bronze Age farmers (Thomas, 1985), but for centuries before that nomadic people who left little sign of their presence other than a few flints had visited the islands. The population has fluctuated and there have been many incomers over the centuries. Not many of the current families can trace their ancestors back more than a few hundred years, usually to the 1640s or 1650s (court records show the Trezise family was in the islands in the thirteenth century). Some are probably descendants of soldiers who came to man the Garrison and married local women. The inhabitants of St Agnes used to be known as Turks as they tended to be short and swarthy and were reputed to have had an exotic ancestry. As on other British islands such as Orkney (Berry, 1985) there has been a continuous stream of people, including Neolithic visitors, Bronze Age and Iron Age inhabitants, pirates, smugglers, Cromwellian soldiers, Royalists, French traders, British servicemen in both World Wars, land-girls, and men and women who came to staff hotels and other establishments. Many of these peoples stayed, married locals, and their descendants have added to the rich mix of heritage in the population.

Population

The resident population of the islands has stayed at around 2,000 for many years. Of these about 1,600 live on St Mary's, with about 160 on Tresco and 100 on each of the other inhabited islands (St Martin's, Bryher and St Agnes). During the summer holiday season visitors approximately double the population.

The Duchy of Cornwall

The Isles of Scilly became part of the original Duchy of Cornwall in 1337 when Edward, the Black Prince, became the first Duke of Cornwall. Today the islands are still owned by the Duchy, administered by a resident Land Steward. The Duchy is governed by a Council, of which His Royal Highness the Prince of Wales and Duke of Cornwall is Chairman. Much of the land on the inhabited islands is in agricultural tenancies, with the exception of the island of Tresco, which is leased to the Dorrien-Smith family, and Hugh Town, which became freehold in 1949 (Mumford, 1987). In 1999 there were some sixty farm-holdings, covering 557 hectares, of which 182 are in horticultural use, mostly bulbs. The average farm on the smaller islands of Bryher, St Agnes and St Martin's is very small, sometimes less than 10 ha, although those on St Mary's and Tresco are proportionally larger. Many fields are equally small, some less than 0.1ha (Pontin, 1999). Some 1,845 hectares of the unfarmed land are now leased to the Isles of Scilly Wildlife Trust, mostly heath, wetland and coast on the inhabited islands and including all the uninhabited rocks and islands.

The Council of the Isles of Scilly

The Council of the Isles of Scilly is a unitary authority (Local Government Act 1972, as applied by the Isles of Scilly Order 1978). This means the Council has unusual powers in that it has all the functions of county, district and parish councils as well as replacing the Environment Agency and the airport authorities in the islands. The islands are not automatically included in all national legislation. There are sometimes specific references or amendments to ensure that legislation also refers to the islands.

TRAVELLING TO THE ISLES OF SCILLY

These days getting to Scilly is no longer the difficult and chancy business it was in the past, and we can easily forget that for earlier visitors the journey was frequently an ordeal. Passengers could arrange to go by sailing ship to the islands, but it was not until the start of the regular mail boat after 1827 that there was an organised service from Penzance to St Mary's. Even so the passage usually took eight to nine hours and at times as much as two days. Things picked up when a steamer service started about 1858, and a year later the railway was extended to Penzance. Then in 1937 the air service started linking Scilly with the mainland, offering an alternative and much quicker route for those reluctant to brave the sea crossing.

The RMV *Scillonian* (Fig. 6) is the third of that name to have carried freight and passengers between Scilly and the Cornish mainland. She sails most days (except Sunday) between spring and autumn, the crossing taking about two and a half hours according to conditions. The *Scillonian* is notorious for her rolling motion, which is due to her shallow draft, designed to enable her to enter the shallow waters around the islands; but the possibility of seeing unusual seabirds, cetaceans and other excitements during the passage makes her popular with many visitors. The alternative routes to Scilly are by air, either fixed-wing plane or helicopter, both of which take about twenty minutes; but neither flies if there is fog. Flying is the only route in winter when the *Scillonian* is laid up. A second ship, the MV *Gry Maritha*, now transports most freight to the islands. Inter-island launches meet the ships in St Mary's and transfer goods of all kinds to the 'off-islands', as the other four inhabited islands are known locally.

FIG 6. The RMV *Scillonian* in harbour after her two-and-a-half-hour sail from Penzance. July 2006. (Rosemary Parslow)

Tourism

It was not until after World War II that Scilly became really popular as a holiday destination, with hotels and guesthouses opening up to accommodate many more visitors, including many naturalists. In 2003 Scilly attracted 122,000 visitors (Isles of Scilly Tourist Information). Tourism now accounts for some 85 per cent of the island economy, although apparently a significant amount of the profits goes off the islands to the mainland-based owners of holiday property and hotels. Most visitors stay in holiday accommodation on the islands, including hotels, guesthouses, cottages and camp sites. Others arrive and stay on their yachts and motor cruisers.

THE UNIQUENESS OF THE SCILLONIAN FAUNA AND FLORA

We will see in later chapters that the Isles of Scilly aptly demonstrate the phenomenon of island biogeography. In all groups of flora and fauna there is a paucity of species compared with Cornwall, and this is a theme to which we will return. This paucity is readily attributed to the distance from the mainland, the much smaller land area and the limited range of habitats compared with those in Cornwall, with no rivers, only a few tiny streams, no acidic mires (bogs) and only granitic bedrock, with none of the slates, serpentinite and other rock types of the mainland. Widespread exposure of habitats on the Isles of Scilly may also account for the absence of some species that are susceptible to wind-blown salt spray. For example there are currently about 217 bryophyte species (57 liverworts, 3 hornworts, 157 mosses). Of these, six liverworts and five mosses are species introduced in Britain. Compared with Cornwall the total bryophyte flora is much poorer, with only about 36 per cent of the overall Cornish total of 167 liverworts (including hornworts) and 37 per cent of the total of 430 mosses. Scarcity of basic soils on the Isles of Scilly may also account for the absence of some other species common in Cornwall.

The number of species of land birds in Scilly is also small. Visitors to the islands are usually surprised to find many common passerines, let alone owls and woodpeckers, missing or in very low numbers. Equally the very confiding nature of blackbirds *Turdus merula* and song thrushes *T. philomelos* will soon be remarked on. The Isles of Scilly have hardly any land mammals, and no predators such as foxes *Vulpes vulpes* or stoats *Mustela erminea*. There are no snakes and very few resident species of butterflies or dragonflies; this is common for all groups. But on the other hand there are species that are only found in Scilly, such as the

Scilly shrew *Crocidura suaveolens cassiteridum*, several rare lichens and many other examples of interesting and uncommon species.

Lusitanian and Mediterranean influences

References will be made in the following chapters to Lusitanian influences. The geographical position of the Isles of Scilly has led to a number of unique aspects of the flora and fauna. Many species are at their northern limit in Scilly and southwestern Britain. These are species from the Atlantic coastal regions of southern Europe, based on the former Roman province of Lusitania, and into the Mediterranean. A visit to parts of Spain or Portugal will reveal many species of plants that are commonly seen in Scilly, but that are rare of absent from the rest of Britain. There are also lichens, invertebrates and other groups with Lusitanian species that reflect the same distribution, and in the marine environment many species found in southern or Mediterranean waters that also occur in the Isles of Scilly and the Channel Islands. In the *New Atlas of the British and Irish Flora* (Preston *et al.*, 2002) the floristic elements of the flora are described: the Mediterranean–Atlantic and Submediterranean–Subatlantic are plants that are associated with these biogeographical regions.

NATURE CONSERVATION DESIGNATIONS

Currently the Isles of Scilly are covered by a plethora of designations relating in some way to nature conservation.

- The whole coastline of the Isles of Scilly was designated a Heritage Coast in 1974.
- Scilly is a candidate Special Area of Conservation (cSAC) under the European Habitats Directive.
- A Special Protection Area (SPA) (for birds) covers 4.09km².
- Scilly is a Ramsar site, an international important-wetland designation.
- Scilly was designated a Conservation Area in 1975.
- Twenty-six sites have been designated Sites of Special Scientific Interest (SSSI) by English Nature. Of these five are geological sites.
- The Isles of Scilly has been a Voluntary Marine Park since 1987 – this includes the whole area within the 50m depth contour line.
- Scilly was designated an Area of Outstanding Natural Beauty (AONB) in 1975 – it includes 'all the islands and islets above mean low water that together form the Isles of Scilly'. The total area covered is 16km². Scilly is the smallest

AONB in the country; also the only one under a single local authority. The Management Plan for the AONB was published in 2004.

STUDYING THE FLORA AND FAUNA OF THE ISLES OF SCILLY

Although many of the visitors to the Isles of Scilly over the centuries have commented on the natural history of the islands, most of what has been written has concentrated on the most obvious groups. Authoritive books have covered plants, birdlife, butterflies and moths, but many of the marine species, insects and more difficult groups are the subject of papers in scientific journals or rather inaccessible unpublished reports held by English Nature and other bodies. Recently there has been a resurgence of interest in these other groups, especially invertebrates and marine life, which had otherwise been left to a small number of specialists.

For many years botanists have been well served by a *Flora* (Lousley, 1971), but it is now due for an update as there is a great deal of new botanical information available. Some plant hunters whose aim is to record rare plants, and especially alien species, are regular visitors to the islands.

Birds have tended to attract the lion's share of attention since the late 1950s, when the St Agnes Bird Observatory became a focus for birdwatchers hoping to see rare and unusual migrant and vagrant species. October is still the most popular month for birdwatchers to visit Scilly. This is an extraordinary phenomenon; it has to be seen to be believed. Hundreds of enthusiasts, bristling with telescopes, pagers and binoculars, arrive in Scilly intent on seeing rare migrant birds. These birders mostly have well-defined patterns of behaviour, usually travelling en masse to wherever there is news of some exciting bird. So it is not unusual to see them all gathered in one place, behind lines of telescopes waiting patiently for a glimpse of their quarry. In the evenings many will attend the 'count', when the tally of the day's finds are recorded.

The marine habitat might seem to be rather neglected. Although there are organised field trips to Scilly to study marine ecology, most of the information stays in student dissertations. But for every child visiting the islands half the fun is exploring rock pools. Now, with plenty of opportunities to dive or snorkel, the underwater life is becoming much better known. Underwater safaris, glass-bottomed boats and swimming with seals and seabirds are making this fascinating medium much more accessible to the general public.

Some of these visitors to Scilly are going to take more than a casual

interest in what they see. Hopefully they will contribute records and notes that
will lead to further expansion of our knowledge of the natural history of the
islands. Since its inception the Isles of Scilly Bird Group has produced a report
that also includes notes, short papers and reports on natural history subjects
other than birds – the *Isles of Scilly Bird & Natural History Review*. Perhaps this
book too will encourage an interest in the fascinating natural history of the Isles
of Scilly.

The chapters that follow are arranged to give an overview of the geology,
something of the history, the people who contributed to our knowledge of the
natural history of the islands, the individual islands, the main habitats, and the
major groups of flora and fauna. Descriptions of some of the plant communities
are included as an appendix.

CHAPTER 2

Geology and Early History

There are signs of Bronze Age man on every island in Scilly.

Charles Thomas (1985)

GEOLOGY

AT FIRST GLANCE the Ordnance Survey's geological map of the Isles of Scilly appears to be something of a disappointment: almost the whole of the land shown on the map is coloured in the same shade of red-brown, representing granite. A granite batholith, the Cornubian batholith, extends as a series of cupolas or bosses along the Southwest Peninsula from Dartmoor to Land's End and the Isles of Scilly, ending at the undersea mass of Haig Fras 95km further on and slightly out of line, presumably due to faulting (Edmonds *et al.*, 1975; Selwood *et al.*, 1998). Originally the rocks were a softer, slatey rock called killas; this was altered by pressure from the granite boss as it was extruded and pushed up into the killas, which was later eroded and now only exists as rock called tourmalised schist, found as a narrow dyke-like patch on the northwest of St Martin's (Anon., *Short Guide to the Geology of the Isles of Scilly*).

The Scilly granite is very similar to that found in Cornwall, and was classified by Barrow (1906) into different types, the main ones being the older, coarse-grained G1, which is found mainly around outer the rim of the islands, and G2, which is finer-grained and is mostly in the central part of the islands and has often been intruded into G1. The two types of granite merge into each other without any obvious line of demarcation. Characteristically the granites are made up of quartz and crystals of feldspar, muscovite mica, biotite mica and other

FIG 7. Loaded Camel Rock at Porth Hellick, St Mary's, May 2006. (Richard Green)

minerals. Much of the rock is beautifully striped through with veins and dykes, mostly narrow and usually white or black according to the infilling; white quartz or black tourmaline crystals can be found in these dykes, and rarely larger crystals of amethyst quartz. A vein of beautiful amethyst quartz that runs through some of the rocks to the north of St Agnes at one time had large, visible crystals, but most have since been taken by collectors. It is still possible to find smaller veins of crystals, and some beach pebbles have small layers of crystals running through them.

Another characteristic of the granite is the weathering along the veins and softer areas in the rock. The cooling and pressures have already formed these into very distinctive vertical and horizontal cracks, and erosion by weather and the sea then combine to produce the most extraordinary natural sculptures. Some of the most impressive examples can be seen on Peninnis Head and along the east coast of St Mary's, but all the islands have examples. Some of these rocks have been given fanciful names: Pulpit Rock, Monk's Cowl, Tooth Rock, Loaded Camel (Fig. 7). A curious type of formation seen frequently in Scilly is a rock basin in the top of a granite boulder where rainwater has weakened feldspar and released quartz crystals, which apparently have blown round and round to form a natural bowl.

Surface geology

When the granite weathers it eventually becomes reduced to sand. Blown sand is an important constituent of the soils of all the islands as well as forming the beautiful white beaches and the sand bars that link many of the higher parts of the islands. Ram (also known as head or rab) is a cement-like material formed by the breakdown of periglacially frost-shattered granite fragments that forms deposits around the bases of granite carns, in valleys and especially in the cliffs (Fig. 8). It is often excavated from 'ram pits' to be used by the islanders as a mortar in building work and sometimes as a road surface. Alluvium is found under the Porthloo fields, and at Lower and Higher Moors. Small patches of gravel found near the daymark on St Martin's and at a few other places are probably of glacial origin – see below.

FIG 8. Ram shelf at the base of the cliff on Samson. (Rosemary Parslow)

FIG 9. An example of a raised beach at Porth Killier, St Agnes, where former beach levels can be seen above the present beach. May 2003. (Rosemary Parslow)

Raised beaches

Raised beaches are especially common throughout the southwest of Britain, and the Isles of Scilly have many examples. The raised beach at Watermill is a classic site with a conglomerate of clast-supported rounded cobbles and boulders, over-lain by well-sorted medium sand (Selwood *et al.*, 1998). There are many places all around the coasts in Scilly where former shore levels with beach deposits are exposed in the cliffs above the present beaches. There are raised beaches at Hell Bay, Bryher; Porth Killier, St Agnes (Fig. 9); Piper's Hole, Tresco; Shipman Head, Bryher and many other places.

Glaciation

Although it was long thought that glaciation had missed Scilly, there is evidence that a tongue of ice from the southern edge of the Late Devensian ice sheet, the Irish Sea Ice Stream, probably reached the northern islands of Scilly 18,000 years BP (before present), eventually leaving deposits on White Island off St Martin's, and on Northwethel (Scourse *et al.*, 1990). The evidence for this lies in a great variety of rocks exotic to Scilly such as flint, sandstone and associated 'erratics'. The best example of glacial till in the islands is within the Bread and Cheese

FIG 10. The bar to White Island is a former glacial feature, probably a glacial moraine. June 2002. (Rosemary Parslow)

formation at Bread and Cheese Cove sssi on the north coast of St Martin's: the overlying gravels, the Tregarthen and the Hell Bay gravels, are interpreted as glaciofluvial and solifluction deposits respectively. There are erratic assemblages with both deposits (Selwood *et al.*, 1998). Recent work suggests that some of these deposits, such as that at Bread and Cheese Cove, may not be in their original positions (Hiemstra *et al.*, 2005). Other sites with glacial links occur in the bars in the north of the islands, such as the ones at Pernagie, the one connecting White Island to St Martin's (Fig. 10), and Golden Bar, St Helen's: these are probably glacial moraines, not marine features (Scourse, 2005).

EARLY HISTORY – THE SUBMERGENCE

Twenty thousand years ago most of Britain was under the last glaciation, extending as far south as the Wash and south Wales. At this time sea level would have been as much as 120m below Ordnance Datum. Then the climate ameliorated and by 13,000 BP the Devensian ice had almost disappeared (Selwood *et al.*, 1998).

Four thousand years ago, before the sea inundated the land, Scilly would have had a very different landscape, with low hills and sand dunes surrounding a shallow plain (Fig. 11). Based on the present-day undersea contour lines, there would at that time have been three main islands: the principal one would have included the present-day St Mary's, Tresco, Bryher and St Martin's, the Norrard Rocks, the Eastern Isles and the St Helen's group; Annet and St Agnes would have made up a smaller second island group; and the Western Rocks would have been the third. Later the islands became parted as the sea rose still further. The long isolation of St Agnes from St Mary's and the rest of Scilly may possibly explain the differences in the flora – for example why the least adder's-tongue fern *Ophioglossum lusitanicum* is restricted to St Agnes.

Most accounts of the submergence of the Isles of Scilly are based on the model proposed by Thomas in *Exploration of a Drowned Landscape* (1985). Thomas suggests that sea level rose rapidly and reached to within a few metres of present-day levels by 6000 BP, although final submergence of the island of Scilly to

FIG 11. A map showing how the main islands may have appeared prior to the submergence. (After Thomas, 1985)

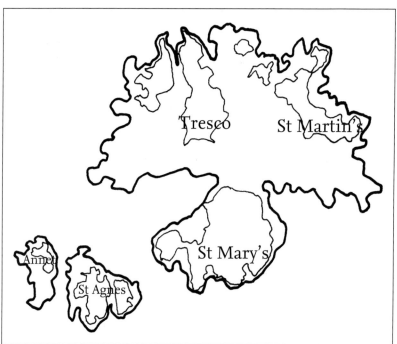

create the present archipelago may not have been effected until post-Roman times. Archaeological and historical evidence show that although sea was rising on a unitary island about 2000 BC, 'submergence began in earnest during Norman times and was effectively completed by the early Tudor period' (Thomas, 1985; Selwood *et al.*, 1998). However, Thomas recognised that although his model assumes a gradual process of submergence, there is an alternative picture with a series of dramatic events such as tidal surges. According to Ratcliffe and Straker (1997), submergence may have been even more gradual than Thomas proposes. The most controversial aspect of Thomas's model is his suggestion that separation of the islands did not occur until early Tudor times. Although the exact details of when and how the marine inundation took place are unclear, remains of huts, walls and graves on areas now covered by the sea are irrefutable evidence that it took place.

THE EARLY LANDSCAPE

During glaciation, land south of the ice sheet would have been bare tundra, cold, with sparse vegetation and probably few animals (Yalden, 1999), and certainly few that are still found in Britain today. It is difficult to imagine what Scilly was like at the time of the earliest human visitors, who were probably Mesolithic hunter–gatherers who left only a few flints as evidence of their passing. We have already seen that the islands would have been a considerably larger landmass than the present-day scatter of islands. Much of the land was covered in birch woodland, sparse grassland and marshy land with sedges. These conditions of the Mesolithic period persisted across southern Britain, then part of Continental Europe, and most of the steppe species that were present then have either died out or retreated to more northerly areas. During the Neolithic period people may have started to settle in Scilly and begun clearing the land, but pollen evidence shows some forest clearance was followed by woodland regeneration and agricultural decline. There are a few artefacts from this time, but it is likely these were only temporary occupations (Ratcliffe & Johns, 2003).

EARLY MAMMALS AND OTHER FAUNA

Very few remains of the early fauna of the islands have been found, but one small rodent, the root or Pallas's vole *Microtus oeconomus* (very similar to our field vole

M. agrestis) was present, as was the red deer *Cervus elaphus*, and both were still present in Scilly in the Bronze Age.

Modern Scilly is poor in mammal species, and the written records are sparse. Bones found in the Iron Age sections of the excavations on Nornour included Scilly shrew, wood mouse or long-tailed field mouse *Apodemus sylvaticus* and root vole. The first two are still extant in Scilly, but the root vole is believed to have become extinct at some later period, no remains having been found after Romano-British times (Turk, 1984; Ratcliffe & Straker, 1996). Root voles are no longer found in Britain although there are isolated (relict) populations still in the Netherlands, Scandinavia and eastern Europe (Mitchell-Jones *et al.*, 1999). In late summer 1978 my daughter and I found a vole mandible and two molars in storm debris on the boulder beach below the Porth Killier Bronze Age midden, along with scraps of bone and shards of coarse pottery. These were sent to the Natural History Museum, where the vole remains were identified as root vole (Gordon Corbet, *in litt.*). Later, in 1982, I had the opportunity to go to Hungary and was able to visit root vole habitat near Lake Kolon, in Kiskunsági National Park. This is an area of rough grassland and *Phragmites* swamp, which would seem to be typical habitat of the vole. An interesting note by Mitchell-Jones *et al.* (1999) is that root voles migrate from wetland to dunes or drier habitats in winter, and even into houses.

Other animal remains that have been found from archaeological sites include seals, various cetaceans, red deer, toad *Bufo bufo* (an amphibian no longer native in Scilly), as well as numerous fish and bird species and domestic horse, ox and sheep, all from Bronze Age sites. Roe deer *Capreolus capreolus*, seals, cetaceans and domestic animals have been recorded from Iron Age/Romano-British sites. At coastal sites seals, small cetaceans and fish were clearly an important part of the diet of the human inhabitants. Although not listed among the remains of fish and molluscs that have been recorded, the boulder beaches and rock pools can support several species of easily caught edible fish, for example rocklings, the larger gobies and grey mullet *Chelon* sp. Today the large freshwater pools on the islands also contain very large eels *Anguilla anguilla*, and these may also have been present in the past.

Further discussion on the early mammal fauna is included in Chapter 15, and prehistoric and historical records of birds are discussed in Chapter 16.

THE EARLY HABITATS

Of particular interest is Thomas's (1985) description of the reconstructed palaeoenvironment of the early Scillonian landscape and the mapping of four main types of habitat. Some of the evidence for this he based on the pollen records, which unfortunately were limited to the few peat deposits and archaeological digs, and also on the distribution of some significant plants in Lousley's *Flora* (1971). The four habitat types he described were stream-drained marsh, woodland, sand dune and open ground (including heath).

There are still marshlands in Scilly today, although they are nowhere near their former extent. Some of the land now under the sand flats between the islands could have been low-lying and boggy, but all that remains now are small wetlands at Higher Moors, Holy Vale and Lower Moors on St Mary's, now much contracted in area. Even as recently as the 1960s there were wet fields from near Porthloo Pool and Rose Hill through to Lower Moors with yellow iris *Iris pseudacorus*, lesser water plantain *Baldellia ranunculoides* and hemlock water-dropwort *Oenanthe crocata*. Although these areas are still there they are now much drier and less species-rich. Another similar wetland area is now flooded and forms the Great Pool on Tresco. All the other streams and marshy areas are now lost under the sea, but some can still be traced from the geological record. Between Teän and St Martin's is the deep channel of Teän Sound, which probably marks the route of a prehistoric stream.

One of the most interesting theories propounded by Thomas is his mapping of the ancient woodland cover on the islands by looking at the distribution of woodland species in Lousley's *Flora*. From the pollen samples analysed by Dimbleby (1977) from Innisidgen and by Scaife (1984) from Higher and Lower Moors it would seem that Scilly was once covered in woodland. This woodland consisted of oak *Quercus robur* and birch *Betula* spp. with an understorey of hazel *Corylus avellana* and alder *Alnus glutinosa* (probably where there were wetter areas). Pollen evidence also included some ash *Fraxinus excelsior* and traces of yew *Taxus baccata*, and later hornbeam *Carpinus betulus* and elm *Ulmus* sp. Virtually nothing of this woodland is evident today, but support for the pollen evidence and what it tells us about former woodland distribution can be extrapolated from the present-day distribution of plants (known as ancient woodland indicators) that have strong ancient woodland associations, for example wood spurge *Euphorbia amygdaloides* and wood dock *Rumex sanguineus* (Kirby, 2004). In his *Flora of the Isles of Scilly* Lousley (1971) comments on a number of these woodland plants that were growing in non-woodland habitats. These fall in very neatly with the pattern of woodland 2000 years ago, as demonstrated by Thomas (Fig. 12).

Since 1971 additional plant records have reinforced the pattern. So it is possible to visualise the kind of woodland that may have grown on the islands at the time, possibly similar to the present-day Wistman's Wood on Dartmoor, with stunted, twisted trees, wind-pruned into shape and only able to reach any reasonable height where they are sheltered in the hollows between the hills – as happens with the elms in Holy Vale today. The ground cover may have been open, with many of the species that still exist in Scilly. The trees and exposed rocks would also have supported luxuriant ferns and bryophytes. Other evidence of the ancient woodlands that existed on Scilly are the numbers of buried tree trunks that have been found on Tresco in the past, and the few oak *Quercus* sp. trees and woodland plants in the area still known as Tresco Wood. There are also records of submerged tree trunks on St Mary's and, more reliably, St Martin's.

FIG 12. The present distribution of AWI (ancient woodland indicator) plants may indicate where woodland existed before the submergence. (Updated since Thomas, 1985)

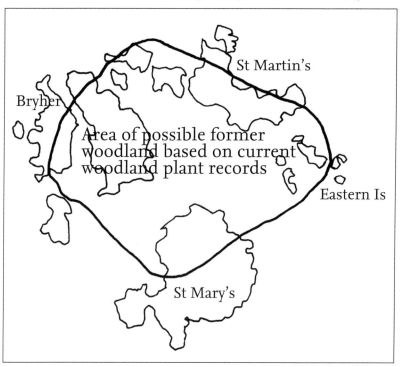

The work carried out between 1989 and 1993 by the Cornwall Archaeological Unit (Ratcliffe & Straker, 1996) on a number of cliff-face and intertidal deposits also provided exciting additional evidence for the deciduous Mesolithic/Neolithic forests. In addition, the CAU found further evidence that these forests were being replaced by heathland, grassland and cultivated plants by the Late Iron Age, as people began to have an impact on the land.

The other main habitats, sand dunes and heathlands, are still present. Many of the dunes have been flattened and have become vegetated with grassland and scrub, or are now cultivated fields. Heathlands and grasslands have resulted from the management of the open habitats over centuries. The land would have been utilised in many ways, from grazing for animals to the stripping of turf from the heath to use as fuel – once the inhabitants had cleared most of the woodland.

Pollen analysis

Pollen analysis of samples from Higher and Lower Moors (Scaife, 1984) shows the distribution of pollen and spores in four levels of the peat below the two mires on St Mary's. Later work investigated more areas of peat (strictly not really peat but humic silts) at Porth Mellon, St Mary's, and Par Beach, St Martin's (Ratcliffe & Straker, 1996). The earliest levels are mostly tree and shrub pollens, oak, birch, hazel, some ash, elm and willow *Salix* sp., also some grass species, sedges, bracken *Pteridium aquilinum*, other ferns and some aquatic plants. These all point to a landscape with woodland, mire and open-water habitats. The record for Lower Moors has less tree pollen and may fit the theory that the ancient woodland was distributed mainly on the north and east of the island (Thomas, 1985). Pollen samples also show there was some further clearance of the secondary woodland that regenerated after the earlier clearances. This coincided with the more open landscape and evidence of arable, heathland, mire and coastal habitats associated with the Iron Age and Romano-British communities then inhabiting the islands. John Evans (1984), excavating an Iron Age field system at Bar Point, found the kind of plant remains that would be expected to follow after most of the woodland had been cleared. These charred fragments were mostly plants of heathland or acid grassland: grasses, ribwort plantain *Plantago lanceolata*, vetch *Vicia* sp., *Galium, Medicago*, broom *Cytisus scoparius*, elder *Sambucus nigra*, gorse *Ulex* sp., false oatgrass *Arrhenatherum elatius*, as well as oak.

EARLY AGRICULTURE

It was not until about 2000 BC that the first settlements may have started on
Scilly (Ashbee, 1974; Thomas, 1985). The evidence from pollen deposits, and from
sources such as middens and other archaeological deposits, shows changes in
the palaeoenvironment after the clearing of the forest, resulting in more open
landscapes with grass and heathland species (Ratcliffe & Straker, 1996). These
clearances coincided with the early settlement of Scilly, when it is presumed the
woodland was cleared for timber and firewood, as well as to open up areas for
cultivation. The growing of cereals (and possibly other plants that produce
edible seeds) and the use of the plough must have happened quite early after
the arrival of the first settlers. The excavation of the Iron Age site at Bar Point
graphically illustrates the agricultural practice at that time (Evans, 1984), with
evidence of stone banks to produce individual fields – not apparently for keeping
stock in, but to demarcate ownerships. Cultivation marks left by the rip-ard
(a primitive plough) and mattock as well as burnt charcoal from gorse were
found, and also hoof prints of domestic animals – horses, cattle, and sheep or
goats. Pollen analysis indicated open land without trees or shrubs (although
a small amount of oak, alder and hazel pollen was found in one location), and
the presence of cereal pollen points to cereal cultivation. Ribwort plantain was
'in consistent but low abundance', which suggests cultivation and grazed land.
The evidence for deforestation is based on the association of ribwort plantain
with pasture and cultivation and its intolerance of competition with woody
plants (Godwin, 1975).

Once the islands had been successfully settled one presumes a period of
stability and expansion of the human population followed. This is when the
great changes in the landscape, the vegetation and animal life in Scilly would
have really begun. As the woodland was cleared, perhaps leaving only small
areas, more and more land would have been broken up and cultivated to meet
the demands of the increasing human population. Farm stock would have
been grazed on the open land, cliffs, dune grasslands, coastlands or around the
marshy areas. Bell heather *Erica cinerea*, ling *Calluna vulgaris*, reed *Phragmites
australis* and bracken would have been cut for bedding and thatching. Beaches
would have been scoured to search for edible seaweed, molluscs and fish.
Widespread cultivation and grazing became prominent during the second
millennium BC, with many evidences of farming in the pollen and charcoal
plant remains, querns for grinding grain, bones of farm animals and so on

FIG 13. The remains of an Iron Age and Romano-British settlement are still visible on Halangy Down, St Mary's. March 2006. (Rosemary Parslow)

(S. Butcher, *in litt.*). Also the field walls, settlements and lynchets across some fields indicate the impact on the landscape. Cultivation of the islands must have continued over many centuries, as is demonstrated near the Romano-British settlement at Halangy Down (Fig. 13), where Charles Thomas and Peter Fowler found traces of earlier fields with ones on a different alignment underneath.

There are numerous field walls that are now only seen at low water spring tides in the sea off Samson, Teän and some other islands (Fig. 14). These all point to there having been much more land available for grazing or cultivation before it was lost to the sea with sea-level rise. Their presence also suggests that not all the low-lying land was marsh; but only reasonably accessible land would have been divided into fields.

FIG 14. At low tide the lines of ancient field walls are visible in the sand flats off Samson. June 2002. (Rosemary Parslow)

Arable cultivation

Early cereal crops on Scilly included six-rowed (and possibly two-rowed) barley *Hordeum vulgare* in both the hulled and naked varieties, which have been identified from several archaeological sites. Other crops that have been recorded are emmer wheat *Triticum dicoccum*, Celtic bean *Vicia faba* var. *minor* and oats *Avena* sp. The origins of domestication have been identified in the area of the Near East some 9,000–10,000 years ago, and barley and other crop species must have gradually made their way to Europe with the early inhabitants and through trade (Smith, 1995).

There is evidence of arable cultivation in the Isles of Scilly at least as far back as the Bronze Age. On Samson archaeologists found a cache that consisted of a cleaned crop of naked barley, probably six-rowed barley, confirming this was grown in the Early Bronze Age. Six-rowed barley (and possibly also two-rowed barley) was clearly an important crop in Bronze and Iron Age Scilly both in the hulled and naked forms – although most of what has been found is the naked variety. Hulled barley has been found at Middle and Late Bronze Age sites. Barley has also been identified from post-medieval deposits at Steval Point, St Mary's. Emmer wheat and Celtic bean were found with both kinds of barley at sites at Porth Cressa, St Mary's, and Porth Killier, St Agnes. At Halangy Down, besides the older lynchets beneath those of the Romano-British settlement, a pot was found nearby with impressions of grain in the clay. One intriguing find was of a large number of seeds in the post-occupation layers of a hut at West Porth: these were dated to Late Bronze Age/Early Iron Age and are of great interest as they were of common arable weeds (Ratcliffe & Straker, 1996). Unfortunately there are very few records or remains of plants to give more than a hint of the wild flora of arable fields.

Arable weeds identified from Bronze Age sites in Scilly include vetches, knotgrass *Polygonum* sp., chickweed *Stellaria* sp., black bindweed *Fallopia convulvulus*, small nettle *Urtica urens*, corn spurrey *Spergula arvensis* and red goosefoot *Chenopodium rubrum*. A curious occurrence was ploughman's spikenard *Inula conyza*, a plant more usually growing on calcareous soils. It is possible that some plant seeds (for example corn spurrey and knotgrass) were eaten in a kind of porridge. Certainly weed seeds continued to be found from archaeological sites after the Bronze Age, as did emmer and barley. Unfortunately there is not a great deal of evidence of Iron Age cultivation. Only two sites are recorded, Shipman Head, Bryher, and Halangy Porth, St Mary's (Ratcliffe & Straker, 1996).

There is little information on arable plants from the Late Roman and Early Medieval periods, although there are unspecific barley and oat records from the seventh/eighth-century layer and wheat and barley from the tenth to thirteenth centuries. Weed seeds, most of which could be arable weeds, were also recorded. Some of the plants that are still found in Scilly are believed to have been early introductions as contaminants of seeds or goods brought in from the Continent, even from as far away as the Mediterranean.

LIMPET MIDDENS

There are shell middens in many places on the Isles of Scilly, refuse heaps that in some cases date back to the Bronze Age. They contain bones and other rubbish thrown out by the inhabitants, especially common limpet *Patella vulgata* shells. There seems to be a correlation between the size of the limpet shells and the living conditions of the people at that time: the smaller the shell apparently the tougher life had become for the people, as the shells were being harvested before they had reached full size. It is reported that they are very chewy and uninteresting, but presumably they were at least an easily accessible food and protein source. However, the University of Bristol Expedition in 1978 declared limpets were delicious in a risotto!

Limpet shell middens have been found at many archaeological sites on Scilly, on any islands that have been inhabited at any time. Middens were often in use up to the nineteenth century, and frequently can be dated by pottery shards and other remains layered in with the shells and other rubbish. When the inhabitants of Samson were evacuated from the island in 1839 they left behind a huge pile of limpet shells. Some of the beach pebbles used to knock limpets off the rocks were also found. There is evidence that some limpets were collected for fishing bait, but it is also very probable they were eaten even in quite recent times (Ratcliffe & Straker, 1996). Although limpets were the main species taken, remains of other edible molluscs have also been identified from the middens. These are mostly the species that would be expected: cockles, scallops and topshells, all of which are still common around the islands.

CHAPTER 3

Later History – People and Their Influence on the Islands

Back to the sunset bound of Lyonesse –
A land of old upheaven from the abyss
By fire, to sink into the abyss again;
Where fragments of forgotten peoples dwelt,
And the long mountains ended in a coast
Of ever-shifting sand, and far away
The phantom circle of a moaning sea.

Tennyson, *The passing of Arthur*

THE HISTORY OF England and how it was reflected in the Isles of Scilly is perhaps peripheral to our story of the natural history. But throughout the centuries there has been commerce with the mainland of Britain, as well as short-lived invasions, and a variety of traffic between Scilly and the Continent, at least as far as the Mediterranean. People bring all manner of goods with them when they travel – but it is often the unrecorded or accidental materials they may have carried that are of greatest interest to us.

MEDIEVAL SCILLY

The early history of Scilly is shrouded in the mists of time. An archipelago of small islands just visible on a clear day off the coast of Cornwall was bound to seem mysterious and attractive. There are many tales and legends associated with the islands, many of them bound up with tales of giants, Vikings and especially King Arthur. In the absence of written records, however, real history can only be deduced from the artefacts and remains left by the early occupants on Scilly.

There is little material evidence of trade from abroad prior to Roman times, although some finds suggest that the islands were not totally isolated. By Roman times finds of Samian and other wheel-made pottery, pipe-clay figurines on Nornour and Roman coins indicate links with France, elsewhere on the Continent and the Mediterranean (Ashbee, 1974). These contacts were very likely to have been instrumental in the importation of plants – both deliberately for food and accidentally as weed seeds, among seed corn or caught up in goods and packaging – that may have been some of the early colonists of cultivated fields.

Later, during the early Middle Ages, long-distance trade increased between western Britain, Ireland, France and the Mediterranean. Scilly was in an excellent position to benefit from ships calling in for fresh water and supplies, and in return to acquire goods such as amphorae of wine and olive oil from the eastern Mediterranean and wine and pottery from Gaul. A site on Teän was possibly a small trading post at the time (Ratcliffe & Johns, 2003).

During the twelfth century Tavistock Abbey administered the northern part of the Isles of Scilly. At this time a Benedictine Priory was established on Tresco, with small churches on the other islands. This would have been significant in the botanical history of the islands, for the monks were much involved in long-distance trade all around Britain and the Continent and would, deliberately or accidentally, have been another vehicle for the introduction of plants. Scilly produced dried seabirds and fish, which were exchanged for goods from further afield (Ratcliffe, 1992). The monks are credited with the introduction of various herbs, some of which still occur in Scilly, such as soapwort *Saponaria officinalis* and tansy *Chrysanthemum vulgare*. They may also have reintroduced elder, and they are said to have brought the first narcissi to Scilly, as they had done already on St Michael's Mount in Cornwall. Whether or not this is true, it is from those original narcissi growing semi-wild around the former priory that eventually grew some of the flowers that centuries later became the foundation of the bulb industry.

In the early fourteenth century Ennor Castle, on the hill above Old Town, St Mary's, was held by Ranulph de Blanchminster, who was charged with keeping the peace and who was expected to pay the king an annual tribute of 300 puffins *Fratercula arctica* or 6s 8d. Apparently puffins counted as fish and so could be eaten in Lent; their feathers were also valuable. What is not clear is whether the 'puffins' were actually puffins or Manx shearwaters *Puffinus puffinus*, which at one time were known as 'puffins' (as is suggested by their scientific name). There is a record that during Ranulph's occupation he imprisoned the king's coroner for taking away a whale that had been beached on his land and only released him on payment of 100 shillings. In 1337 Scilly became part of the original Duchy of Cornwall when Edward the Black Prince became the first Duke of Cornwall.

ELIZABETHAN SCILLY

It was Queen Elizabeth I who in 1570 leased Scilly to Francis Godolphin, initially for 38 years at £20 per annum. This link with the Godolphins was to continue, more or less, until the heir to the Godolphins, the then Duke of Leeds, gave up the lease in 1831 and the Duchy of Cornwall resumed control. The next period in Scilly's history seems to have been a nervous time, with the threat of invasion ever in the offing. Despite this nothing much was done to prepare to repel possible attack during the early years of Queen Elizabeth's reign, despite, one would have thought, there being a very real threat of invasion by the Spanish Armada. Then, near the end of Queen Elizabeth's reign, Star Castle was built, followed by the first defences on what is now the Garrison.

THE CIVIL WAR IN SCILLY

During the Civil War the Garrison defences were improved and King Charles's Castle was built on Tresco to defend the harbour at New Grimsby. The islands passed from Royalist to Parliamentary hands and back again. Unfortunately the Royalist command by Sir Richard Grenville led to the islands becoming a base for piracy, which annoyed not only Parliament but also the Dutch. It was not long before both the English fleet and the Dutch set sail to capture the Isles of Scilly. Eventually the Royalists surrendered to Admiral Blake after the Garrison had come under relentless fire from his ships and from Oliver's Battery, which had been built on Tresco, and the Dutch backed off. Later, another fortification known as Cromwell's Castle was built in a better position overlooking the harbour of New Grimsby (Fig. 15), to ward off further attack by the Dutch (the fortifications at Charles's Castle on the hill overlooking Tresco Channel being so badly placed as to be useless for defence).

In 1660 the monarchy was restored, and the Godolphins returned to Scilly. But it does not seem to have been quiet for long. Spain became a threat again, and in the second half of the century there was a massive programme of building on the promontory of the Garrison and elsewhere to strengthen the defences.

Turk (1967) refers to a comment by Richard Ligon in the *True and Exact History of the Island of Barbadoes* (1673), where he mentions puffins 'which we have

FIG 15. Cromwell's Castle and the ruins of King Charles's Castle, Tresco. Photographed from near Hangman's Island, Bryher, March 2005. (Rosemary Parslow)

from the Isles of Scilly ... this kind of food is only fit for servants'. So clearly puffins (or shearwaters, which were considered a delicacy) were being exported from Scilly at the time.

NAPOLEONIC WARS

For the next century life in the Isles of Scilly remained quiet once again, and very little of note happened. During the Napoleonic Wars (1803–15) Scilly again seemed vulnerable and some additional defences were built. Life in Scilly was very hard at this time. Attempts to relieve the poverty and distress of the islanders by establishing a pilchard and mackerel fishery were not very successful, and famine conditions continued for some years, especially on the off-islands (Bowley, 1990). In 1834, just three years after taking over the lease from the Godolphins, the Duchy of Cornwall leased the Isles of Scilly to Augustus Smith in an effort to get rid of what had become an acute embarrassment to them. The arrival of Augustus Smith was to have a profound effect on Scilly and the Scillonians, as well as on the flora of the islands (see Chapter 13). In 1863 the Garrison defence force was eventually disbanded.

WORLD WAR I AND WORLD WAR II

During the two World Wars Scilly was host to large numbers of servicemen, and the islands were considered very vulnerable to attack or invasion. In World War I a naval seaplane base was established, first on St Mary's but later transferred to Tresco, and almost a thousand men were based on the Garrison on St Mary's. During World War II Scilly became important as a lookout post for German submarines, and additional fortifications were built on St Mary's, with fighter planes and air-sea rescue launches stationed there. Even so a number of air raids occurred and there was some bomb damage on the islands. It was just prior to World War II that the population of Scilly reached 2,618, the highest yet (excluding temporary summer populations now). This was also the time when the greatest amount of arable land was under cultivation (Lousley, 1971).

THE KELP INDUSTRY

For some hundred and fifty years from the late seventeenth to the early nineteenth century the burning of kelp was an important local industry that involved almost every family on Scilly (Fig. 16). When kelp burning was in progress, 'wreaths of smoke rising amidst the dun verdure and hoary carns of these pretty isles' apparently made them look all the more 'pleasing and picturesque' (Woodley, 1822). This might have seemed picturesque from a safe distance, but it is known that the clouds of acrid smoke polluted the air and stank out the houses and the washing lines for weeks on end. James Nance introduced kelp burning to Scilly in 1684, at a time when their more 'usual' means of livelihood, smuggling and wrecking, had been curtailed by the introduction of lighthouses and a customs house (Over, 1987). Activities such as collecting the seaweed, stacking it to dry and processing it would have involved the whole family. When it was burned it produced soda ash, which at the time was essential for the making of glass. Although the seaweeds collected were generally called 'kelp', they were mostly different species of the large wracks. The species mostly involved were the following:

- knotted wrack *Ascophyllum nodosum*
- bladder wrack *Fucus vesciculosus*
- serrated wrack *Fucus serratus*
- driftweed *Laminaria cloustini*

- sugar wrack *Laminaria saccharina*
- driftweed *Laminaria digitata*

According to Over (1987) only the fucoid seaweeds would have been a significant part of the harvest in Scilly because of the difficulty of collecting the big *Laminaria* seaweeds that grow in deeper water. However, storms frequently drive masses of seaweed onto the shore where it can be collected, and use of a boat could also have made it possible to access the *Laminaria* beds at low water springs.

Starting in March, families would collect the seaweed and carry it to places where it could be heaped up and dried. Deep stone-lined pits just above the shore were used to burn the seaweed, and these were kept going continually until the mass of weed began to liquefy, when it was stirred in a particular way and left to solidify. This lump of 'kelp ash' was eventually shipped off to Bristol or Gloucester to be processed for use in glass making, as well as for the manufacture of soap and alum.

It was necessary to haul huge amounts of the algae up the shore (it took

FIG 16. Burning kelp in pits by the shore to produce soda ash was a stinking and unpleasant task. The industry lasted for some 150 years until about 1835. (Gibson collection)

some 3–4 tonnes of weed to produce 127–152kg of crude ash before refinement), which could mean a family was collecting something in the order 268 tonnes of wet seaweed in a year. This would have had a considerable denuding effect on the shore and must have been quite devastating to those species associated with the algae. In some years it seems the crop of algae was not enough to go round. There is some indirect evidence of this in the court cases recorded at the time that refer to islanders infringing the rights of others by taking kelp they did not own. By law, 'no person was to cut … off an inhabited island where a horse could go among the rocks at low tide', presumably as these stands of kelp were already allotted. One would imagine that when the kelp was not so abundant and families became hard-pressed to find enough to fulfil their requirements, life must have been increasingly hard (Over, 1987). Kelp collecting was not confined to the inhabited islands: for example, some islanders spent the summers on Great Ganilly collecting seaweed.

The kelp industry spread all around the coasts of Britain, although it was not initially popular everywhere; in Orkney, the islanders of Stronsay rioted in 1762. But soon the high prices paid for the soda ash ensured that the practice became the main means of livelihood for many coastal and island communities (Berry, 1985). This was helped by wars and protective tariffs that blocked off the usual foreign sources of alkali, particularly 'barilla' glasswort *Salicornia* sp. from Spain. Eventually the industry fell into decline after the Napoleonic Wars, and it never recovered once it was found easier to manufacture soda chemically. Presumably the shores soon recovered and the algae soon grew again unchecked.

There are few signs now of this extraordinary industry, just a few abandoned kelp pits above the shoreline and the remains of a handful of quays from which the kelp was exported. There is a good example of a kelp pit below Kittern Hill on Gugh, with others on White Island, St Martin's, on St Martin's itself and on St Mary's – and there are several on Toll's Island, St Mary's. These are now just shallow stone-lined basins in the turf, not as deep as they would have been when in use. There are ruined quays at Pendrathen and on Teän, as well as on White Island, on Toll's Island, and at Watermill (Bowley, 1990).

Seaweed was also used to manure the fields, a practice which was in use until quite recently in the 1960s and 1970s. In the past both sheep and cattle would also graze on 'oar weed' (Borlase, 1756). A few farmers and householders still take seaweed to use on their crops, usually composting it until it has rotted down and the rain has washed out some of the salt.

PIRACY AND SMUGGLING

Scilly had been a base for pirates during the early twelfth century, at which time it was left to the resident monks to attempt to control the practice. Later, Lord Admiral Seymour (the widower of Catherine Parr, the surviving queen of King Henry VIII) was hanged in 1549 for piracy and treason after spending only two years on Scilly. Smuggling has long been associated with the southwestern counties of England, and Scilly is uniquely suited to it, with plenty of hidden places around the islands and fleets of gigs capable of sailing to the coast of France. At one time smuggling was one of the main occupations of the islanders, alongside the legitimate occupations such as piloting.

WRECKS

Over the centuries there have been hundreds of wrecks in the Isles of Scilly. Besides the accidental passengers they may have carried, such as rats, their spilled cargoes frequently washed ashore and may have introduced some plants and animals to the islands. From the published lists of cargoes we know the

FIG 17. The SS *Castleford* ran aground on the Crebawethans in fog in June 1887. Most of the cattle from the ship were later taken to Annet. (Gibson collection)

ships were frequently carrying hides, corn and seeds. When cattle were rescued from wrecks we know that the survivors were landed on uninhabited islands, Samson in one case and Annet in another (Fig. 17). One supposes the islanders would also have taken supplementary feed to the cattle during their enforced marooning. This may have resulted in grasses germinating from fallen seed from the hay.

One animal that may have reached Scilly as a stowaway is the wood mouse, now resident on St Mary's and Tresco. The black rat *Rattus rattus* may also have arrived by boat. At one time they had colonised Samson and would have been on many of the islands; later the brown rat *R. norvegicus* also presumably arrived on ships.

FARMING

The observations of the many people who visited the Isles of Scilly over the centuries give only the most tantalisingly incomplete account of the life of the people at the time, and very little detail about the farming. Maddeningly, most authors have not confined themselves to their own first-hand experiences but have quoted liberally, repeating, frequently without acknowledgement, the observations of their predecessors. One gentleman who visited the islands, the Reverend George Woodley (1822), was also very scathing about his predecessors, Robert Heath, who spent a year on the islands, and John Troutbeck, who was the chaplain of the islands. Troutbeck published his account in 1794, but his information in turn appears to be based on the reports of Robert Heath (1750). From all the accounts it seems that one of the most important crops at the time was potatoes in great quantity, and in good years the islanders might get two crops a year. The islands were not very good for growing wheat, but barley, rye, oats, pillas (an oat-like grain eaten as a porridge, which even up to quite recent times was being grown alongside corn and root crops), peas, beans and roots all did well. Salads, gooseberries, currants, raspberries, strawberries – anything that can be sheltered below walls could be grown. Garlic, both cultivated and wild, samphire for distilling and pickling, all grew locally. Rock samphire *Crithmum maritimum* still grows around all rocky shores (Fig. 18), but it is no longer pickled and exported in small casks (Heath, 1750; Woodley, 1822).

According to Woodley (1822) the local horses were small and had to survive on poor fare that included gorse, which they bruised with their hooves before eating, the sheep were small, long-legged animals similar to those on the Scottish islands, and both the sheep and the small black cattle subsisted on seaweed when

FIG 18. Rock samphire collected from the shore was once used for pickling and distilling. (Rosemary Parslow)

there was no hay for them. The local hogs would also have to be fed on seaweed and even limpets at times, causing their flesh to be reddish in colour and giving them an unpleasant fishy taste.

Several of the uninhabited islands were used as summer grazing, as well as places where there were colonies of rabbits *Oryctolagus cuniculus* and seabirds that could be utilised to provide rabbit meat and gulls' eggs. Sheep and deer were grazing on the Garrison, St Mary's, when Walter White (1855) was there in the mid nineteenth century. He also describes hayfields, arable fields of grain, root crops and potatoes (the latter were sent to market at Covent Garden).

Sheep were kept on the islands until the beginning of the twentieth century, and although there are now very few they have never completely died out. There are sheep pictured beside the Punchbowl Rock on Wingletang, St Agnes (Mothersole, 1919), and the last time sheep were on the island was in 1926 at Troy Town. Goats were kept throughout the centuries and are still present on several holdings on the islands. Donkeys were very common at one time and were used to carry baskets of kelp up from the beach. The Gugh donkey Cuckoo became famous when Leslie Thomas wrote about him in *Some Lovely Islands* (1968). Until the mid-1950s horses were still used on some farms, but the only horses now on the islands are for riding, other than the Shetland ponies that are being used for conservation grazing on some of the important nature conservation sites.

One curious industry between about 1840 and 1880 was straw-plaiting for making hats (Matthews, 1960). Besides using wheat and rye straw various hollow-stemmed grasses were also utilised, including crested dog's-tail *Cynosurus cristatus* and yellow oatgrass *Trisetum flavescens*. Crested dog's-tail is still a common grass in the islands and yellow oatgrass was found on Teän as a relict of farming but has now disappeared.

THE EVACUATION OF SAMSON

Sir Walter Besant's romantic tale of Armorel of Lyonesse (1890) has coloured the island with a totally unrealistic, fictitious past; there is even a ruined cottage on the island reputed to be Armorel's cottage. Sadly the reality is quite different: although the island was inhabited for many years, life for the islanders was hard and eventually Samson was abandoned in 1853–5 during the 'reign' of Augustus Smith.

Samson has many archaeological sites from the Bronze Age, mostly burial monuments but also a field system and hut circles on the south side of South Hill and another field system on North Hill. At some time the island became deserted and may have then been uninhabited for centuries. Finds of pottery from below dunes in East Porth may point to a lone cleric or other person living there in the thirteenth century (Thomas, 1985). In 1669 five people were living on Samson, possibly in a single dwelling, when Cosmo III, Grand Duke of Tuscany, made his short visit to Scilly. At some time after this the population rose to some thirty or forty people; between about 1755 and 1780 was probably their most settled time.

The main difficulty with living on Samson was the very poor water supply. The wells were slow or silted up, and the water was bad. At times water had to be fetched in barrels from Bryher or Tresco. It must have been a hard existence, based on fishing, which was the islanders' major occupation, growing a few basic crops, corn and potatoes, and keeping stock. From the limpet shell middens they left behind there clearly were difficult times, when shellfish became a major part of their diet. Other sources of income, piloting and kelp burning, were important but never enough to sustain the population.

At the time of the greatest population, in 1829, there were nine cottages and thirty-seven people. The islanders grew their crops in small strip fields or lynchets. Even their tiny fields were subdivided into even tinier plots, in keeping with the custom of the time that when a man died his holding would be divided between his sons and sometimes also widowed daughters and daughters-in-law. The boundaries of these divisions were often based on earlier lynchets or were laid out strip-fashion. There were no trees for fuel so turf would have been cut from the tops of the hills (the top of North Hill is still very bare to this day, possibly from turf cutting or later fires). It was reported by Captain Robert Welbank, a Trinity House visitor in 1841, that both bracken and dried seaweed were used for fuel, and any driftwood would also be precious (Thomas, 1985). At that time there were twenty-nine people living on Samson, seven being children. There were only seven households: four farmers, one farmer's widow, two fishermen. By this time Augustus Smith was introducing his reforms and imposing them on the other islanders in Scilly, and he soon prevailed on the tenants on Samson to relocate to St Mary's or other islands, with the benefits of education for their children and better occupation for themselves. The last inhabitant is said to have left in 1855. After that the houses would have been stripped; they soon began to collapse and are now all ruins (Fig. 19). Shortly after the evacuation Augustus Smith built a large stone-walled enclosure around the top of South Hill in which he attempted to keep a herd of fallow deer *Dama dama*. The deer, however, soon escaped and tried to get to Tresco. Some accounts say they drowned, but the distance is not very great and at low tide they might have walked across. A herd of cattle was also grazed on the island.

FIG 19. Ruined cottages on Samson, photographed during a visit to the island by a party of geology students in the 1890s. (Gibson collection)

FIG 20. On Samson primroses still grow near the ruins of the cottages. (Rosemary Parslow)

Besides their ruined dwellings, kitchen middens and other artefacts, the inhabitants of Samson left other mementos. They left behind several trees, tamarisk *Tamarix gallica*, elder, privet *Ligustrum ovalifolium* hedges (the latter now apparently lost, as only wild privet *L. vulgare* is found on the island today), burdock *Arctium minus* and primroses *Primula vulgaris*, which are still found not far from the ruins (Fig. 20). They also left the stone hedges that marked the boundaries of some of their tiny fields. Despite the history of Samson, Kay (1956) was of the opinion that it was the sort of place where a couple of enterprising young men could earn a healthy living with a flower farm and a few cattle. He had earlier heard of a Scillonian who had been offered a deal on the island, £10 per year rent for twenty years, then £250 per year afterwards. His friend did not take up the offer, his new wife not fancying a life on an uninhabited island – and it is probably fortunate for Samson that it has remained uninhabited by humans.

CHAPTER 4

Naturalists and Natural History

A singular circumstance has been remarked with respect of these birds [woodcock],
which, during the prevalence of strong gales in a direction varying from East to North,
are generally found here before they are discovered in England, and are first seen about
the Eastern Islands and the neighbouring cliffs. May not this circumstance tend to
elucidate the enquiries of the naturalist relative to their migration?

George Woodley (1822)

SOME OF THE early visitors to Scilly played their part in contributing to our knowledge of the flora and fauna of the islands, and some of them will be mentioned in these pages. Today, Scilly is a popular holiday destination, and many naturalists visit the islands. Universities and other groups also make field trips to Scilly to study various aspects of the ecology, especially the marine biology. Another large group that has contributed greatly to scientific information about Scilly is the diverse body of professional biologists who continue to carry out surveys and all manner of research projects on the flora and fauna, often on behalf of statutory agencies such as English Nature. Clearly there are now too many people to do more than acknowledge the contribution of a few of their number. The selection is necessarily subjective, covering mainly the earlier naturalists, but also people I know, and those whose work I have drawn upon. It is becoming increasingly difficult to acknowledge everyone who has added to our knowledge of the natural history of Scilly – especially when it comes to birds and plants. So I hope those mentioned here will stand as representative of the rest.

Prior to the early 1900s the only notes on the natural history of the Isles of Scilly were occasional comments in reports of broader interest such as that by

Robert Heath (1750), after he had spent about a year in Scilly. When J. E. ('Ted')
Lousley published his *Flora* in 1971 he gave a comprehensive account of botanists
who had contributed to the discovery of the flora of the islands. In this he commented on the paucity of botanical records from Scilly before the early twentieth
century, which he put down to the inaccessibility of the islands. So when Sir
William Hooker, the first Director of the Royal Botanic Gardens, Kew, spent ten
days in Scilly in spring 1813, visiting all the larger islands and making only the
most miserable of comments on a few species he had observed, Lousley is
scathing in his assessment of the great opportunity lost.

Fortunately things picked up a little from then on. In 1821 a Warwickshire
botanist, the Reverend William Thomas Bree, visited Scilly and listed a few
plants, including the first record of balm-leaved figwort *Scrophularia scorodonia*.
Other botanists also visited the islands: Francis King Eagle collected white
mignonette *Reseda alba* in 1826, and Matilda White discovered orange bird's-foot
Ornithopus pinnatus in 1838 (Fig. 21). Fifteen species of Scilly ferns identified by
Edward William Cooke were published by North (1850). The year 1852 was
apparently a good one, with four excellent botanists visiting the islands in the
shape of Joseph Woods, John Ralfs and the two Misses Millett. These ladies
spent five weeks on Scilly in June and July and listed 150 flowering plants and
ferns. Lousley is full of praise for the competence of the sisters and only regrets
they did not include localities for their finds. Another botanist who paid a short
visit to Scilly was Frederick Townsend, who stayed at Tregarthen's Hotel on

FIG 21. Miss Matilda White discovered orange bird's-foot on a visit to Tresco in 1838.
(Drawing by Alma Hathway)

St Mary's (the hotel is still there). Although he only spent ten days in the islands, he recorded 348 species and published his list in 1864. Unfortunately Lousley found 21 records on the list were probably mistakes, some of which were later corrected by Townsend himself in his own copy of the report (Lousley, 1971). As botanists at the time did not have the competent floras and identification aids we have now, I have nothing but admiration for their achievements.
As more and more botanists managed to get to Scilly, some of them made a greater contribution than others to the flora; their records are acknowledged by Lousley (1971).

It was fortunate that Ted Lousley, a well-known and respected amateur botanist, visited the Isles of Scilly in September 1936, when he personally added western ramping-fumitory *Fumaria occidentalis* to the flora. He was so taken with the islands that he continued his visits, recording many additional species and experiencing every month from March to September during the next four years. The first manuscript version of the *Flora* was completed in 1941 and then hidden away during the war years to be finally completed and published in 1971. The last visit Lousley paid to Scilly was in May 1975 when he stayed at Star Castle Hotel on St Mary's, conducting a group of botanists around the islands and showing them dwarf pansy *Viola kitaibeliana*. Lousley, by profession a bank manager, was at some time Honorary Curator of the South London Botanical Institute. As it happened this was where many of the specimens, correspondence and manuscripts from botanists who had visited Scilly had been deposited. Among those whose material he had access to were Hambrough (visited Scilly 1845), Woods (visited 1852), Beeby (visited 1873) and Townsend (visited 1862).

Lousley's own herbarium specimens are now at Reading University. Some of his notebooks, letters, photographs and papers, as well as the manuscript of the *Flora*, are held in the archives of the Isles of Scilly Museum on St Mary's. He also wrote a number of reports on the flora for the Nature Conservancy Council during 1946, 1954, 1957 and 1967, of which the latter three have been consulted in preparing this book, the earliest report having apparently been lost.

It was an early visit by Cambridgeshire classics don and well-known amateur naturalist John Raven to St Agnes in March 1950 that added the least adder's-tongue fern and early meadow-grass *Poa infirma* to the flora (Raven, 1950). Raven spent ten days in March and April in Scilly accompanied by his father and Dr R. C. L. Burges. He found early meadow-grass was abundant and widely distributed on St Mary's, Tresco and St Martin's but not on St Agnes (he did not get to Bryher). While having a picnic on Wingletang Down, St Agnes, Raven found the least adder's-tongue fern. He had seen dead fronds on a previous visit but it was too late to identify them. Another plant that he discovered was dwarf

FIG 22. In 1950 naturalist John Raven found several new plants on Scilly, including dwarf pansy on Tresco and St Martin's. (David Holyoak)

pansy: two colonies on Tresco and also some plants on newly dug fields on St Martin's (Fig. 22). John Raven wrote a number of books and papers on plants, including *Mountain Flowers* in the New Naturalist series.

Besides acknowledging the many botanists who had contributed the records that formed the basis of his *Flora*, Lousley also refers to the first attempt to classify the common plant communities in Scilly by Oleg Polunin in 1953. At that time Polunin was the much-respected biology teacher at Charterhouse School, Godalming. He produced short descriptions of the plant communities in *Some Plant Communities of the Scilly Isles* (1953) as a handout for the boys he took on field trips to Scilly. Later in the 1950s he was Botanical Society of the British Isles (BSBI) recorder for West Cornwall, when he also found time to visit Scilly.

Polunin is probably now better known as the author of a number of photograph-based field guides to European plants.

Not everyone who recorded plants in Scilly was a botanist. W. S. Bristowe was an arachnologist who visited Scilly twice and wrote two seminal papers on the spiders (Bristowe, 1929, 1935). What is particularly remarkable is that he managed to land on so many of the small islets during his visit and not only collect spiders but also record the vegetation. In some cases until recently his were virtually the only records we have for some of the least accessible islands. Apparently he had a period of unprecedented calm weather for his stay that allowed him to make so many landings.

Someone else who seemed to manage to get onto many of the small rocky islands was a local photographer and keen naturalist. C. J. King lived on St Mary's and owned a photographic business, sold postcards and gave lectures on natural history. He published an account of the birds and other wildlife as *Some Notes on Wild Nature in Scillonia* (1924). This is a small volume but full of his own very personal and interesting observations. He seems to have made many expeditions to uninhabited islands and scrambled among rocks to get close to the birds or seals he wanted to photograph, even spending the night there on occasion.

The association of the Dorrien-Smith family with Scilly, especially Tresco, has been of considerable significance to the natural history of the islands ever since Augustus Smith first leased the islands from the Duchy in 1834. During his stewardship Augustus Smith was responsible for many introductions, besides plants. Some of these introductions were quite eccentric: different coloured rabbits, deer, and even 'ostriches' – although from the photographs in Cowan (2001) and Llewellyn (2005) and the probable source of the birds (Augustus Smith apparently having 'kidnapped' the first one from a ship that had come from Rio) it would seem these were in fact South American rheas *Rhea americana*.

Augustus Smith also had an interest in birds, and many shot on the islands ended up in the Abbey collection. He also regularly had shooting parties, especially on Tresco, that sometimes resulted in flushing unusual species – which were shot. After the death of Augustus Smith, his nephew, Mr Thomas Algernon Smith-Dorrien (who in keeping with his uncle's wishes changed his name to Smith-Dorrien-Smith, later shortened to Dorrien-Smith), took a leading interest in the new flower-growing industry (Vyvyan, 1953). The Dorrien-Smith family inherited the lease of all the islands, but when Major Arthur A. Dorrien-Smith ('the Major') succeeded his father Thomas Algernon he returned the lease to the Duchy, retaining only Tresco and the uninhabited isles. Although the Dorrien-Smiths have been mainly interested in plant acquisition for the Gardens, they also continued to add to their large collection of stuffed birds, mostly taken in the islands (generally only one of each species was collected). Between 1922 and 1940 the Misses Dorrien-Smith (Gwen and her niece Ann) made a collection of Scilly wild flowers. What Lousley describes as an 'unreliable' list of these, without localities, appears in Vyvyan (1953). But I think Lousley was a little harsh, as most of the 260 species are plants that are still on the Scilly list.

The Major took a particular interest in natural history, especially birds. He contributed regularly to *British Birds* and the reports of the Cornwall Birdwatching and Preservation Society. Commander Thomas Dorrien-Smith, the only son of the Major to survive World War II, was the Nature Conservancy Council (NCC) honorary warden until the 1960s and also held a unique licence under the 1954 Protection of Birds Act from NCC to take bird specimens to add to the family's private Abbey collection. 'The Commander', as he was known, was very disappointed when he was not told about the 1958 northern waterthrush *Seiurus noveboracensis* (the first for Britain), as he would have liked to add it to the collection! He was persuaded that rare birds should be left alive for others to enjoy and this was apparently why he stopped collecting (J. Parslow, *in litt.*). The last specimen shot for the Abbey collection was taken by Fred Wardle, the estate gamekeeper, about 1956. Later Peter MacKenzie persuaded the Commander to allow the bird collection to be moved from the Abbey to the basement of the recently opened museum on St Mary's. While the collection was in the Abbey it was housed in a dark corridor; unfortunately when moved to the museum the specimens were exposed to strong light, eventually resulting in loss of colour and some deterioration. The Commander leased Tresco from 1955 until his death in 1973; his son Robert Dorrien-Smith succeeded him. Over the years the Abbey Gardens have been the source of most of the alien plants and animals now established in Scilly.

Collecting bird specimens as mounted skins was a perfectly respectable hobby among gentlemen in the nineteenth century. One collector, Edward Hearle Rodd, was author of *The Birds of Cornwall and The Scilly Isles* (1880), although he died while the book was in production and the final editing had to be carried out by his friend James Edmund Harting. Although there are references to Scilly throughout the text, the main section on Scilly consists of the collected letters from his nephew Francis Rashleigh Rodd, written to his uncle when staying on Tresco between 1864 and 1871. Rodd was a well-known collector of bird skins, and many specimens from Scilly ended up in his collection, eventually passing to his nephew on his death. F. R. Rodd was also a sportsman and collector, and shot many birds both for the pot and to add to his collection of stuffed birds. He also had dead birds sent to him from Scilly. One of his trophies that clearly delighted him was a bittern *Botaurus stellaris* that he 'knocked down' on Christmas Day 1864. He decided to have it mounted with the neck feathers 'rampant' rather than 'couchant'. One interesting letter comments on how the gentlemen of the county were giving up their hobby of falconry and were now shooting birds instead. Collections of birds' eggs and stuffed birds became very popular at the time. When his uncle died Rodd inherited his bird collection and housed it at Trebartha Hall in Cornwall with his own specimens. Everything was lost when the Hall was burned down in 1949 (Penhallurick, 1978).

Leslie and Clare Harvey moved to Scilly soon after Leslie retired as Professor of Zoology at Exeter University. Clare Harvey had also been a lecturer at the university and had specialised for many years in the study of seaweeds. They lived in a bungalow on the Garrison that was approached through a sally port (one of the stairways through the granite walls connecting one level with another). Ducking your head to descend the precipitous stairs to the garden, you were aware of all manner of plants, wild and cultivated, that ran riot on the walls and in the narrow garden. Clare was a great collector, and it is perhaps fortunate for future botanists that the high walls of the Garrison imprisoned most of the plants within the garden. During their sojourn on the islands the Harveys were the focus of all that was botanical, and in 1970 they started a wild-flower table in the museum, exhibiting live specimens during the summer months, replenished weekly by a group of local enthusiasts known affectionately as the museum 'Flower Ladies'. Clare was BSBI recorder for Scilly until the 1980s, but sadly, despite an unrivalled knowledge of the wild flowers, she kept no records, wrote very little and rather lost heart without Leslie's company after he died in 1986. Despite increasing frailty and failing sight, Clare still took an interest in the plants and continued to write to me and send specimens until just before her death in 1996 when she was in her nineties. The 'Flower Ladies' continued to put out their weekly display of local wild flowers until 2004, when the last team retired. But Julia Ottery (who produced a book of her wild-flower paintings in 1966), Celia Sisam, Elizabeth Legg, Lesley Knight and others were responsible for adding many plant records to the flora. Another resident who contributed to what we know about the flora was Peter Clough, who was head gardener at Tresco Abbey from 1973 until 1984. Besides being a notable horticulturalist, Peter was also a keen botanist and took a great interest in the wild flowers on Tresco. He maintained a card-index of plant records during his time on Tresco which he allowed me to copy into the database of the Isles of Scilly plants.

The Isles of Scilly Museum was opened in 1967 by the Isles of Scilly Museum Association with the aim of providing a permanent home for the finds from the archaeological site on Nornour. The present purpose-built building was built by the Council of the Isles of Scilly, financed by subscriptions, donations from the

Duchy of Cornwall, various trusts and generous well-wishers, including a
handsome interest-free loan from the late Mr K. M. Leach, a benefactor with
a great interest in Scilly and especially the wildlife. Many natural history
collections are held in the museum, including the Tresco Abbey bird collection,
seashells, lichens and many other specimens. The museum also houses a small
library of books on Scilly and many photographs, maps and artefacts. As
honorary curator, Steve Ottery ran the museum for many years, assisted by a
team of devoted and knowledgeable volunteers. Recently, Amanda Martin was
appointed as part-time curator, although she too relies on a rota of volunteers
to help deal with around 12,000 visitors annually and enquiries from all over
the world. Another well-known resident of Hugh Town is the potter Humphrey
Wakefield. Humphrey has contributed to many aspects of the work of the
museum, both archaeological and natural history, as well as being the first
chairman of the Environmental Trust.

A former senior curator of another museum, the Royal Cornwall Museum
in Truro, the late Roger D. Penhallurick wrote a number of books and papers
on the natural history of Cornwall and the Isles of Scilly, including *Birds of the
Cornish Coast* (1969), *The Birds of Cornwall and the Isles of Scilly* (1978) and *The
Butterflies of Cornwall and the Isles of Scilly* (1996).

The MacKenzie family on St Mary's had been very much involved in the
setting up of the local museum. Peter Z. MacKenzie was the veterinary surgeon
on the islands and also an enthusiastic naturalist and amateur archaeologist who
contributed much to what was known at the time, especially on birds and plants.
In 1971 he was appointed part-time honorary NCC warden. Until David Hunt
arrived, Peter and his great friend Ron Symons, plus Hilda Quick and the young
Francis Hicks on St Agnes, were the only resident birdwatchers on the islands.
As honorary warden, Peter was responsible, among other things, for setting up
the first nature trail at Lower Moors. Also at this time the NCC were bought a
boat, the *Marius Neilson*, by Mr Leach (who had helped with the loan to set up the
museum), and this enabled Peter to warden the uninhabited islands and count
seals. Until Peter's untimely death in 1977 his boatman was a young islander,
Cyril Nicholas. In 1979 Cyril was taken on as the NCC's and later English
Nature's boatman/estate worker, running the *Marius Neilson* and then her later
replacement *Melza*. Over the years Cyril has taken many survey teams around
the islands and has been particularly adept at tricky landings on the smaller
uninhabited islands. He has also contributed a great deal to the knowledge of
the natural history of Scilly.

Someone who made a huge contribution to the understanding of the early
Scilly environment was Frank Turk, who had lived in Cornwall from 1939 with a

collection of 14,000 books and a private museum of specimens. Dr Turk was a polymath whose interests ranged from Chinese and Japanese culture to poetry, Siamese cats, art and music, and the natural sciences. He wrote papers on many natural history subjects; he was an expert on mites, myriapods, false scorpions, mammals and animal bones from archaeological sites. His studies of animal bones found on archaeological sites in Scilly have given us a detailed picture of the species of birds and animals that formerly inhabited the islands. His wife Stella Turk worked in tandem with her husband for many years, supporting his work. Stella Turk was born in Scilly, on St Mary's, but emigrated with her family to New Zealand when she was two, returning to Cornwall when she was seven. Stella is perhaps best known for her work on land and marine molluscs and other invertebrates, as well as her book *Sea-shore Life in Cornwall and the Isles of Scilly* (1971). Stella retired from her work at the Cornwall Biological Records Unit in 1993, since when she has continued to give her time voluntarily, entering thousands of records on the 'Erica' database of Cornish records. In January 2003 Stella's contribution to Cornish natural history was recognised when she was awarded the MBE in the New Year's Honours.

It was when I first visited Scilly and stayed at the St Agnes Bird Observatory at Lower Town Farm that I met Hilda Quick, the resident birdwatcher and a force to be reckoned with. Miss Quick, as she was always called, moved to her cottage just a few metres from Periglis beach, St Agnes, in 1951. When the bird observatory first started up in 1957 she was at first greatly opposed to the use of mist-nets and would cut birds out of the nets if she found them.

FIG 23. 'Birdwatching from a boat'. A woodcut by Hilda Quick of herself, from her book *Birds of the Scilly Isles* (1964).

FIG 24. 'Seabirds'. Another of Hilda Quick's woodcuts, produced in her tiny cottage by Periglis beach, St Agnes.

Fortunately she was eventually won over and although she probably merely tolerated ringing, she nevertheless became a stalwart friend and supporter of the bird observatory. She wrote *Birds of the Scilly Isles* (1964), a small volume illustrated with her own woodcuts (Figs 23 & 24), and also edited the Scilly records for the *Cornwall Bird Report* for many years. Her hand-printed and very original Christmas cards were a delight to receive. If especially favoured, you might be invited in for a glass of wine made from local wild flowers. In this she was quite an expert and enjoyed demonstrating the difference between wine made from ling flowers and that made from bell heather. Miss Quick kept her elephant-size copy of Audubon's *Birds of America* propped open for visitors to admire in her cottage.

The St Agnes Bird Observatory was started by a group of enthusiastic London birdwatchers and ringers. The first year they camped, but in 1958 they moved into Lower Town Farm. The founder and organiser was John Parslow, then working at the British Trust for Ornithology's Ringing Office, based in the Bird Room at the Natural History Museum. John later went to join David Lack's team at the Edward Grey Institute of Field Ornithology in Oxford, working on bird migration. The unoccupied farmhouse building was rented from Lewis and Alice Hicks of the Lighthouse Farm, who took a great interest in the doings of the birdwatchers. It was in Lewis Hicks' boat *Undaunted* that many of the ringing expeditions to the bird sanctuary island of Annet were made. Perhaps part of their interest was due to their youngest son Francis, who was a small boy at the time and an avid birdwatcher. Before he went away to school on the mainland Francis had an extraordinary bird list, with many great rarities, but no woodpeckers, owls or other common birds! Francis now runs the farm, still finding rare birds; he always wears a pair of binoculars, even when working on his tractor.

Two other enthusiastic birdwatchers at the time were Ruth and Gordon George. Gordon was a farm labourer who worked for Lewis Hicks, and he and his wife Ruth lived in a cottage (now the Turk's Head pub) by the quay at Porth Conger. They not only kept a lookout for any new birds that had arrived, but encouraged the birdwatchers to stop off at their cottage for a 'second breakfast' after the morning circuit of the island. This usually ensured a coffee and a generous wedge of the fruit cake Ruth baked specially for the birdwatchers.

The early days of running an observatory on a small, inhabited island had their problems, such as when the young daughter of the island's postmaster and her pony rode into a mist-net. Even in its short life, the observatory carried out very valuable work as part of a network of bird observatories around the country. Unlike the big, manned observatories with resident staff, places like St Agnes were run on a shoestring, with a committee who organised the finance and bookings as well as the teams of volunteer ringers and observers. During the life of the observatory it attracted many of the well-known 'names' of the ornithological world. Some stayed in the hostel-type accommodation at the observatory and others brought their families and stayed at guesthouses on the island. Many of these have remained loyal to the islands and have returned many times since.

Over the eleven years of its existence the Observatory Committee recorded breeding success, migrants and ringing in an annual report. Although it officially closed in 1967 when the farmhouse became uninhabitable, the logs were maintained for another two years (the logs are now lodged in the Alexander Library, Oxford). Sadly, once the observatory closed the main focus of ornithological work in Scilly was lost for a time. More recently there have been ringers on a regular basis, as well as individuals carrying out scientific work, seabird surveys for example. Most of this work is now coordinated by the Isles of Scilly Wildlife Trust. Perhaps the best-known spin-off from the observatory days was the upsurge of the 'twitching' phenomenon, which started with a group of London birdwatchers some of whom were regular visitors to the observatory. They had found that the cyclonic conditions in the Atlantic in autumn could lead to the arrival of North American birds on Scilly, as well as the European migrants that arrived with easterlies. Now autumn in Scilly is a phenomenon in itself, with the arrival of hundreds of birdwatchers every October.

Frank Gibson is the fourth generation of the Gibson family to be a professional photographer in Scilly. Many of Frank's superb photographs of landscape, seas and wildlife have been reproduced in numerous books and publications about Scilly, including several on plants and other natural history subjects. Several photographs from the Gibson collection (which includes photographs by earlier members of the Gibson family) are reproduced in these pages. One of Frank's collaborators on several books and booklets about the natural history of

Scilly was David Hunt, who came to Scilly in the early 1960s, initially as gardener at the Island Hotel on Tresco. Later he moved to St Mary's, where over the years he carved a niche for himself as the 'Scilly Birdman', despite great difficulties in making a living as an independent guide, lecturer and local bird expert. He was responsible for writing a 'code of conduct' for birdwatchers which helped to improve relations between islanders and birdwatchers. David's autobiography, *Confessions of a Scilly Birdman* (1985), was published posthumously after his career came to an untimely end in northern India in 1985, when a tiger killed him as he was leading a birdwatching tour. When I saw him shortly before his final trip, he mentioned his need to get a good photo of a tiger; his camera was recovered after the accident and when the film was processed he had indeed secured a good picture of the tiger that killed him.

After David Hunt's death his friend Will Wagstaff continued the slide shows and guided walks that had become very popular with visitors. Will had, like many other birdwatchers, first come to Scilly on holiday, returning every year from 1975 until he eventually moved to St Mary's in 1981. For a while Will worked for the Isles of Scilly Environmental Trust (now Wildlife Trust) as field officer until becoming a self-employed tour leader and lecturer. When the Isles of Scilly Bird Group was started in 2000, by a group of resident birdwatchers, Will was the first Honorary President. The ISBG publishes the excellent *Isles of Scilly Bird & Natural History Review* annually. With a nucleus of resident birders on the islands there has been an increase in observations during the winter months, and indeed throughout the year. This has culminated in the production of another book on the birds of Scilly (Flood *et al.*, in press).

During the twelve years he lived on St Mary's Peter Robinson carried out ringing and population studies as well as organising surveys on behalf of RSPB, JNCC and English Nature, including 'Seabird 2000' and the Breeding Bird Atlas. In 2003 his interest in the islands and their ornithology culminated in the publication of *The Birds of the Isles of Scilly*. This monumental work reviewed the birds of Scilly from historic references up to the present day.

The Environmental Trust for the Isles of Scilly was set up in 1986. In 2001 the Trust became the Isles of Scilly Wildlife Trust, the forty-seventh member of the Wildlife Trusts partnership in the UK. Based on a total land area of 3,065 hectares at LAT (lowest astronomical tide), the Trust is responsible for 60 per cent of Scilly, with 1,845 ha leased from the Duchy of Cornwall. A very small trust, with only three members of staff in 2006, they have an unusually challenging operation, working in an island situation where all the tools, machinery and volunteers have to be transported by boat from St Mary's to other islands for a day's practical management work. During 2000 the Trust took on the disused

1900 Woolpack gun battery on the Garrison, which has now been refurbished and is used as a custom-built volunteer centre with accommodation for thirteen volunteers, including an underground meeting room.

Many films and TV programmes are made on Scilly. Andrew Cooper first visited Scilly in 1981, and made several films about the natural history of the islands, *Isles Apart, Secret Nature* and *Lost Lands of Scilly*. He also wrote *Secret Nature of the Channel Shore* (1992) and *Secret Nature of the Isles of Scilly* (2006). While working on the films Andrew spent many months in Scilly, observing and filming the wildlife. He was the first person to photograph caravanning behaviour of Scilly shrews. Andrew is Vice-President of the Isles of Scilly Wildlife Trust.

In recent years a number of other naturalists, both local and visiting, have made their unique contributions to our understanding of Scilly's wildlife. Local diver Mark Groves has written and lectured on the marine life of the islands, photographing many underwater subjects. St Agnes farmer Mike Hicks records and writes about moths, and local restaurateur Bryan Thomas's superb photographs are a regular feature of the *Isles of Scilly Bird Report and Natural History Review*. Martin Goodey, who runs Trenoweth Research Station, is also an enthusiastic photographer of birds and insects. For many years Stephen Westcott has been studying the Scilly population of grey seals *Halichoerus grypus* (Fig. 25). He works from a kayak, which enables him to get very close to the animals with minimal disturbance.

FIG 25. Grey seal among tree mallow. (David Mawer)

Lower plants have not been forgotten, and have been studied by Bryan Edwards (lichens), David Holyoak, Jean Paton and Robert Finch (bryophytes). Insects have been getting more attention too, with the papers by Ian Beavis, and a number of other entomologists, including local birdwatchers in Scilly who have now extended their interests into recording bush-crickets, stick insects and other groups. Molluscs, ferns and plants have also had their disciples. The production of the *Isles of Scilly Bird Report and Natural History Review* has encouraged visiting and local naturalists to publish their records and papers, making information much more readily available. A number of contributors to the *Review* have been very generous with information and illustrations for this volume and are acknowledged elsewhere.

CHAPTER 5

St Mary's

Not a tree to be seen, but there are granite piles on the coast such as I never saw before, and furze-covered hills with larks soaring and singing above them.

George Eliot (1857)

ST MARY'S IS THE largest of the Isles of Scilly at 649 hectares (above MHWS) and approximately 4km × 3km from coast to coast. Only on St Mary's is there enough metalled road to merit any kind of bus service or any traffic as such. There are just over seventeen kilometres of road that link most of the communities on St Mary's. Besides being busy with local and farm traffic, the sightseeing buses, the hire bikes and the taxi cabs all use the road to provide a service for the holidaymakers who flock to the island in the summer (bringing your own car to Scilly is not advised).

Away from the sea the interior of the island is gently undulating with a slightly more 'mainland' feel due to a largely cultivated landscape with small hamlets scattered among the farms. Many of the fields are arable and often have interesting weed floras, usually including some of the arable plants now becoming increasingly rare in Britain. The field boundaries, consisting of pine windbreaks, evergreen and elm 'fences' (hedges), and stone 'hedges', all have their particular natural history and landscape features. The unfarmed land, comprising grassland, wetlands and heath, is mostly around the coast. Also around the coastal areas are spectacular rocky headlands, cliffs, sandy bays and dunes. The 'main' road forms a figure of eight round the middle of the island, with a few other small sections of made-up road linking the hamlets. Farmland away from the road is generally inaccessible to the general public except were served by footpaths. There is a coastal path round the island and a system of footpaths that mostly link the roads with the coast, or access the nature reserves.

THE BUILT-UP AREA

Around the main harbour on the west of St Mary's is Hugh Town (Fig. 26), the principal town in the islands, the administrative 'capital' where most of the main business of the islands takes place, with the Council offices, shops, banks, hotels, museum and the nearby industrial estate at Porth Mellon. The Council of the Isles of Scilly has unusual responsibilities, and although representing a very small population of approximately 1,600 (c.4,000 in summer) it has virtually the same powers as a county council. The offices of the Duchy of Cornwall (the landlord of the Isles of Scilly), the Wildlife Trust and other organisations are also mainly based in Hugh Town. The passenger ship RMV *Scillonian* sails from St Mary's harbour, and with the airport forms the main link with the mainland. The present quay is built over an island, Rat Island, and out into St Mary's Pool. From the harbour the inter-island launches and the 'tripper' boats link with the off-islands and run sightseeing trips.

FIG 26. A view of St Mary's harbour, Hugh Town and the Garrison, May 2003. (Rosemary Parslow)

Much of the town is on the low-lying land that was originally a sand bar joining the promontory of the Hugh to the rest of St Mary's between the Pool (harbour) and Porth Cressa. From there the town spreads up the slopes of the Garrison and Church Street. The proximity of the harbour and the beach has resulted in many coastal plants having become residents in the town. Portland spurge *Euphorbia portlandica* grows at the base and on top of some walls, tiny sea spleenwort *Asplenium marinum* ferns grow in crevices on many walls and four-leaved allseed *Polycarpon tetraphyllum* and rock sea-spurrey *Spergularia rupicola* along cracks in pavements. Some plants have become strongly associated with Hugh Town, including sand rocket *Diplotaxis muralis*, sweet alyssum *Lobularia maritima* and cineraria *Pericallis hybrida*. With all the small gardens around the town many garden plants and more exotic plants are able to escape into alleys and byways, so part of the fun for a botanist wandering around the streets is not knowing what discovery might be waiting around the next corner!

During the summer holiday season Hugh Town can be quite a bustling place. Every morning the holiday people stream down the main streets to the harbour, where they join the queue on the quayside for tickets and then embark on one of the launches that will take them to one of the other inhabited islands or, if the weather is good and the seas calm, on a trip around the Eastern Isles or Annet and the Western Rocks. On the calmest days there will perhaps be a boat going as far as the Bishop Rock lighthouse. This can be an exciting trip that guarantees close views of seabirds and seals. There is always a sea running beyond the Western Rocks, even in the calmest weather, giving the passengers something to boast about in the pub later. But sailing out among the Western Rocks, among the savage beauty of jagged islands and myriad splinters of rock just breaking the surface of the waves, is a graphic reminder of the hazards associated with the sea and Scilly. Reaching Bishop Rock means sailing over another long stretch of restless water beyond the Western Rocks towards the long finger of the lighthouse pointing skywards in the distance. As you sail beneath the lighthouse there is little sign of the rock on which it is built, and looking up at the tower above is an utterly awesome experience. The return of the tripper boats results in a reverse flow back up the main street from the quay as everyone returns for the evening. For a little while now the shops are busy. And if you are a birdwatcher it is time to check the blackboard where bird news is chalked up, hoping all the time you have not missed anything exciting.

On the opposite side of the island to Hugh Town is the hamlet of Old Town (Fig. 27). This was the main town and former harbour (the quay can still be seen) on St Mary's in medieval times, with a castle where the Governor lived, but it was superseded by the better-fortified Hugh Town. There is little left of Ennor Castle

FIG 27. Old Town harbour with its old granite quay and the church, January 2000. (Rosemary Parslow)

now, just the mound on which it stood; presumably it was demolished and the stone used to build Star Castle. Despite improved sea defences and rebuilding of the sea wall and the road in 1996 it is not unusual to see sand-bags propped up against front doors or seaweed in the street in winter; the lower part of Old Town is another area under constant threat from the sea. Overlooking the Bay is Old Town Church, where the surrounding churchyard, with its different levels and terraces, surrounded by trees, provides a haven for many unusual species of plants. It is impossible to overlook the multi-coloured cinerarias that have escaped from cultivation and rampaged over all the walls, paths and old graves. Other plants growing in the churchyard include grassland species, ferns or garden escapes that find refuge among the gravestones and walls. Migrant birds are often located in the churchyard, and the sheltered conditions also attract many insects and even bats on calm evenings. Some of the nearby fields behind the church also have good arable weed floras. Not far from the church along the edge of the bay is a large isolated rock, Carn Leh, which is an important site for rare lichens.

INLAND ST MARY'S

Inland the countryside is slightly undulating farmland served by the 'main' road. The island bus service only drives around the main part of the interior, some roads being very narrow. Between the fields, both pasture and flower fields, the boundaries are formed both by stone 'hedges' with a rich cover of ferns, grasses and other plants, and by tall, clipped evergreen 'fences' (Fig. 28). Many of the roadsides are fringed with elm trees, predominately Dutch elm *Ulmus* × *hollandica*. In sheltered areas the elm trees are able to grow tall, those in the valley of Holy Vale and around Maypole being some of the finest. Crossing the island are several conifer shelterbelts (Fig. 29), which in places include the distinctive silhouettes of Monterey pines *Pinus radiata*, where remnants of earlier plantings still survive.

FIG 28. Inland St Mary's: evergreen fences near Porth Hellick, August 2006. (Rosemary Parslow)

FIG 29. A pine shelterbelt and an arable field covered in corn spurrey near Watermill Cove, June 2005. (Rosemary Parslow)

CLIFFS AND COASTS

Most of the coastland of St Mary's consists of cliffs, not very high, but spectacular enough at times when gales drive the waves in onto the rocks. In places a few small bays break the coastline and there are two large promontories, the Garrison in the southwest and Peninnis Head in the south. In many places there are granite carns (tors) eroded into extraordinary, fantastical shapes: Pulpit Rock, Tooth Rock and the Loaded Camel are just a few well-known examples (Fig. 30). Above the cliffs and steep slopes along the west coast are typical maritime-cliff plant communities, dense bracken communities on the deeper soils, heather-dominated heath and short grassland on the shallower soils and over rocks. Among the shrub species growing on the coast are both common gorse *Ulex europaeus* and western gorse *U. gallii* and scattered patches of broom. Along the coastal edge the maritime grassland sometimes extends inland as a series of pastures that in summer are bright with the yellow flowers of common cat's-ear *Hypochaeris radicata* amid a colourful mixture of grasses and forbs.

At Carn Morval, on the steepest part of the coast, part of the nine-hole golf course is perched on a rocky promontory above the slope. The rest of the

FIG 30. Pulpit Rock on Peninnis Head, St Mary's, May 2006. (Richard Green)

FIG 31. Bant's Carn on Halangy Down, St Mary's, probably the best known of the Bronze Age entrance graves in the Isles of Scilly. March 2006. (Rosemary Parslow)

golf course sits high above at the top of the slope, where its manicured greens frequently attract migrating birds. As with the airfield this can be very frustrating for the excluded birdwatchers! Beyond Carn Morval is another area of coastal heath at Halangy Down, where in a carefully tended area of grass and mown heather is an important archaeological site managed by English Heritage. These are the remains of an Iron Age/Romano-British village settlement of many small buildings, now marked only by low walls, and the ridges denoting earlier field systems on the nearby slopes. At the top of the hill is Bant's Carn, a large Bronze Age entrance grave, one of the best examples of its type in Scilly (Fig. 31). The whole closely managed and mown site is quite species-rich, and even the walls and banks of the ancient village have an interesting flora that includes western gorse, hairy bird's-foot-trefoil *Lotus subbiflorus*, subterranean clover *Trifolium subterraneum* growing on and among the stones. The turf is also full of chamomile *Chamaemelum nobile*, deliciously scenting the air as you explore. Ruts on some of the paths nearby have a miniature flora of toad rush *Juncus bufonius* and sometimes in spring an unusual but very inconspicuous alien called Scilly pigmyweed *Crassula decumbens*. This is a South African species, probably introduced accidentally with other plants to the nearby Bant's Carn farm. Only very recently has it apparently started to spread away from the farm, and it can now sometimes be seen on the path leading up the hill towards the golf course.

Just beyond Bant's Carn Farm the land slopes down to the sand dunes that form the northern tip of the island at Bar Point. The dune system is very disturbed. Part has been quarried and there is also a part used as a dump. Much of the dune system has become colonised by bracken and bramble *Rubus* agg. communities. There are areas of scattered gorse bushes, where both the rare balm-leaved figwort and Babington's leek *Allium ampeloprasum* var. *babingtonii* can be found. Closer to the quarry and the dump some plants of garden origin have become established so that you can come upon bear's breech *Acanthus mollis*, montbretia *Crocosmia* × *crocosmiiflora*, fennel *Foeniculum vulgare* and even the giant rhubarb plant *Gunnera tinctori*. Somewhere in the dunes near here the fern moonwort *Botrychium lunaria* used to grow under the bracken. It was last recorded by Lousley in 1940, and may have been lost when the area suffered major disturbance some time after 1954, from various activities including re-laying the submarine telegraph cable, winning sand and dumping rubbish. Since then, despite much searching, there has been no further sign of the moonwort.

More areas of bracken communities follow the northern coast of the island all the way round from Bar Point to Innisidgen, Helvear Down, and right down to the narrow inlet at Watermill Cove. On this northern part of the coast there are areas of pine shelterbelts, which extend right round to the eastern side of the island, and large stretches of beautiful heathland near the coast. Patches of tall gorse with an understorey of lower heathland plants grow along the sides of the path as it continues around the coast, also appearing anywhere there are breaks in the bracken cover.

Close to the coast path are two impressive entrance graves, Innisidgen Upper Chamber and Innisidgen Lower Chamber. Around the barrows the vegetation is kept regularly mown, resulting in species-rich lawns of grasses, sedges and typical heathland plants, demonstrating the potential richness of the vegetation if the surrounding overgrown areas could be restored and perhaps maintained by grazing. Beside the path what appears to be a low wall is the remains of the former Civil War breastworks, half-buried in dense vegetation. As the path drops down the hill into Watermill Cove, the Watermill Stream runs into the sea through mats of dense hemlock water-dropwort, fool's-water-cress *Apium nodiflorum* and a group of grey sallow *Salix cinerea oleifolia* trees. Just round the corner there are steep cliff exposures along the section of the inlet at Tregear's Porth, an important geological site, notified as the Watermill Cove Geological Conservation Review site. From here the path continues along the coast, and another one follows the Watermill Stream inland along the heavily shaded lane lined with ferns.

The mosaic of heathland, gorse, bracken and bramble continues along the coast past Mount Todden. In places there are more sections of Civil War fortifications and much earlier archaeological sites. Below the cliffs at Darity's Hole is a very important underwater site where many unusual marine species have been recorded. Towards Deep Point there is an area of 'waved heath' (see Chapter 10), and elsewhere there are patches of heather still beneath the taller bracken, as well as around rocks and paths. Where there is a freshwater seepage down one of the slopes, the understorey consists of broad buckler fern *Dryopteris dilitata*, occasional soft shield-fern *Polystichum setiferum* and marsh pennywort *Hydrocotyle vulgaris*. Near Deep Point in an area of short coastal turf careful searching may reveal another rare lichen, ciliate strap-lichen *Heterodermia leucomela*. It was at Deep Point that at one time the islanders disposed of cars and other rubbish over the cliff. Although the practice has been stopped, the remains of vehicles at the bottom of the cliff in deep water apparently now support a rich marine flora and fauna! At Porth Wreck there is a former quarry in the cliff, often the place to find unusual casual plants.

Porth Hellick Down is one of the largest areas of wind-pruned waved heath on St Mary's. Much of the gorse among the heathers in the area is western gorse, with flowers a deeper golden colour than the yellow of common gorse. Around the Porth Hellick barrow Ancient Monument is a closely mown circle of grass starred with flowers of chamomile, tormentil *Potentilla erecta* and lousewort *Pedicularis sylvestris*, as well as stunted bell heather and other typical heathland plants. Similar vegetation covers the burial mound with a dense sward of low grasses and flowers.

South of the deep bay of Porth Hellick lies the open heathland of Salakee Down with the rather eroded outline of Giant's Castle, an Iron Age hill fort. At Salakee Down is a beautiful stretch of coastal grassland and waved heath, again with common gorse and western gorse, bell heather, ling and other heathland species (Fig. 32). Close to the Giant's Castle are a number of small damp and seasonally waterlogged pits with wetland plants including lesser spearwort *Ranunculus flammula*, bulbous *Juncus bulbosus* and soft rushes *J. effusus* as well as small adder's-tongue fern *Ophioglossum azoricum* and royal fern *Osmunda regalis*. Further towards Porth Hellick are more areas of waved heath, where the heather is deeply channelled into ridges by the wind. These coastal areas are among the best places to look out for migrating birds, especially wheatears *Oenanthe oenanthe,* and even migrating butterflies such as clouded yellow *Colias croceus*. These 'downs' are also home to green tiger beetles *Cicindela campestris*, rose chafers *Cetonia aurata* and other insects.

Between Giant's Castle and Blue Carn one of the runways of the airport

FIG 32. An example of 'waved heath' can be seen near Giant's Castle, an Iron Age cliff castle. Salakee Down, June 2002. (Rosemary Parslow)

interposes itself into the cliff edge. Not a place to linger, although the system of traffic lights at the top of the slope on the edge of the cliff warns of the imminent approach or departure of aircraft. The airport is one of largest areas of open grassland on St Mary's, but access is restricted due to safety considerations. Most galling for the birdwatchers, as the mown grass attracts rare plovers, wheatears and other birds of open habitats. Usually some kind of viewing place is negotiated each autumn so that birdwatchers can see part of the airfield without interfering with the business of flying.

As you round the corner into Old Town Bay you pass the narrow rocky promontory of Tolman Point, between the bay and Porth Minick. Here there are maritime grassland and cliff communities and a small triangular group of planted shrubs including shrubby orache *Atriplex halimus*. On the Old Town side of the headland Hottentot fig and rosy dewplant *Drosanthemum roseum* grow over the rocks and grassland, in places completely submerging native species.

The next headland round the coast is Peninnis Head, the southernmost point on St Mary's (Fig. 33). This rocky promontory is important, with habitats that support rare plants and lichens. The impressive weathering of the granite tors and the lack of glacial features also contribute to the geological significance of the site. In the nineteenth century Peninnis 'was considered one of the pleasantest places on the island by visitors; it was a large open downs with no hedge on the west side of it until you got halfway to Buzza Hill, and it was covered with long heath and wild flowers of various kinds which made it very pleasant in summer time' (Maybee, 1883). The headland is still popular with visitors, who enjoy the dramatic scenery of massive granite carns eroded into natural sculptures and, among the rocks and tumbled boulders, the squat little lighthouse on the Head overlooking St Mary's Sound. This is the place where the islanders have lit ceremonial bonfires in the past, and it was also the site for the Millennium beacon on 1 January 2000. There are the usual stretches of coastal grassland and maritime heath over the granite, with western clover *Trifolium occidentale* and two species uncommon elsewhere, spring squill *Scilla verna* and wild thyme *Thymus polytrichus* at one of its few Scilly locations. The most exposed edge of the headland is noted for its rare lichen flora including *Ramelina siliquosa, Roccella fuciformis, R. phycopsis*, golden hair-lichen *Teloschistes flavicans* and ciliate strap-lichen. To reach the Peninnis headland there is either the track around the coast or the central track from Hugh Town, King Edward's Road, bisecting the cultivated centre of the headland, with arable fields and pastureland either side. The soils here are deep and less sandy than elsewhere

FIG 33. Peninnis Head is a jumble of extraordinary granite tors. May 2005. (Rosemary Parslow)

so a different range of arable weed species is found among the crop: these include some of the goosefoots *Chenopodium* spp. as well as the ubiquitous corn marigold *Chrysanthemum segetum*, docks *Rumex* spp., shepherd's-purse *Capsella bursa-pastoris* and sow-thistles *Sonchus* spp.

Above Hugh Town is the high, rocky promontory of the Hugh, almost completely surrounded by the granite walls of the early fortifications of the Garrison. Here the long history of the Garrison is marked by an array of buildings, defence works and other structures. English Heritage manages most of the historic buildings and walls that form the Ancient Monument. There are some areas of semi-natural vegetation within the fortifications managed by the Wildlife Trust, mainly areas of bracken and bramble thickets, rough heathland and mown grassland. Some of the windbreaks of Monterey pine have died but there are still more pines and other trees on the eastern flank of the promontory. On the slopes of the hill Babington's leek and balm-leaved figwort both grow among the bracken and bramble. And a few stands of the Nationally Scarce wild leek *Allium ampeloprasum* can also be found here, probably overlooked because they were assumed to be the commoner Babington's leek variety. On the exposed southern side of the Garrison there are more maritime habitats from below the walls to the rocky shore (Fig. 34). There is also a row of tiny abandoned gardens perched on the edge of the cliffs. The thin soils on top of the massive granite walls often support a therophyte community (therophyte plants overwinter as seeds and germinate in spring) of dwarfed species of grasses and forbs similar to that seen on natural granite outcrops around the coast. Where they are permitted to flourish, small ferns such as sea spleenwort lodge in the mortar between the granite blocks, as do other plants that are usually found in rock crevices on the cliffs: Danish scurvygrass *Cochlearia danica*, pearlworts *Sagina* spp. and thrift *Armeria maritima* are frequent examples.

Other interesting species of ferns and other plants grow on both sides of the high granite walls. Between the ramparts are mown lawns that in some places are still typical of coastal grasslands with a tight sward of fescues *Festuca* spp., buck's-horn plantain *Plantago coronopus*, sheep's sorrel *Rumex acetosella*, small-flowered catchfly *Silene gallica*, western clover, rough clover *Trifolium scabrum* and other clovers. Besides the usual resident birds, the coastal area and the shelterbelts are good venues at bird migration times to look out for species such as wheatear, wryneck *Jynx torquilla* and black redstart *Phoenicurus ochrurus*. One section of wall near the Woolpack Battery is remarkable for the hundreds of autumn lady's-tresses orchids *Spiranthes spiralis* that flourish there just at eye level in late summer.

FIG 34. Exposure to southern gales restricts growth on the seaward side of the Garrison walls to lichens, tiny ferns and a few other plants. November 2002. (Rosemary Parslow)

QUARRIES

There are a number of former quarries on St Mary's. Most are overgrown or incorporated into fields, and many are unlikely to be noticed. One you cannot miss is on the side of Buzza Hill. Rising up from Porth Cressa beach, the hill is a popular vantage point to look out over the town and beach below. The quarry at the foot of the hill is mainly used as an informal picnic or rest area and has a mixture of scrub and rough vegetation as well as grassland in the base. Among the plants that have colonised the walls of the quarry are Hottontot fig and another South African succulent, lesser sea-fig *Erepsia heteropetala*. Another unusual alien grass, rough dog's-tail grass *Cynosurus echinatus*, also grows all along the sides of the track up the hill, usually with greater quaking-grass *Briza maxima* and tall stands of yellow and occasionally white sea radish *Raphanus raphanistrum maritimus*. Further up the hill yet another unusual alien called wireplant *Muehlenbeckia complexa* scrambles over the walls, covering most of the vegetation and even the ground with dense wirelike growths so it becomes a kind of mad sculpture. Once at the top of the hill you reach Buzza Tower (a former windmill restored to commemorate a visit by King Edward VII), surrounded by scrub, tall grasses and herbs. The shrubs include broom (probably native here) as well as gorse and bramble.

At the top of Buzza Hill you will find you are on the edge of Hugh Town again and there are many houses, some of which are guesthouses. Inland at Carreg Dhu (pronounced, and sometimes written, as Crake Dew) is another former quarry. This has now been developed as a garden open to the public (see Chapter 13). There is also the former quarry on the Garrison, which has now vegetated over and is probably generally passed unobserved. Other small quarries exist all around the island, and may have just been used very locally to produce building stone or ram.

PORTHS AND BAYS

Because part of St Mary's straddles a sand bar there are two bays with sandy beaches, Porth Cressa on the south and Town Beach on the north within the Pool (harbour). Porth Cressa lies between the two headlands of Peninnis, the long promontory stretching to the south, and the Hugh, the hill surmounted by the Garrison with the town creeping up its flanks. Porth Cressa is one of the most accessible and popular bays with families and visitors staying locally, because of its proximity to the town and local amenities (Fig. 35). Although it is usually a sheltered bay, the area has proved extremely vulnerable when there are storms from the south. In the past the sea has broken through on a number of occasions and threatened to wash away the buildings (which are virtually only perched on the former sand dune) and eventually cut through into the Pool on the other side of the island. In recent years major defence works have been carried out along Porth Cressa beach to reinforce the sea bank and protect the town. There is perhaps little of great interest yet along the beach, due to the landscaping when the bank was restored, although arable weeds are reappearing in the flowerbeds and some of the sand-dune plants such as sea radish and yellow horned-poppy *Glaucium flavum* are colonising the beach defences. Town Beach has slightly more muddy sand, and is where all the mooring lines from the smaller boats in the harbour are stretched ashore.

There are several bays on the east coast of St Mary's. Old Town Bay is quite rocky but with clear channels into the harbour, sheltered from all directions except southeast. The harbour is only accessible at high tide. Near the narrow sandy beach are patches of tree-mallow *Lavatera arborea*, smaller tree-mallow *L. cretica*, sea radish, white ramping-fumitory *Fumaria capreolata* and other plants

FIG 35. Porth Cressa, July 2006. (Rosemary Parslow)

that flourish in the disturbed sandy ground. The sea wall was rebuilt in 1996 after severe storms caused a great amount of damage.

Porth Minick is quite a small bay and has also had substantial sea defence works to reinforce the sea bank. One of the best stands of sea-kale *Crambe maritima* grows at the top of the beach, and I once saw an islander collecting leaves of the plants by the sack-load – whether to use as a vegetable or perhaps more likely to feed tame rabbits was not clear. Among the rocks at one end of the beach are clumps of house holly-fern *Cyrtomium falcata* growing in deep crevices where it has been established for many years among the boulders. Fortunately the beach works stopped just before reaching the fern.

Porth Hellick is a large inlet at the seaward end of the Higher Moors nature trail. There is a narrow sandy beach and below it a rocky bay with pools and shallows that attract many birds; at times rare waders will turn up to feed at low water. Between the reedbed around Porth Hellick Pool and the bay there is a narrow strip of tall grassland with wild angelica *Angelica sylvestris*, balm-leaved figwort and bracken. The bank of the Porth is densely planted with clumps of spiky rhodostachys *Fascicularia bicolor*, replacing the New Zealand flax *Phormium* sp. that formerly grew there to consolidate the low dune. The seaward side of the bank supports common dune plants, marram *Ammophila arenaria*, sea sandwort *Honckenya peploides*, sea-kale, yellow horned-poppy and oraches *Atriplex* spp. This is also a good place to look for the distinctive little striped nymphs of the lesser cockroach *Ectobius panzeri*. Greek sea-spurrey *Spergularia bocconii* used to grow near the small granite monument to Sir Cloudesley Shovell at the top of the beach, although it has not been seen there for many years, possibly due to the changes that have been made to the sea bank (recently Greek sea-spurrey has been re-found at other sites on the east coast of St Mary's). The monument marks the spot where the ill-fated admiral's body was first buried (it is now in Westminster Abbey) when it came ashore after his fleet foundered in the islands in 1707. Another very beautiful sandy bay on the east side of the island is at Pelistry, with its sparkling white sands and unsurpassed views towards Toll's Island and a distant view of the Eastern Isles.

There are also sandy bays on the west coast of St Mary's. Porth Mellon is on the edge of Hugh Town and popular for sailing and other activities. There is a degraded sand dune at the back of the bay with some typical species among the marram grass. The next small sandy bay is Thomas's Porth, backed by narrow dunes and dune grassland. A little group of small bulb fields above the bay once

FIG 36. The coastal form of wall rue, with unusually thick and fleshy fronds. St Mary's, June 2004. (Rosemary Parslow)

grew a crop of the original Sol d'Or narcissus. Among interesting arable species in these fields are fumitories *Fumaria* spp., small-flowered catchfly and masses of starflowers *Tristagma uniflorum*. One of the less common *Carpobrotus* species grows beside the footpath and Babington's leek grows in the dunes. At Porthloo the grassland behind the dunes is used for boat standing and boat building; occasionally plants such as hairy buttercup *Ranunculus sardous* and arable weed species can turn up here due to the constant traffic and disturbance. Wall rue *Asplenium ruta-muraria* grows on a wall near here, the only place the fern is known on St Mary's (Fig. 36). The fronds are unusually thick and fleshy, probably due to exposure to salt spray. Porthloo is also a geological s s s i, based on the Quaternary sedimentary deposits in the cliffs, the raised beaches, and organic material that includes pollen indicating former arctic tundra conditions in the palaeoclimate of the island.

WETLANDS

On St Mary's there are two large wetland nature reserves, Higher Moors and Lower Moors. Higher Moors is fed by a stream that arises in Holy Vale and flows down through the Holy Vale nature trail through the tangle of tall elm trees, grey sallow and understorey of wetland plants either side of the raised pathway. The stream continues through an area of rank grassland and yellow iris. In the stream grow tall plants of fool's-water-cress, water-cress *Rorhippa nasturtium-aquaticum* and hemlock water-dropwort. Higher Moors nature reserve and s s s i include both the 'moor' and Porth Hellick Pool. Access to the reserve is via a path leading from the road to the coast. Within the reserve views can be made from the boardwalk through the reedbed and from two bird hides overlooking the pool. Along the path a line of very large tussock-sedge *Carex paniculata* plants usually attract attention as they are up to a metre and a half high and have ferns and other plants growing epiphytically on their trunks. It seems quite shocking now to realise that at one time attempts were made to destroy the plants by killing them with herbicide and burning them. Fortunately, in more enlightened times, clearance of vegetation from around the sedges and cutting back the willow carr has encouraged them to spread. There are also some magnificent stands of royal fern as well as the ubiquitous lady fern *Athyrium filix-femina* throughout the site.

The Lower Moors nature reserve is situated in a low-lying area between Hugh Town and Old Town Bay (Fig. 37). A stream flows through the site to the sea at Old Town. Part of the area is reedbed, part marsh composed of beds of a very lax local variety of sea rush *Juncus maritimus* (the endemic var. *atlanticus*, according to

FIG 37. Lower Moors from the air, February 2004. (Rosemary Parslow)

Lousley), and there are areas of grey sallow carr, as well as a small pool and a scrape with bird hides on the bank. The pools and surrounding vegetation attract rare birds in the migration season. There are ditches, wetter areas and more open areas, all of which support a range of typical wetland plants.

There are also a few other small freshwater pools on St Mary's, although several have generally degenerated into duck ponds. There is a pond beside the road from Porthloo to Rose Hill which, with the two fields on the west and Well Field on the east, is managed by the Isles of Scilly Wildlife Trust as a nature reserve. These fields are composed of a mixture of wetland plants and open grassland. Very little of nature conservation interest remains in the duck pond these days; it has largely been given over to a collection of exotic ducks and a few half-tame moorhens *Gallinula chloropus*.

Two small freshwater pools at Newford, the Argy Moor pools, drain into the Watermill Stream. Originally designed as ponds as part of a failed attempt to grow flax (presumably the ponds would have been used to steep the plants), the ponds are now very eutrophic due to the large numbers of semi-domestic ducks that frequent the site. There are a number of introduced plants around the ponds and a few marginal species such as soft rush, but there now (2006) appear to be no aquatic plants, although prior to the invasion of water fern *Azolla filiculoides* there had been a typical aquatic flora (Lousley, 1971). Whether it was the strenuous attempts to get rid of the water fern using herbicides that also eliminated all the aquatic plants, or whether the conditions of the ponds are no longer suitable, is unclear.

Shooter's Pool, a small pool on farmland behind Lower Moors, is being developed to provide freshwater habitats for birds by the Isles of Scilly Bird Group (in 2005 the pool attracted a black-winged stilt *Himantopus himantopus*). This pool at one time had a population of the rare lesser water plantain, but this apparently disappeared some years ago. It will be interesting to see whether the plant reappears in future.

CHAPTER 6

The Off-Islands

We'll rant and roar, across the salt seas
Soon we'll strike soundings in the Channel of Old England
From Ushant to Scilly is thirty-four leagues.

Spanish Ladies, traditional sea-shanty

IN ADDITION TO St Mary's there are four inhabited islands in the Isles of Scilly. These are called the 'off-islands' by Scillonians. Three were formerly joined to St Mary's when Scilly was mainly one large island many centuries ago (see Chapter 2). St Agnes has been separated from the rest far longer by a deep channel, St Mary's Sound, and as a result always seems to have a different 'feel' and some differences in the flora that may reflect this longer isolation. None of the off-islands has a large population. The majority of the inhabitants are farmers with some involvement with the sea, boats or fishing, and most rely to some extent on tourism.

BRYHER

Lying just to the west of Tresco is the island of Bryher. The island is only 129 hectares above MHWS, 2km long by 1km wide. Even so, the topography is very varied. At the far northernmost tip is the domed headland of Shipman Head Down, 42 metres high and divided from the extreme rocky promontory of Shipman Head by a narrow channel through which the sea boils at high tide. The bay to the west of Shipman Head Down, Hell Bay, is famed for its restless, dramatic seas (Fig. 38). Dominating the west coast of the island are Gweal Hill

FIG 38. Restless sea in Hell Bay, Bryher, May 2006. (Richard Green)

and Heathy Hill, with bays between, Great Popplestone Bay, Stinking Porth and
Great Porth. These end in Stony Porth and the sandy bay and dunes of Rushy
Bay in the south of the island, looking across to the island of Samson. The
eastern side of Bryher is more sheltered and sandy, with dunes facing Tresco
across the shallow channel. Only beyond the post office in the northeast does the
coast become rocky, with a rather sinister small rocky islet topped with a gibbet
emerging from the sea: this is Hangman's Island, where apparently Admiral
Blake, who put down the Royalist uprising in 1651, hanged some of his men
(Vyvyan, 1950). Watch Hill gives a good vantage point for looking out over the
island, as does Samson Hill further to the south.

The centre of Bryher is low-lying, mainly arable fields and pastureland. The
gardens and grounds associated with the hotel occupy a large site dominating
the lower land in this part of the island. Close beside the hotel is Great Pool, a
large brackish pool with a fringe of marshy vegetation. Most people visiting
Bryher for the first time will either head south to the beach at Rushy Bay, a 'must'
for naturalists because of the unusual plants that are found there, or will aim
for Shipman Head across the top of Shipman Head Down to see the notorious
wild seascapes in Hell Bay.

Bryher has many good things to offer, and you do not have to be a naturalist
to appreciate the colour and the beauty of the scenery. The island is small enough
to get round in a day, although it repays a longer visit. Although Bryher does not

have the wealth of bulb-field annuals of other islands it does have some, for example common fumitory *Fumaria officinale*, which is very uncommon elsewhere in Scilly. The dune grassland behind Rushy Bay supports a great variety of dune species, usually in a very stunted form. There are miniature plants of sea spurge *Euphorbia paralias* and Portland spurge, common stork's-bill *Erodium cicutarium*, forget-me-nots *Myosotis* spp. and English stonecrop *Sedum anglicum*, growing virtually in pure sand. Nothing, however, can quite prepare you for the Lilliputian perfection of the rare dwarf pansy, when you eventually find it, growing in the sandy turf and on bare sand. In May the pansy may be in its thousands, but they are often very difficult to find. In the dunes behind the bay there is a population of grey bush-crickets *Platycleis albopunctata* that live mostly in among the marram grass. The very observant may also find one of the tiny lesser cockroaches scuttling across the sand behind the dunes.

Perhaps the next attraction for the naturalist is the Great Pool and surrounding marshy vegetation (Fig. 39). The pool lies close to the shore at Great Porth and is unique in now being the only true brackish lagoon in Scilly. A leat links the pool to the sea in Great Porth. At times the pool is temporary home to shoals of land-locked grey mullet *Chelon labrosus*, trapped until the spring tides can release them again. The pool is very shallow and open and the only aquatic plants are those that can cope with the brackish conditions, usually

FIG 39. Bryher from Gweal Hill, looking towards the saline Pool and Great Popplestone Bay, June 2002. (Rosemary Parslow).

beaked tasselweed *Ruppia maritima* and fennel-leaved pondweed *Potamogeton pectinatus*. Saltmarsh rush *Juncus gerardii*, sea club-rush *Bolboschoenus maritimus* and at least one species of spike-rush *Eleocharis* sp. grow all round the edge of the pool. A few birds frequent the pool. Moorhen usually nest and gadwall *Anas strepera*, mallard *A. platyrhynchos* and mute swan *Cygnus olor* are often seen there. But the salty water restricts the number and species that live in the pool, so dragonflies, for example, cannot breed there. A second very small pool nearby at one time would have been covered in brackish water-crowfoot *Ranunculus baudotii* and one of the starworts *Callictriche* sp., but for some years it was planted up with water-lily and other pond plants. Now these have been removed it is returning to its former state.

Close to the pool on the brow of Great Popplestone Bay, as well as elsewhere on short turf, grows a lovely red form of white clover, *Trifolium repens* var. *townsendii*, often in its most extreme form with purple-red flowers and almost black leaves. And as you walk over the short turf here the unmistakable scent of chamomile rises about you. Spring squill, which is otherwise uncommon in Scilly, is at its best on Bryher. It grows in the short maritime turf along the slopes above Hell Bay, along much of the west side of the island and also below Samson Hill. Even when the flowers are over, the leaves persist for a while, lying curiously twisted on the ground as though they have been poisoned.

On the granite carns where the thin soils become desiccated in summer are areas of typical plant communies (see Appendix) which include plants such as common bird's-foot *Ornithopus perpusillus*, bird's-foot-trefoil *Lotus corniculatus*, English stonecrop, buck's-horn plantain, some of the tiny grasses such as silver hair-grass *Aira caryophyllea* and in a few places the rare orange bird's-foot. Nearby, heathers, grasses and taller plants grow where there are deeper soils, and in some years the tiny orchid, autumn lady's-tresses, also appears here. Where moisture is retained over the granite platform there may be one or two discrete patches of small adder's-tongue fern.

Shipman Head Down in the north of the island is an extensive area of 'waved heath', the wind-eroded heath that is one of the most important habitats in the Isles of Scilly. The dominant species are ling, bell heather and western gorse, with common gorse forming dense scrub along the southeast edge and extending down towards the coast. This is where spring squill can be found on top of the plateau, as well as several species of rare lichens. Getting to Shipman Head itself can only be accomplished by a scramble down steep rocks. The promontory is accessible for a short time at low water across the very deep cleft that separates the Head from the main bulk of the island. Colonies of seabirds are able to breed on Shipman Head in relative isolation.

One curious little gem of social history that has revolutionised visiting Bryher was the building of what the islanders humorously call 'Annekey' or Anneka's Quay. This is a pontoon landing on the beach just north of the old stone quay, built during 1990 as part of one of Anneka Rice's TV programmes, *Challenge Anneka*. This new landing enables boats to get in to Bryher when the tide is too low to land elsewhere. The only alternative in the past was to run the boat up the beach and land passengers by a plank from the bow.

TRESCO

Tresco and Bryher face each other across the narrow channel that forms the sheltered anchorage of New Grimsby Harbour. Tresco is the second largest and arguably the best known of the Isles of Scilly, on account of the famed Abbey Gardens. The island is just over 3km long and 1.7km wide, and covers approximately 298 hectares. At the north end is one of the most extensive areas of waved heath in the islands, on a plateau some 30 metres high. Across the middle of Tresco, almost dividing the island in two, is the long, water-filled gash that is the Great Pool, with the Abbey Pool slightly to the south. North of Great Pool is a broad band of farmland that stretches to Old Grimsby on the east coast (Fig. 40). South of Great Pool are the Abbey Gardens and woodland around Tresco Abbey. Beyond the Gardens and on the eastern side of the island are extensive sand dunes and stretches of dune heathland. Other than rocky Gimble Porth, and the northern fringes of the island, the coastline of Tresco is mainly composed of dunes and sandy beaches.

General impressions of Tresco tend to be coloured by the presence of the Abbey Gardens and the farm, and especially the very large area of planted woodland that dominates the landscape. The island has a much more managed atmosphere than the other off-islands. This may be partly due to its history, but is mainly because almost the whole island is under one tenancy and has been mostly managed as one estate for a very long time. The present incumbent of Tresco, Robert Dorrien-Smith, took on the estate in 1973.

Even before the visitor reaches the Gardens their influence and that of the tenure of Augustus Smith and the Dorrien-Smith family is evident everywhere on Tresco. Apart from the gardens themselves, this influence is most evident in the sand dunes around Appletree Banks and Pentle Bay, where a hotch-potch of exotic plants have become established among the native dune species. Throughout the dunes are clumps of rhodostachys, the very similar Tresco rhodostachys *Ochagavia carnea*, bugle lily *Watsonia borbonica*, *Agapanthus praecox*

FIG 40. Old Grimsby Harbour, on the east coast of Tresco, June 2002. (Rosemary Parslow)

and red-hot pokers *Kniphofia* sp. growing among the marram, with balm-leaved figwort, Babington's leek and sand sedge *Carex arenaria*. Where the dune has become flattened and consolidated, dune grassland and heathland have formed. Rushy Bank, just beside the road from the landing at Carn Near quay, is particularly interesting, with many unusual plants: orange bird's-foot (found some years growing all along the edge of the concrete road) and small adder's-tongue fern can be found here, and on the heathers nearby are rich growths of lichens, including some of the lungworts. Also beside the road at Carn Near there are banks of the extraordinary wireplant moulding itself over the other vegetation in a parody of topiary. Below the dunes, at the back of the beach, is one of the very few places where a few plants of the rare shore dock *Rumex rupestris* grow among the masses of the coastal form of curled dock *Rumex crispus* var. *littoreus* (see Chapter 9). As this section of coast is actively eroding, the future of this shore dock site is probably limited.

Tresco has its own heliport, opened in 1983 (Fig. 41). The island has a hotel, the first to be established on an off-island, and an established time-share business. With the draw of the Gardens, Tresco attracts more visitors than any of the islands other than St Mary's. The heliport is on a beautiful mown stretch of grassland just beside the Gardens and is well worth looking at (but not when

FIG 41. Tresco, looking north from Oliver's Battery across coastal dunes, the heliport and plantations, April 2005. (Rosemary Parslow)

helicopters are landing!). Like the airfield on St Mary's it frequently attracts feeding waders and other birds. In autumn it can be one of the places to look for rare pipits and larks.

Towards the edge of the Abbey Pool (Fig. 42) the grassland is seasonally waterlogged so a band of marsh pennywort, lesser spearwort and other wetland plants extends all round the edge, and similarly around the south side of the Great Pool. When Borlase visited Tresco in 1756 he commented on 'a most beautiful piece of fresh water edged round with Camomel Turf, on which neither Brier, Thistle, nor Flag appears. I judged it to be half a mile long, and a furlong wide.' The chamomile turf is still there but no longer so extensive. The fine silt drawdown zone (much enriched by droppings from gulls and waterfowl) around the edge of the Abbey Pool supports a variable array of tiny wetland plants, depending on how much mud is exposed. During periods of drought some of the submerged aquatic plants become visible as the water level drops, and those growing on the mud spread quickly; six-stamened waterwort *Elatine hexandra*, for example, on these occasions can turn the surface of the mud bright red. Abbey Pool has a resident population of wild and domestic waterfowl, but like anywhere in Scilly it has seen some notable rarities at times.

Great Pool is much more extensive. The lake stretches right across the middle of the island, virtually dividing it in two. Surrounding Great Pool are reedbeds, areas of willow carr and some stretches of muddy foreshore. A painting of the lake and the surroundings by Augustus Smith's sister Mrs Frances Le Marchant, executed in September 1868, shows the lake to be much more open than now, with the reedbeds only marginal (in King, 1985). The lake attracts many water-birds, both migrants and the resident species, including gadwall, mallard and moorhen, and is an important feeding area for migrating waders. Among the reeds and in open patches along the foreshore are many common wetland plants, lesser spearwort, royal fern, bulrush (reedmace) *Typha latifolia* and yellow iris. The rattling songs of reed *Acrocephalus scirpaceus* and sedge warbler *A. schoenobaenus* can be heard from the reedbeds around the lake during summer. Good views across the lake can be obtained from the bird hides that are approached by boardwalks from the track north of the pool. One hide was erected in memory of the late David Hunt, the 'Scilly Birdman', who was resident on Tresco before moving to St Mary's (see Chapter 4).

Much of Tresco is under agriculture, with pasture and arable fields (Fig. 43). The Tresco Estate currently runs a large herd of beef cattle. There is more tree cover generally, so that in autumn the island attracts rare migrant birds from

FIG 42. Tresco Abbey and Abbey Pool, April 2005. (Rosemary Parslow)

FIG 43. Arable fields and pine shelterbelt on Tresco. (Rosemary Parslow)

North America and elsewhere to tease the 'twitchers' who also flock to the islands.

Across the north end of the island is Castle Down, one of the largest areas of wind-eroded waved heath in the islands. This is a fascinating place, a plateau covered in low heather only about ankle height where the plants form long ridges as they are rolled over by the wind, with large patches of exposed bare ground between the waves. This type of heathland is not particularly species-rich but very atmospheric when the heathers are in flower and the whole place is full of the hum of bees. Besides bell heather and ling, there are several common species of grass, patches of English stonecrop, lousewort and bird's-foot-trefoil, and lichens and mosses. The tread of many feet on the pathways across the Down, exacerbated by the eroding effect of wind and rain, have caused the braiding of many pathways. On some places on the paths are many shallow temporary pools with a transient wetland flora of starworts and lesser spearwort. Ruins of all that remains of King Charles's Castle are on one of the high points at the western edge of Castle Down. Besides having a good population of ferns and sea stork's-bill *Erodium maritimum* among its stones, the top of the castle makes a good vantage point for looking down into the Tresco Channel between Tresco and Bryher, and over the tower of Cromwell's Castle on the headland below.

Gimble Porth on the eastern side of the headland is backed with low cliffs where gulls nest, and where some years there is a kittiwake *Rissa tridactyla* colony. Piper's Hole is a deep cavern in the north-facing cliffs that can be approached by scrambling down the cliff, but a boat is needed to explore properly. It was very popular with holiday visitors in the past, and there are still postcards on sale showing it lit up with lanterns in the early 1900s. The cave consists of a long boulder-filled passage over 20m long leading to a large underground pool that can be traversed by boat (a punt used to be kept there in the past) to reach the inner chamber, which is over 40m deep. The cave system was investigated in 1993 by Philip and Myrtle Ashmole and specimens of the cavernicolous fauna collected, including a springtail new to Britain, *Onychiurus argus*, a troglophile species otherwise known from caves in Spain, France and Belgium (Ashmole & Ashmole, 1995).

The plantations and windbreaks originally planted by Augustus Smith and his successors are now coming to the end of their life. Much planting and felling has taken place to remove and replace the fallen timber. The woodlands are a mixture of planted trees and shrubs, escapees from the Gardens, as well as wild plants and ferns – a botanical recorder's headache. Protected by the plantations are the 'subtropical' Abbey Gardens (Fig. 44). These are densely planted with a

FIG 44. Tresco Abbey Gardens, April 2005. (Rosemary Parslow)

great range of plants from countries with a Mediterranean climate, Australasia, the Canary Islands, South Africa and parts of South America (see Chapter 13). Visitors to the Abbey Gardens will also remark on the extraordinarily tame birds. In 2004 the entrance to the Gardens was updated and the tea room moved. If you visit the tea garden, kamikaze robins *Erithacus rubecula* snatch crumbs from your lips and blackbirds, chaffinches *Fringilla coelebs* and other birds will help themselves to cake from your plate. At certain times of the year the odd appearance of the house sparrows *Passer domesticus*, starlings *Sturnus vulgaris* and blackbirds – with bright yellow caps of pollen from drinking the nectar of *Puya chilensis* plants – has occasionally led to them being identified as something far more exotic! Another curious phenomenon in the former tea garden was the pecking of holes in the mortar of a wall by dozens of house sparrows, presumably seeking minerals after the manner of some tropical parrots.

Some of the exotic plants that grow around Tresco and the other islands are spread intentionally when people take cuttings or seeds to cultivate for their own gardens or pass around to their friends. Other plants escape from the Gardens by natural means, blown by the wind or otherwise carried accidentally, to end up elsewhere in the islands. Many of these are now established as part of the Scillonian flora. Perhaps the most unusual inhabitants of the Gardens are the two species of New Zealand stick insects that have been part of the fauna for about a century and are now found elsewhere around Tresco. Recently they have also reached St Mary's. Also from New Zealand but less obvious are the woodland hoppers *Arcitalitrus dorrieni*, the little back amphipods that now live under every rock and log on the island. These are the most obvious and well-known examples, but there are many other insects and other invertebrate species that originally arrived as stowaways with horticultural material from abroad.

It is not just insects and other animals that have arrived in Scilly with introduced plants. A series of discoveries of rare introduced bryophytes began in 1961 when Miss R. J. Murphy discovered two unexpected liverworts on Tresco, *Lophocolea semiteres*, new to the northern hemisphere, and a new species of *Telaranea* that was named *T. murphyae* after her by Mrs Paton in 1965. *Telaranea murphyae* may have been introduced to Tresco from the southern hemisphere, as has happened with many other species such as *Lophocolea semiteres* and *L. bispinosa*, which are found only on Scilly and in Scotland, pointing to introduction with exotic plants. Besides *Lophocolea bispinosa*, found by Mrs Paton in 1967, was a moss *Calyptrochaeta apiculata*, later also found in East Sussex.

Since then, the moss *Sematophyllum substrumulosum* was first recorded as new to Britain on several of the islands (it has since been discovered to have been found, but not identified, in West Sussex in 1964). It was growing on the bark of

Monterey pine in 1995 and again may have arrived with horticultural material (Paton & Holyoak, 2005). Other species recorded have included two mosses rare in Britain (*Chenia leptophylla*, *Didymodon australasiae*) and another that has become very widespread and common (*Campylopus introflexus*). By 2003 some of the alien bryophytes had greatly extended their ranges since the 1960s, with both alien *Lophocolea* species now widespread throughout the islands, and *Telaranea murphyae* had spread from Tresco to St Mary's.

ST MARTIN'S

St Martin's is a long narrow island with a mainly west-to-east axis. It is just over 3km long by 1.5km wide and covers 238 hectares if you include White Island (15ha). First impressions of St Martin's are of long, empty white beaches (Fig. 45), intense turquoise sea, little clusters of houses tucked into the hillside and the strangely modern-looking (it actually dates from 1683) conical red and white banded tower of the daymark on high ground on Chapel Down at the eastern end of the island.

FIG 45. The south coast of St Martin's, looking towards Tresco at low tide with the sand flats exposed. June 2005. (Rosemary Parslow)

As on St Agnes, the individual hamlets are named, rather unoriginally, Lower, Middle and Higher Town. They are strung out along the two-kilometre concrete road from Lower Town quay in the west to Higher Town Bay and New Quay, just over halfway along the length of the island. Beyond the farmland to the east the land rises up to the heathland on Chapel Down. Heathland also extends all along the northern edge of the island; only the insert of the dune grassland of the Plains and in some places wetter areas and a small pool break the continuity. Around the higher and exposed land are rocky promontories and cliffs where seabirds nest. Looking northeast from the cliffs on a clear day you can often see the cliffs of Land's End, 45km away.

The southern shores of St Martin's are mainly sandy, with sand dunes and just a few stretches of low cliff. Along the back of the dunes at Higher Town Bay are small bulb fields, frequently inundated by blown sand (Fig. 46). Indeed, much of St Martin's is composed of blown sand that has been deposited over the whole top of the island in the past. This has led to some of the most impressive arable weed populations in Scilly being found here, including unusual species not found elsewhere in the islands. The sandy soils are also found around Higher Town Bay, where the cricket field is mown maritime grassland dominated by

FIG 46. Bulb fields with rosy garlic *Allium roseum*, whistling jacks and great brome, St Martin's, May 2003. (Rosemary Parslow)

chamomile and several species of clover, including both suffocated *Trifolium suffocatum* and subterranean clover. The cricket field is low-lying and sometimes floods completely – perhaps not ideal for the cricket, but maybe why there is a superb show of chamomile most summers. The sand-dune areas around the quay and along the track ways are also places where some rare clovers are found. Suffocated clover can be difficult to find, as blown sand often drifts over the plants and completely buries them. It also flowers early in the year so has usually dried up and disappeared by early summer. In the corner of the cricket field is a small brackish pool, sometimes covered by the pretty white and yellow buttercup flowers of brackish water-crowfoot.

The dune system along the Higher Town Bay is typical of the NVC (National Vegetation Community) SD7 semi-fixed dune, relatively species-poor but with some interesting herbs such as balm-leaved figwort and Babington's leek. In places bracken and the evergreen shrub *Pittosporum crassifolium* are invading the dune. A sub-prostrate form of wild privet occurs along the edge of the track. There are species of unstable foredune habitats such as sea rocket *Cakile maritima* where there are breaks in the dune. In summer this is one of the best places to see ringlet butterfly *Aphantopus hyperantus*, a recent arrival in Scilly. At the back of Lawrence's Bay is a low cliff with a hanging curtain of the succulent Sally-my-handsome *Carpobrotus acinaciformis*, with its distinctive curved leaves and carmine flowers.

There is a series of rocky headlands with exposed rocks and thin soils along the north side of St Martin's. Wind-eroded heather and gorse heathland cover the area between Top Rock Hill and the separate group of the Rabbit Rocks. The slopes below the hill are covered with bracken and gorse communities on deeper soils and a fringe of maritime grassland towards the coast. At Round Bowl both small adder's-tongue fern and orange bird's-foot have been recorded, but the dune is being invaded by heath and scrub species in this area. Pernagie is a group of small bracken fields below the hill with maritime grassland and a small area of heathland at Pernagie Point. The westernmost headland on St Martin's is Tinkler's Hill. The top of the hill has a cover of gorse scrub surrounding a smaller area of heather. At the bottom of the hill is heathland and coastal grassland alongside Porth Seal, where small adder's-tongue fern may be found. Porth Seal is a geological SSSI on account of the raised beach and important deposits; pollen analysis from the site demonstrated the arctic tundra nature of the Devensian environment. Chaffweed *Anagallis minima* grows along some wet cart ruts across the heathland, but is easily overlooked. Turfy Hill may have got its name from the practice of cutting turf there formerly. Now the area is dominated by bracken communities, with smaller patches of heather and gorse.

Small adder's-tongue fern also occurs in this area, and one of the large species of New Zealand flax, *Phormium colensoi*, is well established and spreading.

Burnt Hill is the small promontory of open land on the north of the island between Turfy Hill and Chapel Down. It consists of mainly heather-dominated maritime heath and grassland. Inland from the promontory the heathland becomes dominated by bracken communities and a large area of gorse. Many areas of gorse and bracken are being managed to encourage the re-establishment of heathland plants. Chapel Down, where the land rises up towards the daymark, is dominated by waved heathland with scattered granite boulders and exposed granite platform very prominent towards the east. Many of the rare heathland plants, including small adder's-tongue fern, orange bird's-foot and chaffweed, are also found here, and this is also the territory of the St Martin's ant *Formica rufibarbis* (see Chapter 14). There are steep cliffs around the edge of the headland with colonies of nesting seabirds during the summer. Above the cliffs are areas of bracken communities and gorse scrub. At Coldwind Pit near the coast there are a number of unusual aquatic plants growing in and around the pool.

On the north side of St Martin's is an unusual open area called the Plains (Fig. 47). Formerly open grassland and low heath that had developed from dune grassland, it is becoming overgrown by gorse and scrub. Formerly small adder's-

FIG 47. North coast of St Martin's, with the Plains and Round Island lighthouse in the distance. (Rosemary Parslow)

FIG 48. Mouse-ear hawkweed is one of the unusual species found in dune grassland on the Plains, St Martin's. (Alma Hathway)

tongue fern was widely distributed throughout the Plains until it became submerged by taller vegetation. Rare plants such as orange bird's-foot and a patch of mouse-ear hawkweed *Hieracium pilosella* at its only known station in Scilly can be found here still (Fig. 48). Above the Plains among the dense thickets of common gorse it is also possible to find the strange pink nets of the parasitic heath dodder *Cuscuta epithymum*, another plant apparently only found in this one place in Scilly. The headlands and slopes along the northern side of St Martin's also have spreading, triffid-like, populations of New Zealand flax, although control measures to reduce their numbers started in 2005. It is likely similar measures will be taken against another invasive alien, *Myrtus luma*, a myrtle-like shrub. Nearer the coast the dune is still active and sea spurge and Portland spurge are among the plants growing on the edge. A sand bar joins St Martin's to the small, uninhabited White Island (see Chapter 7).

ST AGNES AND GUGH

Officially counted as one island, you could be forgiven for considering them two separate islands if you only saw them at high tide, when the sea covers the sand bar that links them. Most days there is a period when the bar is uncovered and it is possible to cross from Gugh to St Agnes. When the Hick family lived on Gugh in the 1970s, if the bar was covered by the sea, their two sons would sometimes have to row across in their small dingy – the Bar Bus – or miss getting to school on St Agnes if it was too rough to row (W. Hick, *in litt.*).

St Agnes is 1.5km long by about 1km wide, and Gugh 1km long by about 0.5km across. The land area they cover together is 145 hectares, of which Gugh is 37 hectares. The St Agnes coastline is very convoluted, so walking around the edge can take a suprising amount of time. In the days of the St Agnes Bird Observatory the daily round of the perimeter of the island, to check what birds had arrived overnight, was said to be five miles (8km), presumably including Gugh.

St Agnes

Most of what could be called the 'middle' of St Agnes is cultivated, mainly as bulb or arable fields, and it includes the three 'towns', Higher, Middle and Lower Town. Inland, St Agnes is a made up of a nucleus of small fields, farms and houses. Many of the fields have a good arable weed flora and between hedges are glimpses of delightful gardens full of exotic plants. Some of the garden walls have some of the best collections of lanceolate spleenwort *Asplenium obovatum* in the islands.

Wherever you are on St Agnes you are aware of the lighthouse perched on the hill in the middle of the island. The fat white tower dominates the landscape and appears to squeeze into every photograph (Fig. 49). St Agnes lighthouse was built in 1680, making it one of the oldest in Britain. Initially the light was supplied by a cresset, a coal-burning brazier, which stood on a platform in the lantern. This was not very efficient and was replaced by copper oil lamps and revolving reflectors in 1790. The wind vane on top of the lantern is 22.5 metres above the ground, 42 metres above mean high water mark (Bowley, 1990). When the Peninnis Head lighthouse came on line in 1911 the St Agnes light was downgraded to a daymark. The lighthouse keeper's house is now a farmhouse. Just below the lighthouse hill is the former parsonage in a grove of trees. In migration times a constant stream of birdwatchers patrol the road outside the parsonage in the hope of seeing some really unusual bird that has been attracted to the dense cover in the garden (Fig. 50). Quite often, if they are lucky enough to glimpse a Pallas's warbler *Phylloscopus proregulus* or some such rarity, it will flit across the road to disappear out of sight behind the massive wall of the lighthouse garden.

The northern part of the island is flat, low-lying and sandy, with a large meadow and a few former hayfields towards the rocky headland of Browarth. From the hill near the lighthouse you can see the almost perfect circle of Big

FIG 49. St Agnes: cattle grazing beside the lighthouse, May 2005. (Rosemary Parslow)

FIG 50. Pied flycatcher near St Agnes lighthouse. The gardens of the parsonage and the lighthouse attract many passage migrants. (D. I. M. Wallace)

Pool in the meadow (Fig. 51). Both the pools here (there is also a Little Pool nearby) are surrounded by grassland on low-lying land with the sea on two sides. The sea occasionally floods the meadow area, although recent sea defences have reduced the frequency. At other times the pools flood after heavy rain and the leat connecting Big Pool to the sea has to be opened at low tide to release the water. So, although usually freshwater, Big Pool may at times be slightly brackish. Around the pools are successive rings of vegetation: sea club-rush succeeded by saltmarsh rush, marsh pennywort, then creeping bent *Agrostis stolonifera*. Big Pool contains a few aquatic species, usually fennel-leaved pondweed but on occasion beaked tasselweed. The pool attracts very few breeding waterfowl, but is important at migration times. There are two resident *Odonata* species, common darter dragonfly *Sympetrum striolatum* and blue-tailed damselfly *Isnura elegans*. Frequently there are very large common eels in the pool and occasionally a heron *Ardea cinerea* will be seen standing in the pool, struggling to swallow one that has wrapped itself around its neck. These drawn-out battles between fish and bird can last for many minutes before the heron manages to swallow the fish or gives up and lets it go.

The meadow is also the local cricket pitch (as well as the tennis court and occasional helipad, especially in winter), with a species list that includes a

FIG 51. Big Pool and the chamomile cricket pitch, St Agnes, February 2004. (Rosemary Parslow)

number of rare and unusual plants including autumn lady's-tresses, chamomile and several rare clovers. Most of the meadow sward around the cricket pitch is kept short by mowing, or elsewhere by rabbit and cattle grazing. The only site in Scilly for common adder's-tongue fern *Ophioglossum vulgatum* is under bracken on the edge of the meadow. Nearby in the cart ruts left by tractors in the sodden turf can be found two species of spike-rush, slender spike-rush *Eleocharis uniglumis* and many-stalked spike-rush *E. multicaulis*, as well as another rarity, early meadow-grass, and tufts of the tiny club-rushes *Isolepis setacea* and *I. cernua*.

Just west of the meadow is the harbour of Periglis. Here are the former lifeboat house and the remains of the longest lifeboat slip in Scilly, although the shallowness of the incline meant it never functioned properly. Periglis is the main harbour for the islanders' boats and is very sheltered from most directions. There is a low dune at the back of the bay with typical dune plants including sea-kale, sea bindweed *Calystegia soldanella* and strandline species where the sandy beach gives way to rocks and boulders towards the north in one direction and towards the quay in the other. Burnt Island is a small island that lies to the northwest of Periglis, joined to St Agnes by a reinforced boulder-filled gabion at Ginamoney Carn. The island is low-lying and rocky, mainly covered in maritime grassland, bracken and thrift. At the furthest extremity of Burnt Island is Tin's Walbert, a large rock promontory that can only be reached at low tide.

To the east of the meadow is a large and very rocky bay, Porth Killier, and round the next promontory into Porth Conger is the main quay where passengers and freight are landed. South of the bar which links St Agnes to Gugh is the large inlet of the Cove, in which is found the very popular small bay of Covean. Besides attracting sunbathers to its warm, white sands, this can often be the stopping-off place for migrant birds, and sometimes there are willow warblers *Phylloscopus trochilus*, flycatchers and other birds flitting in and out of the tamarisks and snatching flies from the sand between the sunbathers. Just above the path from Covean to the Bar is a suite of fields with very sandy soils. Most of these have a particularly impressive arable weed flora and are often very colourful with corn marigolds, the 'whistling jacks' gladiolus *Gladiolus communis byzantinus*, fumitories and smaller tree-mallow.

The whole southern part of the island delights in the charming name of Wingletang Down, an extensive stretch of maritime heath with the twin bays of Wingletang Bay on the east and Porth Askin on the west, with the rocky promontory of Horse Point at the southern tip of the island where the land falls into the sea among short maritime grassland and a great chaos of tumbled rocks. Horse Point is almost separated from the rest of the island by the two bays and a narrow sandy neck of land, and it seems highly probable that one day it will eventually be cut through. In the middle of Wingletang Bay is Beady Pool, so named because it is where the small barrel-shaped brown beads from a seventeenth-century wreck have been found. At the back of the bay yellow horned-poppy, sea-kale and sea spurge surmount the low dune bank. Shore dock once appeared in a sand pit here (illicit digging possibly having exposed buried seed), but died out after a few years to reappear in a dune blow-out on the opposite side of the island beside Porth Askin; unfortunately it soon died out there as well. Wingletang Down is very important botanically: rarities such as orange bird's-foot and small adder's-tongue fern grow here, but it is also the only locality in Scilly for the very rare least adder's-tongue fern, known in Britain only from here and the Channel Islands.

St Warna's Cove is a rocky, south-facing bay on the west of St Agnes. This section of the coast is studded by a number of huge carns that continue right around the west side of the island (Fig. 52). The cove is overlooked by a curiously shaped rock called Nag's Head on the heathland below the distinctive outline of the coastguard cottages (Fig. 53). And close to the shore is a stone-lined well that is possibly of great antiquity – it is reputed to be close to where the saint is supposed to have landed from Ireland in his coracle. Traditionally pins should be dropped in the well to encourage storms to drive a wreck ashore! Castella

FIG 52. Granite carns at St Warna's Cove, St Agnes, August 2003. (Rosemary Parslow)

FIG 53. The Nag's Head and the coastguard cottages, St Agnes, July 2002. (Rosemary Parslow)

Downs, an area of rabbit-grazed coastal grassland and rough heathland further to the west, is where the Troy Town maze, actually a pebble labyrinth, is set in the turf.

Gugh

The island of Gugh might be described as the sixth inhabited island, but it is usually included with St Agnes. At low tide you can cross the Bar – a sand bar, strictly a tombolo – from one island to the other. Immediately at the end of the Bar is a small area of dune and dune grassland merging into the maritime grassland fringe around the island. A dense edge of sea-holly *Eryngium maritimum* marks the dune edge and both sea and Portland spurge are found here with sea bindweed and other coastal plants. The grass bank at the top of the Bar is one of the few places where wild thyme grows; earlier in the year western clover and early meadow-grass are also abundant here. This is another beach where the lesser cockroach has been found. The majority of the island is wind-pruned waved heath or dense gorse and bracken, with maritime grassland around the coastal fringe and on the north and southwest of the island. The summit of Gugh

FIG 54. Named after islander Obadiah Hicks is Obadiah's Barrow, an entrance grave on Gugh, half hidden among foxgloves and wall pennywort. June 2003. (Rosemary Parslow)

is remarkable for the number of archaeological remains that are still visible: on top of the hills that form the spine of the island are a series of Bronze Age barrows, remnants of walls and a standing stone known as the Old Man of Gugh. Another well-known barrow, Obadiah's Barrow, lies among dense gorse on the side of the hill (Fig. 54). For a small island there is an extensive list of rare and unusual plants, lichens and invertebrates.

The former Gugh farm occupies the central area just north of the neck across the middle of the island, between the two heathy hills that make up the body of the island. Two houses now stand there; they were built by a Mr Cooper in about 1920 and they have strange curved concrete roofs, like upturned boats, designed to withstand gales (Fig. 55). When Cooper died he was buried on the island. On the east coast of Gugh is a bay with dazzling white sand called Dropnose Porth. This curious name occurs elsewhere in Scilly, so maybe this is a humorous, descriptive reference to a nearby rock. Many of the granite carns and rocks have been eroded into fantastic shapes. There is a rock near Kittern Hill at the north end of Gugh that, seen from the sea, appears to have been sculpted into a likeness of Queen Victoria – though from a slightly different angle it becomes a Red Indian brave!

The sandy neck between the two hills formed from blown sand has an unusual flora. Growing among the bracken beside the path are dog roses *Rosa*

FIG 55. The tide just covering the Bar (strictly a tombolo) from St Agnes to Gugh, November 2002. (Rosemary Parslow)

canina and an unidentified yellow rose (presumed an escape from cultivation). Balm-leaved figwort is very common here, despite not being found elsewhere on the island. Another plant found in this vicinity is the alien Argentine dock *Rumex frutescens.* This grows on the edge of the abandoned sand pit, originally dug as a reservoir. In the field below the Gugh houses from about 1933 viper's-bugloss *Echium vulgare*, wild mignonette *Reseda lutea* and common melilot *Melilotus officinalis* were found, although not all have been seen recently. Their presence in the field has been attributed to the use of shoddy (a high-nitrate manure deriving from the wool industry) before 1933. In the 1960s this neck area was close-cropped grassy sward, a good place to find mushrooms, where thousands of garden tiger *Arctia caja* caterpillars would swarm and cuckoos *Cuculus canorus* would arrive to feed on them, and where wheatears would also appear on passage (J. Parslow, *in litt.*). When myxomatosis reduced the rabbit population, the neck became overgrown with brambles and bracken, and the open turf and the grass tennis court that was there all disappeared from view (W. Hick, personal communication).

Along the top of Gugh, just above Obadiah's Barrow, there was a heath fire in October 1972 that burned down through the shallow peat soil to the granite. As a result recovery has been slow and even now traces of the fire can still be seen, in blackened stems of gorse and bleached rocks. There have also been changes in the vegetation: yellow bartsia *Parentucellia viscosa*, for example, became very common in the burnt area and for a time English stonecrop and bird's-foot-trefoil were dominant plants on the bare ground. Elsewhere heathland extends along the crest of the island, both north and south of the 'neck'. Sometimes the rare orange bird's-foot can be found on one of the larger carns in the southern half of the island. Here too are extensive colonies of lesser black-backed gulls *Larus fuscus*, herring gulls *L. argentatus* and a few great black-backed gulls *L. marinus.* It is wise to avoid the gull colonies during the breeding season, as the gulls are likely to 'dive-bomb' people who approach too close to their nests, and can be very intimidating.

Small adder's-tongue fern has been found on at least one place on Gugh in the past, but has now not been seen for about a decade. This is not unusual with this group of ferns, so it could reappear again if conditions are suitable. Other rarities, for example golden hair-lichen, certain invertebrates and migrant birds are found on Gugh, just as they are on St Agnes. Manx shearwater and storm petrel *Hydrobates pelagicus* no longer breed, but on dark nights the shearwaters may still be heard revisiting their former haunts. For many years there has been a colony of kittiwakes under the cliffs, but recently the colony seems to have moved elsewhere.

Other than rabbits, there are now no grazing animals on Gugh. Cuckoo, the little donkey described by Leslie Thomas (1968), and Demelza the house cow both left in 1974. Cloven-hoofed animals failed to thrive on Gugh due to cobalt deficiencies in the soil, and the animals had to be given supplements (W. Hick, *in litt.*). Gradually the sandy neck area largely scrubbed over and there is no longer the wide swathe of short grassland that was there in the 1960s. Other farming projects since then have failed, so there are abandoned bulb and asparagus fields which have gone back to dense bracken, but where a flush of daffodils or wisps of asparagus fern still appear in season. Some of the abandoned bulb fields on the farm still have remnant hedges and, where the rabbits have been digging, some of the arable plants, along with both common and orange bird's-foot, may reappear.

Cuckoo the donkey is a reminder that of all places in Scilly, Gugh often used to have the largest and noisiest population of cuckoos, apparently attracted by the extraordinary numbers of garden tiger and other large caterpillars found there some years. They would fly over the island and the Cove in spring in noisy display, their cuckooing echoing across the water until in the past some islander, driven demented by them, would take the law into his own hands and silence them with a shotgun.

CHAPTER 7

The Uninhabited Islands

Nine leagues from the farthest westerly point of England, there is a space of sea, which, in a circuit of seventy miles, embraces a very great number of small islands and rocks, a great part of which are constantly covered with water, and are the cause of more ship wrecks than happens perhaps in all the other seas of Europe together. These islands, which, by modern geographers are called the Sorlings, are, by English, more commonly known by the name of Scilly.

Cosmo III, Grand Duke of Tuscany (1669)

WHAT CONSTITUTES AN island in Scilly is subject to considerable difference of opinion. Each writer seems to have had their own idea as to how many islands there are, their views mostly coloured by their particular interest. In 1542 John Leland estimated there were 140 islands 'that grew grass'; in 1607 William Camden described Scilly as having 'near 145 islands covered with grass or greenish moss', but this is rejected by Bowley (1990) on the grounds that many of the smallest islands only had lichen present. Bowley defined an island as being land surrounded by water at high tide, supporting land vegetation at all times and locally accepted as an island. He then lists 54 islands that fit his criterion of having land vegetation. For the purpose of this account the definition of an island has more to do with its natural history, so in this case the designation is essentially pragmatic: it includes any land obviously separate at high water where any kind of wildlife is present. This means all types of islands are included, not just those with higher vegetation growing on them, and it includes bare rocky islets that have colonies of breeding seabirds or are used as hauling-out places by grey seals.

Most of the uninhabited islands can be considered in three main distinct geographical groups, each having their own special character. Of course the name 'uninhabited' is something of a misnomer. Rather they are islands not inhabited by humans, as there are plenty of other inhabitants – birds, rabbits and other animals. At the furthermost southwestern extremity of the archipelago, completely exposed to the full force of the sea and the prevailing winds, lies the Bishop Rock, surmounted by the lighthouse (Fig. 56). Included in one group with the Bishop Rock, lying just 2.5km away, is the low mass of jagged rocks,

FIG 56. Bishop Rock Lighthouse towers 49 metres above its rock base. May 2005. (Rosemary Parslow)

reefs and small craggy islands that form the Western Rocks. Continuing the semicircle inwards is the larger island of Annet, low-lying and exposed but large enough to be well vegetated. The Norrard or Northern Rocks also lie to the west of the main group of islands and in the path of the worst storms from the west. Islands in this group are also extremely rocky and bare, like the Western Rocks, just the tips of a more extensive mass of granite reefs hidden below the sea. The harsh contours of the Norrard Rocks and the Western Rocks support very few higher plants, unlike the Eastern Isles and the St Helen's group (including Round Island and Teän), which seem much softer islands with their gentler contours and vegetation cover. The Eastern Isles are the most sheltered of all the uninhabited islands, protected by the half-circle of the inhabited islands.

The duplication of names of rocks and islands in Scilly can be confusing. For example there are two Green Islands, two Plumb Islands, two White Islands, and so on. With rocks it becomes even more confusing: twelve Round Rocks, four Seal Rocks, five rocks called Biggal and many duplications in the names of bays and other features. Over two hundred islands have some known natural history interest, and the most significant of these are described below.

SAMSON, WITH PUFFIN, WHITE, GREEN AND STONY ISLANDS

Samson is the largest of the uninhabited islands, 36 hectares above MHWS in extent and just over a kilometre in length, consisting of twin hills linked by a sandy neck. Along the eastern side of the island are wide sand flats stretching across the shallow channel to Tresco. At low tide much of the flats is exposed, revealing the remains of ancient walls. The twin granite hills top 30 metres and have archaeological remains on their summits (see Chapter 3 for more about the history of Samson). Many of the lower slopes of the island are covered in deeper soils, now mostly under bracken. Ruins of several abandoned cottages from the time the island was inhabited can be seen, mainly on the north slope of South Hill. The island was finally evacuated in 1855. Some of the field walls are still standing, especially on South Hill, and are seen clearly when the bracken has died down. Other walls may have been robbed to provide stone for the wall of the deer park. Although the 3.5ha enclosure on South Hill was abandoned by 1860 when the deer escaped, the wall is still clearly visible. The few trees found on the island, tamarisk and elder, are associated with the former inhabitants, as are plants such as primroses that probably originated in their gardens.

A sand bank at the northeast corner of Samson is the usual landing place for visitors, and very popular for sunbathing and picnicking. Behind the landing is an area of sand dune and low scrub with North Hill rising up behind (Fig. 57). On top of the hill and along the ridge is an area of heathland, much of which has been burned on a number of occasions, exposing the line of archaeological sites along the top. The slopes of the hill and much of the rest of the island are covered in dense stands of bracken. South Hill has vestiges of heathland, but

FIG 57. North Hill, Samson, with Scilly Rock in the distance, July 2006. (Rosemary Parslow)

more bracken and bramble. The southern side of South Hill descends to the sea in a jumble of rocks and bracken, with the shallow natural pool at Southward Well by the shore, and above the southwest slope a distinct pattern of field boundaries. Southward Well still has a few wetland plants associated with it; the pool has recently become choked with brambles.

Between the twin hills is a low-lying 'neck' of sand. When the neck was breached in the sixteenth century, the hills may have become separate islands. Later, as deposition of sand and shingle over the next century closed the gap, Samson again became one island (Thomas, 1985). At times the neck area is open sand with scattered plants, but at other times it becomes more vegetated, until opened up again by storms. Woodley was told by an islander there had been 'fine meadows' some time about the 1780s, about forty or fifty years before his visit; although when he was there the area was again covered in sand and one of the two wells that had been dug was choked by the sand (Woodley, 1822). There is a still a small well on the main path leading up South Hill and another hidden among the bracken nearby. Water could have also been obtained from Southward Well, although it was probably always rather murky, situated so close to the shore.

Samson is very important botanically, and it has a number of interesting plants: there is an increasing colony of pyramidal orchids *Anacamptis pyramidalis* in the dunes, which first appeared in 1997 and has since spread; lesser skullcap *Scutellaria galericulata* grows in several damp areas, including Southward Well on the southern shore of the island; balm-leaved figwort is widespread in the bracken areas; and there is a small population of the rare shore dock around the shoreline.

The island is also of considerable ornithological importance for breeding seabirds. The peripatetic common tern *Sterna hirundo* colony has been the subject of a series of experiments to encourage the birds to continue nesting on South Hill rather than moving to a new site every few years. One incident associated with Samson was the wreck of the liner *Minnehaha* west of Bryher in April 1910. The ship was carrying a cargo of cattle, which were swum across to Samson and left there until they could be re-exported. Wrecks of cattle ships were important to the islanders: they were able to claim salvage money for each head of cattle, and even drowned animals had a value. Also on the ship was a large consignment of tropical birds on their way to London Zoo (Seth-Smith, 1910). The birds, all American species, were released – and their subsequent fate is unknown.

At one time there was a colony of black rabbits on the island, their existence being attributed to Augustus Smith, who released rabbits with different coat colours on several islands. These may have now died out, although whether their demise can be attributed to myxomatosis or to eating rat-bait, or to a combination of both, is not known. Attempts to rid the island of rats started in 1992/3 and appeared to have been successful. Continual vigilance is needed, as rats can swim well and could easily find their way back at any time from one of the other islands.

Puffin Island

Lying just off the northern landing beach of Samson is Puffin Island, a small round island with an archaeological site on the top which may once have been part of the larger island (Ratcliffe, 1992). Puffin Island is covered with grasses, thrift and other common coastal plants including curled dock and sea campion *Silene uniflora*. An unusual record is of white ramping-fumitory, discovered in 1984 growing in a crevice among the rocks. It is very likely the plant grew from seed transported by gulls, as has been found on some of the Welsh islands (Gillham, 1956, 1970). A number of gulls also nest on the island, but there are no puffins there despite the name.

White Island

Lying just to the west of Samson is White Island (there is another White Island off St Martin's). There is very little in the way of vegetation on this 1.3ha island, which is mostly bare rock, except for a small amount of spear-leaved orache *Atriplex prostrata*, sea mayweed *Tripleurospermum maritimum*, common scurvygrass *Cochlearia officinalis*, thrift tussocks and a clump of tree-mallow. Lesser black-backed gulls, herring gulls and cormorants *Phalacrocorax carbo* nest on the island. Kittiwakes bred there formerly.

Green Island and Stony Island

Green Island and Stony Island are very small, little more than conglomerations of rocks just off Samson. Neither carries any higher vegetation, and their main interest derives from Green Island having been a former nesting site for roseate *Sterna dougallii* and sandwich terns *S. sandvicensis*. Common terns still nest on the islands some years, but the last time roseate terns successfully bred there was in 1993.

ANNET

Lying just about a kilometre from St Agnes is the well-known 'bird sanctuary' island of Annet (Fig. 58). The island is closed to the public from 15 April to 20 August to protect the colonies of nesting seabirds. Annet is one of the larger uninhabited islands, approximately 1km in length and 22 hectares in extent. It has been designated as an SSSI for its important breeding seabird populations, and also for the well-developed thrift turf, the small population of shore dock and several rare lichens including *Roccella fuciformis*.

The island supports breeding colonies of seabirds: Manx shearwater, storm petrel, lesser black-backed gull, herring gull, shag *Phalacrocorax aristotelis*, puffin, fulmar *Fulmarus glacialis* and great black-backed gull. Some years common terns breed on the island, very rarely arctic terns *Sterna paradisaea* have bred, and until recently a few cormorants. Annet was the main focus of the seabird ringing by members of the former St Agnes Bird Observatory from 1957 until the mid-1960s, mainly Manx shearwaters and storm petrels (*SABO Reports*). A few grey seals occasionally pup on the island.

FIG 58. North West Porth, Annet, with pink-flowering English stonecrop and thrift, June 2002. (Rosemary Parslow)

Annet is about the same size as the island of Teän but has less varied habitats and topography. The main compass of the island is low-lying, thickly covered with grasses, sand sedge, bracken and thrift. At the two northern 'arms' of the island stand huge granite carns, Annet Head and Carn Irish, and from Annet Head a line of triangular carns – the Haycocks – stretches out from the island to give it its characteristic silhouette from a distance. Large areas of thrift turf, often in the form of very large thrift tussocks, dominate much of the island, especially in the north. Elsewhere there are dense stands of bracken with bramble and bluebells *Hyacinthoides non-scripta*, and in places sand sedge and Yorkshire fog *Holcus lanatus* are locally prominent. In one or two places thickets of tree-mallow grow behind the storm beaches. In the south of the island there are also rocky outcrops but on a much smaller scale. The island is almost divided in two by a narrow 'neck' at West Porth. At times the waves wash right across here, leaving a scatter of flotsam among the thrift and sea mayweed.

Perhaps the most impressive feature on Annet is the huge thrift tussocks that cover much of the northern half of the island (Fig. 59). These are so large that it needs a bouncing gait to walk from one mattress-like plant to the next without falling down between them. In May the flowering thrift turns the island a glowing pink, visible from the other islands. The southern half of Annet is mostly bracken and sand sedge with Yorkshire fog grassland where the lesser black-backed and herring gulls nest (Fig. 60). Almost the whole perimeter of Annet is formed of boulder beaches, on some of which colonies of storm petrels nest under the boulders, and where even in daytime they can sometimes be heard 'purring' deep below your feet. Until 1982 there were scattered colonies of the rare shore dock on some of the boulder beaches in the southern half of Annet. After storms swept away many of the overlying boulders the dock also disappeared, with the sole exception of a healthy population growing in a freshwater seepage in the corner of a relatively sheltered beach on the south of the island. Areas of damp flushes near the beaches are marked by species such as brookweed *Samolus valerandi* and sea club-rush.

In a few places above the boulder beaches are stands of tree-mallow. The plant is a very short-lived perennial, often seeming biennial, so there are some years when the tree-mallow is tall and flowering and others when the new plants are growing up among the whitened stems of dead plants. Tree-mallow can be very important both as shelter for nesting terns and also at migration times as habitat for small passerines. Inland from the coast Manx shearwaters nest in burrows, either old rabbit burrows or ones they have excavated themselves. Like the petrels, shearwaters only come in to land on the island on the darkest nights to prospect for nest sites, or later to feed their young. Other seabirds nest on

FIG 59. Annet Head: the whole island flushes pink with flowering thrift in May. (Andrew Cooper)

FIG 60. Lesser black-backed gulls among bracken and Yorkshire fog on Annet, June 2002. (Rosemary Parslow)

FIG 61. Puffins on the water: the smallest of the auks breeding in Scilly.
(D. I. M. Wallace)

the cliffs and above the rocky shore, including a colony of puffins whose burrows are just at the top of the cliffs above one of the bays, where they are subject to frequent scrutiny by tripper boats loaded with holiday visitors who sail in close to the island hoping to catch a glimpse of a 'sea parrot' (Fig. 61).

There are large and noisy lesser black-backed and herring gull colonies on the island, which are a constant hazard for common terns when they also nest there. The accepted 'villains' of the bird world, the splendid great black-backed gulls, are usually solitary nesters. They have a macabre technique of turning their prey, often a Manx shearwater, completely inside out, leaving the skin behind. Bird-ringers have to turn them back the right way in order to retrieve and read the numbers on the leg rings. Other seabirds – razorbills *Alca torda*, guillemots *Uria aalge*, shags and sometimes cormorants – also nest on Annet, both around the coast and on the carns and cliffs.

There are none of the very obvious prehistoric sites on Annet that are found on some other islands. Other than a few walls and other remains including a midden, nothing much is visible now. At one time Annet would have been used for grazing livestock and for hunting seals. Bones of both sheep and cattle were recovered from the midden, indicating that both had been grazed on the island in prehistoric times.

Several of the wrecks that took place off Annet may have had some impact on the natural history. Wrecks are always an obvious source of materials that may get washed up or landed on the islands. The loss of the SS *Castleford*, when she struck the Crebawethans in June 1887, led to some of her cargo of cattle being landed on Annet. Reports suggest there were somewhere between 250 and 450 steers on the island for up to ten days. In a contemporary report Gurney (1889) said the animals trampled everything and would have caused an immense amount of damage at the peak of the shearwater and storm petrel nesting season.

MELLEDGAN AND THE WESTERN ROCKS

Between St Agnes and the Western Rocks is one island on its own, Melledgan. It is not often visited because it is usually a difficult landing due to heavy swell. The island is very exposed and rocky, and in common with similar islands has very few plant species present, mainly tree-mallow, spear-leaved orache and common scurvygrass.

Lying on the fringe of the ring of islands that forms the Scilly archipelago are the jagged rocks, reefs and islands that make up the Western Rocks. Over the centuries they have been a graveyard for shipping and have been instrumental in some of the most notorious shipwrecks recorded. The worst disaster was the loss of the fleet of Admiral Sir Cloudesley Shovell, which came to grief among the Western Rocks on its return from the siege of Toulon in October 1707. Four ships sank with the loss of 1,400 men, including the Admiral. The second major disaster was the loss of ss *Schiller* in May 1875, when 311 passengers and crew drowned. Despite the dangers associated with them, the Western Rocks are a fascinating group of islands, and of great importance for their populations of seabirds and seals (Fig. 62).

FIG 62. Gorregan and the Western Rocks are important for their colonies of breeding seabirds. (John Parslow)

THE UNINHABITED ISLANDS · 115

First impressions of the island of Gorregan are of solidity and square fissured rocks, very different from the disordered jumble of most of the other islands in the Western Rocks. The main block of the island is only 8 metres high and from the sea it does not seem a very great island, but when you try to land it looms over you in towering cliffs. There is very little in the way of vegetation, just a few tufts of common scurvygrass, rock sea-spurrey and orache tucked away out of the weather in deep crevices. Gorregan was at one time one of the best places to see kittiwakes, but now there are more colonies on several other islands.

Rosevear is the largest island in the chain of rocks and islands that form the Western Rocks. It is only 2 hectares in size and 5 metres high, with a relatively flat top so that in storms the spray can wash right over the island. Rosevear is renowned as the island where the workmen lived during the building of the Bishop Rock lighthouse. A group of four cottages were built to house the workmen and the blacksmith's workshop (Grigson, 1948). From a boat it is still possible to pick out the outline of two of the ruins, now half-buried in dense stands of tree-mallow and usually with gulls perched on the gable top of the old buildings. Having landed on Rosevear on several occasions, I find it an intimidating prospect to think of living there. Landing is difficult except in very calm conditions and even then there is a scramble over rocks and boulders to the area around the buildings. The aspect is bleak and exposed; there are altogether only half-a-dozen species of plants growing on the island. Now the area is a tangle of sea beet *Beta vulgaris maritima*, common scurvygrass, orache and the tree-mallow (Fig. 63).

There were Cornish workmen living on the island for over ten years in the 1840s and 1850s. It is said they grew vegetables on the island and even held dances, bringing out women from St Mary's. As the sea spray fetches right across the island, life for the men there must have been very hard, even if they only stayed for a few months in summer. The boats used by the workmen may have landed on a flat area on the south side of the island as there are signs that there may have been a derrick there. All the stone for building the lighthouse was dressed on Rat Island on St Mary's before being shipped across to Rosevear and then to Bishop Rock. During a visit to the island Geoffrey Grigson (1948) describes finding clinkers around the ruins that had once been the blacksmith's shop, a few puffins, scores of razorbills, shags, and great black-backed gulls.

In early October 1990 we landed on Rosevear after there had been a heavy fall of migrants overnight, and the patch of tree-mallow on the island was swarming with small birds in extraordinary numbers. There were dozens of migrating robins, goldcrests *Regulus regulus* and several yellow-browed warblers *Phylloscopus inornatus* all feeding frenetically among the sparse vegetation.

FIG 63. Tree-mallow often provides the only available shelter on some of the smaller uninhabited islands. May 2005. (Rosemary Parslow)

Immediately south of Rosevear is another rocky, craggy island with almost no vegetation. This is Rosevean, all bare rock except where an occasional plant clings in a crack in the rock. The main interest of the island lies in its seabird colonies and seals. In the chain of rocks and islands to the south of Rosevean, Daisy is also recognisable as a separate islet. The pretty name seems rather incongruous for such an inhospitable place. The island is an important haul-out area for the grey seals. To the north of Rosevear and Rosevean there are a number of rocks, most of which are half-hidden under the sea, ending in Little Crebawethan and Great Crebawethan, a mass of rock surrounded by dangerous reefs – the 'death-delivering, ragged and black islets and rocks out towards the Bishop' (Grigson, 1948).

Bishop Rock lies several kilometres off the rest of the Western Rocks; it is hardly much of an island, just the rock on which the lighthouse is built, which barely shows above the waves. Construction of the lighthouse started in 1847, but the structure was swept away when almost complete in February 1850, and work had to begin again. The lighthouse was finally completed in 1858. The tower is 49 metres high, and in the times when the lighthouse was manned (it was automated in 1992) there were occasional sightings of birds and bats around the tower by the lighthouse keepers.

THE NORTHERN OR NORRARD ROCKS

The northern group of islands, although they do not have quite the fearsome reputation of the Western Rocks, have seen many wrecks and incidents over the centuries. Although rugged, they are not quite as fearsome as the Western Rocks. Scilly Rock is reputedly the island from which all the rest of the archipelago was named, although there appears to be no satisfactory explanation of why this should be. Scilly Rock consists of two rocks 22 metres high lying just over 1km off the west coast of Bryher and rather separated from the other Norrard Rocks. According to Kay (1963) there are small patches of 'grass' on the top of the peaks and a small pool on one. Kay's grass seems unlikely, due to the exposure of the site, and the only plants that have been recorded there are rock sea-spurrey and oraches.

South of Scilly Rock are a number of small islands and many rocks. One of these exposed, windswept islands, Illiswilgig, supports a number of plants: tree-mallow, thrift, sea beet, rock sea-spurrey, common scurvygrass, orache and English stonecrop. Several species of seabirds have been recorded nesting on the island, including a few storm petrels (Chown & Lock, 2002). A little way to the east the distinctive outline of Castle Bryher is easily recognised by the high rock tower formation on the edge of the island, which rises 26 metres above the sea. Castle Bryher is also able to support a limited number of plants: sea beet, common scurvygrass, tree-mallow, rock sea-spurrey and orache. Gulls and other seabirds, including storm petrels, nest on the island.

An orache is the only plant recorded on small rocky Seal Rock, whose main interest is as a breeding and haul-out place for grey seals. Between Seal Rock and the next island, Maiden Bower, is a stretch of sea studded by a scatter of vicious rocks called the Garden of Maiden Bower, an ironic name for somewhere so dangerous (Maiden Bower is in fact a corruption of the Old Cornish *Meyn-Meur*, meaning 'great rocks'). No higher plants have been recorded from Maiden Bower. A few gulls nest on the island. Mincarlo is one of the larger islands in the group, about 1.8 hectares in extent, 2km west of Samson and the southernmost of the Norrard group. M.Walpole, who landed there in 1967, reported finding tree-mallow, orache, common scurvygrass and rock sea-spurrey; there are also earlier reports of sea beet (Lousley, 1971). Several species of seabirds nest on the island, including great blacked-back gull, razorbill and shag. Ernest Kay (1963) commented that 'good bird's nesting can be obtained on Mincarlo in the spring.'

ST HELEN'S

At 19 hectares, St Helen's is the largest of the uninhabited islands in the northern part of the Scilly archipelago. Most of the island is a granite hill rising to 42 metres, with steep cliffs on the north side facing Round Island, and a fringe of dune grassland and maritime grassland mainly around the southern coast. The summit of the higher ground has an area of maritime heath and sparse vegetation on thin soils where there had previously been major fires in the 1940s. Wartime incendiary bombs set much of the island on fire, burning away much of the top of the island. By 1987 Hottentot fig had spread right over the native vegetation in this area, but by 2002 much of the plant had gone, having been killed off in the interim (possibly either by unusually cold weather or by salt spray), and heathland had returned. Now the heathland extends over rocky areas of the slopes of the hill, but where the soils are deeper there are dense bracken and bramble communities. There are still some large patches of Hottentot fig both on the heathland and bare rocks and on parts of the shore, so it could easily spread back again. Around the former Pest House building are areas of taller vegetation with hemlock *Conium maculatum* and hogweed *Heracleum sphondylium*, rank grassland with balm-leaved figwort, and a number of unusual plants including grey sallow and wood spurge. There is a large breeding colony of lesser black-backed gulls and other seabirds, including a small number of puffins. Shore dock is no longer found on St Helen's, although it was recorded there in the past (Lousley, 1971). The island is notified as an SSSI with Northwethel and Men-a-vaur for the populations of rare plants and breeding seabirds.

St Helen's is an island with a long history of human habitation, and it seems to have had more human activity associated with it than most. After the early farmers came the establishment of a hermitage in the eighth century, with a tiny oratory and living cell. It is believed the first occupants could have been St Elidius (St Helen's being a later corruption of the name, according to Thomas, 1985) and his followers. In the eleventh century a church was built nearby, and it was extended in the twelfth century when the churches in Scilly came under the juristiction of Tavistock Abbey. The church fell into disrepair in the fifteenth century and was never rebuilt. Even after the abandonment of the Hermitage it is recorded that there was one family with their animals on St Helen's in 1669, when Count Lorenzo Magalotti visited Scilly with his master Cosmo III. In 1764 a 'pest house' was built on the island to use as an isolation hospital for sick sailors from ships coming into the Isles of Scilly. A garden and other cultivation was associated with the Pest House.

Every year on 8 August a boat still goes from St Mary's to St Helen's to celebrate the feast of St Elidius. A service is then held in the ruins of the little church. To allow access for the visit, the tall vegetation is cut down around the Pest House and the Hermitage, and on the path to the landing and the surrounding area. Although only the ruins and the faint signs of fields remain, these activities have influenced the present state of the vegetation and some of the species that were or are found there.

Landing on St Helen's is usually on the south side of the island, where there are still the remains of a rough granite quay. A line of low dunes stretches along the sandy beach, behind which is the flat area on which stands the ruined Pest House and the rough grassland and scrub that once would have been cultivated or grazed. The Hermitage with the Oratory, monk's cell and other buildings are spread around the beginning of the slope of the hill that forms the bulk of the island. Further east, and not always visible among bracken and brambles, are a well and the walls of several small fields.

ROUND ISLAND

The characteristic 'currant bun' profile of Round Island makes it easy to pick out among the other islands in the group, especially with the lighthouse on top (Fig. 64). The lighthouse tower is situated in a commanding position with the lantern 55 metres above the sea (Tarrant, 2000). It is not an easy island to visit: in addition to a difficult landing onto steep steps up the side of the cliff, the island is leased by Trinity House, from whom permission to land must be obtained. Unfortunately when Lousley visited the island in 1957 he apparently made no plant list, other than recording the presence of Hottentot fig. In 1987 I was permitted to spend a short time on the island and was escorted around the top of the island by the then resident lighthouse keepers. This was shortly before the lighthouse was automated and the keepers were withdrawn. At that time the keepers still had a garden on top of the rock, carefully protected by screens from the searing winds. The soil for this garden had originally been transported to the island and hauled up to the top by aerial hoist. Much of the ground between the buildings and the cliff edge was covered in a dense, slippery carpet of the jelly-bean-like succulent purple dewplant *Disphyma crassifolium* and Hottentot fig. There seemed to be no garden weeds in the keepers' immaculate garden; otherwise the sparse flora consisted of the usual coastal species, bird's-foot-trefoil, spear-leaved orache, sea beet, rock sea-spurrey, thrift and tree-mallow, with some fine large fronds of sea spleenwort in crevices in the

FIG 64. Round Island with its lighthouse, seen from the summit of St Helen's, June 2002. (Rosemary Parslow)

granite cliffs. Exposure to the raking seas probably prevents any higher plants persisting for long on the cliff face.

There is an extraordinary account from the 1860s of a Mr L'Estrange who sailed to Round Island through a sea 'speckled with white' for miles upon either side 'by the silvery breasts of innumerable puffins'. Sadly that sort of experience is unlikely to be repeated today, although there are a still a few seabirds in the vicinity, even a handful of puffins. Storm petrels also nest on the island, although this was only discovered when the keepers commented on the black feathers they kept finding. The distinctive sweet smell of the feathers (petrel feathers retain their scent for many years) revealed the identity of the victims and the keepers' cat was banished (P. Robinson, personal communication).

NORTHWETHEL

Another island with a history of human habitation, with the remains of an ancient field system and settlement still visible, Northwethel is 4.6 hectares in extent and lies just off Gimble Porth, Tresco, in the channel to Old Grimsby

Harbour. The story goes that during the Civil War 1,500 Parliamentarians landed on Northwethel under the impression they were on Tresco. It seems amazing that anyone could have mistaken this small tract of land for part of Tresco.

Most of Northwethel is now a dense tangle of bracken and bramble. Lousley recorded 54 species of plants there on one day in May 1957, far more than his total for the considerably larger but windswept island of Annet. The greater plant diversity of Northwethel may also be in some part due to the island having been grazed at one time, plus more varied habitats. There is a sandy beach on one side and a small brackish pool behind the sea bank. The seasonal pool on Northwethel supports unusual plants: sea-milkwort *Glaux maritima*, fennel-leaved pondweed and red goosefoot have been recorded there. Just southeast of Northwethel and the entrance to Old Grimsby Harbour is Foreman's Island, one of the group of low-lying small islets and rocks of importance for breeding seabirds.

MEN-A-VAUR

This island is northwest of St Helen's on the outer, northern fringe of the Scilly archipelago. It consists of three main huge rocks that together form the islet. From its fanciful resemblance to a sailing ship in full sail it is often assumed that the name of this dramatic rock is a corruption of 'man-of-war'. Disappointingly, according to Charles Thomas it is more likely that the name derives from Old Cornish and could mean 'great rock' or 'rock beside, or facing, the hump', in this case the upturned pudding-bowl shape of Round Island. But from some angles the rock does look remarkably like a ship in full sail. It rises to 38 metres almost sheer from the sea, with a deep cleft through the middle, through which a boat can sail at certain tides. There are no higher plants permanently on Men-a-vaur, but there are lichens and algae. It has important colonies of breeding seabirds; raven *Corvus corax* and peregrine *Falco peregrinus* nest here some years.

TEÄN

Teän is only 16 hectares in extent, including the islets Pednbrose, Old Man and Crump Island that are joined to the main island at low water. It consists of low-lying ground linking granite carns and the larger prominent Great Hill (Fig. 65). The undulating coastline consists of a number of bays (porths) and sandy

FIG 65. Teän, viewed here from the top of Great Hill, is home to a number of rare plants and insects. June 2002. (Rosemary Parslow)

beaches, linked to a number of offshore rocks and carns. The sinuous coastline and the hills give Teän far more variety of habitats, and the feeling of a much larger island.

When Lousley wrote about the island of Teän in his *Flora*, he described an island where human influence was still relatively recent and evident (Lousley, 1971). Crispin Gill described it as an open and friendly place, an island likely to attract inhabitants, which it certainly did over many centuries. Remains of Early Period walls have been found and there were two peasant holdings on the island in Roman times. Some of the fields from that time are now under the shallow sea over the sand flats, only visible at extreme low tides. In 1652 a Parliamentary survey noted there was one inhabitant on the island 'whose house is now ruined' (Thomas, 1985). Cattle were still being grazed on the island in 1945 (Grigson, 1948). There had been a thatched cottage with heavy granite walls on the flat area between the two beaches of West and East Porth. This building had been the original cottage occupied by the Mr Nance who introduced kelp burning to the islands in 1684 and whose family lived on Teän for several more generations. The island was inhabited by ten people in 1717, but apparently not in 1744, although Borlase saw ruins and fields of corn in 1752. After that it seems there was the

occasional occupation (Woodley, 1822); the Nances of St Martin's pastured sheep
and cultivated a few acres for a time. There is still a well below Great Hill,
although apparently the water tasted muddy and needed boiling. This well had
been known for three centuries, although in 2002 the remains of the pump had
all but rusted away.

Bracken communities or dune grassland now dominate most of the low-lying
areas of the island. The tops of the largest carns and Great Hill have patches of
heather and heath vegetation. Behind the old cottage building was the original
suite of pastures until at least 1939, which has now all reverted to bracken. False
oatgrass is still in abundance, as is hogweed. Some of the plants associated with
former cultivation, such as yellow oatgrass, have not been seen for many years;
possibly they may reappear if the fields are grazed again in the future.

A number of rare plants occur on Teän, notably orange bird's-foot, shore
dock and dwarf pansy. Balm-leaved figwort and Babington's leek are found
among the tangle of bracken communities, Portland spurge is common around
the sandy beaches and thorn apple *Datura stramonium* and New Zealand spinach
Tetragonia tetragonioides are also occasionally found on the beaches. Several
species of seabirds breed on the island and nearby islets. The island also supports
populations of rare insects; some of the common blue *Polyommatus icarus* and
meadow brown butterflies *Maniola jurtina* represent described island variations,
and the St Martin's ant was found there in 2002 (see Chapter 14).

THE EASTERN ISLES

There are twelve islands in the Eastern Isles group, plus Hanjague further east
and Guther's in the channel between St Martin's and Bar Point, St Mary's. The
whole group forms the Eastern Isles sssi. When, in the past, the sand flats
between the islands were a low-lying plain, what are now the Eastern Isles would
have been a group of low hills (Fig. 66). There is historical confusion over the
names of the islands; it appears that what is now called Nornour was once Little
Ganilly, which makes sense as it adjoins Great Ganilly. What is now Little Ganilly
was at one time known as Little Arthur (Thomas, 1985). The confusion seems to
have arisen as the three hills that make up Great Arthur started to become
separate islands at high tide .

At low tide it is still possible to walk along the boulder ridges between the
'Arthurs' and between Nornour and Great Ganilly. Visiting these islands at
different states of the tide gives a very different impression: at extreme low water
they could be all one large island with several hills, but high water separates the

FIG 66. Nornour and Great Ganilly in the Eastern Isles, seen from St Martin's, June 2005. (Rosemary Parslow)

FIG 67. The Arthurs, seen from Little Ganilly, July 1983. (Rosemary Parslow)

group into individual islands (Fig. 67). The general visitor does not usually get a chance to land on the Eastern Isles, although there are more frequent trips to some of the unrestricted islands. Several of the Eastern Isles are closed to landing during the birds' breeding season (15 April to 20 August) and although a few islanders may land to pick up driftwood, except for fishing and other boat traffic the islands are relatively undisturbed until late summer. In good weather during summer there are daily tripper boats around the islands to look at seals and seabirds; the Eastern Isles are probably the easiest place in Scilly to get close to grey seals. The animals get so blasé during the summer that the older animals do not bother to move off their loafing places, sliding into the water only at the last minute as the boats approach.

Unlike the Western Rocks, which are exposed, harsh and drenched in salt spray, with poor species lists, the Eastern Isles have a more gentle profile and are sheltered from the worst of the westerly gales, and support remnants of habitats that are relatively species-rich. An impenetrable barrier of the bramble *Rubus ulmifolius* on some of the islands makes botanising extremely challenging. When the larger islands were used for summer grazing, stock would have browsed the brambles, so there would have been more grassland and open habitat. Small areas of most habitats can be found on the Eastern Isles: coastal grassland, rock crevices, seabird communities, dunes and heathland. Perhaps one of the most interesting features of the vegetation is the presence of several possible ancient woodland indicators, butcher's-broom *Ruscus aculeatus*, wood spurge and wood small-reed *Calamagrostis epigejos*.

Lousley in his *Flora* recorded 111 species of higher plant on the Eastern Isles, which accords well with the 114 we recorded up to 1999. Each of the islands is slightly different and some have species apparently peculiar to them. For example, Lousley commented on the presence of white ramping-fumitory and an oak tree on Great Ganinick in 1970; the oak had been there when he visited earlier (Lousley, 1940) and was also seen by Geoffrey Grigson (1948). Both those species were still present in 1997. It seems likely the tree may have arisen from an acorn carried there by a bird from Tresco. If it is the same oak that has been growing there for over half a century it has not made much headway: it was still just a twisted gnarled little specimen a few feet high, hunkered down in a sheltered spot. Great Ganinick is the northern of the two Ganinick islands, and is 1.8 hectares in extent. The vegetation is unusually rich in species, and when Lousley visited the island he recorded 74 species. Here too can be found butcher's-broom, wood spurge and wood small-reed. Besides the white ramping-fumitory, Hottentot fig, an *Aeonium* species and rosy dewplant have also been recorded, presumably having originally been carried there by gulls.

The adjoining island of Little Ganinick is 1.2 hectares of typical grassland with seabird colonies and strandline plants.

Great Ganilly is the one of the larger islands, 13.8 hectares in size (Fig. 68). When kelp burning was at it zenith people would spend several weeks each summer on Great Ganilly in a temporary hut. Having a freshwater spring may have made using this island as a temporary home more practical. Kelp was collected from about March to August. Like the island of Samson, Great Ganilly consists of twin hills separated by a low sandy neck with a sandy bay each side, where a number of local sand-dune species including Portland spurge, sea spurge, sea-kale and balm-leaved figwort can be found. Both hills have dense bracken communities covering the lower slopes and maritime heath on the tops of the hills where soils are thinner. It is one of only two places in Scilly where betony *Stachys officinalis* is found, growing in an area of heathland with orange bird's-foot and wild thyme.

Little Ganilly is a smaller, round island of 2.7 hectares, just to the north of Little Arthur. The vegetation follows the usual pattern of bracken communities on the slopes, with maritime grassland and cliff communities round the edge and a small amount of heathland on the summit of the island. On the eastern coast there are several small caves in the cliff face. Seabirds breed on the island and seals haul out on the rocks (Fig. 69).

FIG 68. Great Ganilly, looking south towards Great Innisvouls and Menawethan, June 2002. (Rosemary Parslow)

FIG 69. Grey seals and cormorants breed among the Eastern Isles. (D. I. M. Wallace)

The Arthurs (7.8 hectares) are three islands joined at low water by pebble and blown-sand causeways that form a ragged curve around a large bay. There are some particularly well-preserved entrance graves on Great and Middle Arthur as well as other remains (Ratcliffe, 1992). Great Arthur is the largest of the group. It consists mainly of a low hill with a stony top covered in maritime heath and bare ground with English stonecrop. Around the edge of the island are a wide fringe of maritime grassland and a small area of strandline and dune vegetation. There is a stunted grey sallow on the island, possibly the same tree recorded by Lousley. Middle Arthur is virtually just a granite carn and entrance grave surrounded by a small area of vegetation. There are a few patches of heather on the top of the carn, with maritime grassland and some strandline vegetation on more sheltered shores. Little Arthur is also a granite carn with bracken on deeper soils and heathland on the top, with English stonecrop on more open areas and maritime grassland around the edge. There is a small area of dune and strandline vegetation. Slender St John's-wort *Hypericum pulchrum* is found at one of its few Scillonian localities on Little Arthur.

A very tiny island lies between the main groups of the Eastern Isles. This is Ragged Island, which, despite its small size, has an interesting species list. Besides areas of grassland, thrift, scurvygrass and strandline species there are curious records such as Chilean hard-fern *Blechnum cordatum* and borage *Borago officinalis*. How these species got to the island is unknown, although fern spores can be blown considerable distances.

Nornour is also a small island, about 1.6 hectares in size, just to the north of the larger mass of Great Ganilly. At low tide it is possible to walk from one island

FIG 70. Hut circles on the island of Nornour, June 2002. (Rosemary Parslow)

to the other across a boulder causeway. Nornour probably gets more visitors than other islands in the group, to see an important archaeological site just above the high water mark (Fig. 70). In 1962, when the sea swept away the low dune, the remains of an abandoned Bronze Age and Iron Age settlement were revealed. During Roman times the site had been a shrine where many objects were left as votive offerings, including many beautiful enamel brooches. A former shore dock site there may have been lost during the excavation of the buildings or from erosion by the sea. Nornour consists of one hill mostly covered in bracken communities with a small area of heathland. The eroded and disturbed area around the archaeological site has a large number of species typical of heathland, grassland, sand dune and disturbed ground. The rare plants still found there include Portland spurge, balm-leaved figwort and butcher's-broom. The sea is still washing away this part of the island every time there is a storm, despite attempts to protect the archaeological site.

Great and Little Innisvouls are small rocky islands whose main interest lies in their colonies of breeding seabirds. Great Innisvouls has small areas of bracken and maritime grassland and Little Innisvouls has just some strandline species. On a rock just east of Little Innisvouls called Mouls, Bristowe (1929) recorded a tiny pseudoscorpion, *Neobisium (Obisium) maritimum*, walking around on seaweed between tidemarks.

Menawethan is a steep-sided island, 2.8 hectares in extent, also mainly of interest for its breeding seabirds. There are several well-vegetated areas. Most of the plants are typical of seabird nesting islands with orache, common scurvy-grass and Yorkshire fog. Several large areas are dominated by thrift and sea campion, and others are covered by Hottentot fig. Tree-mallow forms temporary stands and is conspicuous some years. Unusually brookweed grows among the rocks above the shore, apparently associated with a freshwater seepage. Grey seals haul out on the rocks and are often very curious when you land on the island, coming in very close and blowing and moaning gently. This was one of the first islands where English Nature carried out rat eradication.

Coming into Scilly on the *Scillonian* by the high-water route (at low water she has to use the deeper channel of St Mary's Road) the first island you see is the isolated, sugar-loaf stack of Hanjague – the easternmost of the Isles of Scilly, about one kilometre northeast of Great Ganilly. Although there are no plants on the island there are seabirds on the higher ledges (Fig. 71).

West of the Eastern Isles and south of St Martin's is the tiny island of Guther's. At first it appears to be a disordered stack of rocks, but as you sail closer the vegetated middle of the island can be seen. A mat of grass, sea beet and docks grows on top of the island. Among the curious rock formations is a strange, bird-like natural sculpture. The island is a breeding site for shags, great black-backed gulls and herring gulls.

FIG 71. Hanjague, viewed at close quarters from a tripper boat. (Rosemary Parslow)

ISLANDS OFF ST MARY'S

Taylor's Island and Newford Island are two very small islands just a boulder
scramble at low tide off the coast at Porthloo on the western side of St Mary's.
Newford Island is the larger of the two and is mostly occupied by a garden
surrounded by hedges. The rest of the island and Taylor's Island are maritime
grassland with a few tamarisk trees, bracken and bramble.

On the opposite side of St Mary's in Pelistry Bay is the attractive little Toll's
Island (Fig. 72). At low tide it is easy to walk there across the sand bar from
Pelistry Bay. Despite the small size of the island it has a number of interesting
features. Some of these are related to the former use of the island, with evidence
of prehistoric fields and fortifications dating from the Civil War; the battery
known as Pellow's Redoubt is on the highest part of the island. Walls and earth
banks as well as the line of well-preserved kelp pits are evidence of considerable
human activity over the centuries. The main part of the island consists of
maritime heath and grassland. A small area of bracken exists in the southwest
corner, and some gorse in one of the small enclosures. Hottentot fig occurs on
the small bays along the southern shore. Two balm-of-Gilead or balsam poplars

FIG 72. Toll's Island, off the east coast of St Mary's at Pellistry Bay, June 2002.
(Rosemary Parslow)

Populus × jackii grow on the island, having presumably been planted many years ago, and there is also a large daisy tree *Olearia* sp. A small patch of arrow bamboo *Arundinaria japonica* grows by the wall. Small adder's-tongue fern once grew on the heathland, but has not been seen for a number of years.

WHITE ISLAND (OFF ST MARTIN'S)

One of two White Islands, this one is connected to St Martin's by a boulder causeway accessible at low tide. White Island has been designated as an SSSI for biological importance (maritime heath and grassland), for breeding seabirds, and for the geological importance of the dramatic cleft of Chad Girt, which shows a sequence of deposits and is a classic site for interpreting Late Pleistocene succession (Fig. 73).

The island has a sandy short maritime grassland interior sloping up to rocky cliffs with deep clefts between the headlands. A low bank divides the island in two and there are traces of early fields, cairns and other archaeological remains. The slopes of the higher land are covered with rather sparse bracken communities merging into maritime heath along the top of the hills. There are

FIG 73. Chad Girt on White Island, July 2002. (Rosemary Parslow)

rare lichens on some of the steep slopes, one of which is the gilt-edged lichen
Pseudocyphellaria aurata. A shallow depression on the flat grassland just above the
landing area near Porth Morran appears to be a seasonal pool. Small adder's-
tongue fern has been recorded on the dune grassland (in an area now covered
in pebble 'mazes') on the St Martin's side of the bar.

GWEAL

Just off the west coast of Bryher is the small, rocky island of Gweal. The island
consists of two hills joined by a boulder beach. The vegetation consists of typical
species associated with seabird sites: sea beet, rock sea-spurrey, common
scurvygrass and a more extensive area of thrift tussocks, and a group of tree-
mallow on the shoulder of one hill. The island is included in the Norrard Rocks
SSSI, notified for the colonies of breeding seabirds.

CHAPTER 8

The Sea and the Marine Environment

The steamer trip to Scilly however is nearly always rough, even in summer, and is calculated to impress upon the visitor the seafaring qualities of the mariners of four thousand years ago.

Hugh O'Neill Hencken (1932)

T HE SEA HAS ALWAYS dominated life on the Isles of Scilly. The lives of the human population are deeply bound up with the sea around them, as a source of livelihood and as both a barrier and a route to the outside world. The influence of the sea on climate and vegetation is described elsewhere; this chapter deals more strictly with the life in the shallow seas and on the seashores.

The beautiful sugar-white sandy beaches, especially those on St Martin's and Tresco, usually enchant visitors to Scilly. Elsewhere the beaches are rocky, formed of large cobbles with finer sand or the cement-like 'ram' beneath. More extreme types of rocky beach include the boulder beaches of exposed shores, especially around some of the uninhabited islands, as on Annet and the Western Rocks, and the boulder causeways that link some of the rocky islets. Even more extreme situations are seen on isolated stacks such as Men-a-vaur, Hanjague and many of the Western Rocks, which seem to emerge directly from the sea and where it would seem nothing alive could survive the pounding of the waves (Fig. 74).

To put the shores of Scilly into context, the reasons for their importance can be summarised as follows, partly based on Holme (1983):

- The Isles of Scilly are the most southwesterly archipelago in the British Isles, a long way from the mainland and on the edge of the Atlantic. The islands have an exceptionally mild climate with sea temperatures in winter 0.5 to 1°C warmer than around the mainland.

- Wave exposure of the shores of the Isles of Scilly ranges from super-extreme on the outer coasts (an additional grading having had to be added for the most extreme shores by Hiscock, 1984) to the most sheltered conditions within the archipelago.
- With hardly any freshwater input from streams from the islands entering the sea, there are virtually no water-borne pollutants or silts.
- In Scilly the sediments are mainly formed of quartz grains derived from decomposed granite. The type of sand varies within the archipelago, with some places having very fine sands and others very coarse-grained sand, inhabited by species that usually occur offshore in coarse shell or gravel.
- Although there is a similar range of species to those found in Cornwall, there are notable absences, and these are usually species that cannot reach the islands due to isolation from the larval source, because the currents are primarily from the southwest (Harvey, 1969).
- There are many species of southern European and Mediterranean distribution that are common in Scilly but are rare in mainland Britain.
- Some species in Scilly are ones that require milder climates and are usually found in the sublittoral (the area of shore below the lowest tides), but in Scilly are found on the lower shore.

FIG 74. Rocks pounded by the sea in Hell Bay, Bryher, May 2006. (Richard Page)

MARINE BIOLOGY

Several of the early visitors to Scilly, such as G. H. Lewes (1858, 1860), commented on the marine life in their writings, but no systematic studies were made until the marine shells were examined in the 1880s (Smart & Cooke, 1885). Later came studies of the decapod Crustacea (Clark, 1909), then intertidal organisms (Crisp & Southward, 1958).

From the late 1950s to the early 1960s onwards there was an increased interest in the marine fauna and flora of the Isles of Scilly. At this time I was collecting intertidal specimens from St Agnes, targeting specific groups of marine invertebrates and fishes for colleagues at the British Museum (Natural History). Also making collections were members of the London University Sub-Aqua Club, and results from their expeditions were published in the *Journal of Natural History*. These started with a general introduction to the marine flora and fauna of the Isles of Scilly by Professor L. A. Harvey (1969), and have continued to the present day, including in their number many important papers such as that by Turk & Seaward (1997) on the marine molluscan fauna of the islands. Most of these papers were reporting on the sublittoral species collected by divers, but they also include some references to other collections and material.

The Nature Conservancy Council (subsequently English Nature) marine team and other teams of divers have continued the exploration of the sublittoral. This culminated in 1987 in the designation of a Voluntary Marine Park within the islands in an endeavour to protect the rich maritime flora and fauna. Later, in 1994, the area became recognised as an 'Important Area for Marine Life around England'. In 1995 the mudflats and sand flats were put forward as a candidate Special Area for Conservation (cSAC) under the Habitats Directive of the European Community.

Studies of the marine habitats, and monitoring of the health of the eelgrass *Zostera marina* beds and of some of the rare habitats and marine life, continue to this day. In addition, the Isles of Scilly are still a popular venue for students on marine field courses. Groups from Exeter University and from several other colleges and schools have visited Scilly over the years to study the rocky shores and other marine habitats.

SCILLIONIAN SHORES

The topography of the islands is determined by the underlying granite rock. The prevailing winds are from the southwest and it is mainly on those shores that are on the west, southwest and northwest of the islands where there is the greatest degree of exposure. The main islands are somewhat protected from the greatest force of the wind by the islets and reefs of the Western Rocks, which take the brunt of the wave action (Harvey, 1969). Even so, powerful seas pound all round the most exposed coasts of the islands, resulting in spectacular seascapes – especially at Hell Bay and Shipman Head on Bryher, St Warna on St Agnes, Peninnis Head on St Mary's and Shag Point on St Martin's. The most sheltered areas are the extensive sand flats and shallow water enclosed by the ring of all the other islands. The contrast between the savage outlines of the Western Rocks and the more gentle curves of the Eastern Isles graphically demonstrates the difference in the amount of exposure.

ZONATION OF THE SHORE

The shore is divided into zones determined by tide levels. The diagram in Figure 75 indicates the zones and the names used to identify them, ranging from extreme high water springs (EHWS) down to extreme low water springs (ELWS). The abbreviations are generally used when describing the area on shore.

The seashore can be divided into biological zones using the presence of different species of plants and animals. In Scilly for example they range from the extremely exposed Western Rocks, where little other than barnacles can survive, to the gentle, sheltered sandy bays of the inner islands. The sandy shores can look sterile, but most animal life there is beneath the surface and only appears when covered by the tide. The type of the sand, mud or gravel also influences the types of animals found there. Perhaps the poorest habitat for species diversity is a pebble beach, where the stones get rolled about by the waves and very little can survive between them or on their surfaces.

The remainder of this chapter is divided artificially between the two main types of seashore in the islands, firstly the rocky shores and then the sandy shores.

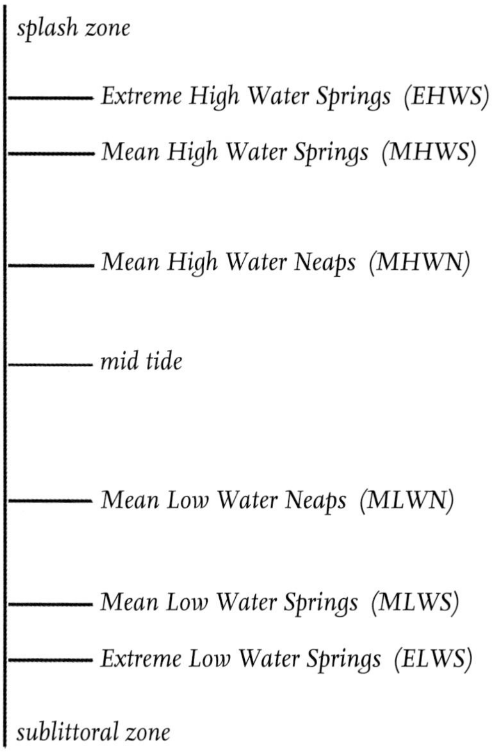

splash zone

———— *Extreme High Water Springs (EHWS)*

———— *Mean High Water Springs (MHWS)*

———— *Mean High Water Neaps (MHWN)*

———— *mid tide*

———— *Mean Low Water Neaps (MLWN)*

———— *Mean Low Water Springs (MLWS)*

———— *Extreme Low Water Springs (ELWS)*

sublittoral zone

FIG 75. Zonation of the shore.

ROCKY SHORES

Rocky shores are classified according to the amount of exposure they receive; the classification described below is based on that originally proposed by Ballantine (1961), modified by Hiscock (1984). Because the shores in the Isles of Scilly have communities indicating more severe wave action than in Ballantine's classification, an extra, 'super' exposed category was added by Hiscock. This classification uses groups of organisms and their position on the shore as a sort of 'rule of thumb' to identify the amount of exposure they receive. Sheltered shores in Scilly are less sheltered than similar shores elsewhere in Britain, and physically close to areas of exposed shore, all of which makes them particularly unusual and interesting.

Extremely exposed shores

These can be divided into super-exposed shores (those that are exposed to the full force of wave action driven by the prevailing winds) and extremely exposed shores (those exposed to very strong action). Most are west-facing shores, composed of steeply sloping bedrock in the most extreme situations, such as in the Western Rocks, where very few species can survive. On exposed stacks and rocks in the splash zone a few species of lichens will be seen (the lichens are able to survive frequent wetting by sea water), as well as some small periwinkles and barnacles. Where the wave action is slightly less extreme limpets become common and there can be several species of periwinkles. Lower down the shore a few red seaweeds start to appear, as well as the brown seaweed bladder wrack and occasionally beadlet anemones *Actinia equina*, and sometimes patches of mussels *Mytilus* sp. may find a niche.

Very exposed shores

These are rocky shores exposed to direct wave action, but where there is less than the full force of the waves due to some slight shelter, usually from rocks, that minimises the effect. This type of shore is much richer in species, so that besides those found on more exposed shores there are more red seaweeds, coralline algae, bladder wrack, limpets, barnacles and periwinkles. Beadlet anemones are common, dog whelks *Nucella lapillus* occur and the large kelps are found on the lower shore.

Exposed shores

These are rocky, sloping shores on seaward-facing shores on the outer islands, but where the position of offshore rocks or the direction they face gives some shelter. Encrusting calcareous algae, patches of thongweed *Himanthalia elongata*, wracks and kelps cover the lower shore. Beadlet anemones often occur in huge numbers.

Semi-exposed shores

Rocky shores on the outer isles that are east-facing and more sheltered are categorised as semi-exposed. These are very similar to exposed shores but are more protected by aspect. Brown wracks are frequent, although upper levels are still very bare in appearance. There are often good rock pools.

Fairly sheltered shores

These bedrock and boulder slopes near open coasts in bays and extending to sand on lower shores are very rich areas with dense algal cover, encrusting algae on rocks, abundant kelp and many molluscs. These shores also have a rich under-boulder fauna. Where this type of shore merges into sand there may be dense mats of the hair-like red algae *Audoinella* sp. on sandy rocks.

Sheltered shores
These are bedrock and boulder shores extending into sand, sheltered from strong wave action. They are densely covered in red and brown seaweeds. There is a rich fauna both under boulders and under the algae.

Very sheltered shores
The least exposed category are coasts where the fetch of the waves reaches less than a few hundred metres. The most sheltered shores here are very species-rich, with many species of seaweeds, especially where there are large boulders on gravel. The sides of the rocks are covered in sponges, tunicates and other encrusting animals.

THE SPECIES OF ROCKY SHORES

There are about 97 kilometres of rocky shores in Scilly, the variations due to the proximity of exposed to sheltered shores being one of the features that make this coastline so interesting. Also the very broken nature of rocks and boulders on the shores often results in very rich under-boulder communities. Scilly does not have the wealth of rock pools found in many places in Cornwall and elsewhere, mainly because of the way granite weathers, but it does have a range of pools of all sizes, and at different levels on the shore. Some of the highest pools may only be replenished by the sea at EHWS, and are subject to enormous fluctuations in salinity and temperature depending on factors such as rainfall, sunshine and evaporation. The larger high pools with their mats of green algae may have temporary populations of grey mullet and occasionally gobies. The inhabitants of smaller pools are more transient, as the pools can dry up completely in summer. Further down the shore the pools may be more like miniature aquariums, with many kinds of algae, sponges, bryozoan colonies, probably several species of anemones, tubeworms, fish and small crabs and prawns.

There are a number of sloping, rocky shores with large rocks that have encrusting species on their undersides and hide a fascinating gamut of species in their shelter. Carefully upending the rocks on the lower shore will reveal a very rich fauna, only accessible just before the tide turns. Many of the more

uncommon species may be trapped here, especially at ELWS. Judicious searching
may even find cup corals, rosy featherstars *Antedon bifida* and unusual species
of fish.

Another habitat that is found in Scilly is the under-boulder cave. These are
often very substantial pools under immense boulders, which may be at least as
large as a garden shed. Usually these habitats are under water the whole time
and only emerge briefly at low water, but at the equinoctial tides they may just
be accessible long enough to wriggle into the hollow under the rock. Some of
the best caves have their walls and roof coated in an array of colourful species –
sponges, colonial tunicates, cup corals and anemones. The pool below will often
be lined with different-coloured varieties of the anemone *Sagartia elegans* and
other species, and may also have a few fish and more lively inhabitants. On one
occasion I found a lobster *Homarus gammarus*, and another time a small conger
eel *Conger conger* under a really enormous boulder.

Lichens

At the top of the beach is the supralittoral or splash zone; this is the region
above the highest fetch of the waves but still influenced by the spray, just below
the start of the higher vegetation. There is a group of lichen species that are
closely associated with the splash zone. *Lichina pygmaea*, a black, seaweed-like
lichen, grows in tufts around high water mark, sometimes overlapping with the
highest seaweeds; sea ivory *Ramelina siliquosa* forms patches of grey-green with
disc-shaped fruiting bodies; *Roccella fuciformis* is a similar species that is frequent
in Scilly. Among the most spectacular lichens in this area are some of the bright
yellow species, including *Xanthoria parietina* and *Caloplaca marina*, that form the
yellow band on the rocks of the shore just above high water mark of spring tides.

Seaweeds

Some of the rocky shores are ideal places to demonstrate zonation, and
numerous groups of students will have been to Scilly for this purpose. The
seaweeds begin just at the lower limit of the lichens, at EHWS, and they continue,
species by species, all the way down the shore to ELWS and into the sublittoral
kelp beds, until there is no longer enough sunlight to allow them to
photosynthesise.

Green seaweeds can be found throughout the shore but are most noticeably
in pools on the upper shore and where freshwater seepages run down the shore.
Some of the large rock basins that only become replenished with sea water at
the spring tides have carpets of the hair-like green algae *Chaetomorpha linum* and
similar species, which in high summer can become bleached almost white. One

very common species, gutweed *Enteromorpha intestinalis*, is frequently found both in pools and where fresh water trickles down the beach, and two other species of *Enteromorpha* also occur in Scilly (S. M. Turk, 1971). The fragile leafy fronds of sea lettuce *Ulva lactuca* can be very obvious higher on shore. *Codium* spp. are also easily identified green seaweeds with velvety, soft cylindrical branches, found mostly on the lower shores.

The brown seaweeds are the ones that show the neatest zones on rocky shores. These include the very important group, the fucoid seaweeds or wracks. At the top of the beach, often overlapping with the lichens, is channelled wrack *Pelvetia caniculata*, a small species that apparently dries up at neap tides and becomes twisted and blackened. This enables the seaweed to survive until the waves reach it again and it becomes soft and brownish-green once more. Below this are the other wracks, bladder wrack (the one with the bladders that children find so satisfying to pop), spiral wrack *Fucus spiralis* and serrated wrack. Knotted wrack is a very characteristic brown seaweed of the more sheltered rocky shores around the islands in Scilly and in places is the most common species. In the most sheltered bays the fronds can grow to several metres long, completely masking the boulders at low tide. The fronds have egg-shaped floats, which give the alga its characteristic appearance and alternative name of 'egg-wrack'; on some there may be additional nodules which are caused by a nematode worm (Coles, 1965; Ingle, 1969). When kelp burning was a major occupation of the population these wracks were very important to the Scillonian economy (see Chapter 3). Below the wracks are oarweeds of the *Laminaria* zone; these kelp beds emerge for a while at low water, the fronds seeming to writhe like a pack of sea otters at the extreme edge of the tide. This is the moment before that audible hush as the tide turns – slack tide – before returning faster than it went out. Kelp grows at low water mark and below into the sublittoral for many metres. A photograph by Mark Groves taken 18m below low water off St Mary's shows the kelp line below which there is insufficient light for the seaweeds to grow (Groves, 1988).

Kelps are very important in forming a protective 'forest' in which many animals take shelter and on which many other algae and encrusting animals grow (Fig. 76). Several species of kelp are frequent around the islands, including the driftweed *Laminaria digitata*, the rare southwest species *L. ochroleuca* and other *Laminaria* spp. including sugar wrack. The holdfasts of the *Laminaria* provide an ideal home for many encrusting animals such as sponges and hydroids and in the crevices there are worms, brittlestars and small crustaceans. The stipe and fronds are frequently home to the beautiful little blue-rayed limpet *Helcion pellucidum*, easily recognised by iridescent blue lines on the shell of the young

FIG 76. Kelp beds exposed at low tide. (Paul Gainey)

animals. Two other species commonly associated with kelp are the cowries, both arctic cowrie *Trivia arctica* and spotted cowrie *T. monacha*, which prey on compound ascidians that also often grow on the stipe. Some of the *Laminaria* can grow to huge sizes, and four metres is not unusual for the larger species. Many of these large algae, furbelows *Saccorhiza polyschides* for example, are annuals and break off in storms, usually leaving the holdfast to grow a completely new frond each year; others, including cuvie *Laminaria hyperborea*, are perennials and will live a number of years in more sheltered situations.

Thongweed (Fig. 77) is a common and very distinctive seaweed. This is a perennial alga that grows every year from a small 'button' on a short stalk attached to the substrate. The buttons often cover large areas of rock; some grow in rock pools, where they apparently do not develop fronds. The fronds or 'thongs' usually grow to about two metres, but in places in Scilly can reach ten metres, forming dense beds between the islands. A similar weed is mermaid's tresses *Chorda filum*, which grows similar long cords, but it is much less common in Scilly than thongweed. Several smaller brown seaweeds are common and easily identified; some have a distinctly southwestern distribution in Britain. One of these is *Cystoseira tamariscifolia*, a pretty brown seaweed found in rock pools that shows blue iridescence when under water; another is *Bifurcaria bifurcata*, a species with a southwestern distribution. *Leatheresia difformis* is a brown seaweed that appears as irregular, hollow brown bubbles that grow on other small seaweeds, and sometimes get washed ashore in large numbers. In recent years an alien invader has become common throughout the islands. This is the notorious japweed *Sargassum muticum*, first reported in the UK in 1973 (Farnham *et al.*, 1973) and in Scilly in 1991. Japweed forms long chains with the branches all hanging from the main stipe like washing from a washing line, and it has become common in shallow bays among the Eastern Isles and elsewhere. It is now very frequently washed up all around the shores on the islands.

There is even greater variety in the red seaweeds than in either brown or green. Approximately 400 species have been recorded in Cornwall and most of these will be in Scilly. Many of the leafy or ferny species are among the most beautiful of the marine algae, although identifying many of them is a specialist skill. It is not always realised that the encrusting species on the rocks that appear like coloured cement are also plants. There are several species present in Scilly, but unfortunately they too are not easy to identify. Many pools have dense carpets of the pink coralline algae *Corallina officinalis* and others that form crisp, beaded, fringe-like growths in rock pools and in crevices along the rocks. Another type

FIG 77. Characteristic seaweeds growing on rocks, including thongweed 'buttons', saw wrack, sea lettuce and carragheen. (Paul Gainey)

of coralline alga that forms dense, soft, chalky masses is *Mesophyllum lichenoides*: it is common in some pools and under boulders. A very unusual red alga found commonly in Scilly in summer is *Asparagonopsis armata*, named from the barbed side branches. This is the gametophyte or sexual generation of a species called *Falkenbergia rufolanosa*, which forms blobs of threads on other seaweeds. *Asparagonopsis* has a very local distribution in Britain; it may have originated from Australia about 1925 (Campbell, 1976). Another quite recent arrival is *Pikea californica* from the Pacific, first found in Scilly in 1967 but not reported until 1976 (C. Harvey and S. Fowler, personal communication). Among the more easily recognised common red seaweeds are *Polysiphonia lanosa*, which forms little epiphytic tufts on knotted wrack, and carragheen or Irish moss, which includes two very similar species: *Chondrus crispus*, with blue iridescence on the fronds, and *Mastocarpus stellatus*.

Shore fish

Fishing in rock pools and searching under boulders at low water can be very rewarding in Scilly when looking for shore fishes. On some islands there are extensive areas of pools on rocky outcrops – although the way the granite weathers frequently results in very awkward-shaped pools for fishing out the inhabitants! But the crevices and overhangs and dense algal cover are ideal hiding places for fish and other marine animals. The rocky shores of southwest Britain have the highest species counts for shore fishes (Hayward, 2004).

Some of the species of fish that may be found in rock pools are more generally associated with the open sea. These are usually free-swimming species that have become stranded when the tide retreats and leaves them marooned in the very highest pools until they can escape on the next high spring tide. Grey mullet are frequently trapped in this way and if not taken by predators appear to be able to survive for weeks if not months. Young stages of some fish such as wrasse can also be encountered onshore. Otherwise the common fishes in the pools are mostly ones that are adapted to conditions that include fluctuations in temperature and salinity. Many of these fish spend their whole lives in the intertidal zone, breeding in the pools or in cavities under boulders. When the larval fish hatch from the eggs they will move immediately into the plankton, while others spend their juvenile stages in the shelter of pools and inshore before moving into deeper water until adult (Wheeler, 1994).

Montagu's blenny *Coryphoblennius galerita* (Fig. 78) is a characteristic species of higher rock pools lined with coralline algae. It is of Mediterranean and Lusitanian distribution and only reaches the southwest of Britain; it is very common in Scilly. In summer this lively little fish can be seen displaying and

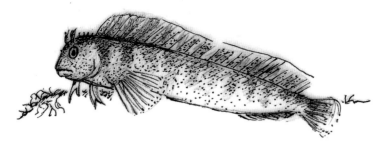

FIG 78. Montagu's blenny is a southwestern species found commonly in rock pools in Cornwall and the Isles of Scilly. (Rosemary Parslow)

dashing out from the crevices in its pool to skirmish with its neighbours. It is easily recognised by the tentacles above the eye that stick up like eyebrows. The males become quite aggressive and territorial; when excited their colours become brighter and more intense. They also appear to parade in front of females, colouring up, often turned almost black and erecting their dorsal fins. Another even more common blenny is the shanny *Lipophrys pholis*. Shanny and Montagu's blennies have several features in common, including their territorial and breeding behaviour, egg-guarding by the males and their ability to rest, apparently basking, partly out of the water. This behaviour, especially as their eyes are high on their heads, is very reminiscent of the mangrove-living mudskippers. Shanny can get quite large, up to 16cm, and have strong jaws and a bulldog-like tendency to bite hard and hold on if anyone is rash enough to use a finger to try and dislodge them from their holes. Another blenny, the tom-pot blenny *Parablennius gattorugine*, may occasionally be found in pools lower on the shore; tom-pots have bulging eyes and even larger feathery 'eyebrows' and dorsal fins.

Gobies are another group of fish commonly found between the tides. Here again there are several species that are common, but they are not easy to identify in the field and can usually only be reliably identified by catching specimens. Some gobies are found in rock pools and can superficially resemble blennies with their large heads and bulging eyes. But unlike blennies they have scales, two dorsal fins and flattened pelvic fins forming a weak sucker. Two-spotted goby *Gobiusculus flavescens* and common goby *Pomatoschistus microps* are small species found in pools or shoaling among seaweeds.

One very rare fish, the Red Data Book giant goby *Gobius cobitis*, with again a southern distribution, lives in deep, bare rock pools usually high on the shore

(Fig. 79). The pools always contain a large boulder or other shelter and usually no seaweeds except for the green *Enteromorpha* sp., often indicating some input of rainwater. This fish appears to be tolerant of brackish conditions. Some giant gobies were found almost twenty years later, in the same pools on St Agnes where I had collected some for the Natural History Museum in 1973 (Potts & Swaby, 1993). There is a concern that giant gobies could be quite vulnerable in these pools as they are the ones regularly fished by local children, but fortunately in Scilly they are apparently still extant. Sometimes another large goby, rock goby *Gobius paganellus*, can be found in the same large pools, but it is more often found under boulders on rocky shores.

Looking under boulders low on the shore may reveal an extraordinary little fish attached to the underside of the rock. This is another species with a western distribution, one of the clingfish, the Cornish sucker *Lepadogaster lepadogaster*, with a dorso-ventrally flattened body with big, blue false eyespot markings. When disturbed, it will move away in a series of jerks as it uses its sucker to slide around the rock to hide. Other clingfishes and sea snails are uncommon on shore, but two-spotted clingfish *Diplecogaster bimaculata*, small-headed clingfish *Apletodon microcephalus* and the tadpole-like Montagu's sea snail *Liparis montagui* all have occasionally been found at the lowest spring tides.

Some bays with large boulder beaches are refuges for many other common shore fish, which hide deep under the boulders or in pools beneath the seaweed.

FIG 79. The giant goby is a very rare, southern fish only found in some deep pools on the upper shore. (Paul Gainey)

Long-spined scorpion fish *Taurulus bubalis* are sometimes exceptionally common. They have spines on their gill covers, and will puff themselves up and spread their spines wide to deter predators. This does not always work: both heron and cormorant have been seen to catch and eat them. Underneath boulders and among seaweeds the thin brown worm pipefish *Nerophis lumbriciformis* can often be found. They have tiny horse-shaped heads and bootlace-shaped bodies. As in the related seahorses, it is the male that takes care of the eggs, carried on the ventral surface of his body until they hatch. Another common species in the same places is the eel-like butterfish *Pholis gunnellus*, usually brown in colour with a line of white-ringed black spots along the sides. Tiny common eels are sometimes plentiful on shore and occasionally a fifteen-spined stickleback *Spinachia spinachia* will be found. The two species of rockling, shore rockling or whistler *Gaidropsarus mediterraneus* and five-bearded rockling (or pettifox locally) *Ciliata mustela* are both found on rocky shores, usually in pools under large rocks. Although fishing in pools is still a common pastime for the local and visiting children, some of the traditional forms of rock-pool fishing may be dying out. At one time, it was traditional to fish for whistlers at Easter, the name apparently referring to the need to whistle when fishing for them – or at least, as was said in a manuscript from the late seventeenth century, 'this fish rarely taking the bait unless they doe (whistle), for whereas if the anglers whistle and make a vocal noise ... they bite very freely' (Turner, 1964). These long brown scaleless fish look somewhat like a catfish with their whiskery faces; they hide under rocks or in deep pools where they could be caught on a hand line. They were considered delicious fried in butter.

Sponges

The sponge fauna of the Isles of Scilly is considered to be very rich in species. Certainly exploring the rocky shores at low tide will reveal a range of encrusting forms in many colours and textures. On some shores the undersides of all the boulders are covered in a deep layer of carpet-like sponge, sometimes so thick they join large boulders together. Some sponges have a distinctive smell. The strong odour of the breadcrumb sponge *Halichondria panicea* is unmistakable: the sickly, sweet–sour smell it is so strong that it clings to everything the sponge has been in contact with. Other encrusting sponges grow over rocks and on seaweeds, especially on holdfasts of the larger brown seaweeds. A few species form vase-shaped or purse-shaped colonies: of these the flattened white purse sponge *Scypha compressa* colonies are common and distinctive enough to have a vernacular name. Although the colours can be very variable this is not necessarily a guide to species, and identification of sponges is mostly based on microscopic study of their internal spicules. Sponges are divided into their two main classes by whether their spicules are siliceous or calcareous. As only one of the groups of encrusting animals on the shore, it is sometimes difficult to distinguish sponges from superficially similar colonies of sea squirts and bryozoans, but pressing a finger on them will sometimes reveal the 'crunchy' feel of the internal spicules of a sponge. While the number and diversity of sponge species still remains a challenge for specialist taxonomists, their importance to the marine environment cannot be underrated. There is a whole underclass of small animals and plants that grow in, on, or among sponges, and the dense mat of sponge acts as an important refuge even for larger animals such as fish and crabs.

Jellyfish, hydroids and allies

Most jellyfish are the well-known floating bell-like medusas found offshore, or onshore as casualties, and occasionally small jellyfish may be found floating in a tide pool, but another group live onshore as small, sessile, stalked jellyfish. The species most likely to be encountered is *Haliclystus auricula*, which looks like a tiny brown umbrella with groups of tentacles on each 'spoke' hanging from fronds of red seaweeds.

There are very many species of hydroids. Some are solitary polyps, tiny sac-like animals with feeding tentacles, but the commonest forms likely to be encountered in the Isles of Scilly are colonial animals. Most are very small and the colony has the characteristic zigzag or branched structure with polyps on the ends of the 'branches'. Superficially they look more like plants than animals, but underwater the hydranth will be seen to emerge and wave its tentacles. There are many species, all very similar in appearance and difficult to identify, but examples are easily found attached to rocks or seaweeds, and they are common around all the islands.

Occasionally found on the lower shore at low spring tides is one of the soft corals, dead-man's fingers *Alcyonium* spp. This is another colonial animal, usually resembling part of an old glove. Underwater it can be seen that the surfaces of the 'fingers' are studded with individual polyps (see Fig. 94).

Sea anemones and corals

The sea anemones are well represented in the Isles of Scilly. Several species are abundant on shore and in rock pools, while others need searching for under overhangs, in caves or buried in deep crevices in the bedrock. Some are cryptically coloured and their patterned discs merge with the background; others are among the most colourful animals on the seashore. Some of the most distinctive are easily identified, but many others are very difficult to determine, especially as they can occur in many colour varieties of the same species. Common species will be encountered in rock pools, where they may be easily observed when their tentacles are expanded. Beadlet anemones are perhaps the most familiar and the hardiest; when the tentacles are withdrawn they are just a tough blob of red, green, or brown jelly in a crevice, sometimes so high up the shore it would seem they barely get a wetting at neap tides. Their name refers to the row of blue beads, the verrucae or acrorhagi, at the base of the red tentacles. At one time believed to be a variety of the beadlet is the larger strawberry anemone *Actinia fragacea*, which when retracted does bear an extraordinary resemblance to its namesake (Fig. 80). It is generally found lower on the shore, but in the warmer conditions of the Isles of Scilly it can also be found in high cracks in the granite.

Also found living with tentacles emerging along the cracks around the base of rock pools is the snakelocks anemone *Anemonia viridis*, in various shades of green and brown, often with lilac tips (Fig. 81). This species usually does not retract when touched, catching at your fingers but without being able to sting. Also in deep cracks in rock pools among coralline algae is another southwestern and Mediterranean species, the gem anemone *Bunodactis verrucosa*; in Scilly it is usually a very pretty pink with grey, green and pink markings on the disc and a

FIG 80. The strawberry anemone appears to live higher on the shore in Scilly than elsewhere. (Paul Gainey)

FIG 81. Snakelocks anemones come in different colour forms, of which the brown and the purple-tipped are the most common. (Paul Gainey)

pink column so it blends with the coralline algae. Another easily identified anemone found lower on the shore, or again in pools, is the dahlia anemone *Urticina felina*; it is variably patterned and coloured, but tends to be short and wide with a coating of sand grains and bits of shell adhering to the verrucae.

Several of the anemones can produce new individuals by various forms of splitting or fission. Snakelocks anemones for example demonstrate this: in an aquarium captive specimens soon colonise the tank by subdividing into two or more individuals over and over again, rapidly forming cloned populations. One of the most fascinating modes of asexual reproduction is the growing of new polyps inside the body cavity, the coelenterum. When specimens are being collected, gem anemones frequently expel these tiny, young anemones from the mouth, quite perfect miniatures with long tentacles.

In the under-boulder caves on the lower shore are pools with swarms of the anemone *Sagartia elegans* in many colour forms, sometimes *Anthopleura ballii* (a very rare Mediterranean species), and one of the prettiest animals found on the shore, the jewel anemone *Corynactis viridis*, again a species of south and west Britain and the Mediterranean. These tiny anemones with knobbed antennae occur in sheltered places under boulders low down on the shore as well as in the caves. They often form large sheets covering the surface of the rock and the patches come in one of several boiled-sweet-coloured varieties: pink, orange or green. Jewel anemones are closely related to the corals. Only one coral, a cup-coral, is likely to be encountered on shore, the Devonshire cup-coral *Caryophyllia smithii*. When retracted, the corallum, the stony cup attached to the rock, is insignificant, but when the polyp opens the coloured disc and knobbed tentacles are exposed. Other cup-corals are found in Scilly, but in deeper water.

Polychaetes

Many species of polychaete worms are common on all types of shore, free-living, buried in sand or in some form of tube. Most are only identifiable in a general way as ragworms, tubeworms, fanworms, scaleworms, paddleworms, lugworms, etc. Some, such as the larger ragworms and lugworms, are better known, mainly because fishermen collect them to use as bait. Collecting the larger ragworms can be a challenging business: these very active worms have an impressive pair of teeth and can give a painful bite. Many of the smaller worms, the scaleworms (with large scales along the dorsal surface) and similar species, can be found not only under rocks but also among seaweeds and encrusting sponges. One tiny one lives in the ambulacral groove of the large edible sea urchin *Echinus esculentus*. Fanworms and tubeworms have fans of tentacles that function as gills and also open out to trap particles of food from the water. When disturbed the fan is withdrawn instantly and only reopens when danger has passed. Most of these species of worms build some kind of tube in which they live. Sometimes the tube is formed of mucus and is stiff and leathery; in others some material such as shell fragments or sand are incorporated. In the serpulid tubeworms a hard white tube is made of calcareous material and fixed to the substrate. The spirorbid worms *Spirorbis* spp. and keeled worms *Pomatoceros triqueter* are well-known examples. Spirorbids have small, white, coiled tubes often seen on rocks, on seaweeds and on other animals such as shells. Keeled worms are similar but larger, with a twisty tube with a triangular cross-section. With patience it is possible to see the tiny tentacles emerge as the worm begins feeding, proving there is still a live animal inside, as the hard tubes survive for a long time after the owner has gone.

Crustacea

Of all the inhabitants of the seashore, the crabs, shrimps and lobsters are among the most easily recognised animals. Many species of marine Crustacea are found in Scilly, and many can also be found onshore in a variety of habitats. One group of crustaceans are the cirripedes, which include the barnacles – although at first sight they would not seem very obviously related to crabs or shrimps, their body form has been so extremely modified. Several species, including *Balanus perforatus* and *B. crenatus*, are very familiar occupants of the bare rocks at the top of the shore. When the tide comes in the plates covering the barnacle open and the 'legs', the thoracic limbs, sweep the water, kicking suspended food into the mouth. Acorn barnacles form dense patches on the upper shore but their close relatives the goose barnacles are only seen when they are washed ashore attached to logs or other flotsam. One of the strangest of the cirripedes is *Sacculina carcini*, a parasite on shore crabs *Carcinus maenas*, forming a large, smooth, yellowish mass under the crab's tail, superficially resembling an egg mass, but with no obvious structure.

There are a number of small crustaceans that are common in pools, under rocks and seaweeds, which are generally lumped together as shrimps or prawns. Opossum shrimps are small, transparent animals with big eyes, which swim jerkily through the water (one species, the chameleon prawn *Praunus flexuosus*, is found in the brackish waters of Bryher Pool). Of the two groups of shrimp-like animals, the isopods and the amphipods, isopods are flattened dorso-ventrally and amphipods are flattened laterally and swim along on their sides. There are many species of isopods in Scilly, some occurring in large numbers under weeds while others congregate where fresh water seeps down the shore. *Sphaeroma serratum* and several related species are stout little woodlouse-shaped isopods. Sea slaters *Ligia oceanica* are like very large woodlice up to 3cm long, sometimes seen scrabbling up rocks and harbour structures (Fig. 82). At one time a very large sea slater appeared to live beside the ticket kiosk at the top of the quay on St Mary's Harbour: it would sit waving its antennae almost on the edge of the window while you bought your ticket. The sandhoppers that are found high up the beach under rotting seaweed are typical amphipods, and some of their close relatives can be found under rocks and in rock pools. Ghost shrimps *Caprella linearis* are long, thin amphipods that are occasionally found low down on the shore among seaweeds. There are several species of prawns, all rather similar transparent animals often seen swimming in rock pools. Prawns need very close examination to identify them; they have a sharp beak-like protuberance on their carapace, the rostrum, the shape of which differs according to species.

Two species of true lobster occur in Scilly, common lobster (see Fig. 94), a deep blue animal in life (the red colour only appears when it is cooked), and the crawfish or spiny lobster *Palinurus elephas*, usually called crayfish in Scilly. The latter is similar to the lobster but is red in life and lacks the big chelipeds, the large first claws. These are not animals usually found on shore except when stranded, or rarely in caves under huge immobile boulders. The large spiny spider crab *Maia squinado* is very occasionally found at ELWS, and the empty carapaces are common on the shore. Small species of spider crabs *Macropodia* sp. are not uncommon lower on the shore, often among seaweeds and clumps of

FIG 82. Sea slaters are often seen scrabbling up harbour walls as well as seaside rocks. (Rosemary Parslow)

hydroids. They are slow-moving and difficult to see due to their cryptic colouring and habit of sticking bits of algae, sponges and other material on their legs and carapace.

Tiny edible crabs *Cancer pagurus* are very common in pools and especially under boulders high on the shore, as are shore crabs. The shore crabs are one of the most ubiquitous animals, found almost anywhere on the shore. They have very variable colouring, especially when young, when almost transparent, fingernail-sized individuals can be discovered among coralline algae or in holdfasts of the large kelps. They are tolerant of the extreme conditions of the high-tide pools and even the brackish lagoon on Bryher. Several other crabs are likely to be encountered between the tides. Many of them can give a painful pinch and should be handled with care, but none is so ferocious as the beautiful velvet swimming crab *Necora puber*, which readily rushes out to attack with claws held wide. This crab has a plush covering of hair with deep blue markings on its swimming legs, and with its vivid ruby-red eyes it can appear very frightening – it will pursue would-be captors until they retreat (Fig. 83). Another 'typical' crab that is quite widespread in Scilly is the hairy crab *Pilumnus hirtellus*, easily recognised by the soft velvety hairs all over the carapace and legs (Fig. 84). Two close relatives, *Xantho pilipes* and *X. incisus*, have smooth but furrowed carapaces and live in similar situations. *Xantho pilipes* is another animal with a strong southwestern associations.

Broad-clawed porcelain crabs *Porcellana platycheles* are very small, hairy, flattened crabs with large chelipeds that live under boulders, where they edge along pressed to the surface of the rock. They are very common in spring. Less

FIG 83. The ruby-eyed and blue-fringed velvet swimming-crab can be aggressive if cornered. (Rosemary Parslow)

FIG 84. Hairy crabs are one of a number of small species of crabs that may be found on the lower shore. (Paul Gainey)

common is a close relative that lives among hydroids and other growths, the long-clawed porcelain crab *Pisidia longicornis*, a hairless animal without the big flattened chelipeds. The delightful hermit crabs, usually living inside periwinkle or whelk shells, are very common sidling about on the floor of rock pools or under blankets of seaweed. Those found on the shore are mostly small species, *Pagurus bernhardus* and *Anapagurus chiroacanthus*. At times they seem to inhabit almost every empty shell. A rare hermit crab, *Cestopagurus timidus*, distinctive in having brilliant violet antennae, was first found in Scilly by students on a field trip, shore collecting at low tide (Harvey, 1964). This is another example of a species found in Scilly that has a more southern distribution: it is usually found around the Canaries and Mediterranean.

Another animal frequently encountered on rocky shores is the common squat lobster *Galathea squamifera* (Fig. 85). One spring, they were so numerous just off St Agnes that when they became trapped and marooned by the low spring tides the slap of their tails could be heard as they tried to escape. When disturbed they swim rapidly backwards and lodge themselves in crevices; they will also use their strong chelae to administer a sharp nip if you try to catch them! Although not a species likely to be found on shore, there have been three records of slipper

FIG 85. Squat lobster, another crustacean that is frequently found onshore. (Rosemary Parslow)

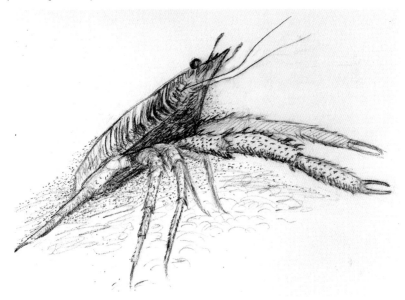

lobster *Scyllarus arctus* from waters around the Isles of Scilly. Slipper lobsters are usually found in the Mediterranean and the eastern Atlantic as far north as the English Channel. The one found in a lobster pot in 2001 eventually ended up as an exhibit in the National Marine Aquarium, Plymouth. It was 13cm long and banded in shades of brown (Herdson, 2002).

Sea spiders

These strange, cryptic animals are not often seen, but may emerge from among red algae and walk very slowly into the open. The one found most often in Scilly is *Nymphon gracile*, usually reddish in colour, with immensely long, thin legs. Sometimes a handful of red seaweed put into a dish of sea water will be found to be alive with them.

Molluscs

Molluscs are among the best-studied marine invertebrates of Scilly, and many specimens have been contributed to collections in the Isles of Scilly Museum and the Natural History Museum (Turk, 1991; Turk & Seaward, 1997).

Shelled molluscs can be divided into three main groups, snail-like gastropods, bivalves (animals with paired shells) and then those few species with multi-valved shells. Usually it is the snail-like gastropods and the multi-valved molluscs that are associated with rocky coasts and *Laminaria* beds; bivalves are more commonly found on the sand flats.

One of the commonest snail-like gastropods of the rocky shores is the rough periwinkle *Littorina saxatilis* (there may be more than one subspecies involved). It can be seen crawling over fronds of brown seaweeds, and comes in several colour varieties, but commonly bright yellow or amber. Although there are four main types of periwinkles found abundantly on the shores, the species are not easily distinguished in the field and are therefore divided by shape for convenience. All the periwinkles are grazers on lichen or algae and have their own region on the shore: periwinkles can often demonstrate zoning very nicely. At the top of the shore and almost a temporary landlubber is the very tiny small periwinkle *Littorina neritoides*, with a pointed, dark-coloured shell. They can be seen in cracks and crevices, even inside the empty shells of acorn barnacles, right into the splash zone – and they may also be found in caves, for example Piper's Hole on Tresco (where the extremely small little ear-shell *Otina ovata* has also been found: S. M. Turk, 1971). Slightly lower down are the rough periwinkles, then another group, the flat periwinkles, again very colourful with amber, bright yellow and banded shells; the empty shells of this animal can be found in huge numbers and are collected locally to fashion shell-craft objects to sell to tourists.

Flat periwinkles graze on brown seaweeds lower down the shore and their jelly-like egg masses can frequently be seen on the fronds. The largest member of this group, the common or edible periwinkle *Littorina littorea*, is extremely rare in Scilly.

Another common, characteristic and well-known group of gastropods are the top shells. The commonest species in Scilly are two very similar animals, the grey top shell *Gibbula cineraria* and the flat top shell *G. umbilicus*, both with banded shells that are often very worn so that the underlying mother-of-pearl layer is revealed. A larger, very pretty conical top shell is the painted top shell *Calliostoma zizphinum* (the name is very appropriate, as the shell does look like the old-fashioned child's toy), which can often be found at low spring tides. The empty shells of all the top shells are found on shell beaches and in rock pools. The toothed top shell *Monodonta lineata* is another species with a southern distribution that has been common in Scilly for perhaps 4000 years, as they have been found in Bronze Age shell middens. They are still eaten as a 'winkle', and at times so many were consumed that the shells were used to fill cart ruts (Turk & Seaward, 1997).

Also with conical shells are limpets, very familiar both as empty shells and as common animals of the upper shore. Limpets are very clearly adapted to a life on exposed shores, both in their shape and in their very thick, strong shells. Two species, common limpet and china limpet *Patella ulyssiponensis*, are found in Scilly, but the one on the most exposed places is almost always common limpet. By approaching the animal quietly it can be detached from the rock with a sharp blow; otherwise their grip on the rock is phenomenal. Where the limpet has been living is a cleaned area of rock and a ring-shaped groove worn by the edge of the shell in close contact with the rock. Limpets graze algae on the surface of the rock and have their own territories, each returning to its own groove at low tide (Yonge, 1949). There are many large limpet middens in Scilly, formed from discarded shells over many centuries from the Bronze Age up to the nineteenth century (see Chapter 3); limpets were even eaten by the workmen on Rosevear during the building of the Bishop Rock lighthouse when they ran out of supplies (Grigson, 1948). They were also eaten during famine years during the early nineteenth century, so clearly limpets were not only vital to the survival of the islanders in the past, but must have been very abundant.

Perhaps one of the most delightful molluscs you can find among the big oarweeds is another limpet, the blue-rayed limpet. These child's-fingernail-sized shells are found on the stipes and fronds of the big *Laminaria*, and as they get larger they excavate pits in the stipe and the holdfast. Often the holes can cut right through the stipe and it has been suggested this can so weaken it that it

breaks off at this point (Norton & Burrows, 1969; Hayward *et al.*, 1996). The blue
rays on the shell are faintly iridescent but gradually fade as the animal grows so
that when the empty shells wash up on the shore they may not be recognised.
Another easily identified limpet that can be found on rocks lower down the shore
is the white tortoiseshell limpet *Tectura virginea*; it has a tiny white shell often
with a fringe of yellow dots around the rim.

There are many gastropods that will be encountered between tidemarks or as
empty shells on beaches. These include whelks, a well-known group with strong,
turreted shells, some of which are common enough to have vernacular names:
dog whelk, thick-lipped dog whelk *Hinia incrassatus* and the similar netted dog
whelk *Hinia reticulata*, for example. These are carrion feeders or, as with the sting
winkle *Ocenebra erinacea*, active predators on other molluscs.

Ginamoney or guinea money is a local name for cowries in the Isles of Scilly.
Tropical cowries are beautiful, large shells that are on sale in local gift shops; the
Scilly cowries are much less well known, although to some of the initiates
collecting cowries is a passion! Two species occur, spotted cowrie and arctic
cowrie, tiny animals scarcely larger than a pea. Cowries are most frequently
encountered as empty shells on shell beaches, although both species can
sometimes be found alive on *Laminaria* seaweed on the lower shore. The living
cowries feed on sea squirts, golden stars sea squirt *Botryllus schlosseri* being a

FIG 86. Cowries live among the kelp, feeding on colonial sea squirts, especially golden
stars sea squirts. (Rosemary Parslow)

common prey. When they are alive and moving around, the cowries have a bright coloured mantle, red or yellowish, which they spread up over the shell from both sides like a cloak, to completely hide the shell (Fig. 86). The name of the large carn on St Agnes, Ginamoney Carn, suggests cowries must have been of interest to Scillionian people in the past; certainly the small shell beach below the carn has been a good source of cowrie shells. It was here in the pre-war Easters that the local children would have a picnic before searching for guineamonies, rock gobies and garlops (shanny) (Mortimer, 1991).

Coat-of-mail shells

Multi-valved shells are represented on Scillionian shores by chitons or coat-of–mail shells, another group of molluscs that are frequently found on rocks, often in pools. Two species are common, bristly coat-of-mail shell *Acanthochitona crinitus* and common coat-of-mail shell *Lepidochitona cinereus*. Again unlike their tropical relatives the British species are small and could be mistaken for some odd kind of woodlouse rather than a mollusc. They graze encrusted rock surfaces and because they adhere very closely and are cryptically coloured are easily overlooked.

Bivalves

Not many species of bivalves live on rocky shores. One group of familiar molluscs that might be expected, but is relatively uncommon in Scilly, is the mussels. A few common mussels *Mytilus edulis* do occur, tucked away in cracks on bare rocks low down on the exposed shores, but they are not found in the huge masses found on rocky shores elsewhere.

Nudibranchs and relatives

The sea slugs include several different families of superficially similar animals, including sea hares, nudibranchs and an unusual family called pleurobranchs. Sea hares, so named for the fanciful resemblance to a hare's face, are large, mobile animals that may be found feeding among the algae. Several species have been recorded in Scilly, and in some years young individuals of the common sea hare *Aplysia punctata* are abundant among seaweeds, on which they feed. For several years the side-gilled sea slug *Berthella plumula* has been found in large numbers under rocks at low tide; they look like small, fleshy lemons until the foot can be seen underneath. Most of these species feed on sea anemones and sea squirts, and sometimes their colouring may be related to their food: the red colour of *Rostanga rubra* is derived from the red sponges it has been grazing. Nudibranchs are fantastically shaped, colourful animals, one of the most extraordinary groups that may be encountered on the shore. Despite their clusters of tentacles, flower-like gills and often vivid colouring, they are surprisingly difficult to see until they move. Juvenile specimens of *Polycera quadrilineata* and similar species are frequently found in rock pools, where they prey on bryozoans, sea squirts or sponges (Fig. 87). Despite their distinctive appearance very few sea slugs have common names, and only some of the largest such as the grey or plumed sea slug *Aeolidia papillosa* are exceptions. Even more like a lemon in appearance than *Berthella* is the sea lemon *Archidoris pseudoargus*, one of several species that leave their eggs on rock surfaces in a white spiral that looks like 'Wonderweb' hem-tape!

FIG 87. *Polycera quadrilineata* is one of the common nudibranchs that are frequently found in rock pools. (Paul Gainey)

Bryozoans (formerly polyzoans)

This group of animals is easily confused with hydroids, being small, encrusting and colonial. Although the colonies frequently grow over the surface of rocks, shells and algae they unfortunately are not an easy group to identify to species. Most bryozoans have box-shaped skeletons in which the tiny zooids live. The only species that is well known is hornwrack *Flustra foliacea*, which frequently gets washed ashore from deeper water and resembles dried-up seaweed when it is found along the strandline. Another species of Mediterranean distribution that also occurs in Scilly is a lace coral *Turbicellepora magnicostata*, which forms thick cylinder-like bracelets around the stipes of some of the fucoid seaweeds.

Echinoderms

Echinoderms are a phylum of five classes of animals, all of them totally marine. They demonstrate radial symmetry, the body pattern repeated round a central mouth, usually with five identical subdivisions (pentamerism), although there are some exceptions to this. The classic echinoderm is the starfish, a recurrent theme in anything to do with the marine environment, as any bathroom ensemble can demonstrate. After the starfish the next easily recognised echinoderm is the sea urchin (urchin from the old name for hedgehog *Erinaceus europaeus*). Visitors to Scilly will see dried tests (shells) of the largest sea urchin, the edible sea urchin, being sold as curios, often by children who clean and varnish the dried tests and sell them for pocket money. At one time they were collected on a commercial scale by divers, with thousands being exported – for example 40,000 in 1984/5 (Bishop, 1985). The other echinoderms are the brittlestars, superficially like extremely long-armed starfish; the crinoids or featherstars, where the long arms have feathery branches; and the holothurians or sea cucumbers, in which the affinities to starfish are not very obvious as they are bilateral and worm-like. In starfish the five divisions of the body are drawn out into arms or rays, giving the classic shape, and the skinny arms of brittlestars and featherstars are similarly arranged. The sea urchin still has the five rays but they are bent around to form the more or less globular shape. In the sea cucumbers the basic shape has been considerably modified and is much less obvious, but they still have five rows of tube feet, the locomotory organs found in other echinoderms.

There are two types of sea urchin, based on their shape: regular urchins are the ones with the round tests found on the rocky shores; heart urchins have a flattened, bilaterally symmetrical shape, and are burrowers found in soft substrates. Edible sea urchins are still very common on rocks on the lower shore, among the *Laminaria* beds and in deeper water. At low spring tides their grey-pink, domed tests can be found exposed on rocks among the seaweeds. They are large animals, 13–15cm in diameter with a dense covering of short, mobile spines. They glide across the rocks on their tube feet grazing algae with the five 'teeth' held in a structure called Aristotle's lantern in the central mouth. Another regular sea urchin, very common in rock pools and on the underside of boulders, is the green sea urchin *Psammechinus miliaris*. This is a small animal, less than 3.5cm, with short green spines, sometimes with purple tips, frequently coated with a disguise of bits of weed and debris.

Everyone recognises the reddish-coloured common starfish *Asterias rubens*, but in Scilly the really common starfish is the larger, blue-grey, spiny starfish *Marthasterias glacialis*. Some of the spiny starfish may be very large, over half a metre in diameter, although those found on shore are usually much smaller. Occasionally larger ones may be found where fishermen have been emptying their crab pots. Very occasionally one of the multi-armed sunstars, the common sunstar *Solaster papposus* or the purple sunstar *S. endeca*, may also be found in pots. Perhaps one of the most dramatic starfish likely to be seen by the casual observer is the seven-armed, brilliant red sea star *Luidia ciliaris*, which is some-times found exposed on a seaweed-covered rock at low tide (Fig. 88). Turning over boulders will reveal tiny, short-armed cushion stars *Asterina gibbosa* clinging to the underside. This species can often be found quite high up on the shore. Most other species of starfish are likely to be only found in deeper water below the low water mark.

Finding your first brittlestar is quite a surprise: suddenly there are the waving arms that you would otherwise have missed due to the cryptic patterning. Several species of brittlestars occur in Scilly. Of those encountered on rocky shores the most frequent is common brittlestar *Ophiothrix fragilis*, a variable species often beautifully patterned, sometimes with the disk and arms in contrasting colours. Black brittlestars *Ophiocomina nigra* are often found in the same places, but are duller colours, black or brown. An extremely tiny grey brittlestar, *Amphipholis squamata*, is common at all levels on the shore, even in holdfasts of seaweeds and especially among coralline algae in rock pools. Also found in holdfasts is the uncommon *Ophiopholis aculeata*.

It is unusual to find a featherstar on the shore, but there are a few places in the Isles of Scilly where they become exposed at ELWS. The rosy featherstar only reveals its true beauty when seen with gently waving arms under water. They can also swim, detaching themselves from the substrate and slowly moving though the water by undulating their arms. The final class of the echinoderms is not very common onshore in rocky areas. Tiny sea gherkins *Cucumaria* sp. turn up occasionally under rocks, but most of the commoner sea cucumbers are found on sandy substrates.

FIG 88. *Luidia ciliaris* is a conspicuous starfish with seven arms rather than the usual five, sometimes seen on the seaweed-covered rocks at low tide. St Agnes. (Rosemary Parslow)

Sea squirts

The name of this group of animals relates to their habit of squirting water out of their siphons when disturbed. The sea squirts are primitive, chordate animals, that is animals with backbones, although in sea squirts this is not evident as the chordate stage is the larva. Most sea squirts have hollow, sac-like bodies with two openings, the siphons. Some are solitary animals looking like little plastic flasks, others are in groups joined at the base, still others occur as sheets of colonial animals encrusting rocks and other flat surfaces. Not many sea squirts are easily identified but two species that are common in Scilly and easily recognised are the gooseberry sea squirt *Dendrodoa grossularia* and the golden stars sea squirt (Fig. 89). The latter can form quite large sheets of blue, purple or other coloured jelly with a pattern of contrasting coloured 'stars' formed by the zooids, the individual animals. A related species, *Botryllus leachii*, is very similar but the zooids are arranged in parallel lines.

FIG 89. In the golden stars sea squirt the individual polyps are surrounded by purple or other coloured jelly. This is the usual prey of the cowrie. (Paul Gainey)

SANDY SHORES

Among the most important habitats in Scilly are the tidal flats between the main islands. Historically we know this was dry land, and at ELWS large expanses of sand become exposed, as do vestiges of stone field walls and hut circles belonging to earlier human inhabitants. Studies of the area have revealed the richness of the fauna, resulting in the flats being designated an SSSI. These areas of sand and fine silts are home for completely different species of animals to those found on the rocky shores. Many of them live buried beneath the surface, and other than their empty shells rarely give much sign of their presence. Besides the invertebrates that live in or on the sand, there are the wading birds that feed there when the sands are exposed (see Chapter 16), and the fish that inhabit the same areas when the tide is in.

The animals that live on sandy shores have to contend with a different set of conditions to those on rocky shores. The sea is less turbulent, and they can burrow into the sand to escape desiccation or to avoid predators. Several groups of invertebrates specialise in a burrowing life, and echinoderms, molluscs, burrowing anemones and annelid worms are well represented in the fauna of the wide sand flats off St Martin's. For animals that tunnel, the type of substrate is critical. If the sand is too stony it may be difficult to penetrate, and some worms also need a soft substrate because, like earthworms, they ingest the sand as they progress.

Exploring sandy shores can be frustrating, as only a few animals leave external signs of their presence. Other than glimpses of some animals in shallow water, and the tops of burrows or tubes in the sand, it is mostly the empty shells or occasionally a live animal stranded by the tide that betrays their being there.

Echinoderms

On the sand flats most echinoderms are living beneath the surface of the sand, but only when the empty dead tests are washed ashore will their presence be suspected. Several species of irregular or heart urchins are found in sand on the St Martin's Flats and other similar areas around the islands. Two heart urchins are well known enough to have common names, the sea potato *Echinocardium cordatum* and the purple heart urchin *Spatangus purpureus*. (When you handle these heart urchins you may find masses of *Montacuta substriata*, a tiny bivalve, clustered around the spines in their ambulacrae or feeding grooves.) The sea potato (Fig. 90) secretes a mucus breathing tube to connect it to the surface; the purple heart urchin apparently manages on the air trapped in the sand and tends

FIG 90. Sea potatoes are burrowing heart urchins. They are sometimes washed up on the beach after storms. (Paul Gainey)

to live closer to the surface. Sea potatoes are vulnerable on the surface although they can dig their way down very quickly; gulls have been seen breaking open the shells and eating them on occasion. A third species, the pea urchin *Echinocyamus pusillus*, is also present in gravelly sands, but the tiny, denuded, oval tests washed ashore may be the only indication of its presence. The empty tests are surprisingly tough and can be found on shell beaches, often with the shells of cowries and other similar-sized molluscs – to the delight of children (of all ages!). The very long-armed brittlestar *Amphiura brachiata* also lives just below the surface of the sand, with just the tips of the arms protruding above the surface.

Worm-like sea cucumbers are found on the sand flats, but only one is found commonly: this is *Labidoplax digitata*, which looks more like a pink burrowing sea anemone and is not immediately recognisable as an echinoderm. Another burrowing cucumber, *Leptosynapta inhaerens*, also occurs on the sand flats (Fig. 91). A sea cucumber sometimes seen from a boat or when snorkelling over the *Zostera* beds is the large black cotton-spinner *Holothuria forskali*, lying in the open on the sand. The reason for this curious name becomes evident if the animal is touched, when masses of sticky white threads are immediately squirted out from the anus to deter any would-be predator.

FIG 91. *Leptosynapta inhaerens*, one of the worm-like sea cucumbers that live under the sand. They appear to 'suck' food off their tentacles. (Rosemary Parslow)

Molluscs

It is on the sand flats that the bivalve molluscs really come into their own. They live below the surface, at a level determined by the length of the siphon that extends to the surface of the sand. They move through the sand quickly by means of a strong, muscular foot – as anyone who has tried to dig up razor shells *Ensis* spp. will acknowledge. Edible cockles *Cerastoderma edule* have short siphons so live close to the surface, while some of the tellins *Tellina* spp. can extend their siphons several times their body-length. Dense populations of some bivalves such as razor shells and thin tellin *Angulus tenuis* live in fine sand, and others such as the rayed artemis *Dosinia exoleta* in coarser gravelly areas. Many other species of bivalves living in the sand flats are only ever seen as empty shells washed up on beaches on St Martin's and Tresco. Perhaps one of the rarest species is one of the hatchet shells, the divaricate lucina *Lucinella divaricata*, a small but rather solid white-shelled mollusc that had only been known as occasional shells until live specimens were found living in muddy, gravelly sand off Tresco (Tebble, 1976). All the venus shells are southern species, and several occur on the flats, including brown venus *Callista chione*, banded venus *Clausinella fasciata* and the smooth artemis *Dosinia lupinus*. Tellins are also southern species; one that is very familiar is the thin tellin, whose pretty oval shells with shiny, pink interiors are common on the shell beaches.

Sometimes the dead shells of molluscs get jammed into the substrate and they form attachment points for seaweeds or even animals such as barnacles or sea anemones. Gastropod molluscs that live on sandy shores have different ways of coping with the sandy substrate: some have a large muscular foot to dig into the substrate; others, like the pelican's foot *Aporrhais pespelecani*, have wide, winged shells; in the necklace shell *Lunatia catena* the foot spreads out around the animal like a snow-shoe so it can slide over the surface of the sand, and turban top shells *Gibbula magus* also live on the surface of the sand.

Many gastropods graze on algae and detritus, while others are carnivores: necklace shells *Polinices* spp. prey on bivalves, boring a hole through the shell (these can be seen on the empty shells) to get at the inhabitant. Netted dog whelks are attracted to dead animals and are frequently found on dead fish or other carrion. The characteristic egg masses of necklace shells are familiar objects on the shore as whorls of web-like collars held together with mucus and sand grains.

Attempts to introduce oysters, both edible oyster *Ostrea edulis* and Pacific oyster *Crassostrea gigas*, to the Isles of Scilly on several occasions in the mid-1980s were unsuccessful; in the latter case although 10,000 spat were laid in Porth Cressa they suffered heavy predation, mainly by starfish (Turk & Seaward, 1997).

FIG 92. The delightful miniature little cuttle sometimes gets stranded in a pool. (Paul Gainey)

A cephalopod mollusc, in this case one of the cuttlefish, the little cuttle *Sepiola atlantica*, can often be found swimming along the edge of the retreating tide hunting for surface-dwelling crustaceans (Fig. 92). The little cuttle is less than 20mm in length, a perfect miniature of its larger relatives, and its camouflage so closely matches the sandy substrate that only its shadow may give it away. When trapped in a net they will propel themselves backwards in an attempt to escape.

Anemones

Only a few species of anemones are found in sandy substrates. The burrowing anemone *Peachia hastata* looks more like one of the burrowing sea cucumbers or a long pink worm with a fringe of tentacles at one end; it is occasionally dug up in soft sand. Daisy anemones *Cereus pedunculatus* and other sea anemones that may be found with their tentacles opened in a circle of the surface of the sand are not free-living, but will be attached to rocks or shells below. Snakelocks anemones also live on the sand flats, frequently attached to the *Zostera* plants.

Ribbon worms

Only one species of these worms is commonly found on the shore. The
so-called bootlace worm *Lineus longissimus* is an extraordinary animal that can
be found under boulders where there is some muddy sand. Bootlace worms are
brown, soft and slimy. One I found on the edge of Periglis beach on St Agnes,
measured almost six metres when uncoiled, although up to 30 metres has been
recorded.

Bristleworms

These worms are often the most numerous animals inhabiting sedimentary
shores, both in species diversity and in biomass. Two main types of the worms
are adapted to living in these conditions: sedentary species and errant or free-
living species. Sedentary worms live in tubes they build from sand grains or shell
fragments anchored to the substrate. Errant worms have tough cuticles to protect
their bodies for a life squeezing through the sand, or they exude thick mucus and
are assisted by a powerful prostomium (the flexible, snoutlike front end) and the
parapodia with tufts of chaetae on each segment (as in earthworms) so they can
also move quickly through the sand.

Sedentary worms, being unable to move about to search for food, have to
collect what they can by using mucus-covered tentacles or by drawing water down
into their tubes and extracting particles of detritus. Several of these worms are
quite abundant although they may only be found at low tide, when there is very
little to see above the surface of the sand. *Cirriformia tentaculata* spreads a mat of
sticky tentacles over the surface of the sand, where they look more like a mass of
red tubifex worms. The sand mason *Lanice conchilega* can be located by the tuft on
the top of its tube sticking out of the sand, the worm itself being invisible below.
A number of other worm species live in similar locations, some in fragile tubes
built of sand, so that only fragments get washed up on shore. *Chaetopterus
variopedatus* is an extraordinary worm that lives in a U-shaped mucous tube in
the sand. They have specialised parapodia that help to collect food from the
water, which is drawn down through the tube and expelled at the opposite end.
Some of the adult worms are a 'lingerie-pink' in colour and look like ragged
cloth if removed from the tube.

Errant worms look more like earthworms. Some have a protrusible pharynx
that assists in moving through the sandy substrate; others have strong jaws
with 'teeth' that can bite quite painfully; and most have appendages such as gills
and other structures that are protected by stiff bristle-like chaetae or can be
withdrawn into the body. One small, squat worm, *Travisia forbesi*, would be
unremarkable if it was not for the fact that its presence is given away by the

garlicky smell of the sand where it lives! The lugworms *Arenicola* spp. are familiar worms, even if all that is usually seen are the worm casts on the surface of muddy sand. Lugworms are found in many areas in Scilly, usually lower on sandy beaches where the sand is muddy, including in the black silt at the bottom of the brackish lagoon on Bryher. They are commonly used as bait for fishing.

Many free-swimming animals inhabit the sand flats when the sea flows across them. Sand gobies *Pomatoschistus minutus* can be seen in shoals over sandy bottoms along with many other species of fish, especially some of the flatfish and others such as the handsome dragonet *Callionymus lyra*. Among the *Zostera* beds there are vast shoals of sand eels, while brown shrimps *Crangon crangon*, prawns and other Crustacea shoal over the sands.

Zostera beds

Although it grows in the sea, *Zostera* is not a seaweed, but a genus of higher plants known as eelgrass that live in sand in shallow seas. The plant grows mostly in the shallow sublittoral down to about five metres, occasionally being exposed by very low spring tides. The long ribbon-like leaves can only grow in areas of sheltered water where the effect of tides is very weak. When storm conditions do disturb the *Zostera* beds they may be ripped up, and torn leaves and plants wash ashore. In the 1930s an epidemic wiped out the eelgrass beds around Britain; after several decades the plant gradually recovered and in Scilly it is now flourishing. Since 1984 there has been an ongoing survey programme to monitor the health of the plants, since they have shown some recurrence of infection by the slime mould *Labyrinthula macrocystis* (Raines *et al.*, 1993; reports by Fowler, Cook *et al.*).

Eelgrass beds are an important habitat worldwide; they are the nursery for the young of many important species of food fish. The *Zostera* beds in Scilly are very extensive, growing in shallow water over the sand flats and sheltered bays all around the islands, especially between St Martin's, Tresco and St Mary's. As *Zostera* needs relatively sheltered situations to thrive, these provide ideal conditions for a rich assemblage of species living on or within them (Fig. 93). Either swimming through the *Zostera* or looking down from a boat, using a glass-bottomed bucket, will reveal shoals of fish, crabs and larger animals. Closer inspection will disclose many epizoics and epiphytes: stalked jellyfish, hydroids, snakelocks anemone in different colours, several species of sea slugs and green algae growing on the leaves; pipefish, sand eels *Ammodytes tobianus* and sand gobies swimming between the long, waving leaves; heart urchins and the flower-like disks of hidden sea anemones on the surface of the sand between

FIG 93. Extensive *Zostera* beds grow on the underwater sand flats between the islands. They are important nurseries for fish and other marine life. (Mark Groves)

the plants. In sandy bays small flatfish such as plaice *Pleuronectes flesus* can be abundant, and in the past local people would spear them with tridents. Rare species such as seahorses *Hippocampus ramulosus* are sometimes found in the *Zostera* beds.

SUBLITTORAL LIFE

Following the tide down to the extreme low of ELWS is a fascinating experience, but always ends in frustration (and usually a wetting) as the tide turns just as you have reached that magic zone with featherstars, colourful encrustations of sponges and sea anemones. For the non-diver, snorkelling gives tantalising glimpses of the world below the waves. In some of the shallow bays it is possible to swim through the *Zostera* beds and over the edge of the huge granite blocks that form the underwater rim of the islands. Seeing animals that are usually just blobs of jelly or half-hidden in rock crevices underwater, when they have expanded into flowerlike anemones or are swimming in the open so you can appreciate what they really look like, is unforgettable. Although the undersea scene in Scillonian waters does not have the bright primary colours of the coral

FIG 94. Lobster against a background of the soft coral dead-man's fingers, with polyps extended. (Bryan Thomas)

reefs we see on our television screens, there are many fascinating and colourful animals, as well as the more subtle hues of seaweeds.

The sublittoral regions are mostly outside the scope of this book, but many of the plants and animals have already been described, as they include several species found at ELWS tides or in the finest rock pools and under boulder caves. Underwater, with no interruption by tides, there are large masses of colourful sponges, colonial sea squirts and hydroids growing over rocks and other life forms. There are also many species of sea anemones, in many different colour varieties. All these encrusting animals form a colourful background to the free-living animals (Fig. 94). Some are species that can just be glimpsed at the lowest extent of the tide, while others are usually only seen by divers: plumose anemones, scarlet and gold cup corals, featherstars, masses of brittlestars, soft corals and rare and fragile sea fans. Some places in Scilly are well known for their rich assemblages of undersea life: Darity's Hole, St Mary's, for example. The islands are very popular with divers, and it is also possible for novices to learn to snorkel and dive while on holiday.

BETWEEN THE ISLANDS

Although the deep waters are also outside the scope of this book there are some animals that are not infrequently met with when sailing between the islands. Several species of cetaceans are frequently seen (see Chapter 15), and harbour porpoises *Phocoena phocoena* in particular often come in quite close to shore and can be seen from the land. Sometimes they seem to be following shoals of fish, probably mackerel. Perhaps the most spectacular sightings are of basking sharks *Cetorhinus maximus*, which can be seen feeding in surface waters on calmer summer days. Usually it is only the two fins that show, but if the water is clear the huge fish can be see cruising along with open mouths taking in plankton. Another fish that appears to becoming increasingly common (or perhaps more frequently recorded) is the ocean sunfish *Mola mola* (Fig. 95). These strange-looking fish are poor swimmers and drift along in currents near the surface; as they submerge they waggle the dorsal fin in a characteristic 'wave'. Another warm-water fish that sometimes strays into Scillonian waters is the grey triggerfish *Balistes capriscus*. Other animals that are encountered are the jellyfish and other floating animals that have been described earlier.

FIG 95. Sunfish are becoming a frequent sight in southwestern waters. (Bryan Thomas)

STRANDINGS

Exploring the beaches to look at the flotsam that arrives on the tides can be very rewarding, as almost anything can turn up on a beach. After storms the big oarweeds get torn from their anchorage and arrive on the shore, whilst other casualties can be some of the animals usually buried in the sands, or those normally floating in the open sea.

Strandings of cetaceans are dealt with in Chapter 15. Turtles are occasionally seen near the Isles of Scilly, usually leatherback turtles *Dermochelys coriacea* following the jellyfish on which they feed, and they too are sometimes stranded or picked up semi-moribund.

But some of the most spectacular strandings are not of large mammals or reptiles but of invertebrates, sometimes in thousands. Among the most frequent of these involuntary arrivals are jellyfish. One is the large purple jellyfish *Cyanea lamarckii*, which can arrive around the islands in huge numbers. Most people are very reluctant to go swimming while they are around. Another very common species is the moon jellyfish *Aurelia aurita*: this is the one with the four purple circles showing through the semi-translucent disc. Sometimes washed ashore at the same time are compass jellyfish *Chrysaora hysoscella*, a brownish bell divided into sections by distinctive V-shaped marks (Fig. 96). The lion's mane jellyfish *Cyanea capillata*, an orange-coloured species closely related to the purple jellyfish, is often very large, 'as big as a dustbin lid', and has a severe sting. Another impressively large species is root-mouth jellyfish *Rhizostoma octopus*, up to a metre across; it too swarms some years in large numbers. There are other species that may turn up from time to time, but none quite as frequent as these.

There are a few other 'jellyfish-like' animals that can be washed up or seen floating offshore that are not strictly jellyfish. Best known, and feared, is the Portuguese man-of-war *Physalia physalis*. This is not an individual animal, but a siphonophore, a floating colony of hydrozoans rather than a jellyfish. Easily recognised, the Portuguese man-of-war consists of a float on the surface resembling nothing so much as an inflated polybag. The dangerous part of the colony is underwater, long strings of stinging cells hanging down for many tens of metres and almost invisible to divers or when caught up on the lines attached to lobster pots. Two other animals that may be encountered floating ashore are not harmful. The little hydroid by-the-wind-sailor *Velella velella* does have stinging cells but they are usually moribund when they reach the shore. The animal consists of a small violet disk with a sail, mouth and fringe of tentacles that bowls along through the water like a child's paper boat. Some years they can

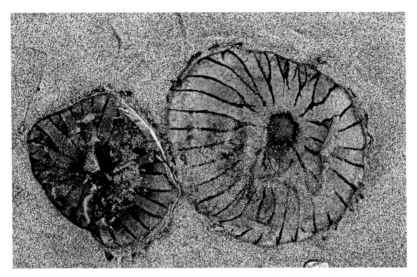

FIG 96. Compass jellyfish are one of several species of jellyfish that are frequently stranded. (Paul Gainey)

be tossed ashore in their thousands, where they may then be eaten by herring gulls (Fig. 97). The others are sea gooseberries, most commonly *Pleurobranchia pileus*. They look very like transparent, colourless gooseberries and sometimes continue to pulse gently when stranded in tide pools.

Goose barnacles *Lepas* spp. are named after the barnacle goose *Branta leucopsis* (they look something like tiny goose heads, and the geese were supposed to have arisen from the barnacles). Quite often goose barnacles are still alive when they come ashore and if kept in sea water will open up and start feeding by 'kicking' food into their mouths. Most of the goose barnacles are attached to some piece of flotsam, a log or plastic rubbish (Fig. 98). One species, the buoy barnacle *Dosima fascicularis*, has its own foam float that resembles a piece of polystyrene.

Species that would not usually be seen can be thrown ashore by severe storms. One such happening was the wreck of masked crabs *Corystes cassivelaunus* in 1904 (Thurston, 1970) and of the beautiful violet sea snails *Janthina janthina* in 1964; at other times you can find animals on the beach that may have been thrown overboard from fishing boats, maybe a snake pipefish *Syngnathus acus*, a common sunstar or a purple sunstar.

The sea mouse *Aphrodita aculeata* sometimes gets washed up after storms, it is a large scaleworm sometimes as much as 20cm long and 3.5cm wide, not at all obviously wormlike, with a dense fur-like covering of bristles and long, shiny,

FIG 97. By-the-wind-sailors can be washed ashore in their thousands and eaten by gulls. (Paul Gainey)

FIG 98. Any object that has been floating in the sea for a long time may be colonised by goose barnacles. (Bryan Thomas)

iridescent chaetae along the sides. It normally lives on the sand flats, where it ploughs its way through the sand to search for food. Other strandings can be plants. Coconuts *Cocos nucifera* even turn up on occasion. It is not always possible to determine whether these have come from the Caribbean or elsewhere in the tropics, or from the cargo of a ship, or if they were thrown or dropped in the sea closer to home. 'Sea bean' is a general name covering a number of seeds of tropical plants that are occasionally washed up. The commonest sea bean found on the beaches of Scilly is *Entada gigas*.

PHOSPHORESCENCE

In her book *An Introduction to Sea-shore Life in Cornwall and the Isles of Scilly*, Stella Turk (1971) describes the romantic atmosphere of a Cornish shore by moonlight: 'The first occasion that one witnesses the sea afire with a scintillating phosphorescence as small waves dash at the rocks is quite unforgettable.' And indeed, however many times I have seen the waves light up along the shore, or a boat's wake turn to 'liquid fire', it still entrances. Equally amazing is to wade into the sea on such a night and see every hair on your legs eerily glowing. A number of different organisms are phosphorescent, or more correctly bioluminescent. One of the commonest is a tiny dinoflagellate, *Noctiluca scintillans*, a small algal member of the plankton with the ability to swim. It is possible to take a bottle of sea water containing these invisible creatures (with a hand lens they just show as tiny transparent dots) into a dark room and by shaking it stimulate a display of ghostly flashes. My children, when small, attributed this performance to 'tinkerbells'. Sea gooseberries are just one of many other species of marine animals that are phosphorescent.

POLLUTION

Despite the recognition of the importance of the Isles of Scilly and the many designations that have been applied to this important and fragile coastline there still seems to be no published Oil Pollution Incident Plan – although there is a St Mary's Harbour Oil Contingency Plan. Should there be a major incident, then the Isles of Scilly Council will have to take advice from the major agencies including Cornwall County Council. With so many fragile ecosystems at risk it is surprising there is no general plan to indicate how to protect them or minimise damage to the beaches, the SSSIs around the coast and the sand flats.

This would seem imperative both for nature conservation and for the tourist industry on which the prosperity of Scilly rests.

There has always been a threat that oil pollution could be devastating to the islands' economy, let alone the marine life. In 1967 the wreck of the tanker *Torrey Canyon* on the Seven Stones (between Scilly and Land's End) threatened Scilly with a massive oil incident. At that time it was extremely fortunate the tides took most of the oil away from the islands and very little reached the shore. Cornwall was not so lucky and the example of the toll on seabirds and damage to the coastline and marine life are a constant reminder of the vulnerability of the islands to a similar incident (Gill *et al.*, 1967). Even so there have been a number of minor spills that have resulted in oil on beaches and unpleasant tarry lumps buried in the sand or stuck on boulders. The continual passage of tankers and container ships past the islands is a graphic reminder of the susceptibility of the islands. In 1997 the wreck of the *Cita* left the islands with an expensive and potentially serious new form of pollution. Part of the *Cita*'s cargo consisted of huge drums of plastic tape, much of which unwound and soon washed onto every beach and into every bay. The plastic material broke up and covered beaches, blew inland and snarled up the fishing grounds. Fortunately that kind of tape appeared eventually to degrade, but other forms of plastic used as packaging can persist for years. Cleaning up after the *Cita* incident demonstrated the lack of any strategy to cope with incidents of this magnitude, and worse still was that there did not seem to be a lead agency to sort out the mess, so that the small local agencies, the Environmental Trust and the Council for the Isles of Scilly, had to cope with an incident that was not only outside their spectrum but was also very costly. In March 2003 a smaller incident, apparently due to a container being lost overboard somewhere off Land's End, resulted in tens of tons of nappy liners coming ashore both in Scilly and in mainland Cornwall.

Since plastic bottles and containers have become the dominant form of packaging the shores and the sea-bed are becoming the depository for huge quantities of rubbish of this sort. Tides and winds influence where the rubbish ends up, and many of the more isolated beaches, including some on uninhabited islands, become covered in this material (see Fig. 207). Much of it is carried by the tide high up onto the shore, where it can get partially buried on the boulder beach and covered in strandline vegetation, and where it stays as a hazardous layer with no realistic method of clearing it away. Other material can get blown by gales onto the shore and may blow well inland to become an eyesore on some of the coastal heathlands, as happened in autumn 2004. Reports from divers suggest that the problem is not restricted to beaches: undersea rubbish tips develop as plastic material gets taken by the tide into underwater sheltered bays and hollows (Mark Horobin, personal communication).

Surveys of litter on beaches have been made to identify the type of rubbish and its source. Litter is not only an aesthetic problem: it can be ingested by marine animals, tangle others and trap some inside containers; ropes and plastic also get wrapped around propellers and fishing lines. Analysis of litter on a representative set of beaches found that on two amenity beaches much of the litter could be attributed to tourists using the beaches. On the other more remote beaches the majority of litter came from the sea. Seventy per cent of all the litter consisted of plastic materials, most of which takes a very long time to break down (Cook *et al.*, 2001).

CHAPTER 9

The Coast

*When Nature addressed herself to the construction of this archipelago she brought to
the task a light touch: at the moment she happened to be full of feeling for the great and
artistic effects which may be produced by small elevations, especially in those places
where the material is granite.*

Sir Walter Besant, *Armorel of Lyonesse* (1890)

ROCKY SHORES

MUCH OF THE coast around the Isles of Scilly is low granite cliff,
rising in places to four metres or more in height. In the cliffs
are areas of the cement-like 'ram' or 'rab'; this also occurs at the
base of cliffs and dune coasts and extends in places under boulder beaches, often
forming a very characteristic shelf (this is one of the places where the rare shore
dock grows). Below the cliff, the shore consists of rocks and boulders before
giving way to sandy areas. Sometimes the boulders almost fill the bay, as in
St Warna's Bay on St Agnes, although even there the huge rocks are capable of
being moved by the more extreme winter storms: for example in October 2004
enormous boulders were flung up into fields above the bay.

Boulder beaches
Boulder beaches are common in Scilly (Fig. 99). They are formed of accumu-
lations of rocks above 20cm in size and are exposed to heavy salt spray, so the
plants living on these beaches are necessarily halophytic (able to cope with
salt deposition). Many beaches are shelving, made up of very large, rounded

FIG 99. Boulder beaches and granite carns are a feature of exposed coasts in Scilly. St Warna's Bay, St Agnes, February 2004. (Rosemary Parslow)

'cobbles', where typical strandline plant species can be found. These include varieties of some common plants that have characteristic coastal forms with thick, fleshy leaves, such as an attractive form of woody nightshade *Solanum dulcamara* var. *marinum* that forms sprawling mats across the rocks. Other strandline species include sea beet, the coastal form of curled dock, both common and Danish scurvygrass (Fig. 100), rock samphire, sea mayweed and some of the oraches.

On some of the low, uninhabited islands, for example Annet, boulder beaches extend around the edge of the island, and inland they become covered in dense mats of grasses, especially red fescue *Festuca rubra* and Yorkshire fog, with oraches and cushions of thrift. Stands of the short-lived tree-mallow are essential refuges for flocks of small passerines during migration, frequently providing the only cover to be found on these very exposed, windswept places. Near freshwater seepages in these areas shore dock might have been found in the past, and in addition some of the boulder beaches are very important as breeding places for storm petrels, which nest in tunnels below the rocks.

FIG 100. Common scurvygrass is a common coastal plant frequently associated with seabird nesting sites. (Rosemary Parslow)

Shingle

Strandline plants usually have fruits or seeds that are adapted to float and survive in salt water. They are carried on the tide until they are thrown up later on a beach above the reach of the tide, where hopefully they will germinate. Some of these plants are common species such as some of the oraches, while others are less common – sea-kale, for instance, or rarities such as shore dock, sea pea *Lathyrus japonicus* and sea knotgrass *Polygonum maritimum*.

Shingle covers a wide spectrum of beach material from very coarse sand up to cobble size (>20cm). Much of the vegetation is the same as that found on boulder beaches. Sometimes there is sand underneath the cobbles so sea sandwort may grow up from the sand between the pebbles. Finer material, grading towards coarse sand, has similar vegetation to that of sandy beaches. Some of the plant communities found on Scillonian beaches do not appear to be very good matches for the NVC communities (Dargie, 1990; Sneddon & Randall, 1994; see Appendix), but one that does occur in places is the SC1 (curled dock – yellow horned-poppy) shingle community (Fig. 101). Curled dock is a common plant , although both yellow horned-poppy and sea-kale are rather local in Scilly. There are good examples of this type of vegetation at Wingletang Bay (Beady Pool), St Agnes, and on some of the Eastern Isles. Another very typical strandline vegetation type is the SD2 (sea sandwort – sea rocket) maritime community. Sea rocket populations fluctuate greatly: in some years there may be very few plants and in other years there may be hundreds (Fig. 102).

FIG 101. Yellow horned-poppy usually grows along the strandline on shingle and sandy beaches. (Alma Hathway)

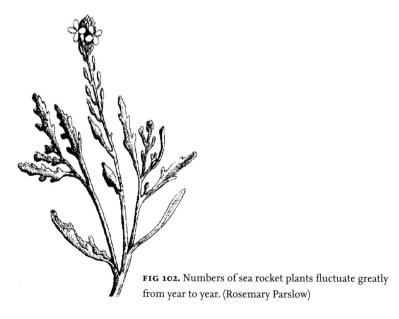

FIG 102. Numbers of sea rocket plants fluctuate greatly from year to year. (Rosemary Parslow)

FIG 103. Waders, including turnstones and oystercatchers, are common on Scillonian shores. (D. I. M. Wallace)

On most beaches Scilly shrews live among the boulders, feeding on sand-hoppers and other invertebrates. Brown rats also favour these beaches, finding rich pickings in the seabird season as well as plant seeds and detritus. A cracking sound heard coming from among the clumps of alexanders *Smyrnium olusatrum* often turns out to be a brown rat sitting in the plant eating the seeds.

Rocky shores are important as feeding areas for many species of coastal birds. At low water the pools and rocks are available to a host of species including waders, gulls, herons and ducks. Some of these, especially waders and gulls, retreat to high-tide roosts on the rocks above the sea (Fig. 103). At high tide the sea will also wash material from the rocks and flocks of gulls will often be seen feeding just offshore.

Lichens and bryophytes

The intensity of the colours in the landscape is one of the attractions of the Isles of Scilly and is frequently mentioned by authors of books on the islands, including Jessie Mothersole (1919) and Geoffrey Grigson (1948). One feature that particularly catches the eye is the lichens growing on the rocks around the coast. From a distance the rocks look grey-green and fuzzy, but a closer look will reveal that not only are the granite rocks made up of different coloured crystals, but also the surface is frequently coated with a crinkly pelt of sea ivory *Ramalina siliquosa* and other *Ramalina* species, as well as a great range of colours and patterns of encrusting lichens (Fig. 104). Some of these latter, the crustose lichens, are the same colour as the rocks and are easily overlooked; others are flamboyant, aniline colours, forming brilliant patches of yellow, orange or green, of different textures and patterns.

The clarity of the air and lack of pollution produce ideal conditions for lichens, the group being very susceptible to sulphur dioxide in the atmosphere. In Scilly the combination of a very favourable set of conditions, clear air, mild and moist climate and the coarse-grained granite rock has enabled a rich and special lichen flora to develop.

In Scilly many lichens are subject to strong maritime influences. There are species that live in the littoral zone, the black zone – for example *Lichina pygmaea* – where they are frequently submerged under the waves. Another lichen, found from high water mark to well above, is the aptly named tar-stain lichen *Verrucaria maura*. Above the littoral is the supralittoral or splash zone, with two groups of lichens, those of the orange zone, the brilliant yellow-orange-coloured *Caloplaca* and *Xanthoria* species, and those of the grey zone, which are above the sea but still catch the salt spray (Gilbert, 2000). The grey zone includes the common species of *Ramalina* and under sheltered recesses on north- and east-facing cliffs is 'the habitat of the frequently elegant *Roccella fuciformis* and *R. phycopsis*, though they

FIG 104. Lichen-covered rocks and boulder beaches on Annet, June 2002. (Rosemary Parslow)

are equally likely to be present as small, gnarled, easily overlooked individuals'
(Gilbert, 2000). Also found in the grey zone are leafy species of the *Parmeliaceae*,
including one that often forms very distinctive patterns on exposed granite rocks
on Annet and elsewhere, *Neofuscelia verruculifera*. As the effect of salt spray carries
many metres, in places up to a kilometre inland, many of the terrestrial as well
as the coastal lichens in Scilly are halophytes. There are also a number of lichens
that are particularly associated with bird droppings: *Caloplaca verruculifera* forms
yellow patches on coastal rocks where gulls perch, and *Xanthoria parietina* is
found on roof tops .

Some of the rarest species in Scilly are Lusitanian or Mediterranean species,
on the northern edge of their range. A suite of rarities is associated with the
coarse-grained coastal granite rock, including *Acarospora subrufula*, *Lecidea
sarcogynoides*, *Pertusaria monogona*, *P. pluripuncta*, *Ramalina chondrina* and *Sarcogyne
clavus*.

Mosses and liverworts are also found in coastal habitats, many being species
that can cope with drying up and apparently disappearing in summer and being
waterlogged in winter. An example of this is the liverwort *Gongylanthus ericetorum*.
Bare ground on coastal heath in Scilly is frequently covered by the distinctive
pattern of the *Riccia* liverworts that frequent these areas. Other coastal species
include the moss *Calyptrochaeta apiculata*, originally from the southern
hemisphere. Although not a great rarity, one moss that causes great interest
when found is goblin gold *Schistostega pennata*, which occurs in some coastal
caves in Scilly. This attractive species has the ability to refract light and can
appear luminous when growing inside dark caverns.

Cliff vegetation
Although the granite cliffs on Scilly are not very high compared with their Land's
End counterparts, they are similarly weathered to form impressive and bizarre
shapes. Some of the cliff landscapes are quite dramatic, and among the most
impressive are those on exposed headlands such as Shipman Head on Bryher,
Peninnis Head on St Mary's and St Martin's Head. Some of the rock islets thrust
up directly from the sea like granite icebergs, and Hanjague, Rosevean and the
38-metre high Men-a-vaur are especially impressive examples. These steeper
cliffs are scoured by the sea and support little or no vegetation, at most a few
lichens. It is on the extensive low cliffs around the islands that we find the
characteristic maritime cliff plant communities (Rodwell, 2000).

One of the commonest vegetation types found on rocky shores is the
maritime rock crevice community, which is found all around the coasts with
good examples also on man-made structures such as the outer wall of Cromwell's

Castle, Tresco, and on the Garrison wall on St Mary's. Typically there are scattered plants of rock samphire, thrift, rock sea-spurrey and red fescue with Danish scurvygrass, buck's-horn plantain and the coastal variety of wild carrot *Daucus carota gummifer*, and where there is some shelter sea spleenwort grows in crevices in the granite or between the stones of the walls, where it is partially protected from full exposure to wind and sea spray (Fig. 105). Below this zone are only the lichens of the splash zone. Higher up on the cliffs, where the soils over the rocks are very thin, is a community of plants adapted to excessively arid conditions. This type of vegetation is also common on the tops of man-made structures, for example on the top of sections of the Garrison walls near the coast. It is also frequent on the rocky carns and other outcrops where in summer the shallow turf becomes baked by the sun, but where there is enough moisture held in the granite for the plants to survive.

Where there are seabird communities on the coast or on some of the smaller uninhabited islands, very distinctive types of vegetation result from their occupation. Sometimes these may be discrete patches around nesting sites and quite localised, but where colonies are extensive a whole section of cliff or top of one of the small islands may be affected. The vegetation on the small islands of

FIG 105. The thick and leathery fronds of sea spleenwort are one of the features of rocky coasts in Scilly. February 2004. (Rosemary Parslow)

Little Innisvouls and Menawethan includes examples of both the MC6 community, dominated by fleshy-leaved forms of sea beet, common scurvygrass and sea mayweed, and MC7, with a fleshy form of common chickweed *Stellaria media*, common sorrel *Rumex acetosa* and several species of grasses. In summer the smell of guano and the flattened and mired appearance of these areas is very obvious and even evocative to a seabird enthusiast! Also on many of the smaller islands clumps of tree-mallow may be significant, such as on Rosevear in the Western Rocks and on some of the Norrard Rocks.

Another distinctive maritime cliff community consists of thick 'mattresses' of red fescue, often with some thrift and other species. One of the most extraordinary vegetation communities is found on Annet, where massive thrift tussocks predominate, like giant cushions completely covering the ground over large areas, with only small amounts of red fescue and often rock sea-spurrey on the bare ground in the gaps between the tussocks.

SANDY SHORES

Flying into the islands, the fine white sand beaches are often visible before any other features can be seen. The dazzling whiteness is due to the composition of the sand, which is formed from crystals of quartz and especially feldspar from the decomposing granite. The most extensive sandy beaches are on St Martin's and the southern part of Tresco. Other good examples exist on St Mary's, St Agnes, Bryher, Samson (Fig. 106) and Teän. There are particularly striking small sandy coves on several of the uninhabited islands, for example on Little Arthur and Great Ganilly.

One of the curiosities of the sands in Scilly is how much they vary from place to place. On many beaches the sands are like fine grit, and those in Wingletang Bay are very coarse-grained, strongly resembling speciality coffee sugar. Most of the sand on St Agnes is quite useless for building sand castles, as it cannot hold a shape – as my children found in the past. Tresco and St Martin's have finer white sand beaches and the especially fine, soft sand from Porth Mellon on St Mary's was once exported for drying ink on letters before the days of blotting paper, and also for polishing pewter (Heath, 1750).

Just above high water mark on sandy beaches there is typically a band of strandline plants similar to those found on shingle: sea sandwort, some of the oraches, sea mayweed and in some years sea rocket may be very abundant, forming dense stands, especially on recently formed sand banks such as the one at the northeastern tip of Samson. One plant that used to be often found on

FIG 106. Typical sandy beach with sea rocket, sea spurge and red fescue, Samson, August 2003. (Rosemary Parslow)

sandy beaches was prickly saltwort *Salsola kali* but it is now very uncommon on the inhabited islands, possibly because the unpleasant experience of sitting on the prickly stems has led to it being ripped up by holidaymakers. At the top of the beach is also where sea-holly (Fig. 107), sea bindweed, yellow horned-poppy and in some places sea-kale are found, usually with sand sedge and some typical grasses. Where the dunes start there is often a narrow strip of sand couch *Elytrigia juncea* foredune, just before the typical dune dominated by marram grass.

Among the entertaining aspects of sandy beaches in Scilly are the occasional appearances of unusual plants, especially rare ephemerals. In the past these have included New Zealand spinach, thorn apple, tomato *Lycopersicon esculentum*, as well as the occasional appearance of sea pea, sea knotgrass and Ray's knotgrass *Polygonum oxyspermum*. Sea pea has not been seen in Scilly since 1982, but sea knotgrass was found in 2003 after almost a century, and Ray's knotgrass the following year. These latter species are ephemeral species in Scilly, none as yet having become established. Other novelties that can turn up are some of the sea beans, the commonest of which is *Entada gigas*, and wrecks of other sea creatures from by-the-wind-sailors to tiny razor shells (see Chapter 8).

FIG 107. Sea-holly has an extremely long root system, anchoring it in the edge of the dune. Gugh, June 2003. (Rosemary Parslow)

Most of the animals that live on the beaches hide in the vegetation at the top of the beach and sally out across the beach to feed among the detritus on the tideline. Often turning over driftwood or rubbish in this area reveals animals such as sandhoppers, the lesser cockroach, springtails (Collembola), beetles and other arthropods. Sandhoppers make burrows in the sand from which they emerge at night to hop along in front of the tide; a nocturnal stroll along the beach will send them hopping away with a sound like rain on a roof. Butterflies, moths and other insects may also have a temporary place on the beach among some of the coastal flowers. Perhaps one bird more than any other characterises the sandy beaches in Scilly – the sanderling *Calidris alba*, whose twinkling toes spirit them along the edge of the waves like clockwork toys. Other waders, ringed plover *Charadrius hiaticula*, oystercatcher *Haematopus ostralegus*, dunlin *Calidris alpina* and little stint *Calidris minuta*, also frequent sandy beaches.

Sandy beaches are prone to movement due to tidal currents and they can change markedly throughout the year and especially over years. The accreting, growing sand spit on the northern end of Samson had already dried out by 1998 and was becoming vegetated with sea spurge, sea rocket and grasses. By 2006 the vegetation had stabilised and formed a dense cover of grasses, sea beet and oraches. The Bar, between St Agnes and Gugh, is always very mobile and rarely stays the same for many tides. And in the Eastern Isles a long sandy spit has been growing out between the islands and St Martin's, gradually obscuring the channels that the boatmen use to navigate this shallow stretch of water.

Dunes

Dunes in Scilly are not the spectacular formations seen elsewhere in Britain, as most are quite low and relatively small. The largest dunes are at Appletree Banks on the south of Tresco. The dune area here extends right across the south of the island, with mobile dune along the shore and continuing around to Pentle Bay and up the east coast (Fig. 108). From there the dunes extend inwards to form dune grassland and heath over blown sand. The Tresco dunes look rather unusual due to having been planted up with all manner of exotics from the Abbey Gardens, giving them an oddly 'foreign' appearance.

Other dune systems occur on St Martin's, where a dune ridge stretches along large parts of the southern shoreline, as well as at Great Bay on the north side of the island, where the dune extends inland as a sandy slope called the Plains. At the north end of St Mary's are the highest sand dunes in Scilly: these extend from Bar Point out into Crow Sound. Bar Point is the only example of a foreland dune

FIG 108. Pentle Bay, Tresco: sandy beach backed by dunes. April 2005. (Rosemary Parslow)

in the Western Approaches of Britain (Dargie, in Barne *et al.*, 1996). Foreland dunes develop on shores where the sand supply comes from two different directions and they gradually extend seawards. Elsewhere the dunes are smaller and so flattened as to hardly seem like dunes at all. These low dunes are found at several places on Bryher, St Mary's and St Agnes and on many of the uninhabited islands such as Samson and St Helen's.

Most of the dunes start at the interface between the sandy shore and the slope of the island. One of the first plants encountered is usually sand couch, a bluish, stiff-leaved grass that quickly forms clumps, producing rhizomes as it moves through the sand. Sand couch frequently gets immersed at the high spring tides and appears to be very resistant to salt water. In places sand couch itself forms low dunes, but usually it grows just along the seaward edge of dunes dominated by marram grass. As part of sea defences at the time, the coastal dunes were planted up with marram grass from about 1830, although it is believed to have already been native to the islands (Lousley, 1971). Later still Augustus Smith planted Hottentot fig, intending the large spreading South African succulent to assist in stabilising the dunes and to stop the sand storms which were a great nuisance to the islanders, submerging their crops and blowing into their houses. The marram, like sand couch, also grows in clumps linked by rhizomes that form a network within the dune (Fig. 109). However much blown sand gets deposited on it, marram has the ability to grow upwards and through the sand so that it is very efficient at knitting the dune together. One of its characteristics is that there is always open sand beneath the canopy of stiff leaves, enabling other plants to get a toehold. Bracken invades dunes in some places where the sand is more acid, growing among the marram or forming dense patches, often with low-growing bramble, at the back on the dune as at Higher Town Bay, St Martin's. Close to the shore, the interface between the beach and low dunes can be blurred, so that typical shore species such as sea bindweed and sea sandwort grow among the marram and sea couch grass (Fig. 110).

Quite frequently the dunes can be subject to 'blow-outs'. These usually happen on the outer edge of the dunes and often occur where people or vehicles have fractured the surface of the dune and broken the network of rhizomes and roots that bind the whole structure together. This can often be seen on paths, especially on short cuts to the beach or where people have dug little shelters into the dunes for sunbathing. Blow-outs can seriously affect the stability of the dune, which can be of concern where the dune is the primary coastal defence. The inherent instability of dunes can be seen where storms have ripped into the seaward edge and swept away much of the sand, as can be seen on the path behind Higher Town Bay to English Island Point on St Martin's. Here a large

FIG 109. Dune coastline dominated by marram grass on St Martin's. (Rosemary Parslow)

FIG 110. Sea bindweed also helps to bind the sand in the dunes. June 2003 (Rosemary Parslow)

section of the dune has gone completely and the islanders have tried reinforcing the area with tree branches to stabilise the remaining sand.

Dune slacks with shrubs, tall plants and open water or water plants are not found in Scilly. There are some areas among the dunes that are waterlogged, for example between Great Pool, Tresco, and the dune ridge. Here plants such as many-stalked spike-rush, common spike-rush *Eleocharis palustris*, several different rushes, creeping bent, silverweed *Potentilla anserina* and marsh pennywort can be found. Another area on Rushy Bank, Tresco, has an unusual flora with red fescue, sand sedge, small adder's-tongue fern and much bare ground.

Some of the exotic plants planted out on the dunes at Appletree Banks have now become completely established. The commonest non-native to become naturalised was probably the *Agapanthus*, but another that appears to be spreading is the extraordinary spikey, agave-like rhodostachys and the very similar Tresco rhodostachys. Other exotic plants that have become established include red-hot pokers, the tall white bugle lily and montbretia. Hottentot fig and possibly the similar Sally-my-handsome have invaded areas away from the shore, and close to the landing at Carn Near a stand of the curious twisted stems of the wireplant grows over other vegetation.

Other than exotic species the dunes support a range of common plants. Besides marram and sand couch there are other grasses, often including the blueish form of red fescue *Festuca rubra juncea*. In the areas behind the marram edge, it is usual to find ragwort *Senecio jacobaea*, both Portland and sea spurge, smooth sow-thistle *Sonchus oleraceus*, madder *Rubia peregrina*, bramble, balm-leaved figwort and early dog-violet *Viola riviniana*. Near Bar Point on St Mary's is where the rare fern, moonwort, used to grow in the dunes. On the edges of dunes, for example those on the edge of the Bar on Gugh and Rushy Bay on Bryher, there are now healthy stands of sea-holly. This attractive plant became quite uncommon for a time in the 1960s when it was popular in dried flower arrangements.

Dune grassland grows on the flat sandy area behind the dunes and is often the stage before the succession to dune heath, when the sand becomes sufficiently stable to support heather. The most important plant here is sand sedge, whose rhizomes spread out in all directions through the sand, quickly forming a network of plants and runners to stabilise the surface. Quickly following are many rosette-forming species, tiny annuals or closely spreading perennials: miniature forms of stork's-bills, scarlet pimpernel *Anagallis arvensis*, English stonecrop, grasses such as early hair-grass *Aira praecox* and some clovers are frequent, but some taller plants such as Portland spurge and common centaury *Centaurium erythraea* soon follow. Grassy areas will be dominated by red fescue, again often including the blue form. In places such as Rushy Bank on Tresco, the flat sandy area merges into a very open area of heathland with ling, bird's-foot-trefoil, common and orange bird's-foot, as well as a rich cover of lichens. Another very common species is one of the parasol mushrooms, probably *Macrolepiota procera*, that produces very tall mushrooms with large caps often 20cm across. The younger fruiting bodies are a distinctive drumstick shape. The parasols grow both on dune grassland and on heathland, sometimes in large numbers.

Although the big sand blows of the past may no longer happen, sand still gets blown inland at times. On most islands, and especially St Martin's, many fields are composed of very sandy soils that originated from the blown sand in the past. Borlase (1756), describing the Plains on St Martin's, refers to the sand 'blown in from some Northern Coves below' and goes on to comment on the 'sheep-run being two miles long, but below this Turf, there is nothing but sand for a great depth'. Some bulb fields to the east side of Higher Town Bay are almost pure sand. These fields have recently been more or less abandoned and are becoming invaded by bracken. Where the sand is still unvegetated or has been excavated and disturbed, there can be patches of common bird's-foot, sheep's sorrel and even the rare orange bird's-foot, plants more generally associated with heathland.

There are probably no birds that are specifically associated with the dunes, other than the common terns that have occasionally nested at Pentle Bay and Appletree Banks on Tresco (Fig. 111). For a while the helicopters avoided over-flying the colony when landing on Tresco. This was a precaution to prevent the

FIG 111. Common tern on nest: one of the few birds associated with sand dunes. (Ren Hathway)

terns from all flying up when disturbed, exposing their vulnerable nests to predators, but the helicopters still fly in and the terns still nest there at times.

A number of invertebrate species are found in the dunes, perhaps the most obvious of which are the bush-crickets, with their loud insistent songs. Grey bush-crickets are found among the marram stands on Bryher and both long-winged *Conocephalus discolor* and short-winged *C. dorsalis* cone-heads also frequent dunes. Although marram appears to be an unappetising plant, with hard, sharp, inrolled narrow leaves that would seem unpalatable to any grazing animals, it does support a few moth species. Some species of snails and other invertebrates, including spiders, beetles and ants, also appear to be able to survive among the stands of marram.

SHORE DOCK, AN EXAMPLE OF A PLANT ON THE BRINK

Shore dock *Rumex rupestris* is sometimes said to be the 'rarest dock in the world' (Fig. 112). It is an endemic species found only along the Atlantic seaboard of western Europe from Galicia (Spain) in the south to Brittany, the Channel Isles, southwest England and Wales (McDonnell & King, 2006). The rarity of shore dock has led to it receiving special protection: it is on Schedule 8 of the Wildlife & Countryside Act 1981, it is listed on Annexes II (b) and IV (b) of the European Habitats Directive 1992, and it is a Priority BAP species (UK Biodiversity Action Plan 1995) with an individal Species Action Plan (Davis, 1999). As a result of all this legislation the shore dock has received considerable attention as part of English Nature's Species Recovery Programme, with surveys of sites in Cornwall and Devon and in the Isles of Scilly from 1994, followed by further surveys funded by Plantlife (Neil *et al.*, 2001).

Although docks may be generally considered rather difficult to identify – and even uninteresting – shore dock at least has the advantage of growing in interesting places. It is a medium-sized perennial plant with either one or multiple stems, the basal leaves often have a smooth, bluish appearance, and the whole plant may appear reddish in colour. Although not particulary distinctive, the 'jizz' may become familiar to the expert, but it is always necessary to examine the 'tepals' (actually the perianth, which in docks is not differentiated into sepals and petals) when the seeds are ripe to be 100 per cent certain of correct identification. This is especially important where there are coastal populations of curled dock *Rumex crispus* var. *littoreus*, which can frequently look very similar, especially where plants have been broken off and stunted by storms. Although

FIG 112. The rare shore dock grows just above high water mark, where it is vulnerable to storm surges. Samson, August. (Rosemary Parslow)

both curled and shore dock have large tubercles on all three valves of the tepals, those of shore dock are more prominent and obscure the valves whereas in curled dock the valve shows clearly.

Lousley, both in his *Flora* (1971) and in the BSBI *Handbook* (Lousley & Kent, 1981), describes shore dock as locally common in Scilly. So it was not until 1982 that I first realised that the plants growing on the shores were not, as we had assumed, shore dock, but the coastal form of curled dock. Searching the shorelines on St Agnes and St Mary's in 1982 and 1983 failed to reveal any shore dock among all the hundreds of dock plants growing around the coasts. So the following year, funded by a grant from the British Ecological Society, two weeks in Scilly were spent surveying the shores, including most of the uninhabited islands (Parslow, 1984). Fortunately, due to a period of unusually calm and dry weather and the use of the Nature Conservancy Council boat *Marius Neilson*, it was possible to land on almost every small island where the dock might possibly grow. The only islands not visited were the Western Rocks (they were visited a few years later). Two weeks and three pairs of plimsols later about fifty shore dock plants (or clumps) had been located on only five islands.

Since 1984 the conditions necessary to repeat the complete survey have not been available, but partial surveys have continued and the colonies have been monitored whenever possible. In 1994 a further survey was carried out and known sites, plus former localities, those recorded in Lousley's *Flora* and any accessible shore that looked 'right' were visited (Parslow & Colston, 1994). This time there were two of us to land and check the plants and collect some 'seed' (fruit and tepals), and we again had Cyril Nicholas as boatman. We recorded 150–200 plants, although what actually constitutes a plant proved difficult in the field, as the dock not only grows in clumps that may be one plant or several, but also has roots that run along under the rocks so that apparently separate plants may all be on one root system. As part of this survey potential sites for reintroduction were identified, as the dock was still only growing on five islands and some known sites had been lost since the 1980s. When possible, annual counts were made of the known sites until 2001, and since then monitoring has mostly been carried out by the Isles of Scilly Wildlife Trust.

In 2001 a further report on the status of shore dock in the Isles of Scilly pulled together what was known about the plant to date (Parslow, in Neil *et al.*, 2001). The discovery of some of Lousley's papers and notebooks in the archives of the Isles of Scilly Museum had thrown new light on the status of the plant historically and the interpretation that had been put on records and sites in the *Flora*. In their review of the Cornish flora Margetts and David (1981) describe *Rumex rupestris* as 'frequent' in Scilly. Their comments are based on the *Flora*, where Lousley had said the plant was 'common', although he did also comment on the decline of the species in mainland Britain and northern Europe. By examining what Lousley actually says about the distribution and status of the plant on each of the islands in his *Flora* and by reference to his notebooks, a clearer picture is emerging of the history of shore dock. Previously it was assumed that the dock was still present on all the islands listed by Lousley in 1971 when his *Flora* was published. But many of the records were collected prior to the first draft in 1940, and much of his additional material now seems to have been collected in the 1950s. It is now certain that the plant was already in decline and had gone from some previous localities.

The colonies by island

By comparing records for each island, using the entries from Lousley's *Flora*, his notebooks and subsequent records, some idea of the history of each colony of shore dock can be elicited. The results are shown in Table 2 (overleaf).

The future for shore dock in Scilly

The fruits of shore dock with their large tubercles are very light and buoyant (Fig. 113); they can be seen blowing along the beach and floating in the sea so should easily be carried to other beaches. Some plants must arise from the germination of seeds carried in this way, but it seems many do not survive long.

FIG 113. Shore dock 'seeds'. Samson, July. (Rosemary Parslow)

TABLE 2. Summary of records of shore dock by island.

SITE BY ISLAND	FIRST RECORDED	YEAR KNOWN PRESENT	LOUSLEY'S FLORA REFERENCE	LATEST RECORD	2001–2006
St Mary's	1873		reference	1873	extinct
St Agnes	1877		reference	1877	extinct
St Agnes A	1984			1985	gone, transient site
St Agnes B	1993			1999	gone, transient site
Gugh	1893	1905	still there	before 1971	extinct
Tresco	1904	1954	still there	2005	still there but declining
Bryher	? before 1961		three sites	before 1971	extinct
St Martin's	1904		? gone	1904	extinct
White Island	1956		yes	1956	extinct
Samson	1954	1982	several sites	2006	still there on several sites
Annet	1950s		several sites	1982	extinct
Annet A	1982			2004	still there
St Helen's & Northwethel	1957		scarce	1957?	extinct
Great/Middle Arthur	1938		reference	1938	extinct
Normour	? 1950s		specimen	before 1971	extinct
Teän	1984			2005	still there

Transient colonies have been recorded on several occasions in Scilly. The St Agnes colonies, one on Tresco and a second site on Teän are good examples, having apparently germinated in unsuitable places where the plants clearly could not thrive, and subsequently dying out within a year or two. Similar circumstances have arisen in artificial (garden) conditions where seed has fallen from pot-grown plants and germinated, in one case in a raised container with alpines and in another case in the gravel drive. In both cases dock plants grew quickly, flowered and set seed themselves, but never made the strong rhizome mass that supports the perennial plant. From pot-grown plants it is clear that they need fresh water to root into, and that they also germinate freely in fresh water – but soon die if the substrate dries out. This has been seen in the field, where plants growing on the ram shelf at the base of the cliff died when the seepages dried up in summer 1996.

It is now apparent that shore dock in the Isles of Scilly is a much rarer plant and has been declining much longer than previously thought. By the time Lousley's *Flora* was published the dock may only have been present on eight islands. Interestingly, the sites on Tresco and Samson visited by Lousley are still in existence and one, the Tresco colony, may have been present for over a century. Unfortunately this colony is gradually being washed away as the site erodes, and unless seed gets washed to a suitable place nearby may soon be lost; there were only two mature plants in 2005. There are still plants at one site on Annet, although not where Lousley had seen them; those were washed away in the winter of 1982/3. Other colonies known to Lousley have not been found since and probably had gone before the early 1980s, when the first systematic surveys were carried out (Parslow, 1984, 1996; Parslow & Colston, 1994). New sites were located on Teän and St Agnes, although unfortunately the St Agnes sites and one on Teän have proved short-lived.

There is already evidence that shore dock is losing out to higher sea levels, storm surges and the 'squeeze' of the narrow strip above high water mark where the plant grows. If sea levels continue to rise at the predicted rate, the present sites may be lost completely and the available habitat for recolonisation restricted. A rise of 30–50cm will encroach onto most of the beaches where shore dock grows at present, although it may be supposed that as long as there are new beaches to be colonised then the plant should be able to utilise them. Higher summer temperatures could also cause the freshwater seepages the plant requires to dry up. Around the coastal fringe of the islands the rock platforms, the ram shelves where many docks grow, are already frequently swept bare by extreme high tides. On Samson by 2006 the ram shelves where the docks used to grow had become very eroded by the sea and deposits of seaweed suggest they can no longer support shore dock. These shelves are close up against the cliff edge, so there seems to be nowhere for the plants to retreat. Even so, there are still beaches, especially among the uninhabited islands, that appear to have the conditions shore dock requires, and the plants produce great quantities of viable seed that can float in the tide. So why are no new colonies arising? Although the populations are known to fluctuate, the trend in Scilly still seems to be downward. Perhaps, as with the larvae of marine animals, the prevailing currents do not favour deposition of seed on suitable beaches.

CHAPTER 10

Grassland and Heathland

There are downs covered with the golden glory of the gorse, with the pink of the sea-thrift, with the purple of the heather; there are hills clothed with bracken breast-high in summer, and changing from green-gold to red-gold as the year advances.

Jessie Mothersole (1910)

GRASSLANDS

T HERE ARE A number of related habitats in the Isles of Scilly that can loosely be described as grassland. Some of these are types of maritime grassland that are included in the maritime cliff communities of the National Vegetation Classification (see Appendix). These include a distinctive short sward that forms a band around the perimeter of the islands, between the edge – mostly delineated by a low cliff – and the main body of the island. On the cliffs this is usually a short turf maintained by rabbits or wind-pruning. On some of the lower-lying islands, as on some of the Eastern Isles, related grassland with an intimate mixture of red fescue, thrift and mayweed with bird's-foot-trefoil forms a flower-studded fringe around the coast.

On the inhabited islands there are more extensive areas of grass fields, some of which would previously have been hay meadow – but which are now mostly pasture. Many of these have been agriculturally improved in some way. A few examples of hay-meadow grassland, close to U4 grassland (*Festuca ovina – Agrostis capillaris – Galium saxatile*) still exist, with sheep's fescue replaced by red fescue – as is typical in Scilly. These grasslands are not particularly species-rich, although the lack of rarities does not necessarily indicate agricultural improvement

(Rodwell, 1992). A field on St Agnes with oxeye daisy *Leucanthemum vulgare* and other meadow plants appears to have been sown, using a commercial wildflower meadow mixture. Some fields on St Mary's fall within U1 grassland (*Festuca ovina – Agrostis capillaris – Rumex acetosella*), again with red fescue replacing sheep's fescue. In places these converge on the heathland and so frequently include heath plants. Small areas with plants such as knapweed *Centaurea nigra*, meadow vetchling *Lathyrus pratensis*, sweet vernal-grass *Anthoxanthemum odoratum* and red fescue are found on odd corners around St Mary's, such as at the edge of the airfield. These are presumably remnants of larger grasslands now lost. Another distinctive type of grassland is dune grassland found growing over almost pure sand, which includes dune grasses and sand sedge.

The recession in the flower industry towards the end of the twentieth century has led to many bulb fields being put down to grass. They were mostly sown with a rye-grass seed mix, sometimes with the addition of crested dog's-tail grass and white clover *Trifolium repens*, or they may have been left fallow. These fields may be topped, or possibly grazed with cattle, and generally have little nature conservation interest. Other fields may have received little treatment other than the natural application of farmyard manure. Sometimes lime is added to 'sweeten' the grassland. On St Martin's there is a group of fields with an MG5 hay-meadow type of grassland that is now grazed. These fields are often a mass of the white umbels of flowering pignut *Conopodium majus* in May, and in June have patches of white clover with some extreme colour varieties (var. *townsendii*), ranging from pink florets through pink with darker edges to deep purple, and frequently also with purple-suffused leaves. In spring the bluebells carpet the edges of the field, flowering before the bracken grows up.

Wet grassland and rush pasture

Mostly on St Mary's, although there are examples on other inhabited islands, are some rather tussocky, wet fields that are mosaics of tall grasses and rush pasture (Fig. 114). Most of these areas have a history of grazing with cattle and/or horses. The other feature they have in common is a high water table, although one field near Porthloo, St Mary's, has patches of more species-rich grassland on higher ground within the matrix. Another field, also near Porthloo, frequently had standing water in winter. This field has now been partially drained and is dominated by yellow iris – but still includes a number of typical wetland plants, including tubular water-dropwort *Oenanthe fistulosa* and lesser spearwort. Another similar field typically had a large population of the very poisonous hemlock water-dropwort – until this was sprayed out with herbicide, presumably to protect stock pastured there.

FIG 114. Wet grassland with rushes, buttercups, lesser spearwort and lady's smock on St Mary's, May 2003. (Rosemary Parslow)

Coastal grassland

Coastal grassland occurs on all the islands and is one of their most attractive features. On some islands it may be grazed by cattle, but in many places, including the uninhabited islands, are short swards that are generally rabbit-grazed. Where there are no rabbits, and very little trampling by visitors, the sward appears to be maintained entirely by the dwarfing affect of wind and sea spray on the vegetation. The short, tight turf of the coastal band consists of several of the varieties of *Festuca – Armeria* grassland (Rodwell, 2000). It was in this type of grassland that Coombe first discovered western clover on the Lizard (Coombe, 1961; Coombe & Morisset, 1967). These grasslands are predominately mosaics frequently dominated by fescues, both red fescue and sheep's fescue, often with Yorkshire fog and sometimes creeping bent. Thrift is often a feature, sometimes dominating sections close to the shore completely. Buck's-horn plantain, yarrow *Achillea millefolium*, wild carrot and English stonecrop are also common, sometimes with common centaury, lesser hawkbit *Leontodon saxatilis*, white clover and tiny plants of rock samphire. In very early spring western clover is a highlight of these grasslands with its flowering heads tightly adpressed into the

FIG 115. Western clover is often in flower early in the year before the similar white clover appears. May 2005. (Rosemary Parslow)

short turf (Fig. 115), and mainly on Bryher the tiny blue heads and corkscrew leaves of spring squill can be found. Where the soils are very thin over the rocks some areas are dominated by the species-rich therophyte community with miniature forms of buck's-horn plantain, English stonecrop, western clover, red fescue, thrift and, where the open conditions allow, tiny annuals such as early hair-grass and silver hair-grass. It is in this sort of habitat on Wingletang Down on St Agnes that the extremely rare least adder's-tongue fern grows throughout the winter. On the top of many of the exposed headlands such as Heathy Hill and Shipman Head, Bryher, there is an intimate mosaic of wind-pruned grassland sward and short heathland communities.

Perhaps the most consistent influence on some of these grasslands is wind-blown salt spray, which in Scilly can be carried right across the islands, so that few places are not influenced by salt deposition to some extent. Deposition of salt drops off rapidly, however, even in very windy places, so that on the Lizard only 20 per cent of the salt was deposited 100 metres inland compared with the cliff edge (Malloch, 1972). This gradation can be seen very clearly on Scilly, as the more maritime plants of the cliff edges tail off away from the sea and there is a gradual change to a more inland type of plant community. But in many places, especially on the smaller islands, the influence of salt spray continues right across from one side of the island to the other.

Dune grasslands (Chapter 9) in many places merge into more typical grassland, especially as so much of Scilly has been subjected to blown sand. One plant that is found on coastal grasslands as well as further inland is the small orchid, autumn lady's-tresses (Fig. 116). In some years the tiny spiral flowering stems are very common and widespread, while in other years there may be very few.

Perhaps the most attractive characteristic of some of the grasslands in Scilly is the presence of chamomile, whose evocative scent rises from the ground when

FIG 116. Tiny autumn lady's-tresses orchids in flower on the grassy top of the Garrison wall, St Mary's, August 2003. (Rosemary Parslow)

the plant is trampled and whose white flowers star the ground in summer. Chamomile is becoming an uncommon plant nationally, but in Scilly it is still widespread and common on all the inhabited islands. It did not appear to grow on the uninhabited islands, until it was recently found on Annet. Chamomile is common in the grass/heathland mosaics such as on Wingletang Down, St Agnes, and around much of the coasts of the inhabited islands. Many of the mown grasslands, for example the cricket fields and those surrounding some of the ancient monuments, are also full of chamomile as well as some of the unusual species of clover. It would appear that mowing these areas replicates the effect of close cropping by rabbits or sheep. These managed grasslands are thought to be very like former closely grazed habitats. Some of the cricket pitches, such as those on St Agnes and St Martin's, can also be very wet, especially in winter. These low-lying meadows have been subject to periodic inundation both by the sea and from rainwater and can be under water for several weeks. This leaves the meadows in a temporarily very rough state, although they soon recover, usually in time for the next cricket season.

Moving away from the coastal edge there are more verdant grasslands. Some very attractive examples of this are a suite of fields along the west coast of St Mary's and on Halangy Down (Fig. 117). Often the grass merges into heath,

FIG 117. A coastal field on St Mary's showing the interface between grassland and heathland. St Helens and Round Island in the distance. (Rosemary Parslow)

with patches of grassland continuing right through the heathland. This mixture of grassland and heathland, frequently as very intimate mosaics, is a recurring feature in Scilly.

HEATHLANDS

Other than the coastal habitats, heathland is regarded as the most important wildlife habitat in the Isles of Scilly. Besides supporting many of the rare species found in the islands, the downs (as heathlands are called in Scilly) are also among the most evocative and colourful places at any time of year. Heath is typically a habitat dominated by dwarf ericaceous shrubs that has been maintained by the intervention of man over centuries; their present-day appearance and composition has resulted directly from the actions of the early inhabitants of Scilly. From the archaeological evidence we know there were heathers and other heathland plants in Scilly during prehistoric times. Charred heathland vegetation has been found at two Bronze Age sites, Bonfire Carn on Bryher and Porth Killier on St Agnes. At Bonfire Carn remains of woody vegetation that had probably been used as firewood were found. The resulting charcoal cannot be identified specifically, but has been recognised as coming from gorse and/or broom, heather/ling and rose/bramble. Besides the charcoal there were other burnt remains, also of gorse and ling, and of heath-grass *Danthonia decumbens*. These species are all still present on the heathland in Scilly today, confirming there were similar areas in the vicinity at that time (Ratcliffe & Straker, 1996). Over the centuries people would have utilised everything they could from the land: turf, bracken, gorse, broom and heather were stripped from the heaths and used for fuel, bedding and thatching, and this would have prevented the invasion of the heath by scrub and kept the landscape open (Page, 1988). On St Mary's the heaths were subdivided by stone fences, presumably to mark ownerships rather than to contain animals. Many of these boundaries can still be seen.

Distribution of heathland

Heathland is found on all the inhabited islands in Scilly where there are thin soils over the granite. Often the extremities of the inhabited islands are all still either heath or coastal grassland, open landscapes with minimal management – now open access. Some of the uninhabited islands also have quite extensive areas of heath: the top of North Hill, Samson, for example or the higher land on St Helen's. On some other islands the amount of heath is quite tiny, just localised patches of ling, bell heather and other heathland plants on the tops of the hills,

FIG 118. Heathland in the Eastern Isles is usually confined to the tops of the hills. (Rosemary Parslow)

as on Teän and several of the Eastern Isles (Fig. 118). These are typical ericaceous shrub heath, but in other places there are areas of gorse scrub or bracken. In the latter areas poking around under the canopy of tall plants may reveal there is still an understorey that includes heather or at least some of the other typical heathland plants.

Many of the present heathland areas are very open, with granite boulders breaking the surface in a very picturesque way. To the uninitiated many of these rocks are indistinguishable from the stone remains of archaeological monuments scattered over the islands – many of which have incorporated natural boulders. On the inhabited islands many rocks, including those that were part of monuments, have been removed by later generations to use as building stone and in some cases to enable the land to be cleared for cultivation. On Tresco it seems that around 1870 the downs were cleared of rocks by blasting, the gorse uprooted, and grass seeds sown (Grigson, 1948). Certainly some of the early stone hedges and houses would have been built from the rocks that had been cleared from the land.

Waved heath

On most of the Isles of Scilly the heathland is very low-growing, and a visitor to Tresco in 1886 described the 'ling and the gorse being about the same height in a very windswept part' (Vagabondo, 1886). What the visitor probably saw was almost certainly heath that had been pruned by the wind to produce a very tight, low-growing heather carpet. In the most exposed places this develops into an extreme example of wind-eroded heath, known as 'waved heath', as can be seen on many areas including Shipman Head on Bryher, Castle Down on Tresco and Chapel Down on St Martin's. There are also extensive areas of waved heath on Wingletang Down on St Agnes, on the top of Gugh and on Salakee Down, St Mary's. Waved heath is so called because the plants form 'waves' as they are rolled over by the wind, leaving bare ground and exposed roots on the side towards the prevailing wind with the leaves and flowers concentrated along the front of the plant away from the wind. At its most extreme, wide ribbons of bare ground form between the lines of heather plants so that it almost appears to have been ploughed into ridges (Fig. 119). Although most waved heath consists of heather plants, where western gorse grows in Scilly it is often in close association with heathers and can also be closely wind-pruned. There are even areas where a sculpting by the wind produces a similar effect on grassland. There are examples of this on Castella Down, St Agnes, and near Heathy Hill, Bryher. Although this heathland is typically species-poor, being dominated by the two species of

FIG 119. An extreme example of 'waved heath' on St Martin's, June 2002. (Rosemary Parslow)

heather, there are several other characteristic plants associated with this type of heathland: close circles of pink lousewort, different coloured milkworts *Polygala* spp. and skeins of yellow-starred tormentil can be found growing through the heather.

It seems unimaginable now that earlier generations used turf as thatch, even as walls for their cottages, as well as for fuel, but possibly there were larger exploitable amounts at that time. Peat (this is not the same kind of peat found in deep deposits in acid bogs, but a thinner layer formed under close heather cover) or turf formed mainly from ling, grass and other heathland plants was the main type of fuel on the islands after most of the woodland had been cleared. Once the trees had gone, other than collecting driftwood, utilising turf, gorse and bracken, even seaweed, would have been the only alternative, but it must have been a struggle to collect enough material, especially with the populations on the off-islands at times being greater than today. Constantly stripping turf for fuel could not have been very sustainable, as it would not have regrown very quickly. There are references to damage being done to the downs by removing turf and peat in the past (Woodley, 1822; North, 1850). This practice was eventually curtailed on the orders of Augustus Smith, as Lord Proprietor (King, 1985). The name Turfy Hill (St Martin's) may relate to the gathering of turf there. The practice of using heather as thatching material for houses continued until replaced by straw, or more often reeds. Not all houses were built of stone, and turf was even used to build some cottages (Ashbee, 1974). At one time it is said the houses in Hugh Town were built of turf with thatched roofs, but they all burned down and were then replaced with stone cottages (Mothersole, 1910). Thatched cottages had either ropes or a net woven from straw cast over the roof and either pegged down or weighed down with boulders to stop them being ripped off by gales.

Two species of gorse occur in Scilly, common gorse and western gorse. The former is a large shrub with bright yellow flowers, whereas western gorse in Scilly is mostly low-growing and has more orange flowers. In former times gorse would have been utilised for everything from hedging to fuel and this would have kept it in check. Common gorse can be very invasive and at times has completely overrun some important heathland sites such as large areas on Wingletang Down, St Agnes. Western gorse in Scilly appears to be non-invasive, and it is also restricted to far fewer sites; Salakee Down and Carn Morval have good stands. It appears to have been lost from St Agnes in recent years and may be more vulnerable to fire than the common species.

On deeper soils bracken soon becomes dominant. It is now found in dense stands over large areas of the islands and has the ability to quickly invade areas of abandoned cultivation. It, too, was at one time utilised by the local people, who would have used it for thatching, fuel and animal bedding. On St Mary's the bracken areas were divided into 'fern splatts' where individuals had rights to cut the ferns. This would have kept the bracken in check at the time. On Annet too, people from St Agnes used to cut bracken to use as fuel, which would also have made a considerable impression on the vegetation. Attempts have been made in recent years to curb the extravagant growths of bracken where it has invaded former pastures by spraying with the herbicide asulam. Unfortunately other ferns, including the adder's-tongues, frequently grow under the bracken and are equally susceptible to the chemical. Asulam has at times also been used to clear small patches of bracken from Annet, when there was a concern the fern appeared to be overwhelming the huge thrift hummocks that are a feature of the island, and under which Manx shearwaters breed. Natural limiting factors for bracken are exposure to salt-laden winds, which stunt growth and in more extreme cases leave fronds burnt and blackened, and soil depth, as the rhizomes are unable to grow in very shallow soils. Even in a normal winter damaged areas of bracken can be seen on exposed hillsides, but as the underground rhizomes are rarely affected the fern soon recovers.

Important heathland plants

Several of the plants of Scillonian heathlands are national rarities that are found only in Scilly and do not occur on the mainland of Britain. Four taxa of the adder's-tongue fern family (*Ophioglossaceae*) occurred in the Isles of Scilly until recently. One species, moonwort, has not been recorded for many years, but possibly may be found again one day. The former site was under bracken on the dunes at Bar Point, St Mary's, which was heavily disturbed when the telegraph cable was installed and the fern was not seen subsequently (Lousley, 1971). The remaining three adder's-tongue ferns are all still extant in Scilly, although St Agnes is the only island where all three are known to occur. Least adder's-tongue is listed in the Red Data Book as vulnerable due to its restricted locality and few colonies, and is protected under Schedule 8 of the Wildlife & Countryside Act 2001. It is endemic in the British Isles and the Channel Isles. Small adder's-tongue occurs in Europe, the Azores and also Iceland; in Britain it is confined mainly to coastal areas along the north and west of Britain, the New Forest and the major island groups from the Channel Islands to Shetland. In Britain it is considered Nationally Scarce. Adder's-tongue has no conservation status, but is extremely rare in the Isles of Scilly.

Least adder's-tongue fern is a very tiny, primitive fern, usually no more that 2cm high, growing in short turf in the heathland/grassland mosaic on Wingletang Down, St Agnes (Fig. 120). The original colony was found in 1950,

FIG 120. Least adder's-tongue fern on St Agnes. (Paul Sterry)

since when a number of other sites have been found within the same area of heathland. Certain colonies are now suffering from a steady increase of competitive vegetation, mainly grasses, gorse and bramble, resulting from the lack of grazing generally. One of the reasons least adder's-tongue was overlooked for so long was probably due to its life history. The plant is below ground for much of the year, emerging usually in late autumn to early winter, with some fronds exceptionally emerging in October or even earlier in a few places. By January the fertile fronds are ripe and shed their spores before turning yellow and dying off by about April. Over a number of years several botanists visiting the islands have mapped the distribution of least adder's-tongue and have expanded the known distribution, although almost all the colonies are within the same heathland area, and they are all on St Agnes. Because the fern is tiny and often quite difficult to find, it is now unclear whether the latest colonies have always been there but overlooked, or whether it has been spreading to new sites over the past twenty years (Parslow, 2006).

Small adder's-tongue is so like least adder's-tongue in appearance that there has been considerable confusion between the two. There is also an overlap between their growing seasons which means least adder's-tongue is just going over as small adder's-tongue emerges; they also share some of the same localities and the emerging young fronds of small adder's-tongue are frequently mistaken for the smaller species. Generally small adder's-tongue emerges in April, is often only about 3cm tall (except in certain flooded sites where the fronds may be larger) and is over by midsummer. Where it shares sites with least adder's-tongue the larger species is in the deeper soils around the edges of rock platforms; but it also grows in pastures, waterlogged hollows and under bracken. There does not appear to be any competition between the two species. Although there has been a recorded decline in this species in Scilly in the past twenty years due to habitat loss and degradation, some new sites have been identified – they too may just have been overlooked in the past. Small adder's-tongue is found on all of the inhabited islands but has not been recorded from any uninhabited ones. It has yet to be confirmed whether this is the true distribution, or whether it may occur but is missed because visits by botanists have generally been too late in the season to find it.

Adder's-tongue has only been reliably recorded from one site in Scilly, a damp, sandy grassland area under bracken between Big Pool and Browarth fields on St Agnes. It is suspected that other records for the species in the past were due to confusion with clones of small adder's-tongue that had larger fronds. Common adder's-tongue ferns have much larger, flatter sterile fronds and taller fertile spikes generally with many more sporangia. The fern emerges in May when the bracken is at the 'crozier' stage, and dies down by the middle of summer, becoming impossible to find after a few weeks as it is quickly hidden by bracken.

Another of the heathland rarities is orange bird's-foot, also a Red Data Book plant, endemic to the Isles of Scilly and Channel Islands. In Scilly it is found on all the inhabited islands, including Gugh, and on the uninhabited islands of Great Ganilly and Teän. Orange bird's-foot is an annual so has 'good' years and poorer years when there are not many plants in the usual sites. In exceptional years it may also produce a second generation. It is predominately a plant of heathland habitats, but in Scilly also occurs in disturbed sandy areas such as abandoned bulb fields. It is one of the more unusual weeds in the Abbey Gardens on Tresco.

Dune heath usually occurs at the dune and heathland interface as on St Martin's, Gugh and several other islands. This is usually on consolidated sand dune sites where sand sedge is generally one of the dominant species, with some ling and bell heather and dune plants such as Portland spurge and stork's-bills.

Lichens and bryophytes

On coastal heath, especially among stands of heather and gorse, there can be rich growths of lichens. Lungworts, especially *Lobaria pulmonaria* and *L. scrobiculata*, and other similar foliose species are frequently found in these situations, although they usually grow on the bark of trees (corticolous) elsewhere. One large foliose lichen, gilt-edged lichen, once known from several islands (Ralfs, in Ranwell, 1966) is now only known from one site in the islands. Another rare lichen of the coastal area is the beard-lichen *Usnea subscabrosa*, which is not known on the mainland (B. Edwards, *in litt.*). Other areas of heathland have rich lichen communities growing both on the ground and on the heather stems. Both reindeer moss *Cladonia* spp. and some of the lungworts are particularly common in this type of heathland, and give the heather a characteristically hoary grey appearance (Fig. 121). Other terricolous lichens, those that grow directly on the ground, prefer the short wind-pruned maritime grassland; the rare and declining ciliate strap-lichen is presently know from seven localities in Scilly, favouring the edges of hollows on very exposed headlands in the open, MC5 maritime therophyte communities (Edwards, 2002). Another *Heterodermia*, *H. japonica*, is also found in coastal turf on several headlands.

Perhaps the most celebrated lichen in Scilly is the golden hair-lichen, as beautiful as the romantic name suggests (Fig. 122), another very rare species known only from southwest England and west Wales. In Scilly it is found on St Agnes, Gugh and St Mary's, growing both on rocks and on very short

FIG 121. An area of lichen heath on Wingletang, St Agnes, January 2000. (Rosemary Parslow)

FIG 122. Golden hair-lichen and *Xanthoria ectaneoides* on a granite boulder, St Agnes, November 2002. (Rosemary Parslow)

heathland turf, where it is vulnerable to both fires and being collected, despite being a protected species (Dobson, 2000).

Several species of lichens now growing either on heather or rocks or in more open situations are elsewhere considered ancient woodland indicators. These include *Nephroma laevigatum*, *Sticta sylvatica* and *Lobaria pulmonaria*. It would be very interesting to map these species to see whether they conform to the modelled location of the former ancient forest in Scilly (Thomas, 1985; see Chapter 2).

The management of heathland in Scilly is very important to the survival of lichens, including many of the rare species. The invasion of heathland by gorse and the lack of grazing threaten the terricolous lichens. Heathland fires, if quick and controlled, can be a useful management tool where there is no stock grazing, and the reindeer moss *Cladonia portentosa* is one species that can take advantage of the open ground that results. Unfortunately many heathland fires are uncontrolled, and in the past some have burned for days, destroying the peat, exposing the underlying granite and completely killing all the lichens on some of the large heathland boulders. The lichens then take many years to return and recolonise the bare rocks. There are also some slow-growing lichens that occur on the bark of very old gorse bushes, so some gorse should always be retained.

Several interesting and uncommon native bryophytes occur in the Isles of Scilly, including two nationally rare species, the liverwort *Gongylanthus ericetorum*, which is found on coastal heathlands, and the moss *Tortula solmsii*, which occurs on several low cliffs. Among those that are Nationally Scarce are the liverworts *Cephaloziella turneri*, *Fossombronia crozalsii*, *F. maritima* and *Kurzia sylvatica* and the mosses *Bryum bornholmense*, *B. torquescens*, *Campylopus pilifer* and *Pleurochaete squarrosa*. *Ophioglossum* ferns also frequently grow in shallow soils among patches of moss.

Vertebrates

The heathland in Scilly is very poor in vertebrates and there are none that are only found there. With no reptiles (other than the recently introduced slow worm *Anguis fragilis*), few species of breeding land bird, and few mammals in Scilly, there are not many particularly associated with the heathland. Rabbits are usually widespread (at least when myxomatosis is not active) and when very abundant will graze small gorse plants into very characteristic, rabbit-height, topiary pyramids. The most typical bird is the stonechat *Saxicola torquata*, whose 'chacking' call from the top of a gorse bush or one of the rock carns can be heard at any time of the year (Fig. 123). Blackbirds are also very common on the downs, where they frequent the gorse thickets. During migration times it is worth

FIG 123. Stonechats frequently perch on a vantage point. (D. I. M. Wallace)

looking more carefully at blackbirds, especially if they have an unusual call, as
they might turn out to be ring ouzels *Turdus torquatus*. Also at migration times
the upright figure of a wheatear may be seen, as they often arrive in very large
numbers and may be seen all over the open heath. Rock pipits *Anthus petrosus*
can also be encountered on heathland areas, where some breed, although they
are more common around the coast. Dunnocks *Prunella modularis* and wrens
Troglodytes troglodytes are also widespread, especially where there is gorse.
Common terns and ringed plovers occasionally nest on the downs, where they
are very vulnerable to disturbance from people and dogs. Open patches of
grassland can attract waders and other birds as feeding areas, or as roosting and
preening places for gulls. These latter areas are very obvious by the hundreds
of feathers scattered around.

Invertebrates
Spend any time in heathland areas, especially on a sunny day, and it will be
apparent there is a huge range of invertebrate animals living there. Several
species of spiders are common on heathland and a good shake of a gorse bush
will reveal all manner of insects and arthropods. Some of the larger and obvious
beetles are frequently encountered on the Scilly heathland (Chapter 14). These
include the carnivorous green tiger beetles that in summer characteristically
fly across the top of the heather, crash to the ground and run very fast. Metallic
shining green rose chafers are most obvious when they too fly low, buzzing, over
the heather before crash-landing. Several butterflies are widespread, including

meadow brown and speckled wood *Pararge aegeria*. In Scilly the speckled wood is found along the edge of gorse thickets and in more open habitats than is usual on the mainland. Other butterflies that may found on heathland, especially in areas of grasses, include small copper *Lycaena phlaeas*, common blue and occasionally small heath *Coenonympha pamphilus*. In some years migrant clouded yellows may be seen flying fast across the heath, although they rarely stop and have no real affinity with the habitat. None of the typical heathland orthopterans found on the mainland occurs as yet in Scilly, but field grasshoppers *Chorthippus brunneus* are very common in the grassland edge of the downs.

Management of heathland: 'Waves of Heath'

Lowland heath is one of the most important habitats nationally, and there are many very good examples in Scilly. In 2003 a £233,000 grant by the Heritage Lottery Fund was made as part of a UK initiative 'Tomorrow's Heathland Heritage', run jointly by the Heritage Lottery Fund and English Nature, towards the restoration and management of maritime heathland in Scilly. The 'Waves of Heath' project has enabled the Isles of Scilly Wildlife Trust to embark on a five-year programme of practical and promotional work to restore and improve the heathland in Scilly both for nature conservation and for people. Much of the management work is directed towards clearing dense gorse scrub, controlling bracken and recreating former areas of heathland. This work is very intensive and the funding has enabled some machinery such as bracken rollers to be purchased.

Bracken has an unfortunate reputation that seems to bring out extreme attitudes in many land managers. This undeniably beautiful fern has few champions and seems by its detractors to be categorised as a sort of plant equivalent to the brown rat! Unfortunately, it has now overtaken such huge areas of land that it is important to reverse the spread. As there is no danger it is ever going to be completely eliminated on Scilly it can take fairly robust treatment. Discrete areas of bracken are important as a habitat and these should be recognised, for example where adder's-tongue ferns grow under its canopy. On Annet nesting Manx shearwaters and gull chicks may also receive some protection from bracken. Although spraying bracken with herbicides, especially ones based on the pteridocide asulam, can be effective if carried out systematically, in Scilly this would not generally be recommended because of the susceptibility of all ferns to the chemical. The alternative method of controlling bracken now being used in Scilly is cutting and rolling (crushing) the fronds several times in the growing season. This needs to continue for a number of years until the bracken is reduced to an acceptable level. Grazing the area afterwards would be helpful. Where bracken control has been continued for a number of years, for example along the northern side of St Martin's, the beneficial effects are already becoming apparent, with heather and other heathland species reappearing where the bracken has been 'knocked back'.

Burning is frequently used to control gorse, but where the heath has been burned too deeply into the shallow peat soils and exposed the granite it may take years to recover (there are occasional exceptions – for example on Samson, where heather appears to be growing on almost bare rock). The vegetation can show the effects of these 'hot' fires for many years, even decades. Ideally when burning is used the aim is for very quick burns that just flash across the vegetation without burning into the peat. By only burning small areas at a time the damaging effects of fire on invertebrates or lichens can be minimised. It is important to follow up burning with stock grazing if possible. Otherwise the bare ground may become invaded by weed species, or most likely by an explosive germination of gorse seedlings.

The dramatic waved heath of the most exposed headlands and hilltops is generally maintained by the natural pruning effect of the wind, and there seems very little evidence that it is necessary to carry out any active management on this kind of heathland. In Scilly stands of heather rarely get tall enough to need cutting.

The success of the experimental use of Shetland ponies to manage heathland on Bryher has been expanded with additional ponies and the introduction of a small breed of native cattle, ruby red Devons (Fig. 124; see also Fig. 208). Other

FIG 124. Shetland ponies have been introduced to graze heathland on Bryher. June 2002. (Rosemary Parslow)

222 · THE ISLES OF SCILLY

small breeds of cattle such as Dexters are being used on heathland sites elsewhere and might also be suitable in Scilly. Some of the rare British breeds of sheep might be considered, especially if there is ever a need to graze the larger uninhabited islands. Hardy breeds that shed their wool naturally would be ideal in such situations. With the changes in island farming that may have to occur over the coming decades, there may be increased stock on the islands and possibly more grazing of heathland and grasslands.

CHAPTER 11

Woodland and Wetland

Not so much as a shrubb, except Brambles, Furzes, Broom and Holly, and these never grew above four feet high. Nor is there in all these islands one Tree.

Robert Heath (1744)

WOODLAND

I N 1857 GEORGE ELIOT visited the Isles of Scilly with George Lewes, arriving on 26 March and staying until 11 May. She wrote that 'there is not a tree to be seen' (Lewes, 1860). In August 1868 the Dean of Canterbury, the Reverend H. Alford, also commented that 'in the whole Archipelago there is not a tree, that is, one which would pass for a tree on the mainland'. As has been noted earlier, there is now no true semi-natural ancient woodland on the Isles of Scilly. Photographs of the islands taken 150 years ago show stone hedges and a virtually treeless landscape (Fig. 125). Exceptions were the already planted windbreaks around the Abbey on Tresco and elm trees in Holy Vale on St Mary's. A photograph from the top terrace of the Tresco Abbey Gardens taken at the time of Augustus Smith's tenure shows the beginning of the tree cover he had planted to protect the gardens (King, 1985). Nothing of the woodland of prehistoric times seems to have survived, having long ago been cleared by the earlier inhabitants of the islands. Pollen evidence indicates the former presence of oak, hazel and birch (Dimbleby, 1977). Just a few oaks may be a link with this former woodland – in an area traditionally known as Tresco Wood. This area was possibly in the tithe that was cleared by the monks in the time of King John (Woodley, 1822). Even if it was, it has long since been planted with other trees.

FIG 125. Treeless nineteenth-century landscape at Higher Town, St Martin's. (Gibson collection)

Other indications that there may have been woodland there comes from the ground flora, which includes species that have strong associations with woodland, such as woodland speedwell *Veronica montana*, grey sedge *Carex divulsa* and wood sedge *Carex sylvatica* (Lousley, 1971). On Tresco dense planting has now produced a type of plantation woodland with a mixture of native plants and planted or escaped exotics. These areas are often home to bird species such as tits and goldcrests, although still lacking the resident woodpeckers or owls that would be expected in a woodland on the mainland.

Some time in the 1870s Cornishman Richard Lynch, Curator of Cambridge University Botanic Garden, had been to an area known as 'the Wilderness' next to the Valhalla at Tresco Abbey where there was 'a grove of alders, Cornish elms and sycamore', but there is no sign of this area any more. Lousley (1971) also comments on the rapid development of elm copses on the islands, which have produced a type of pastiche woodland with a ground flora of bluebells, three-cornered leek (three-cornered garlic) *Allium triquetum*, ivy *Hedera helix hibernica* and ferns under the elm canopy. Where the substrate is wetter, lady fern is abundant under the trees and lady's-smock (cuckooflower) *Cardamine pratensis* may be found occasionally. Also in wet habitats are copses of grey sallow (willow carr). These areas are quite distinctive; and are slowly invading the wet ground except where active management is keeping the trees in check. This type of woodland community is very close to the NVC community W1 (grey willow – marsh bedstraw woodland) although it does not include birch, oak or other tree species that are usually found in this type of plant community. On Scilly the typical wetland ground flora frequently includes interesting species; the huge tussock-sedges at Higher Moors are legendary (Fig. 126). These willow carr sites contain a large amount of dead wood and are a rich feeding ground for birds and invertebrates, attracting large numbers of migrant birds (and the accompanying birdwatchers) during migration seasons. At Lower Moors the willow carr encompasses a number of pools as well as the stream, so that wetland plants associated with the stream grow right through under the trees – yellow iris, fool's-water-cress and hemlock water-dropwort for example.

Holy Vale is an interesting combination of elm copse and willow carr (Fig. 127). The elm trees are among the tallest on the islands, growing in the most sheltered valley on St Mary's. The original trees were planted about 1650. By 1695 one of the trees had a trunk over three feet (90cm) in circumference (Turner, 1964). It was reported that there were fine trees growing there about 1800 (Woodley, 1822). There are still fine, large trees in Holy Vale, although in

FIG 126. Grey sallow, huge tussock-sedges and three-cornered leek grow beside the stream through Higher Moors. March 2005. (Rosemary Parslow)

FIG 127. Holy Vale nature trail, November 2002. (Rosemary Parslow)

2003 some were showing signs of stress, possibly due to the very dry summer. Many of the trees grow on a raised bank, possibly a former field boundary, where their roots are vulnerable to changes in the water table. Turner also commented that the same seventeenth-century manuscript describes how trees grew well on other places on the island until they reached the top of the protecting walls, when they stopped growing upwards and gained no more height. The Holywell stream flows through the valley, eventually making its way through Higher Moors to Porth Hellick and the sea. Beneath the sallows in the wettest areas is an understorey of yellow iris, hemlock water-dropwort, purple-loosestrife *Lythrum salicaria* and, in the stream, more than one species of water-starwort *Callitriche* spp. Frequently the surface of the water is covered in duckweed, both common duckweed *Lemna minor* and least duckweed *L. minuta* – the latter a recent arrival probably introduced by waterfowl. Further up the valley towards Longstone, away from the stream, the ground flora is growing in drier and shadier conditions. Here brambles and ferns are the typical species. This is one of the few places where soft shield-fern is found.

Although Scilly is not well wooded, there are lichens associated with trees, for example *Bacidia incompta*, found where there are wounds on mature elm trees, and the rare *Ramalina portuensis*, which is locally frequent on willows in small areas of carr woodland.

Shelterbelts

Shelterbelts are a relatively new type of habitat in Scilly. The first shelterbelts were probably elm, and when Sir William Hooker, who later became the first Director of Kew Gardens, visited Scilly in 1813 he commented on 'wretched plants of elm and tamarisk'. Elms would not have been ideal as shelterbelts and were superseded by conifers that were able to cope with the salt winds. The first Monterey pines were probably planted on Tresco in the 1850s during the 'reign' of Augustus Smith, as a result of an observation by his nephew Thomas Algernon Dorrien-Smith. After many trees had blown down in a storm, he was sailing up the channel to Tresco and saw one tree still standing, taking a bearing on it. He found it was a Monterey pine (Grigson, 1948, quoting Hunkin, 1947), and subsequently the Monterey pine was planted widely, including as shelterbelts on St Mary's. Small numbers of Monterey pine and Monterey cypress *Cupressus macrocarpa* were also planted on the other inhabited islands, where a few may still be seen.

Monterey pines remained very popular until about 1964, when lodgepole pine *Pinus contorta* began to be planted. The loss of a large number of mature Monterey pines in severe gales over previous years hastened the use of lodgepole pines and they are now gradually replacing the former species. Regrettably, the distinctive silhouette of the huge Monterey pines is becoming a rarity (though fortunately one or two farmers have begun growing Monterey pines again).

The shelterbelts are a curious habitat; the larger ones on St Mary's that skirt the northern edge of the island are quite extensive, and walking through them on the thick cushion of pine needles muffles all sound. There is very little growing under the shelterbelt, except where there is a break in the canopy or near the edge. Scattered red campion *Silene dioica*, wall pennywort (navelwort) *Umbilicus rupestris*, common cat's-ear and occasional ferns or fungi, sometimes a straggling bramble, are virtually the only plants you see here. The incredible silence also seems to extend to birds so that the twittering of a passing flock of tits seems quite disruptive.

More recent attempts have been made to establish broad-leaved trees. A mixed planting in a sheltered, wet field at Rose Hill, St Mary's, has been made with a mixture of native British trees. Most of these do not occur naturally in Scilly and it is too soon to know how they will cope with the conditions. On the north side of St Mary's another mixed planting has been made on the side of the hill. Where conifers have been planted on St Martin's these are thriving, but the broad-leaves planted in the same area are not doing so well.

WETLAND

There would have been more wetland in early Scilly, both along the stream valleys and possibly in the dune slacks that may then have existed. The remnants of 'peat' beds (more accurately minerogenic intertidal sediments containing varying amounts of organic matter) found on several beaches suggest that there were more extensive mires before the central plain between St Martin's and St Mary's was inundated (Thomas, 1985).

Anyone visiting Scilly in recent years will be well aware that water is a problem, especially potable water to support the population when it is inflated by visitors in the summer months. This has been somewhat mitigated by the establishment of a desalination plant near Mount Todden in 1992, after the catchment had been depleted by three years of low rainfall. Most guesthouses and hotels post small notices in their bathrooms warning visitors that water is scarce and needs to be carefully conserved. This is a particular problem on the off-islands. Probably most visitors do not realise quite how precious the water really is. When I first went to St Agnes in 1958, our water came from a storage tank that collected rainwater from the roof of the farm buildings. It had to be boiled and strained before it could be used. Most people at that time collected their water from rooftops: the Lighthouse Farm, for example, collected rainwater from the balcony around the top of the lighthouse. During later visits to St Agnes during the 1970s, water for the cottage where we stayed came from a well near the shore that was pumped on the high tide and frequently suffered from saltwater intrusion. On occasions the water was so brackish as to be almost undrinkable. There are a number of springs on the islands, but most run very slowly and are insufficient to sustain the requirements of modern households, and nobody now takes water from Big Pool on St Agnes as they did in the past (Woodley, 1822).

From the 1980s boreholes were drilled on St Agnes and other off-islands; these are shared between groups of households, who take turns to pump water to refill the storage tanks. This may have produced sufficient water to sustain the resident population of the islands, but at times was insufficient for the additional requirements of summer visitors. Rainwater collected from roofs is now not considered acceptable for drinking water due to contamination from droppings of gulls and starlings. A further complication was the discovery that the aquifer under the islands contained traces of agricultural chemicals from the heavy pesticide regime formerly operated in the bulb fields. As a precaution the local children had to be given bottled water. Although the islanders now have better systems for filtering and sterilising water, more boreholes were drilled in 2004 on St Agnes to tap into the aquifer and increase the amount of available water. It is not known whether there are still residues of agricultural chemicals in the aquifers. The possibility of using desalination to increase the water supply, as already happens on St Mary's, may have to be considered on the off-islands in future. Currently half the water used on St Agnes comes from boreholes and half from rainwater. On such tiny land areas there are concerns that increasing the number of boreholes may result in saltwater intrusion or contamination from cesspits. Even the use of seawater-flushing lavatories is no longer acceptable practice, as the untreated waste goes straight into the sea near bathing beaches.

The need for a water supply for the human population has had an effect on the important wetland sites. This is most obviously seen in the depletion of the stream at Lower Moors on St Mary's and the consequential drying out of the marshes. Water from both Lower and Higher Moors is extracted for the public water supply, although recently water derived from desalinated sea water has reduced the dependence on water from the Moors. The Higher Moors stream is the only one of any size on the islands. It rises at the top of Holy Vale and winds its way down through the nature trail and across Higher Moors to flow into Porth Hellick Bay. Some of the other 'streams' on St Mary's, Watermill Stream for example, now exist only as roadside ditches. Salakee Stream was described by Lousley as 'a malodorous ditch', which is still an apt description, as it flows through the farmyard before descending the hill to where the large fronds of the alien fern *Blechnum cordatum* grow on the edge of the ditch. Unfortunately, in recent years the main ditch has dried up, so it no longer flows into a small field on the farm that was formerly very waterlogged. This has resulted in the probable loss of the colony of wetland plants that grew there both beside the ditch and on the cattle-poached mud; these included the rare Cornish moneywort *Sibthorpia europaea* and ivy-leaved crowfoot *Ranunculus hederaceus*. Cornish moneywort (Fig. 128) is now found only along the side of the Watermill Stream; at one time it also grew along wet roadside gutters and other ditches, but was lost from most of these when the roads were asphalted (Lousley, 1971).

On the uninhabited islands fresh water is found only in a few pools, springs and coastal seepages. The springs and freshwater pools were essential for the establishment of the early habitations and would have been an important factor in the ability of the now uninhabited islands to sustain populations in the past. There are wells still on Samson, Teän and St Helen's, as well as pools both there and on other uninhabited islands. Some of the wells could have at least supported any stock put out to graze there for the summer.

FIG 128. Cornish moneywort was once found in roadside ditches and along streamsides on St Mary's but is now very rare. (Alma Hathway)

Peatlands

The deep valley mire beteen Holy Vale and Porth Hellick, which provided peat for fuel for the islanders, appears to have been cut some time in the medieval to Tudor period. This peat, unlike the turf 'peat' cut on heathland, is more typical peat formed under wet, acidic conditions. Peat was also cut on Tresco, resulting in what is now the Great Pool, and remains of former peat baulks and trenches on Lower Moors also confirm that this area was extracted and exhausted in the past. From pollen work it has also been confirmed that a freshwater lagoon existed at Lower Moors, as is also shown in a map of 1585, and similarly a freshwater pool at Higher Moors (Scaife, 2006). In more recent times these moors have become drier and would probably have been grazed by cattle, as is evidenced by traces of the former field boundaries.

Lousley (1971) describes a small, very acid boggy area at the southernmost point of the Holy Vale Nature Trail. Although only a few square metres in extent, it supported common cottongrass *Eriophorum angustifolium*, as well as marsh St John's-wort *Hypericum elodes*, bog pimpernel *Anagallis tenella*, marsh willowherb *Epilobium palustre* and other characteristic plants. The area is now under sallows and the acid flora has disappeared. Another area with cottongrass on Higher Moors also appears to have been lost more recently, possibly through drying of the marsh.

Freshwater and brackish pools

Nowhere in Scilly is far from the sea. At any time, but especially during storms, salt spray gets blown into any pools around the coasts. Other pools have a direct link with the sea either through a leat or by percolation through the dune bank. How brackish an individual pool is fluctuates with conditions such as proximity to the sea (several pools have sluices that can be closed to prevent sea water backing up into them) and the force and direction of gales. Many of the smallest pools are seasonal, and even some of the largest may dry up completely in drought conditions. Flooding caused by heavy rain or from high seas can cause pools to overflow and inundate the surrounding meadow and even adjoining farmland. Coastal reinforcements have reduced the effect of the sea at places like Porth Killier on St Agnes, but it is not unusual to see extensive winter flooding of low-lying meadows around pools such as on St Martin's. On heathland, cart ruts and depressions over the granite platform often fill up with rainwater, and these often support wetland species: for example lesser spearwort, toad rush, marsh pennywort and chaffweed, which will persist even when the temporary pools have dried up. As well as plants, the pools may also have a transient population of invertebrates, water beetles for example. Another kind of temporary pool found on the coastal edge of the islands is formed at the base of large granite boulders. Examples of these pools are to be found on Horse Point, St Agnes, and some of the headlands on St Mary's where some have been colonised by sea-milkwort. Closer to the shore and salt spray they may have a flora of green filamentous algae.

Great Pool, Bryher, is the only true brackish lagoon in Scilly. It is linked to the sea by a leat through the bank at Popplestone Bay that can be closed by a sluice gate (Fig. 129). It was called the New Pool in 1652 (Pounds, 1984) but

FIG 129. Bryher Great Pool is the only true saline lagoon in Scilly, connected to the sea via a leat. March 2005. (Rosemary Parslow)

whether it formed naturally when a sand bar formed across a bay or was partly man-made is not known. There may also be some percolation of sea water into the pool through the bank at high tide. For most of the time the water has the same salinity as sea water and can therefore support truly marine species. The inhabitants of the pool are ones that can cope with the very stressful conditions concomitant upon lagoons with such variable salinity, temperature and pH (Bamber *et al.*, 2001). Among the animals that are found in the pool are large numbers of shore crabs, fish – including sand gobies and grey mullet – chameleon prawns, and several species of worms, including a small ragworm, and lugworms that at times are so abundant the worm-casts cover the bottom of the pool. The brackish water sand-shrimp *Gammarus chevreuxi* has also been recorded in the past (Bamber & Barnes, in Barne *et al.*, 1996). Grey mullet frequently become landlocked in the pool for several weeks, their shoals making high-speed manoeuvres through the shallow water until released by the next spring tide. The fluctuating conditions can also cause the beaked tasselweed in the pool to form dense mats for a while. Around the shoreline is a narrow fringe of plants that include several salt-marsh species, lesser sea-spurrey *Spergularia marina*, rock sea-spurrey, sea-milkwort, common saltmarsh-grass *Puccinellia maritima* and saltmarsh rush. These species continue along the sides of the leat, where lesser sea-spurrey sometimes also grows on the sand at the bottom, frequently overlooked because the flowers close up in the afternoon. Due to the salinity of the pool no dragonflies are resident, and although many birds visit the pool for feeding and bathing, only a few such as moorhen are resident.

Bryher's Little Pool is a very small, figure-of-eight-shaped pool in the marshy area near Great Pool. Recently it had been planted with a white water-lily *Nymphaea* sp. and bulrush, presumably in an attempt to make it more attractive. In 2004 these plants were removed and hopefully the pool will recover naturally and the former flora of common spike-rush, lesser marshwort *Apium inudatum*, marsh pennywort and lesser spearwort will return.

Almost circular in shape, Big Pool on St Agnes is in the north of the island surrounded by a low-lying meadow; in the past the sea frequently inundated the whole area. It is probable the pool was man-made but it has been in existence since the eighteenth century (Borlase, 1756). Over the past fifty years improved sea defences around the bays of Periglis and Porth Coose, and most recently a sea wall around Porth Killier, have kept the sea at bay, but the area is still vulnerable to storm surges and the continuing and fluctuating salinity of the pool indicates a link to the sea through groundwater fluctuations (Foster, 2006). A sluice with a non-returnable valve drains the pool into Periglis, but prevents seawater incursion at high tide. Big Pool still floods in the winter or after periods of heavy rain, so there are concentric rings of vegetation expanding out from the pool margins. These bands of vegetation show up in the browns of sea club-rush and saltmarsh rush, with greens of marsh pennywort and grasses and the green, white and yellow of hairy buttercup and chamomile. Lesser spearwort is growing in a spreading patch among the sea club-rush, having arrived a few years ago, presumably spread by birds from one of the wetland areas on St Mary's. At times the pool is full of beaked tasselweed and on other occasions fennel-leaved pondweed may dominate, plants that are superficially very similar in appearance and can tolerate brackish conditions. The pool has a resident population of coot *Fulica atra*, moorhen and mallard, and frequently has visiting gulls, other ducks and occasional rarities, especially crakes and rails. Common darter dragonflies and blue-tailed damselflies breed in the pool.

Nearby on St Agnes is the Little Pool, which is usually hardly large enough to merit a name, but on one occasion contained enough water for grey phalaropes *Phalaropus fulicarius* to swim there (K. H. Hyatt, *in litt.*). Otherwise Little Pool stays wet most years and provides a feeding area for snipe *Gallinago gallinago* and other birds. It is also surrounded by sea club-rush, saltmarsh rush and creeping bent; the latter in some years may completely invade the pool. The damp grass around the pool is full of silverweed, chamomile and clovers, especially subterranean clover.

On St Martin's there is a small man-made pool in the corner of Pool Green, the meadow just behind the quay at Higher Town that serves as a cricket pitch and a place for laying out fishing nets. The pool is sometimes covered in a carpet of white and gold brackish water-crowfoot. At times there may be other aquatic plants, fennel-leaved pondweed and one of the starworts, for example. It is not clear whether these plants are there all the time and reappear from time to time from buried seed, or whether fresh material is introduced by water birds. This pool is also always a focus for birdwatchers, as it frequently attracts migrants.

Also on St Martin's there are other small pools, most of limited interest. Near Turfy Hill on the northern edge of the island, among heathland, is a small, bleak pool at the oppressively named Coldwind Pit with floating mats of bulbous rush, plus common spike-rush and a fringe of marsh pennywort.

Similar small pools are found all over the islands, but usually they support little in the way of vegetation and may dry out completely in summer. On Northwethel is a pool with a clear 'drawdown zone' sometimes rimmed by fringes of red goosefoot and sea-milkwort. At Southward Well on Samson is a similar pool with lesser skullcap, docks and common spike-rush. The species composition of these pools can also vary from year to year. Many can at times become overgrown with dense vegetation – but apparently usually recover, possibly due to grazing by rabbits or the effects of drought.

Tresco has two very large water-bodies (Fig. 130). Great Pool is a kilometre-long lake that was the site of the peat-filled valley that cut through the island in prehistoric times (Thomas, 1985). Abbey Pool is smaller, roughly circular, and separated from the Great Pool by a roadway and from the heliport by heathland and mown grassland. Botanically Abbey Pool is the richer lake, with a fluctuating edge of silty sand around the perimeter that sometimes extends for many metres in drought years. On other occasions, after heavy rain, the water overflows into surrounding grassland. This 'drawdown zone' supports a rich flora of higher plants and at times one of the stoneworts *Chara globularis* var. *fragilis* has been recorded growing both on the mud and in shallow water. This plant community appears to be unique in Scilly. Among the species found here are several that are uncommon in the islands: water-purslane *Lythrum portula*, shoreweed *Littorella uniflora*, sea-milkwort, marsh pennywort, chaffweed, bog pimpernel, lady's-smock, allseed *Radiola linoides*, brookweed, six-stamened waterwort and a very tiny form of lesser spearwort. In drought years the whole surface of the mud will be coloured red by the waterwort. Among the other aquatic species in the pool are fluctuating communities of beaked tasselweed and fennel-leaved pondweed. Great Pool also has a narrow muddy edge with some of the same species, but it is

FIG 130. Great and Abbey Pools and the plantations around Tresco Abbey. (Rosemary Parslow)

FIG 131. Porth Hellick Pool, Higher Moors nature reserve, seen from the hide. August 2006. (Rosemary Parslow)

usually relatively narrow, much less species-rich and backs onto the broad band of reeds that continue around the margin of the lake. The reedbeds in one place have grown almost right across the lake. Beaked tasselweed, pedunculate water-starwort *Callitriche brutia* and fennel-leaved pondweed are some of the common aquatic plants in the lake, sometimes getting washed up after storms. At its northwestern end the lake is cut off from the sea by a narrow strip of land containing some of the buildings of the Abbey Farm and a row of time-share cottages. The southeast extremity is protected from the sea at Pentle Bay by a broad belt of dunes. Although Great Pool is essentially fresh water, there does seem to be some slight saline influence at times, as evidenced by the aquatic species above; there is a link with the sea through a ditch and sluice near Abbey Farm.

There are a number of pools, ponds and wet habitats on St Mary's. The largest area of open water is Porth Hellick Pool in the Higher Moors nature reserve (Fig. 131). The pool is about two hectares in extent and is surrounded by mire habitats. A leat controlled by a sluice connects the pool to the sea in Porth Hellick Bay, and fish occasionally enter the pool. Usually freshwater, as with most of the larger lakes in Scilly there is occasional saltwater intrusion, so at times the water can be slightly brackish. Surrounding the pool is a wide fringe of reeds and, along the muddy edges, clumps of sea club-rush and sea rush.

At the top of Watermill Lane are two small, shallow pools known as Argy Moor that flow into Watermill Stream. Lousley (1971) described them as the best examples of non-brackish pools, with a plant population of brackish water-crowfoot, water-cress, lesser marshwort, small sweet-grass *Glyceria declinata* and common duckweed. Sadly, the ponds are now very eutrophic due to the large numbers of semi-domestic ducks that occupy them and none of the former marginal plants survives, other than some soft rush. Just on the edge of the road behind Porthloo is another small duck pond. This, too, had nature conservation interest in former years, but is now largely given over to a collection of exotic ducks and a few moorhens. Behind the pool is a wet grassland field and a small reedbed managed by the Wildlife Trust. Another pool, Shooter's Pool on the edge of Lower Moors nature reserve, was reprofiled and extended by the Bird Group to form a birdwatching scrape. Lesser water plantain formerly grew here, but only lesser spearwort, bog pondweed *Potamogeton polygonifolius* and creeping forget-me-not *Myosotis secunda* have so far recolonised the scrape.

Reedbeds and mires

Most of the reedbeds in Scilly are typical reedswamp communities dominated by common reed, such as those found around Tresco Great Pool and at Higher Moors on St Mary's. These areas formerly contained deep peat deposits that were extracted several hundred years ago, leaving open water, willow carr and marshland (Scaife, 1984, 2006). The reedbeds around Tresco Great Pool are rather different from those on St Mary's, as they mainly form a fringe around the pool edge. They have an understorey of herbaceous plants under the reed stems, mostly lesser spearwort, royal fern, balm-leaved figwort and other plants. On Higher Moors and especially on Lower Moors the reedbeds are a mosaic of reeds and rushes that in places give way to marshy areas dominated by sea rush (Fig. 132). The latter in Scilly is apparently all the form var. *atlanticus* with very lax stems and a shorter lower bract, as described by Lousley (1971). It does seem to be significantly different from the mainland form, especially in autumn when the stems have gone yellowish-brown. In the early nineteenth century Lower Moors was described as being low and marshy, overgrown with reeds, and the marsh was liable to flood with sea water at spring tides so that a drain had to be dug 'to carry off the water but needs keeping clear' (Woodley, 1822). The situation has not changed very much since then, although a sluice has been built in the drain and the flooding with sea water occurs less frequently. As then, 'fine mullets and eels' can also be seen there in summer. Extraction for the water supply and the development of willow carr has lowered the water table.

FIG 132. The reedbed on Higher Moors, St Mary's, is an intimate mix of reed and sea rush. May 2003. (Rosemary Parslow)

Both at Lower and Higher Moors there is now a dense, tangled understorey of herbaceous plants growing under the reed/sea rush swamp. Lesser spearwort, purple-loosestrife, royal fern, tussock-sedge, hemlock water-dropwort, greater bird's-foot-trefoil *Lotus pedunculatus* are often common, with sprawlers such as the pink-striped form of hedge bindweed *Calystegia sepium roseata*, marsh bedstraw *Galium palustre* and woody nightshade prominent in some places, and marsh pennywort, toad rush, tubular water-dropwort, tussock-sedge, many-stalked spike-rush, lesser marshwort and starworts growing in wet hollows at ground level. More local and unusual species that occur in these habitats include yellow loosestrife *Lysimachia vulgaris* in the willow carr areas of Lower Moors, from where it is spreading into the reedbed, and southern marsh-orchid *Dactylorhiza praetermissa* in both the St Mary's marshes.

CHAPTER 12

Cultivated Habitats – Bulb Fields and Arable Plants

Long live the weeds and the wilderness.

Gerald Manley Hopkins

V ISITORS TO THE Isles of Scilly in spring and early summer will find the small bulb fields full of colour, not only from cultivated plants but also from wild flowers, the arable field plants or 'weeds'. Anywhere there is some open soil there will be the wild colonists of disturbed ground, but among the rarest and most interesting species are those most often associated with the bulb fields. Arriving by air in the early months of the year

FIG 133. Unpicked narcissus in full flower in winter, February 2004. (Rosemary Parslow)

the visitor will see white and bright yellow fields of narcissus (Fig. 133), while later in the spring the yellow will be corn marigolds among the crops. And as the airport bus whisks passengers down the narrow lanes into town they will get tantalising glimpses of fields fringed by three-cornered leek and Bermuda-buttercup *Oxalis pes-caprae*. The typical arable landscape of the Scilly flower farms consists of winter narcissus in small fields, surrounded by tall evergreen hedges – though recently there has been a move away from growing bulbs, so some fields are now being used for the growing of pinks and other summer flowers, as well as other crops such as vegetables. Before the arrival of bulb farming there was an earlier arable landscape of fields and low stone hedges.

EARLY ARABLE WEEDS

While there is evidence of arable cultivation at least as far back as the Bronze Age, not much is know about the weed flora of that time. A large number of seeds found at West Porth, Samson, in the post-occupation layers of a Late Bronze Age/Early Iron Age hut, are of great interest as they were from common arable plants, giving a tantalising glimpse of the weeds then common (Ratcliffe & Straker, 1996). Unfortunately there are few records or remains of plants from later finds to give more than a hint of the wild flora of arable fields. Some of the typical arable plants we now associate with bulb fields, buttercups and fumitories for example, have apparently left no traces of their existence. But we do not know if this is because they were not in Scilly then, or because they were mostly post-Medieval arrivals, or perhaps more simply because their pollen or seeds just have not survived. A few weed seeds from a midden on Teän dated between the third and sixth century AD (Late Roman to Early Medieval) were all common species, as were other finds from later remains from St Martin's. Two weed species that were identified, corn spurrey from a Bronze Age deposit and corn marigold from occupation debris in the Civil War Battery at Steval Point on the Garrison, St Mary's, are both found as arable weeds on the islands today (Fig. 134). Corn marigold is not a native of Britain but an archaeotype, a plant that became naturalised prior to AD 1500; it has been known in Britain from the Iron Age (Preston *et al.*, 2002).

When Cosmo III, Grand Duke of Tuscany, visited the Isles of Scilly in 1669, and William Borlase in 1756, they described the arable crops grown at the time, but not in much detail, and neither made reference to arable weeds. There are no references to arable weeds either in the account of his visit to Scilly by Robert Heath (1750). So it just has to be assumed that weeds growing with

FIG 134. Corn marigolds have been known in Scilly since the Middle Ages. (Rosemary Parslow)

the crops included species introduced over the years from outside the islands.

Early trade, from the Bronze Age onwards, between Scilly and the Mediterranean as well as further afield, may account for the presence of some species, especially those of more southern distribution that are now found in the islands. During the nineteenth century too, there was considerable trade from Scilly to the Mediterranean, exporting surplus produce, mostly potatoes, and returning with cargoes of fruit – ideal for introducing wild seeds. This trade gave an impetus to both agriculture and shipbuilding in Scilly; in 1835 the Road (just off St Mary's) was described as full of merchantmen, in for repairs or supplies (Mothersole, 1910). All this coming and going between Scilly, the mainland and further abroad could have enabled plant and other material to be introduced accidentally or even deliberately throughout the years, a process that is still continuing today.

THE ORIGINS OF THE WEED FLORA OF
ARABLE FIELDS

The domestication of wild plants and animals in the Near East gradually spread around the Mediterranean and eventually into northern and northwestern Europe including Britain. The societies would have been mainly hunter–gatherers and would have added a few cereals, legumes and livestock as minor additions to their way of life (Smith, 1995). Over time they would gradually have developed their own version of agriculture suitable to their region and circumstances. It can be seen that many wild plants would have 'hitched a ride' with cultivated species, either as contaminants of crop seeds or carried among goods. Trade routes through the Mediterranean and the Atlantic coast of Europe provided a continual source of seeds over many centuries, some of which would have found the Isles of Scilly an ideal venue, both in habitats and especially in climate. Many plants that are found in Scilly are also common around the Mediterranean and the Iberian peninsula.

Some evidence of the species of plants that were present in Scilly in the past can be gleaned from the plant remains and pollen that are derived from archaeological sites (Table 3). The final column in the table adds present-day data to the information published by Ratcliffe and Straker (1996)

THE START OF THE FLOWER INDUSTRY

In 1879 or thereabouts (the date is disputed), an enterprising gentleman reputed to be William Trevellick (but it might equally have been Mr Moyle or Mr Mumford, as there are several versions of the story) sent a few bunches of cut Soleil d'Or narcissus to Covent Garden in his wife's hatbox. The flowers are said to have sold for 7 shillings and 6 pence. He received 15s for the next consignment, 30s for a third and then £3 for a fourth box – and so started the cut-flower industry (Vyvyan, 1953). Those first narcissi sent to Covent Garden would have been picked from the semi-wild flowers which were then to be found on St Mary's and Tresco. Some had originated from bulbs dug up around the islands, such as those that had been found growing in the ruins of the Abbey on Tresco, where they are believed to have resulted from ones planted by the monks. Others were said to have been found flowering in the moat of Star Castle on St Mary's, originating from bulbs given to the wife of the Governor, who boiled some and, finding them inedible, flung them all into the moat (Kay, 1956).

TABLE 3. Arable weed species recorded from archaeological sites in Scilly. (Based on Ratcliffe & Straker, 1996)

SPECIES		BRONZE AGE
Brassica sp.	mustard etc.	✓
Raphanus raphanistrum/maritimus	wild or sea radish	✓
Hypericum sp.	St John's-wort	✓
Cerastium sp.	chickweed	✓
Stellaria media group	chickweed	✓
Stellaria cf. *pallida*	lesser chickweed	✓
Spergula arvensis	corn spurrey	✓
Montia sp.	blinks	✓
Chenopodium album	fat-hen	✓
Atriplex sp.	orache	✓
Malva sp.	mallow	✓
Vicia/Lathyrus sp.	vetch/tare	✓
Vicia/Pisum sp.	vetch/pea	
Trifolium sp.	clovers	✓
Trifolium/Medicago sp.	clover/medick	✓
Potentilla erecta	tormentil	✓
Potentilla sp.	tormentil	
Polygonum aviculare group	knotgrass	✓
Polygonum lapathifolium	pale persicaria	✓
Fallopia convolvulus	black bindweed	✓
Rumex acetosella group	sheep's sorrel	✓
Rumex sp.	sorrel	✓
Urtica urens	small nettle	✓
Urtica dioica	stinging nettle	✓
Plantago lanceolata	ribwort plantain	
Inula cf. *conyza*	ploughman's spikenard	✓
cf. *Anthemis cotula*	stinking mayweed	
Chrysanthemum segetum	corn marigold	
Cirsium/Carduus sp.	thistle	
Juncus sp.	rush(es)	✓
Bromus hordeaceus/secalina	lopgrass/rye brome	✓
Bromus sp.	brome	✓
Phleum sp.	cat's-tail grass	✓

IRON AGE – ROMANO-BRITISH	ROMANO-BRITISH – MEDIEVAL	POST-MEDIEVAL	PRESENT STATUS
			Several crop species or charlock still present as arable weeds
✓			Both still present, one as a weed, the other coastal
			H. humifusum occasional in arable fields
			Common arable weed
			Common arable weed
			Mostly dunes
✓			Common arable weed
✓			Occasional arable fields
✓			Arable fields etc
			Arable fields etc
			Arable fields
✓	✓		Arable fields
		✓	Arable fields
		✓	Arable fields
✓			Arable fields
			Occasional fields
		✓	Possible fields
✓	✓		Arable fields
			Fields and damp areas
			Arable fields
			Heaths and fields
✓			Often fields
			Arable fields
			Fields/disturbed ground
✓			Still present
			Not known in Scilly today
		✓	Abundant in arable fields
		✓	Disturbed ground
			Some species found in arable fields
			Several species found in arable fields
	✓		Several species found in arable fields
			Infrequent

Collecting bulbs soon became all the rage. Eight varieties were described by Thomas Algernon Dorrien-Smith as found in the islands in 1865: '*Telamonius plenus, Odorus major* (Campernelli), *Tazetta ochroleucus* (Scilly White), *Tazetta aureus* (Grand Soleil d'Or), *Tazetta* Grand Monarque (two vars.), *Biflorus poeticus* fl.pl. and *Poeticus recurvus*.' Some of those varieties, or their descendants, are still grown. Then in 1885 a William Trevithick (who was almost certainly the same William Trevellick) wrote to the *Gardener's Chronicle* listing about forty *Narcissus* varieties then being grown on St Mary's. He also commented that the 'natives' White and Grand Monarque were supposed to have been on the island for 200 or 300 years. Some varieties, Sols (Soleil d'Or) from Morocco and Algeria, Scilly Whites from Vigo, Spain, were said to have first been brought to the islands by sailors, and given by them to soldiers and farmers in the pubs (Vyvyan, 1953). Thomas Algernon Dorrien-Smith started growing narcissus on a large scale and other farmers soon followed his example (Nelhams, 2000). In 1881 he visited Holland, Belgium and the Channel Islands to study the methods used by their bulb-growers and to buy new varieties. The great advantage that Scilly had over all these other countries was that the climate enabled the flowers to be produced a month earlier than anywhere else (King, 1985). By 1886 when the first Flower Show was held on St Mary's, Thomas Algernon showed more than 160 varieties of narcissus. When a party from the Penzance Natural History and Antiquarian Society went to Scilly in August 1889 they heard that Mr T. A. Dorrien-Smith had nearly 'ten acres of land in narcissus alone, and more than £10,000 a year came to the islands from the sale of flowers'.

When new varieties of bulbs were introduced from Holland the farmers of Scilly soon adopted them. In a very short time the flower industry had become a major part of the local economy. Trials of many new varieties resulted in some of these becoming popular and replacing some older varieties. Despite this many of the original narcissus, Soleil d'Or, Paper White and Pheasant's Eye, remained the mainstay of the trade. For many years the Scillonians relied on their field-grown flowers being produced earlier than those from other sources. Now the Scillonian farmers are unfortunately facing competition from flowers grown cheaper elsewhere, and the production of scented narcissus is no longer the major industry in Scilly.

ARABLE PLANTS OF THE BULB FIELDS

From its early beginnings bulb and daffodil farming grew quickly, until by the end of the nineteenth century it was the mainstay of the island economy.

Alongside the cultivated bulbs there has arisen a particular community of wild plants: the bulb-field weeds. Many of the plants that make up the weed flora of arable fields in Scilly are species that are now uncommon on the mainland. Others are species that can only survive in the mild, humid, Scillonian climate with its relatively frost-free winters. Many are winter annuals, often species of a Lusitanian and Mediterranean distribution that germinate in late summer/ autumn, growing throughout the winter to flower early in the year so that they shed their seeds just before the fields are cultivated. Another group of plants found in the bulb fields are alien plants, introduced species that have also found the conditions hospitable. Some plants were originally cultivated varieties, such as whistling jacks gladiolus, that after a time have fallen out of favour but still persist as arable weeds. Usually these grow from bulbs or corms, so are not easy to get rid of. A further group of plants have invaded the bulb fields from other, more natural habitats, from heathland or dune grassland for example, having also found the sandy bulb fields to their liking.

Even when the narcissus or other bulbs are not flowering (and they are generally picked green), the fields can be remarkably colourful (Fig. 135). Some will be all golden with corn marigolds, while around others are radiating

FIG 135. Field with fumitory, corn marigold and other arable species, June 2005. (Rosemary Parslow)

bands of the yellow and white of Bermuda-buttercup and three-cornered leek. Fumitories are smoky pink, and there can be magenta spears of the whistling jacks. Or a field will be just a riot of pink, white and yellow from all the different buttercups, spurreys, mallows and other flowers, with sometimes a touch of blue or red from speedwell or scarlet pimpernel.

Cultivation of bulb fields

When flower farming was at its zenith in the 1950s and 1960s, the weed flora flourished alongside the crop, germinating in autumn, growing throughout winter to flower in spring and early summer and seeding before the bulb fields were cultivated. After flowering the bulbs were left in the ground for the foliage to die back, then the haulms were removed by burning over the fields, often using straw, hay or any cut material to produce a quick hot fire which also had the effect of bringing forward the flowering time of the Soleil d'Or bulbs. When straw became too expensive in the 1960s and 1970s the fields were burned over by tractor-mounted propane burners, which was found to be equally effective, especially if several passes were made. This effectively cleaned the field, including the weeds, and left bare ground, the smoke apparently acting as a growth promoter due to its ethylene content (Tompsett, 1997). It has been suggested that some arable weeds respond positively to burning by germinating quickly, but in any case the bare ground, whether or not the bulbs were lifted and the ground cultivated, provided an excellent medium for germination. The present treatment for the bulb fields involves covering the fields with clear polythene and forcing smoke underneath. These methods are very effective in the production of the two traditional and most popular *Tazetta* narcissus varieties, Soleil d'Or and Paper White.

The advent of a range of agricultural chemicals to protect the crops had the effect of reducing some weed species; some buttercups, for example, appear to be particularly vulnerable to herbicides. Other species such as Bermuda-buttercup (an *Oxalis* despite its name) continued to flourish, despite the use of pesticides, as cultivation spreads the small bulbils through the soil. More recently the decline in the cut-flower trade may have reduced the amount of chemical used, it being no longer cost-effective to use so much expensive herbicide. But some of the herbicides being used are persistent in the soil and it is not known what effect this has on the weed flora.

Other arable fields

Some farmers have gone over to bulb production rather than cut flowers, or to alternative cut flowers such as pinks, or have even put some fields down to grass.

A few farms have also always grown other bulb crops, for example belladonna lilies *Amaryllis belladonna*, *Agapanthus*, *Sparaxis grandiflora*, *Ixia campanulata* and *I. paniculata*. Even though bulb fields have attracted most interest, other arable crops are grown in Scilly and some, such as early potatoes, have at one time been very important. These fields also have a weed flora – but due to differences in cultivation often have a slightly different suite of species to those of the bulb fields. Some of the larger arable fields, for example some on St Mary's, usually have a more typical 'mainland' type of weed flora with fat-hen *Chenopodium album*, black bindweed, small nettle, scentless mayweed *Tripleurospermum inodorum* and corn spurrey. Other fields are now growing vegetables, salads, soft fruit and other crops.

The importance of arable weed communities has only gained recognition since it was realised so many of the common cornfield plants were disappearing from the landscape in the mid twentieth century (Wilson & King, 2003). The plant communities found in disturbed habitats are addressed in the final volume of *British Plant Communities* (Rodwell, 2000), and two of the classifications are particularly associated with Scilly. One, ov2 (lesser quaking-grass – small-flowered catchfly community), only occurs in Scilly and ov6 (sticky mouse-ear – common ramping-fumitory) is restricted to Scilly and the extreme southwest of Cornwall. Both these rare plant communities are associated with the bulb fields (see Appendix).

A group of plants associated with arable fields that are generally overlooked are bryophytes, the mosses and liverworts that grow between the crop and especially on bare headlands. *Sphaerocarpus michelii* and *S. exanus* are rare thalloid liverworts that occur in Scilly and appear to be dispersed by agricultural practices. The liverwort *Riccia crystallina* and the mosses *Chenia leptophylla* and *Bryum valparaisense* are both rare species that are also best looked for in arable fields (Preston & Finch, 2006).

HEDGES AND WINDBREAKS

The stone hedges on the Isles of Scilly in some cases are of great antiquity. Similar stone field boundaries are now under the sea, where they can be seen at spring low tides – especially off Tresco and Samson. Scillonian stone hedges can be of several types: some are similar to Cornish hedges, with double granite walls filled with a soil core, which can be up to a metre or more in width; others are single lines of dry stone walling without the soil infill. Both types of hedges are common field boundaries, but an inherent lack of stability in the drystone walls means they do not stand up well to people climbing over them, as some of the birdwatchers have found out in the past!

Where the hedges have earth infill and tops there is invariably a close covering of vegetation. Many of these hedges are important as refugia for plants, including some of the most interesting arable species, especially western ramping-fumitory (on St Mary's) and similar scramblers. Further into the open countryside, for example towards the north of St Mary's, the hedge tops and sides have rich growths of more heathland plants, such as sheep's-bit *Jasione montana*, bell heather, restharrow *Ononis repens*, sheep's sorrel and common bird's-foot. Greater quaking-grass grows on the top of walls on St Martin's and elsewhere. Other hedges have rich displays of ferns (Fig. 136), bird's-foot-trefoil, wall pennywort and rock sea-spurrey. As Lousley found, the granite hedges were a place where many of the plants 'reproducing from bulbs ... found sanctuary while the fields were being cleaned'. Frequently there are still Bermuda-buttercup, three-cornered leek and discarded narcissus growing in or at the base of the hedge.

The Garrison walls and similar stone structures are different from the stone 'hedges', having no soil core, being built from granite masonry, often with mortar

FIG 136. Lanceolate spleenwort is a fern with a southwestern distribution in Britain, and is a feature of Scillonian stone walls, especially on St Mary's and St Agnes. (Rosemary Parslow)

between the blocks. They do, however share some features. The mortar or cracks between the granite blocks support several species of ferns, plants such as ivy-leaved toadflax *Cymbalaria muralis*, some of the unusual clovers, both common and Danish scurvygrasses and wall pennywort. The top of the Garrison walls also has a shallow layer of turf growing on a thin substrate of broken granite and soil. This arid strip is a rich mixture of grasses, tiny dicotyledons and, where the turf is deeper, autumn lady's-tresses, small-flowered catchfly and other arable plants. These latter were possibly accidentally introduced when there was an attempt to grow grass on the wall top.

On the inhabited islands the kaleidoscope patchwork of colours within the tiny fields gives the impression of a foreign landscape, quite at odds with the surrounding windswept heathland and granite headlands. With their little coffered bulb fields or 'squares', the inhabited islands have a character, an identity so established, it is difficult to remember that this kind of farming is a recent practice. Surveys carried out when Augustus Smith was Lord Proprietor of the islands (1834–72) showed the field pattern of all the tiny landholdings of the times, these having resulted from the tradition of dividing farm holdings up between all the succeeding sons. It was this system of small strips and plots that was to some extent incorporated into the present pattern of small bulb fields.

A century earlier, Borlase (1756) had already commented on the need to plant more shelter if the crops were going to amount to much:

and whatever rises not above their Hedges do very well; and even these would do better, if they would provide against storms, by planting shelters of Elder, Dutch-elm, Sycamore, and the like, in Clumps and Hedge-rows.

Elms were in fact planted before Borlase visited Scilly, but they only do well in the most sheltered places on St Mary's, and most elm hedges in exposed places are stunted. It was the later planting of shelterbelts and hedges of evergreen shrubs that enabled the farmers to develop the flower trade.

Tall, clipped evergreen hedges around the small fields where the bulbs are grown look as though they have always been there, but they only relate to the start of the flower industry. When flower farming started towards the end of the nineteenth century the fields were very open and the crop was often damaged by storms and wind. Then the only protection came from stone hedges, reed screens, and low hedges of elm and tamarisk (Fig. 137), neither of which forms a very effective shelter.

Later plantings included hedge veronica *Hebe × franciscana*, *Escallonia macrantha*, *Myoporum laetum*, evergreen spindle *Euonymus japonica* and other

FIG 137. Tamarisk in flower, with holly blue butterfly. Tamarisk was introduced to the islands as a hedging plant. (Rosemary Parslow)

FIG 138. *Pittosporum* in flower, now the most common hedging species in Scilly. (Rosemary Parslow)

hedging shrubs. Screens of reed and other materials were still also used to protect the fields; even so the crop was extremely vulnerable to gales and salt-laden winds. Then some of the shrubs introduced from New Zealand during the time of Thomas Algernon Dorrien-Smith began to be grown as shelter hedges. One of these shrubs was *Pittosporum crassiflorum*, first recorded in Tresco Abbey Gardens in 1890 (King, 1985). *Pittosporum* was not mentioned (other than as in the Abbey Gardens) by Jessie Mothersole (1910), and it is not shown in any of her illustrations of flower fields, so had not yet become widespread. But it was soon found that this was a very fast-growing shrub, with tough, shiny leaves impervious to salt, that can form dense windproof screens up to five metres; a bonus was that the cut branches and trimmings could be fed to cattle in winter. Soon *Pittosporum* was replacing other hedge plants round the fields and for several decades it became the dominant species (Fig. 138). *Pittosporum* began to be spread all around the islands by birds attracted to the sticky seeds, often growing out of cracks in the rocky carns and even becoming established on many of the uninhabited islands. All was well until severe weather in January 1987 devastated the *Pittosporum* hedges, killing or severely cutting them back, so the shrub fell out of favour. Since then, although it is still grown, it has been partly supplanted by a range of different hedge species, including daisy trees, also from New Zealand.

OTHER FLOWER CROPS

Scillionian farmers did not just stick to growing narcissus. Over the years they have grown other flower crops including *Oxalis*, violets, arum lilies, wallflowers, anemones and iris, and have tried a wide range of other species of bulbous plants. These have had varying success and some were eventually abandoned, but residual plants have since become established members of the flora. Spanish iris *Iris xiphium*, *Ixia*, *Sparaxis* and the whistling jacks gladiolus are still found among other crops in the bulb fields. Montbretia is widespread on hedgebanks on all the inhabited islands. Naturalised whistling jacks were considered something of a pest for years, but have recently come back into favour; corms are now sold in bulb shops. Several kinds of *Oxalis* were grown and some of them became very invasive. There are still new plants being introduced for the flower trade and for islanders' gardens. Pinks (cultivated *Dianthus*) are now an important summer crop for their cut flowers. Rejected and unwanted bulbs and flowers are frequently dumped on waste tips, on banks behind the beaches and alongside hedges, from where they frequently become naturalised; there is still the potential for further additions to the weed flora. Much of the work on developing new crops and on better methods of farming is undertaken by the small research station at Trenoweth, St Mary's. Originally started by MAFF to study and promote the *Tazetta* narcissus, the station is now run privately as a commercial enterprise to improve the profitability of the island farms, to evaluate new species of bulbs and other plants and to investigate other aspects of horticulture relevant to the islands (Tompsett, 1997).

BULB FIELDS AND HERBICIDES

For many years the flower farmers have battled with what to them are pernicious weeds invading their crops. The particular monoculture regime of bulb growing has favoured some annual plants. Recent changes of timing and methods of cultivation, as well as different crops, may not be as ideal for all the arable weeds as it was fifty years ago, but there are still times when the fields are left undisturbed for a period before they are cultivated, which has allowed them to flourish. Many of these arable species produce prolific seed, which can sometimes persist for years in the seed-bank. Others produce bulbils that can readily take advantage of any disturbed ground. There has been heavy use of herbicides, particularly when flower production was at its height. This has had a marked effect on the weed flora, enabling the resistant species to become over-abundant, while others, such as some of the buttercups, have been severely depleted on some farms. Perhaps one of the most dramatic examples of the effect of herbicide use was the St Martin's buttercup *Ranunculus marginatus* var. *trachycarpus*, which was virtually eradicated by spraying in the 1980s. Fortunately it returned after a few years and a small population still occurs on the farm.

Other plants have also succumbed to farming practices. It was probably farming methods that eliminated balm-leaved figwort from St Agnes (it has recently reappeared) and the distinctive Babington's leek (Fig. 139), which is also rarely found on St Agnes. On St Martin's, where Babington's leek is very common, it is not unusual to see whole cartloads of the plant being carried away to be destroyed. Spraying granite hedges with herbicides may until recently have kept some of the larger and more conspicuous plants such as western ramping-fumitory from expanding their range.

FIG 139. Babington's leek and corn marigolds, St Mary's, June 2005. (Rosemary Parslow)

ON ARABLE PLANTS

It is now considered important to refer to the wild plants that grow in arable fields as arable *plants* rather than dismiss them by the derogatory term *weeds*. To farmers these plants are unwanted weeds; to the botanist or natural historian they are an important element of the flora in their own right. Also, as mentioned earlier, some of the arable plant communities in the Isles of Scilly are unique. Three plants found as arable plants in the Isles of Scilly are listed in the UK Biodiversity Action Plan: western ramping-fumitory, small-flowered catchfly and shepherd's-needle *Scandix pecten-veneris*. Others are also Rare or Scarce plants that either do not occur generally in mainland Britain or are restricted to the extreme southwest.

Small-flowered catchfly is quite a widespread plant in Scilly and is found in arable fields on all the inhabited islands. It also turns up in gardens and disturbed ground. A rather impressive display of the plant has occurred on top of the Garrison walls at times, probably resulting from seeds accidentally introduced with soil there. Resembling a small campion with white or pink flowers, the whole plant is hairy, the capsules and top of the plant very sticky.

At one time the beautiful variety of the plant var. *quinquevulnera,* with red-spotted petals, resembling a miniature sweet William, was found in Scilly, but it now seems to have died out in the wild. Fortunately some plants were preserved in gardens on St Mary's, from where they occasionally escape.

Of all the fumitories western ramping-fumitory is the largest and most splendid (Fig. 140). Usually it is found as a scrambler over hedges but it sometimes also grows among the crop. Since Lousley published a distribution map in his *Flora,* western ramping-fumitory has extended its range on St Mary's and is now also found on St Martin's. It does not seem to have reached any other inhabited islands as yet. Although shepherd's-needle occasionally turns up as a casual on St Mary's, the only significant population is restricted to a few fields on St Martin's.

Several other species of plants that are quite widespread in Scilly are otherwise rare outside the southwest. One is the dainty little lesser quaking-grass *Briza minor,* an annual that closely resembles the perennial quaking-grass *Briza media* of old meadowlands, and another is four-leaved allseed, a small, inconspicuous, all-green plant found not only in the fields but also between cracks in the pavement and in gardens. Smaller tree-mallow has been becoming more widespread in the past ten years and on some farms is common. It can be

FIG 140. Western ramping-fumitory only grows on St Mary's and St Martin's. (Rosemary Parslow)

FIG 141. The bright red cage fungus is sometimes found on the edge of bulb fields. (Ren Hathway)

distinguished from common mallow *Malva sylvestris* by its paler flowers and by the epicalyx, the double cup of sepals below the calyx, being fused at the base. Occasionally its larger relative, tree-mallow, will be found on field margins near the coast.

Several species of buttercups are found in arable situations. One is rough-fruited or Scilly buttercup *Ranunculus muricatus*. It is quite a chunky plant with small, pale yellow flowers and very distinctive spiky fruits. The extremely rare St Martin's buttercup is only known from one field on St Martin's. Often found in the same fields with rough-fruited buttercup is musk stork's-bill *Erodium moschatum*. Another robust plant, it has the same distinctive fruits with a very long 'beak' as the common stork's-bill.

Among the lower plants found in arable fields, one that is impossible to ignore is the cage fungus *Clathrus ruber*, a rare species of a southern and Mediterranean distribution (Fig. 141). The extraordinary and very distinctive fruiting body emerges from an 'egg' rather as in the stinkhorn fungus; it looks like a ball of bright red netting and it is frequently found on the edge of the bulb fields or alongside the hedges.

In the late 1960s Mrs J. A. Paton discovered that the thallose liverwort *Riccia crystallina* that is very common on bare ground in bulb fields on Scilly was an apparently introduced species, not the *R. cavernosa* of lake and reservoir edges elsewhere in the British Isles, with which it had previously been confused.

THE STATUS OF ARABLE PLANTS

Table 4 (pp 258–61) lists scarce arable plants in Scilly, showing their national and local status. In 2005 a new Red Data List was produced which categorised plants according to the degree of threat they are under (Cheffings & Farrell, 2005). This follows the guidelines produced by the International Union for the Conservation of Nature (IUCN), which are very different from those used in the Red Data Books (RDB), the latest of which was produced in 1999 (Wigginton, 1999). The new Red Data List is based on the number of 10km squares the plants occupy (Preston *et al.*, 2002) and on the national survey of scarce plants (Stewart *et al.*, 1994). None of these lists, however, appears adequately to reflect the status of arable plants in Scilly. Many of the arable plants are long-established introductions but have no conservation status at present. Additionally, as Scilly is currently included in vice-county 1 (West Cornwall), any differences in rarity and status are often not reflected in the Atlas. Finally, as many arable plants are considered to be neophytes, they may not receive the consideration and importance reserved for native species.

SPECIES ACCOUNTS

The following plants are some of the more interesting species that are closely associated with bulb and other arable fields in the Isles of Scilly.

Rough-fruited or Scilly buttercup *Ranunculus muricatus*
This is a robust buttercup that can be identified by its tiny flowers followed by distinctive spiny achenes (Fig. 142). It seems particularly susceptible to herbicides and much less common than twenty years ago. It tends to flower early in the year and is fruiting in May and June.

Small-flowered buttercup *Ranunculus parviflorus*
Another of the buttercups found in bulb fields and other disturbed habitats. The flowers are very small and pale yellow, and the achenes are quite unmistakable, covered in tiny hooks all over the surface with a large hook on the beak. The whole plant is a pale green.

FIG 142. Rough-fruited or Scilly buttercup has distinctive spiny achenes. (Rosemary Parslow)

Hairy buttercup *Ranunculus sardous*
Found mainly in two different habitats in Scilly, both as a bulb-field annual and as a perennial in wet meadow situations. Hairy buttercup is similar to bulbous buttercup *Ranunculus bulbosus* but is pale yellow and has distinctive warts on the achenes. It can also be mistaken for St Martin's buttercup where they grow together as both have pale yellow flowers. The achenes are distinctive – those of St Martin's buttercup have larger tubercles on the surface, those of hairy buttercup form a ring around the wide border (Fig. 143).

St Martin's buttercup *Ranunculus marginatus* var. *trachycarpus*
Not a particularly spectacular plant, a sprawling buttercup with pale yellow flowers and a distinctive pattern of small thorny tubercles all over the surface of the achene. There is a photograph of the field on St Martin's in the Isles of Scilly Museum in which the field is a sea of yellow buttercups. Unfortunately the buttercup was considered a pest and it was sprayed with herbicide so that by the early 1980s only a few plants remained. Within a few more years it had

TABLE 4. Rare and uncommon plants found in arable fields on the Isles of Scilly.

SPECIES	
Rough-fruited buttercup	*Ranunculus muricatus*
Small-flowered buttercup	*Ranunculus parviflorus*
Hairy buttercup	*Ranunculus sardous*
St Martin's buttercup	*Ranunculus marginatus trachycarpus*
White ramping-fumitory	*Fumaria capreolata*
Western ramping-fumitory	*Fumaria occidentalis*
Tall ramping-fumitory	*Fumaria bastardii*
Purple ramping-fumitory	*Fumaria purpurea*
Common fumitory	*Fumaria officinalis*
Four-leaved allseed	*Polycarpon tetraphyllum*
Corn spurrey	*Spergula arvensis*
Small-flowered catchfly	*Silene gallica*
Trailing St John's-wort	*Hypericum humifusum*
Smaller tree-mallow	*Lavatera cretica*
Thale cress	*Arabidopsis thaliana*
Field penny-cress	*Thlaspi arvense*
Scarlet pimpernel, blue form	*Anagallis arvensis arvensis*
Scilly pigmyweed	*Crassula decumbens*
Hairy bird's-foot-trefoil	*Lotus subbiflorus*
Orange bird's-foot	*Ornithopus pinnatus*
Bithynian vetch	*Vicia bithynica*
Toothed medick	*Medicago polymorpha*
Slender trefoil	*Trifolium micranthum*
Clustered clover	*Trifolium glomerata*
Rough clover	*Trifolium scabrum*
Knotted clover	*Trifolium striatum*
Subterranean clover	*Trifolium subterraneum*
Suffocated clover	*Trifolium suffocatum*
Bird's-foot clover/fenugreek	*Trifolium ornithopodioides*
Musk stork's-bill	*Erodium moschatum*
Bur chervil	*Anthriscus caucalis*
Shepherd's-needle	*Scandix pectin-veneris*
Knotted hedge-parsley	*Torilis nodosa*
Shoo-fly plant	*Nicandra physalodes*
Green nightshade	*Solanum physalifolium*
Leafy-fruited nightshade	*Solanum sarachoides*

NATIONAL STATUS		STATUS IN SCILLY
RDB	RED DATA LIST	
Scarce		Local & declining
		Local
		Local
		Rare, St Martin's only
		Common
Scarce		Local, St Mary's & St Martin's only
		Common
Scarce		Probably extinct
		Local, mainly Bryher
Rare		Common
	Vulnerable	Frequent
Scarce	Endangered	Common
		Local
	Waiting List	Local, mainly St Agnes & St Martin's
		Local
		Locally common
		Local
		Rare, only St Mary's
Scarce		Local
Rare		Local
Scarce	Vulnerable	Rare
Scarce		Local
		Local
Scarce		Local
		Local
		Local
		Common
Scarce		Local
		Local
Scarce		Common
		Rare, St Martin's
Scarce	Critically Endangered	Rare, St Martin's
		Rare
		Rare, Tresco & St Mary's
		Rare, mainly St Mary's
		Rare, St Martin's

TABLE 4. – *cont.*

SPECIES

Kangaroo-apple	*Solanum laciniatum*
Bugloss	*Anchusa arvensis*
Cut-leaved dead-nettle	*Lamium hybridum*
Henbit dead-nettle	*Lamium amplexicaule*
Field woundwort	*Stachys arvensis*
Balm-leaved figwort	*Scrophularia scorodonia*
Weasel's-snout	*Misopates orontium*
Round-leaved fluellen	*Kickxia spuria*
Sharp-leaved fluellen	*Kickxia elatine*
Green field-speedwell	*Veronica agrestis*
Grey field-speedwell	*Veronica polita*
Common cornsalad	*Valerianella locusta*
Corn marigold	*Chrysanthemum segetum*
Common cudweed	*Filago vulgaris*
Jersey cudweed	*Gnaphalium luteoalbum*
Argentine fleabane	*Conyza bonariensis*
Italian lords-and-ladies	*Arum italicum neglectum*
Babington's leek	*Allium ampeloprasum babingtonii*
Whistling jacks	*Gladiolus communis byzantinus*
Lesser quaking-grass	*Briza minor*
Silver hair-grass	*Aira caryophyllea multiculmis*
Great brome	*Anisantha diandra*
Ripgut brome	*Anisantha rigida*
Compact brome	*Anisantha madritensis*
Rescue brome	*Ceratochloa cathartica*

RDB: data from the *Red Data Book* (Wigginton, 1999).

Red Data List: data from the *Vascular Plant Red Data List* (Cheffings & Farrell, 2005).

The RDB uses the numbers of 10km squares where the plant has been recorded in Great Britain, based on the *New Atlas of the British and Irish Flora* (Preston *et al.*, 2002): 1–15 for nationally Rare and 16–100 for nationally Scarce.

The Red Data List is based on 'threat' rather than rarity and gives plants categories that range from EW (extinct in the wild), CR (critically endangered), EN (endangered), VU (vulnerable), NT (near threatened) to WL (waiting list, for species that need determination of their status).

NATIONAL STATUS		STATUS IN SCILLY
RDB	RED DATA LIST	
		Rare, Tresco & St Mary's
		Common
		Local
		Rare
	Near Threatened	Common
Rare		Common
	Vulnerable	Local
		Very rare
		Local
		Common
		Rare
		Common
	Vulnerable	Common
	Near Threatened	Common St Mary's, rare elsewhere
		Rare, St Mary's
		Rare, St Mary's
Scarce	Near Threatened	Common
		Common
		Very common
Scarce		Common
		Subspecies found mainly in bulb-fields
		Locally common
		Local
Rare	Waiting List	Uncommon
		Local

Hairy Buttercup

St Martins buttercup

Small-flowered buttercup

Rough-fruited or Scilly buttercup

FIG 143. Diagram showing the differences between the achenes of the buttercups of arable fields.

apparently disappeared completely and was seen no more for several years despite annual visits to the site. A few buttercups were found in 1997, and by 1999 the plants had started to spread and soon amounted to several hundred in one field and half-a-dozen in an adjacent field. About 2000 a large packing shed was built on the field where the buttercup grew, and the crop was changed to growing pinks – under plastic, so the amount of bare soil was greatly reduced. In 2003 a few buttercups were seen growing in a flowerbed outside the packing shed. Since then a small population has been located in another field on the farm, so it is hoped that the population may persist.

Common poppy *Papaver rhoeas*
The common or cornfield poppy is found on all the inhabited islands, but is much less common than long-headed poppy. There is a beautiful form with large black blotches at the base of the deep red petals that seems to be common on St Martin's and at a few sites on St Mary's.

Long-headed poppy *Papaver dubium*
This is the frequent poppy in Scilly. The flowers are a lighter red than those of common poppy and drop their petals within a few hours of opening.

White ramping-fumitory *Fumaria capreolata*
This fumitory has a more restricted range on St Agnes and St Mary's, where it often seems to be found on field boundaries and along lanes as well as in bulb fields.

Western ramping-fumitory *Fumaria occidentalis*
This is the largest and most splendid of the fumitories. It is more often found as a scrambler over hedges, but does also grow among the crop. Since Lousley published a distribution map in his *Flora* (1971) it has expanded its range on St Mary's and also occurs in a few places on St Martin's. This could contract over the next decades if the current downturn in arable farming continues.

Tall ramping-fumitory *Fumaria bastardii*
This and the next species are probably the most widespread and common fumitories in Scilly, found on all the inhabited islands. Sometimes they may be in such profusion that they turn the fields a hazy pink.

Common ramping-fumitory *Fumaria muralis boraei*
With *F. bastardii* this is one of the most common and widespread fumitories in the bulb fields. It is also one of the most variable fumitories.

Purple ramping-fumitory *Fumaria purpurea*
Recorded from a suite of bulb fields on St Mary's near Old Town church, but it has not been seen since 1989.

Common fumitory *Fumaria officinalis*
In Scilly this is an uncommon plant. Puzzlingly Lousley recorded it as frequent, but other than on Bryher it is only recorded occasionally elsewhere.

Small nettle *Urtica urens*
Common annual in bulb fields and other cultivated ground such as allotments. It was present in Scilly in the Bronze Age.

Fat-hen *Chenopodium album*
This common arable weed was present in Bronze Age and Iron Age/Romano-British Scilly (Ratcliffe & Straker, 1996). It may have been used as a food plant from early times.

Springbeauty *Claytonia perfoliata*

This common bulb-field weed on occasion is so abundant that it almost dominates the crop. A native of North America, it may have been introduced originally as a salad crop (Lousley, 1971). Since 1928, when it was first recorded in Scilly, it has spread rapidly throughout all the inhabited islands.

Four-leaved allseed *Polycarpon tetraphyllum*

A tiny, inconspicuous, low-growing, green-flowered plant that is easily over-looked. In the 1970s it became locally rare due to herbicide application. Since then it has recovered and is now abundant in bulb fields again as well as gardens and other disturbed habitats including cracks along pavements and gutters.

Corn spurrey *Spergula arvensis*

In some fields corn spurrey may be the dominant weed species (see Fig. 29); it is otherwise found generally among crops or on disturbed ground. There are records from Bronze Age and Iron Age/Romano-British sites.

Sand spurrey *Spergularia rubra*

Occurs mainly on field margins and pathways. It seems to be one of a small number of plants that can colonise the bare, compacted field edges left by heavy herbicide treatment.

Small-flowered catchfly *Silene gallica*

Common in cultivated fields, gardens and other disturbed habitats. For example there are usually some large plants on the top of a wall on the Garrison, St Mary's. The whole plant is hairy and the fruits are very sticky. Although usually white, the flowers can also be a dirty pink colour or rarely red-blotched like a miniature sweet William in var. *quinquevulnera*. The latter variety had apparently disappeared from the wild, but has recently escaped from gardens were it has been maintained.

Black bindweed *Fallopia convolvulus*

Still a common arable weed, also found in Bronze Age deposits.

Smaller tree-mallow *Lavatera cretica*

At one time this species, also called Cornish or Cretan mallow, seemed to be declining, but since the 1980s it has been spreading on St Agnes and St Mary's. As the plant grows quite tall it can be very unpopular with farmers when it gets into the crop (Fig. 144). In the fields the plant is annual, but on field boundaries

FIG 144. Smaller tree-mallow flowering in a bulb field with corn marigold and small-flowered catchfly. (Rosemary Parslow)

it can persist as a short-lived perennial. Some plants on St Mary's may have arisen as the result of spreading material from the Council incinerator and dump to surface paths.

Wild pansy *Viola arvensis*

Very common. Usually with pale yellow flowers but plants with purple dorsal petals may cause confusion with *V. tricolor*.

Thale cress *Arabidopsis thaliana*
Formerly a common arable species, thale cress has apparently recently declined. Interestingly the plant has been used in experiments due to its very short life cycle and was the first species to have its genome mapped (Rose, 2006).

Field penny-cress *Thlaspi arvense*
Uncommon in arable fields throughout the inhabited islands. The large, winged fruits are very distinctive.

Charlock *Sinapsis arvensis*
This common, yellow-flowered crucifer sometimes appears in arable fields. It can be confused with other yellow-flowered crucifers.

Wild radish *Raphanus raphanistrum raphanistrum*
A frequent plant found on disturbed and cultivated ground. In Scilly it can have either white or yellow flowers and can be confused with charlock. *R. raphanistrum maritimus* occasionally occurs in fields on the coast. As with most crucifers, the fruits are almost essential for identification.

Hairy bird's-foot-trefoil *Lotus subbiflorus*
This uncommon plant occasionally forms large mats in bulb fields on sandy soils. On occasion it may become locally dominant.

Bithynian vetch *Vicia bithynica*
An attractive plant with bicoloured white and purple flowers. It is very rare in Scilly. The last record was of a field on St Martin's with many plants in 2001.

Toothed medick *Medicago polymorpha*
A scarce plant found in bulb fields and other cultivated habitats. Very similar to spotted medick but without the spot on the leaves.

Spotted medick *Medicago arabica*
Very common both in cultivated fields and on disturbed ground, sometimes in lawns. In many plants the black spot on the leaves can be extremely large.

Knotted clover *Trifolium striatum*
Usually associated with sandy grassland, but also found as a weed in bulb fields. Several other species of clover may also occasionally occur in arable fields.

FIG 145. The oxalis called Bermuda-buttercup is neither a buttercup nor from Bermuda. (Rosemary Parslow)

Bermuda-buttercup *Oxalis pes-caprae*

This pretty little yellow oxalis is one of the most well-known and widespread bulb-field species (Fig. 145). Although usually flowering in spring, it can be found in flower at any time of the year. The tiny bulbils it produces ensure it is a very persistent weed. It can completely cover the ground between the rows of narcissus and is frequently co-dominant with three-cornered leek.

Musk stork's-bill *Erodium moschatum*

Widespread and locally common on all the inhabited islands. The spectacular large seeds of this plant are sometimes mistaken for shepherd's-needle, especially where they occur together (Fig. 146). The seeds have a remarkable ability to bore their way into the ground: when the seedheads ripen and dry the individual sections (mericarps) twist into a corkscrew and visibly drive themselves into the ground. A pretty trick is to hold them on your hand and watch them twist and squirm as they dry in the sun, trying to bury themselves.

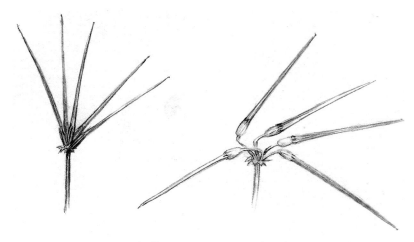

FIG 146. Shepherd's-needle (left) and musk stork's-bill (right) both have spiky seeds. (Rosemary Parslow)

Bur chervil *Anthriscus caucalis*
This small white umbel is known only from a few fields on St Martin's and Tresco. It can be distinguished from other similar plants by the very distinctive fruits covered in hooked spines.

Shepherd's-needle *Scandix pecten-veneris*
Restricted to a suite of fields on St Martin's with occasional records from St Mary's. Another white-flowered umbel with divided leaves similar to carrot. The long-podded, spiky fruits are distinctive. Changes in the management of the St Martin's fields may threaten the population.

Shoo-fly plant or apple-of-Peru *Nicandra physalodes*
Found mostly in bulb fields on Tresco and occasionally as a casual elsewhere.

Black nightshade *Solanum nigrum*
Very frequent in all cultivated fields and disturbed ground. There is a sad account of the death of the daughter of a gardener on Tresco in 1966 from eating 'deadly nightshade berries', which Lousley ascribes to this species.

Green nightshade *Solanum physalifolium*
Uncommon; looks very much like black nightshade but with greenish fruits, partly hidden by sepals, and with paler green foliage.

Leafy-fruited nightshade *Solanum sarachoides*
Very rare. Similar to above but fruit green and completely hidden by sepals. Only recorded from St Martin's.

Kangaroo-apple *Solanum laciniatum*
Generally found on disturbed ground rather than in fields. The large purple flowers, orange fruits and divided leaves are unmistakable. Not infrequent on Tresco and St Mary's. Occasionally can form a large bushy shrub-like plant.

Thorn-apple *Datura stramonium*
This distinctive plant occurs mainly on Tresco and St Mary's, usually in cultivated habitats or other disturbed land. It bears large, spiny fruits.

Common forget-me-not *Myosotis arvensis*
Very common in arable and disturbed situations. Changing forget-me-not *M. discolor* is also sometimes found in cultivated fields.

Bugloss *Anchusa arvensis*
Bristly annual with blue flowers found on all the inhabited islands.

Purple viper's-bugloss *Echium plantagineum*
This beautiful, rare plant was known at one time from arable fields on Tresco, but is probably now extinct. The occasional plants that have turned up recently have always proved to be of garden origin.

Cut-leaved dead-nettle *Lamium hybridum*
Widespread in bulb fields and other cultivated habitats.

Henbit dead-nettle *Lamium amplexicaule*
Known only from one locality on St Martin's.

Field woundwort *Stachys arvensis*
Very frequent in cultivated fields and other disturbed land.

Balm-leaved figwort *Scrophularia scorodonia*
Although usually associated with scrub habitats on the coast, balm-leaved figwort is frequently found in arable habitats.

Weasel's-snout *Misopates orontium*

Also known as lesser snapdragon, this is another plant that can appear from the seed-bank when land is disturbed, for example when the foundations for the St Martin's hotel were being dug, when hundreds of the plants appeared. Otherwise an uncommon plant, although recorded from all inhabited islands (Fig. 147). Does not persist if ground is uncultivated.

FIG 147. Weasel's-snout growing amid the crop in a vegetable field, Bryher, March 2005. (Rosemary Parslow)

Sharp-leaved fluellen *Kickxia elatine*
Sharp-leaved fluellen in Scilly has much rounder leaves than the 'halbert'-shaped leaves of mainland plants, and this may have led to confusion with round-leaved fluellen *Kickxia spuria*, which is rarely recorded. Sharp-leaved fluellen is not a common plant, but may be quite numerous in individual fields, sometimes forming a dense web across the surface of the ground.

Green field-speedwell *Veronica agrestis*
One of the common speedwells found growing in the bulb fields, often forming a sprawling mass at the base of the crop. Other arable speedwells include common field-speedwell *V. persica*, grey field-speedwell *V. polita* and wall speedwell *V. arvensis*.

Field madder *Sherardia arvensis*
A common bulb-field species. It is a prostrate plant with very tiny pink flowers and leaves in whorls.

Common cornsalad *Valerianella locusta*
Found in all kinds of cultivated habitats. There are records of several other rare species of cornsalad. Identification is based on the seeds.

Corn marigold *Chrysanthemum segetum*
An attractive plant that is often a real feature in some of the bulb fields, sometimes in such profusion it can turn whole fields golden. Locally it is called 'bothams'. Although the flowers are usually deep yellow in colour, on one farm on St Mary's there is a pale cream variety. The flowers are attractive to bees, hoverflies and other insects.

Scentless mayweed *Tripleurospermum inodorum*
Very common in some arable fields. Near the coast the very similar sea mayweed *T. marinum* may occur.

Scented mayweed *Matricaria recutita*
Uncommon, apparently restricted to a few bulb fields on St Mary's and St Agnes, where it may be locally abundant – for example on field headlands.

Common cudweed *Filago vulgaris*
A common plant on St Mary's but rarely found on the off-islands.

Jersey cudweed *Gnaphalium luteoalbum*

Found on only one site on St Mary's. It is interesting to speculate where the plants came from: the Channel Isles are a possible source.

Argentine fleabane *Conyza bonariensis*

Apparently a recent arrival in Scilly but already spreading in arable situations.

Spanish bluebell *Hyacinthoides hispanica*

Common in bulb fields, especially on St Agnes, and hybrids with wild bluebell *Hyacinthoides non-scripta* are quite common in and near arable fields.

Babington's leek *Allium ampeloprasum* var. *babingtonii*

This variety of wild leek is endemic in southwest Britain. It is a large and very conspicuous plant, growing up to 2 metres when in flower, still widespread in

FIG 148. 'Whistling jacks' gladiolus: blowing across the leaves produces the whistle. (Rosemary Parslow)

the Isles of Scilly, common in cultivated fields as well as among bracken and bramble communities and at the back of dunes. In the bulb fields it can interfere with cultivation: for example where the farmers need to cover the field with plastic sheeting they have first to cut the tops off the leeks. Some farmers tolerate the plants, but in other cases they may all be pulled up and destroyed. Wild leek *Allium ampeloprasum* var. *ampeloprasum* is a rare plant in Scilly, only found among bracken on the Garrison.

Whistling jacks *Gladiolus communis byzantinus*

Originally introduced as a crop species for the flower trade, it was later abandoned and has persisted as a weed (Fig. 148). Recently the corms have become marketable, especially for sale to visitors who have seen the flowering gladiolus growing 'wild' in the fields.

GRASSES

A number of species of grass are found in the bulb fields and other disturbed ground. Those described below are the typical species; there are many other grasses that occasionally occur as casuals

Squirreltail fescue *Vulpia bromoides*

A grass of many habitats, frequently occurring as a 'weed' in the bulb fields, where it can grow much taller than elsewhere.

Rat's-tail fescue *Vulpia myuros*

Not as common as squirreltail fescue, but found in similar places.

Lesser quaking-grass *Briza minor*

A very common species in bulb fields and cultivated habits throughout inhabited islands (Fig. 149). Lesser quaking-grass is an annual species and very similar to the common, meadow perennial species *Briza media* of the mainland.

Early meadow-grass *Poa infirma*

A small annual grass that flowers very early in spring. Not usually a species of bulb fields, but occasionally found on tracks and trampled ground.

FIG 149. Lesser quaking-grass and pineappleweed *Matricaria discoidea* are both found on arable land in Scilly. (David Holyoak)

Silver hair-grass *Aira caryophyllea*
A very common grass found in many different habitats in Scilly. The bulb-field form is often the variety *multiculmis*.

Early hair-grass *Aira praecox*
A small annual grass that is often common in bulb fields on sandy soils as well as in the more usual heathland and dune habitats.

Great brome *Anisantha diandra*
One of the very large and handsome grasses found in the bulb fields. Great brome is very widespread and appears in other cultivated habits. Found on most of the inhabited islands but has not been recorded from Tresco.

Ripgut brome *Anisantha rigida*
An unusual, tall species of grass found occasionally in the bulb fields. Recorded from Bryher, St Agnes and St Mary's.

Compact brome *Anisantha madritensis*
Another very large species of grass that occurs in bulb fields. The compact heads are quite distinctive. Recorded only from Bryher before 1971, now known from St Agnes and St Mary's.

Rescue brome *Ceratochloa cathartica*
Another large grass found in some bulb fields. Rescue brome is known only from St Martin's and St Mary's.

Cockspur *Echinochloa crus-galli*
This large grass is found occasionally in arable fields.

CHAPTER 13

Gardens

The boundaries between wild and cultivated flowers have become extremely difficult to fix. So many foreign plants have been introduced at one time or another and then the climate does the rest: they thrive and romp and scatter themselve in their new home as if they were natives.

Vyvyan (1953)

I F ONE HAS THE slightest aspiration to be a gardener it is impossible to ignore the gardens on the Isles of Scilly. To many visitors the impression you are walking around in Kew Gardens 'with the lid off' is a major part of the attraction of the islands. Much of the inhabited part of the Isles of Scilly is like a series of extended gardens. All around the islands in cottage gardens, on granite walls, in odd corners and along roadsides all manner of exotic plants have established and become an important part of the scenery (Fig. 150). What a challenge for the visiting naturalist! With a flora half of which are aliens, Scilly frequently attracts a particular type of botanist who relishes this disparate group. But even if you do not attempt to identify anything other than the 'natives', the *Aeoniums*, *Echiums*, *Pittosporum* hedges and all the attractive little succulents growing along the walls are impossible to ignore – if nothing else they will find their way into your holiday photographs!

This rash of introduced plants is usually believed to have started with the Abbey Gardens on Tresco. But even before the gardens were planted there were exotic plants growing around the islands, some undoubtedly having been brought in by sailors and visitors. The islanders found they grew happily in the mild climate. There is a reference to an 'American aloe' (the name is puzzling: was it an aloe or an American agave?) growing in the moat at Star Castle before

FIG 150. Sky-rocketing *Echiums* may reach five metres. (Rosemary Parslow)

Augustus Smith arrived in Scilly (Woodley, 1822). That is not to say Tresco has not been responsible for the main body of introductions. The Gardens have been the source of most of the common exotics that have naturalised around the inhabited islands. Also we know that Major Arthur Dorrien-Smith deliberately planted all manner of garden plants in the dunes on Tresco and 'poked them into cracks' in walls as he passed or anywhere he though they might grow. Clearly many of them 'took' readily enough. The islands would probably have looked very different if it had not been for the Abbey Gardens and the Dorrien-Smiths, a brief résumé of whose association with the Gardens is outlined below. Not to be forgotten are the other introductions that came along on the back of the plants for the Gardens. The liverworts *Telaranea murphae* and *Lophocolea bispinosa*, various bryophytes and fungi, the New Zealand woodland hopper, stick insects, flatworms, spiders and other invertebrates – all are thought to have become established first on Tresco after having arrived along with shipments of plants.

TRESCO ABBEY GARDENS

When Augustus Smith leased the Isles of Scilly from the Duchy of Cornwall in 1834 he soon needed to have somewhere to live 'in the style and comfort he was used to'. Initially settling on St Mary's, he soon looked for somewhere rather more spacious and private to make his home. Eventually he chose Tresco, where the ruins of the former Benedictine Priory on the island seemed the perfect place for his new home and garden (Fig. 151) (Nelhams, 2000).

The first step towards the Garden was the erection of a high wall to shelter the area from the gales and salt-laden winds that raked the island. There were virtually no trees on the island, probably only gorse thickets and low granite walls. References to elder trees ('Innisschawe [i.e. Tresco] ... bereth stynkkyng elders'; Leland, 1535–43), suggest they were common on the island at one time. There are only a few elder bushes there today. Augustus Smith used gorse to shelter his plantings, and 'as he walked about he scattered gorse seed brought from the mainland and was gratified to find that it not only established itself surprisingly quickly but was as effective a barrier as he had hoped' (Dorrien-Smith, 1954). It has been something of a puzzle as to why Augustus Smith brought gorse seed from the mainland, rather than collecting it locally; perhaps it was more readily available, and one can speculate that it may have been western gorse that was the more common species in Scilly at the time, lower-growing and therefore less useful for sheltering young trees. Very soon it became obvious gorse could not provide enough protection, so he began planting shelterbelts of

FIG 151. Ruins of the former priory in the Abbey Gardens, Tresco, May 2003. (Rosemary Parslow)

trees. The first shelterbelt plantings were mainly deciduous trees, elm, sycamore *Acer pseudoplatanus*, oak and poplar *Populus* sp.; later he introduced Monterey pine and Monterey cypress, fast-growing and ideally suited to coastal conditions (King, 1985).

Several features that can still be seen in the present Gardens were laid down in Augustus Smith's time, notably the three main terrace walks and the dramatic long flight of steps from the top to bottom of the garden known as Neptune's Steps. During his stewardship Augustus Smith was soon in contact with, and obtaining plants from, other horticultural-minded gentlemen as well as from Kew Gardens. Many of the plants were of South African, New Zealand and Australian origin. These were also arranged in special areas within the garden named after the parts of the world from which the plants originated. By the time Augustus Smith died in 1872, the gardens and the island were already becoming well known and attracting visitors including shooting parties, horticulturalists and water-colourists.

After Augustus Smith died there was a hiatus until his nephew Thomas Algernon Dorrien-Smith eventually took over as Lord Proprietor of the Islands.

'Algy' had been the only one of his nephews (Augustus had no direct heir) to show any interest in Tresco. In 1874 Thomas Algernon arrived in the islands to take over the work started by his uncle and continued to develop the Gardens. At the time Scilly was suffering from a serious lack of prosperity. The mainstays of the Scillonian economy had been fishing, shipbuilding and producing early potatoes. During this period the building of wooden ships ceased on St Mary's and Bryher, and St Mary's harbour lost its importance as a port. Distance and the difficulties of getting to mainland markets killed the fishing industry and the Channel Islands overtook the Isles of Scilly in growing early potatoes. It was Thomas Algernon who had recognised the potential for the cut-flower trade based on narcissus from the semi-wild plants that grew on the islands.

Thomas Algernon had also recognised the value of the salt-resistant Monterey pine and Monterey cypress as shelter-trees, and he planted them in huge numbers to provide protection for the Abbey Gardens. He continued to develop the Gardens and to support flower shows on the mainland, where many tender shrubs and other plants were introduced to the gardeners of Cornwall. Thomas Algernon died 1918 and was succeeded by his son, Major Arthur Dorrien-Smith, who had already established himself as a plantsman, horticulturalist and collector. Arthur Dorrien-Smith had married a fellow enthusiast and soon he and his wife Eleanor were undertaking plant-collecting expeditions and bringing back many new and interesting specimens. When his father died, Major Arthur returned to a Scilly suffering from the aftermath of the Great War and the run-down state of the farms. Eventually Major Arthur surrendered the leases of all the other inhabited islands to the Duchy and concentrated on managing Tresco.

During the time of his stewardship Major Arthur continued to introduce many new species of plants to the Abbey Gardens. A list produced in 1935 named nearly 3,500 species and varieties (Nelhams, 2000). Most of the introductions were again species from the warmer climates of New Zealand, Australia, the Canary Islands, South Africa and Mexico. World War II meant most of the garden staff had been called up, so Major Arthur and his wife were very busy just keeping the gardens running with the few remaining staff. Of their four sons, three were killed in the war, including the eldest, Robert, already a promising horticulturalist. After the war the Major (as he was known) carried on planting and 'many self-sown seedlings began to appear on the hillside' (Nelhams, 2000). This was probably the start of the grand exodus of exotic species from the Gardens, to become what is now the remarkable alien flora of the Isles of Scilly. Also about this time, in the early 1950s, the Gardens were opened to the public for an entrance charge of 2s 6d, the first time there had been a formal charge.

The next Dorrien-Smith was Lieutenant Commander Thomas Dorrien Smith, known as the Commander. He took over the Gardens in 1955, and although originally his interests were not so much horticultural as in developing the tourism and economy of the island, under him the gardens thrived. More plants were added to the collection. The Commander's mother, Eleanor, also continued her interest in the gardens. From 1973 until 1984 the head gardener was Peter Clough, who besides being a notable horticulturalist was also a keen botanist and took a great interest in the wild flowers on Tresco as well as the cultivated plants. Among the exotic plants in the Gardens is an interesting 'weed' flora, with many typical Scilly arable plants and even orange bird's-foot and other rarities growing in the flowerbeds, in gravel paths and in the mown lawns. A fine show of common broomrape *Orobanche minor* growing on the treasure flower *Gazania rigens* in one of the flowerbeds has attracted the admiration of visiting botanists for many years (Fig. 152).

When the Commander died in 1973 the lease of Tresco passed to his son Robert, who has continued to expand the Tresco Estate, including the holiday cottage and time-share business started by his father. The Gardens have continued to develop their collections of plants and are now one of the best-

FIG 152. Common broomrape growing as a root parasite on *Gazania* in a flowerbed. Tresco Abbey Garden. (Rosemary Parslow)

known and most important subtropical gardens and plant collections in Britain. Many of the trees and other plants have now reached maturity and even more have spread, not only self-seeding within the confines of the garden but also escaping over the walls into the woodland areas outside. Plants are also spread around the other islands by being passed around as cuttings and seeds and, as a result, the inhabited islands all to some extent share in the 'subtropical' aspect of Tresco. Perhaps not generally realised is that the Gardens are particularly important for epiphytic lichens, although some species have been lost as the host trees have been killed by frost or gales (B. Edwards, *in litt.*).

A considerable remodelling of the Gardens has taken place over recent years since Mike Nelhams became head gardener and then curator. Major damage to the shelterbelts by the 1990 hurricane, coming shortly after the unprecedented snows of January 1987, had killed or cut back many trees and shrubs, leaving fallen timber and lots of gaps in the plantings. The effect of the hurricane had been particularly devastating; most of the windbreak trees were Monterey pines that had been planted at around the same time between 1870 and 1890: these were top-heavy trees with large shallow root-plates and they went over like ninepins. This left huge gaps that allowed the wind to wreak havoc within the Gardens, where many specimen trees were also blown down, bringing walls and other structures down with them. Over the four-hour duration of the storm on the morning of 25 January eight hundred trees were toppled on just one hillside; worse still, in many places the falling branches took with them young trees planted as replacements after the 1987 snows (Nelhams, 2000). During the work to replant the windbreaks and repair the damage, it was an opportunity to take advantage of the situation and make improvements and additions to the plantings. Many other major gardens, including Kew Gardens, sent replacement plants to Tresco, and many of these were specimen trees and shrubs, so that within a short time the Gardens were restored almost to their former splendour. Among the changes that took place included moving the former vegetable garden and orchard to a new area at the west side of the garden. An interesting aspect of this work, probably not one appreciated by the gardeners, was that the newly cultivated land threw up a great flush of 'weed' plants, presumably from buried seed, to add to the wild flowers that make up the weed flora of the gardens.

There is also a small but well-stocked garden around Tresco Hotel. It was as gardener here that David Hunt first came to Scilly and started his birdwatching career on the islands (see Chapter 4). Tresco Estate has now extended their interests to the island of Bryher, having taken over the hotel there. In 2003 the gardens and surroundings of the hotel were landscaped and planted up with shrubs and perennials. Undoubtedly some of these have the potential to spread, and join some of the other exotic plants already growing on the island. Bringing in shrubs and other plants is likely also to transfer with them some of the alien invertebrate species from Tresco, as well as some species of wild plants that currently do not grow on Bryher.

CARREG DHU GARDEN

This small garden has been constructed in a disused ram pit (quarry) on St Mary's, planted up by a devoted band of local enthusiasts. The project was begun in 1986 by Richard and June Lethbridge. The garden is designed to be a community garden, with all the work done by volunteers and money collected to buy plants etc. The whole site is only about a hectare in size, but it is densely planted with the shrubs, trees and herbaceous plants typical of Scillonian gardens. These are all tucked into the bowl of the quarry interspersed with lawns and pathways. The garden forms an area of warmth and shelter that is attractive to birds, butterflies and other insects. Many of the wild flowers growing among the cultivated plants are plants of disturbed ground, while others are heathland species that may have already been present in the quarry. So besides enjoying the well-stocked garden the weed flora is well worth investigating by any visiting botanist.

Close to the garden an area has been planted as a display plot of old varieties of narcissus. Many species and varieties that are no longer in cultivation are being collected and grown here to save them for research and as a reference collection.

PRIVATE GARDENS

The gardens of the houses in the Isles of Scilly are often quite remarkable, with mixtures of plants from warmer climates all growing with complete abandon, spilling over rockeries and walls and jumbled up in the tiniest gardens. Dozens of beautiful and unusual species, often originating from Tresco and specialist nurseries, flourish in cottage gardens. Many of the gardens are allowed to be exuberant, probably because it is impractical to maintain a rigorous weed-free regime, and this enables some of the native plants, including some usually associated with arable fields, to flourish. Other species seem to be particularly common in gardens and in weedy corners around Hugh Town. Sand rocket is often seen in gardens round the Parade, and greater quaking-grass is also frequent around the town, sometimes growing in the gutters. One very common 'weed' that surprises visitors is the ubiquitous cineraria, more familiar as a pot-plant, that appears in many colour forms all over Hugh Town, not only in gardens but along walls, up flights of steps, in corners of pavements and anywhere it can get a toehold. Cinerarias grow freely all over the churchyard in Old Town, St Mary's, as do many other former garden plants. Four-leaved allseed is also a frequent weed in the built-up areas, found in gutters, crevices in pavements and gardens on all the inhabited islands.

The astonishing range of native and alien wall plants attracts the attention of even the most casual observer, and features in many holiday postcards. This is hardly surprising, as many of the plants are colourful and exotic in appearance: they are exceptionally photogenic (Fig.153). One group of wall plants are the plants called collectively 'mesems', the dewplants, South African species that look like brightly coloured daisies with succulent leaves. All the dewplants are attractive, like the hot-coloured varieties of *Lampranthus*, although some of the most interesting are not as showy. Walking through New Grimsby after landing on the quay, or through Hugh Town or any other 'town' on the Isles of Scilly, has something of the atmosphere of wandering through a village abroad, in Portugal perhaps, because of the vegetation. Besides the daisy-flowered dewplants, there

FIG 153. *Agapanthus*, originally from South Africa, are both garden plants and established on dunes and hedgebanks. St Agnes, June 2002. (Rosemary Parslow)

FIG 154. *Aeoniums* grow freely in many gardens, and some have occasionally been found on uninhabited islands – presumably taken there by gulls. (Rosemary Parslow)

are giant houseleek-shaped *Aeoniums* that throw up great spikes of yellow flowers even in winter (Fig. 154); spiky agaves (there are some so huge they completely fill cottage gardens), sky-rocketing blue echiums *Echium pininana* and the ubiquitous cabbage palm tree *Cordyline australis*. Some of the plants that are now found on all the inhabited islands have only recently spread to them. One is the fleshy-leaved little yellow *Oxalis megalorrhiza*, another is the now widespread and showy Madeiran geranium *Geranium maderense* that I first saw growing in the wild on Bryher in the 1960s, although it had been in Tresco Abbey Gardens for several decades (King, 1985). It is easy to be beguiled by the succulents and other plants that look so invitingly easy to grow, and carrier-bags full of *Aeoniums*, *Agapanthus* lilies, Madeiran geraniums and others are taken home to the mainland by holiday visitors, where most of them will turn into mush at the first frost or lead sad, etiolated lives in cold greenhouses.

CHAPTER 14

Insects and Other Terrestrial Invertebrates

It is impossible to visit the islands without wanting to know more about them.

Harold Wilson (1963)

O NLY A FEW OF the groups of invertebrates found in the Isles of Scilly have been well studied. So although there are good checklists and accounts of the Lepidoptera, Odonata, Aculeate Hymenoptera, terrestrial Mollusca and some of the larger and more obvious insects, many others are only accessible to the specialist. This account can only give a brief outline of the invertebrate fauna of Scilly; it is based on published reports and on personal observations.

One of the interesting aspects of island fauna is how quickly situations can change. Many of the more mobile species that have arrived in the islands as migrants have become established very quickly, and others can become extinct just as rapidly. The small size of the islands does not give much leeway when it comes to survival.

DRAGONFLIES AND DAMSELFLIES

Until the early 1990s there were only two species of resident Odonata in the Isles of Scilly. The blue-tailed damselfly and common darter both occur on Tresco, St Mary's and St Agnes where there are suitable water-bodies. Many of the pools on Scilly are slightly brackish at times and only species that can tolerate such conditions have become established (Fig. 155).

There have been sporadic records of other species of dragonflies and

FIG 155. Common darters can tolerate the slight salinity of some of the pools in Scilly. (Martin Goodey)

damselflies, more frequently since birdwatchers have shown an increasing interest in the group; Norman Moore (1987) has described dragonflies as the birdwatcher's insect. Some of the migrant species that have increasingly been reaching Britain from the Continent and North America have also been recorded on Scilly. The occurrence in 1998 of a North American species, the green darner *Anax junius*, was an exciting event that even distracted committed birdwatchers from their normal pursuits! The following species account is based on personal observations as well as on published reports in the *Cornwall Dragonfly Group Newsletter* 6–8 and the *Isles of Scilly Bird & Natural History Review*.

Blue-tailed damselfly is the common damselfly on the islands, breeding in Big Pool on St Agnes, Lower Moors and Porth Hellick Pool, St Mary's, and Great and Abbey Pools, Tresco. The males and non-breeding insects are frequently found well away from water. On St Agnes they are often seen basking along hedgebanks in Barnaby Lane (Fig. 156). The only other small blue damselfly recorded in Scilly is common blue damselfly *Enallagma cyathigerum*, with records of an ovipositing female at Lower Moors, St Mary's, in 1994 and a male found at Longstone in June 2004 (M. Scott). A large red damselfly *Pyrrhosoma nymphula* turned up at Longstone in June 2005.

FIG 156. Barnaby Lane, St Agnes, a good place to shelter from gales for birds, butterflies and dragonflies. (Rosemary Parslow)

There are a number of records of migrant hawker dragonfly *Aeshna mixta* from both Tresco and St Mary's. This dragonfly is anticipated to be the next species to become established as a breeding species on the islands. It has been recorded from both Tresco and St Mary's and suspected of breeding on occasion. It was also recorded on St Agnes in 1997, but only a moribund individual at Horse Point.

Several of the larger dragonflies have been recorded in Scilly, but so far none of them has become established. These include southern hawker *Aeshna cyanea* from St Mary's in 1992 and from St Mary's and Tresco in 1996, and common hawker *A. juncea* on the Great Pool, Tresco, in 1992. Golden-ringed dragonfly *Cordulegaster boltonii* is usually found near running water, and is common on rivers in Cornwall; one was seen on Tresco in 1996. Black-tailed skimmer *Orthetrum cancellatum* was recorded on St Mary's in 2005 and on two occasions in 2006.

The emperor dragonfly *Anax imperator* is a distinctive species, and there are records from St Mary's in 1992, 1996 and 2001, and from Tresco in August 2005. In October 1998 I saw what was possibly an emperor dragonfly on St Agnes, but could not be positive as at that time there were green darners in the islands.

Green darner is a North American species that is similar in appearance to the emperor; several individuals were recorded in September and October 1998. I spent a long time watching an individual female that was resting on a tree trunk on Tresco, and just before it flew away observed a subtle change in its colour as it warmed up (Parslow, 1999). The lesser emperors *A. parthenope* that turned up on St Mary's in September 2005 and June 2006 follow the apparent increase in records of this rare migrant.

The only common breeding species of dragonfly found on Tresco, St Mary's and St Agnes is common darter. This species is frequently seen well away from water and can often be seen basking on the top of the hedges or patrolling up along the bramble patches in the sun. Numbers fluctuate from year to year. Sometimes the old male insects can become deep red in colour and can resemble the ruddy darter *Sympetrum sanguineum*. In 2003 a genuine ruddy darter was found and photographed by Bryan Thomas near the pool on the cricket field, St Martin's. Two other darter dragonflies have turned up in Scilly, and both are migrants that are becoming more frequent in Britain. Red-veined darter *S. fonscolombei* is now breeding in Cornwall, and two individuals were seen on Tresco in May 1962. A yellow-winged darter *S. flaveolum* turned up on St Mary's in 1995 at a time when there was an influx nationally.

GRASSHOPPERS AND RELATED INSECTS

The status of the Orthoptera (grasshoppers, crickets and their allies) in Scilly is relatively well known due to the work of a handful of dedicated orthopterists, both visitors to Scilly and residents. Since the advent of small, hand-held bat detectors that can pick up stridulations of grasshoppers and bush-crickets, the study of these insects has been revolutionised. As a result several new sites and species have been discovered since the mid-1990s.

According to Haes (1999) the orthopteroids currently resident in Scilly can be divided into two main groups. First there are those that have been present since the time when Scilly was still linked to mainland Britain. Second there are the recent immigrants, which have either arrived naturally, flying in for example, as long-winged cone-heads must have done, or which have arrived accidentally, probably with garden plants, such as speckled bush-cricket *Leptophytes punctatissima*, or washed up on the shore on flotsam, as Haes suggests short-winged cone-heads may have done. The very surprising arrival of at least three male large cone-heads *Ruspolia nitidula* at the same time in 2003 (see below) may presage the eventual colonisation of Scilly.

Over the last hundred years a number of orthopteroid insects have been recorded in Scilly that so far have not become established. These include oak bush-cricket *Meconema thalassinum* (1906), dark bush-cricket *Pholidoptera griseoaptera* (1906), blue-winged grasshopper *Oedipoda caerulescens* (1903), mole cricket *Gryllotalpa gryllotalpa* (1930) and several lesser earwigs *Labia minor* (1907). Both desert *Schistocerca gregaria* and migratory locust *Locusta migratoria* have been recorded occasionally, usually after there had been Saharan dust storms.

Among the long-term residents great green bush-crickets *Tettigonia viridissima* are the most noticeable and most easily recognised, due to their loud stridulations during both day and night in late summer and autumn, audible for several hundred metres. Great green bush-crickets are restricted in their distribution along hedgebanks on St Mary's and Tresco, and although easily tracked down by the sound, they are almost impossible to locate among the vegetation because they seem to have the ability to throw their 'voice'. When you do find them they are impressive insects, strikingly large and very green (Fig. 157).

Grey bush-crickets are found only on Bryher, although there is the possibility they might have spread to Tresco, stridulating having been reported from the quay area in 2003. There is frequent boat traffic between the two islands so it is possible a bush-cricket might get transferred between the islands, or one might

FIG 157. Great green bush-crickets can be heard on summer evenings along hedgebanks on St Mary's. (Bryan Thomas)

FIG 158. Field grasshopper is the only species of grasshopper resident in the islands. (Martin Goodey)

even have hopped across when the channel dried out at a spring tide. On Bryher the bush-crickets are mainly found in the dunes and dune grassland around Rushy Bay, the marram fringe of Green Bay and in the area around the Pool. In May 2003 I observed dozens of tiny early-instar crickets hopping along pathways between the dunes at Rushy Bay.

The only grasshopper resident on Scilly, field grasshopper, is very common and widespread on all islands where there is enough suitable vegetation (Fig. 158). As elsewhere, it can occur in several different colour forms, including occasionally all black and an all-over purple variety. Field grasshoppers have been recorded on all the inhabited islands including Gugh, and many of the uninhabited: St Helen's, Teän, Northwethel, Samson and most of the Eastern Isles including Great and Little Arthur, Menawethan, Great Ganinick, Great and Little Ganilly.

Around the shores it is possible to see a tiny cockroach, the lesser cockroach, not much larger than a grain of wheat. It is probably quite widespread but easily overlooked. The early instars with dark bands around their bodies are the ones usually noticed, especially when they scurry across the sand at the top of the beach – but they may also be found under pebbles. The adult females may also attract attention as they carry their large pod of eggs around. Since 1990 the lesser cockroach has been found on Gugh, Teän, Bryher, Samson, Tresco, Norwethel, St Martin's, St Mary's, St Agnes and Annet.

Cone-heads are a family of bush-crickets so called from the distinctive shape of their heads. Short-winged and long-winged cone-heads are both recent arrivals in the Isles of Scilly. They are not easy to tell apart, but are most easily identified by their song: the stridulation of short-winged cone-head is not audible to most people but easily picked up using a bat detector. A third species that turned up in Scilly in 2003, the large cone-head, was discovered when their unusual song drew attention to them. The first large cone-head was located on the Garrison, St Mary's, by Ren Hathway and Paul Stancliffe when they were looking for speckled bush-crickets in August 2003 (Fig. 159). The song was recorded, and with the help of Martin Goodey the cone-head was located, caught, examined and photographed before being returned to the same area, where it stayed for several nights stridulating from gorse bushes (Haes, 2003; Hathway *et al.*, 2003). At the same time, two singing males were discovered on St Agnes by Mike Hicks with his sons Murray and Ross, one of which was caught and sent to Chris Haes, who confirmed the identification (the cricket was kept in captivity until it died, when it was presented to the Natural History Museum). Currently the closest population of large cone-heads is in Brittany, so we can only speculate on more being carried up on air currents, eventually to colonise Scilly.

Most people can recognise earwigs. Two species are found in Scilly, common earwig *Forficula auricularia* and Lesne's earwig *F. lesnei*. Superficially, they look alike, with the smaller Lesne's being distinguished from small common earwigs only by their total lack of wings. Lesne's earwig appears to have been overlooked on Scilly until C. J. Timmins started finding them in the hollow stems of hogweed in 1993 (Haes, 2001). Since then they have been found in bushes and in 2002 they were found in large numbers with common earwigs in the dead, hanging leaves of cabbage palm trees. The species is now known from St Agnes, St Martin's, St Mary's, Bryher and Samson. Common earwigs are ubiquitous; they have been found on all the inhabited islands and also on all the uninhabited ones so far checked for their presence.

Another group that everyone can recognise are the stick insects, and two species have been established on Tresco for almost a century. The prickly stick insect *Acanthoxyla geisovii* (Fig. 160) and the smooth stick insect *Clitarchus hookeri* both originated from New Zealand. It is believed they arrived with plant material for the Abbey Gardens originating from Treseder's Nursery in Truro, the importer of plants from New Zealand at the time (Lee, 2003). They are mainly found in the Abbey Gardens or in the vicinity, although recently the prickly stick insect has been found at several places away from the Gardens on Tresco. Recent sightings have also been made on St Mary's, where it has presumably been introduced, either deliberately or with plant material from Tresco. A third

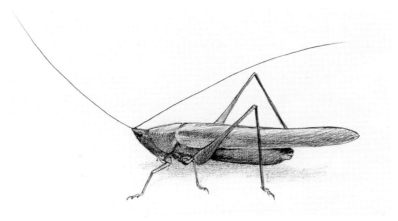

FIG 159. Large cone-head. Three individual males located on St Mary's and St Agnes in August 2003 were the first recorded in Britain. (Ren Hathway)

FIG 160. Prickly stick insect, one of the three species of stick insects now found in Scilly. (Bryan Thomas)

species of stick insect, Mediterranean stick insect *Bacillus rossius*, was discovered on Tresco in August 2002 (Laney, 2003). In 2004 breeding was confirmed when Brian Laney found three nymphs in the same area.

Other species of orthopteroids may be encountered in Scilly as the situation changes and new species reach the islands. There is now a thriving colony of common groundhoppers *Tetrix undulata* near the Pool on Tresco. House crickets *Acheta domesticus* are spreading from the dump on St Mary's, possibly to reinvade Hugh Town, as unfortunately are the alien cockroaches *Blatta orientalis* and *Blatella germanica*. Cockroaches were reputed to have been 'very troublesome Flies' on Scilly when the islands were visited by Borlase (1756). He was told that they were thought to have been introduced from the West Indies in a surgeon's chest. He was sufficiently impressed by them to include an illustration in his account. Speckled bush-crickets are already spreading from their present nucleus near the Garrison; there are plenty of sheltered gardens to provide suitable habitat for them.

BUGS

The Hemiptera are the true bugs, a group of insects which have mouthparts adapted for piercing plant or animal tissues and sucking out the juices. There are three groups of Hemiptera, but only the Heteroptera, which include the shield bugs, and the Auchenorhyncha, which include the frog-hoppers and the aphids, are likely to be generally familiar. One Heteropteran common in Scilly is the hawthorn shield bug *Acanthosoma haemorrhoidale*, which is widely distributed, often on bramble thickets. As hawthorn *Crataegus monogyna* is uncommon in Scilly it must rely on some other food plant. Of the approximately 46 species of bugs recorded in the islands there are several rare species including a ground bug *Emblethis griseus* and a subspecies of the beet leaf bug *Piesma quadratum spergulariae* that lives on rock sea-spurrey (Alexander, in Spalding, 1997). *Dicranocephalus agilisis* is found on Portland and sea spurge plants on the dunes, but unfortunately like most bugs it is not very well known or easily identified except by specialists.

Trioza vitrioradiata is a jumping plant louse that has become a pest on *Pittosporum* (it presumably came in with other plant material and spread to *Pittosporum*). It was first recorded in Cornwall in 1993 and soon after was found in Scilly, where it is now found on all the main islands including Gugh. The larvae feed on the young leaves, making light-green pits in them. They cause considerable damage, but not enough to kill the trees.

CADDIS FLIES

Only one species of caddis fly has so far been recorded in Scilly, *Limnephlus marmoratus*, a pale brown insect found on St Mary's by Ian Beavis (*in litt.*).

LEPIDOPTERA

Moths

At least 269 species of macrolepidoptera (excluding butterflies) and 270 micro-lepidoptera have been recorded from the Isles of Scilly (Smith, 2002). This is little more than half the number recorded from mainland Cornwall, a reflection of the far smaller range of habitats and the smaller and scattered land area of Scilly (Hicks & Hale, 1998). Although there are relatively few species, eleven of those recorded on the Isles of Scilly have not been found in Cornwall (Smith, 2002). Three species of moth found in Scilly are classed as nationally rare. One is the yellow V *Oinophila v-flava*, a small moth with a distinctive yellowish Y on the brown wings, first recorded on St Mary's in 1993. It is normally associated with cellars and other places indoors but in Scilly lives in the open (as do some species of spiders in Scilly) and has been found under the bark of *Pittosporum* bushes. Another of the nationally rare moths is *Nothris congressariella*, which is restricted to its food plant, balm-leaved figwort. The third rarity is *Homoeosma nimbella*, about which very little is known (Spalding & Sargent, 2000). There is a better chance of seeing a monarch butterfly *Danaus plexippus* or clouded yellow in Scilly than in most places on the mainland, and several of the large and impressive hawk-moths are regularly recorded, including death's-head hawk-moth *Acherontia atropa*, convolvulus hawk-moth *Agrius convolvuli* and striped hawk-moth *Hyles livornica* (Fig. 161).

As most moths are nocturnal and are usually only encountered when they come to lights, records are largely dependent on moth-trapping. There are also a few species of day-flying moths that may be encountered at times, and some of the nocturnal species may be disturbed from their resting places during the day. Over the past half-century a number of visiting and resident lepidopterists have run moth traps and added hugely to the knowledge of the moth fauna of the islands. The unique position of the Isles of Scilly enables many migrant species of moths and butterflies to reach the islands, and some from the Continent are recorded most years. Species from North America have turned up at the same time as the regular bird migrants and are equally exciting. There is a growing

FIG 161. Striped hawk-moths are among the rare hawk-moths that occur regularly. (Bryan Thomas)

interest on Scilly in these migrants, and special moth 'viewings' are now some-times arranged for devotees to see them before they are released. Every year new species of moths are caught, adding steadily to the island list.

Two species of red and black day-flying moths are very common on heath-land and dune grassland, including on the uninhabited islands. One is the six-spotted burnet *Zygaena filipendulae stephensi*, with delta-shaped wings and clubbed antennae, the other the cinnabar *Tyria jacobaeae*, whose conspicuous black and orange, football-jersey-striped caterpillars feed on ragwort, heath groundsel *Senecio sylvaticus* and related plants (the warning coloration draws attention to their poisonous nature). Another moth frequently encountered on heathland is the rush veneer *Nomophila noctuella*, a pyralid migrant that in some years arrives in thousands so that they fly up in great clouds when disturbed. Another day-flying moth is the pretty little yellow shell *Camptogramma bilineata*, which superficially resembles a small yellow-ochre butterfly as it flits along the hedgerows.

Several moths also have particular colour forms in Scilly. The lesser yellow underwings *Noctua comes* have a beautifully marked form, *sagittifer*, and there are different forms of the feathered ranunculus *Eumichtus lichenea scillonea* and shuttle-shaped dart *Agrotis puta insula* (Spalding & Sargent, 2000). Some years a distinctive golden-yellow form (a southwestern variation according to A. Spalding, *in litt.*) of the usually brown grass eggar *Lasiocampa trifoli* larva (a Nationally Scarce moth) is common on coastal grasslands. On St Agnes in 2005 among the hundreds of yellow caterpillars were also a small number that were soft grey in colour. In 2006 a few 'normal' dark brown larvae were seen with the yellow form.

Where there is heathland and open grassland the large woolly bear caterpillars of garden tiger and the furry larvae of the grass eggar can be found. Cuckoos, the only birds able to cope with such hairy items, can often be seen where the caterpillars swarm all over the paths and open ground. At times the swarms of caterpillars can be quite spectacular. On one occasion in the early 1960s the numbers of garden tiger caterpillars amounted to 90 per square metre on the short grass in the centre of Gugh (J. Parslow, *in litt.*), and a similar occurrence had been noted by Frohawk (1904). Sometimes garden tiger moths can also be found hiding in vegetation during the day; when disturbed the sudden warning flash of orange underwings may draw attention to them.

Some of the most spectacular moths are the hawk-moths; most are rare immigrants that in some years may appear in unusual numbers. A regular immigrant is convolvulus hawk-moth, which at times arrives early enough to breed and produce larvae. Occasionally death's-head hawk-moth occurs, and its dramatic, large caterpillars have been found in potato fields, where they feed on the plants and can squeak when touched.

The moth that attracts most attention is the hummingbird hawk-moth *Macroglossum stellatarum* (Fig. 162). This species is recorded annually; they often arrive early in spring and can sometimes still be present in November. Very rarely hummingbird hawk-moths have been known to overwinter, and there is a record of one which spent 12 December 1995 to 18 January 1996 in the open porch of John Hale's house on St Agnes (Hicks & Hale, 1998). The hummingbird hawk-moth usually attracts attention because of its distinct resemblance to a hummingbird, flitting from flower to flower, hovering and inserting its long proboscis to feed on the nectar. Certain plants seem favoured, including fuschia *Fuschia* sp., red valerian *Centranthus ruber*, honeysuckle and *Escallonia macrantha*. One of the curiosities of hummingbird hawk-moths is that they often roost at night, in crevices in the stone walls (where John Hale found them) or in the evergreen hedges – where I once disturbed one early one morning, still with dew on its wings.

Another moth frequently seen both in the day and coming to lights at night is silver Y *Autographa gamma*, a common migrant that can also arrive in hundreds

FIG 162. Hummingbird hawk-moths may occasionally overwinter in Scilly. (Bryan Thomas)

in some years. Sometimes clouds of small moths may be seen flying around the top of a *Pittosporum* hedge or around conifers. These usually turn out to be the Nationally Scarce red-necked footman *Atolmis rubricollis*, which swarms some years. In June 2005 thousands of the moths could be seen flying around pine trees all over St Mary's.

Butterflies

Although the number of species of butterflies may not be high, several of them are abundant, and they may even have slight differences in markings that mark them as distinct island variations. Perhaps the most interesting aspect of the butterfly fauna of Scilly is those species that do not occur in the islands or only as very rare vagrants. Several very common British butterflies are still rarities in Scilly. The gatekeeper *Pyronia tithonus* is not known as a resident on Scilly; one I saw on St Agnes in late summer 1978 was apparently a migrant. Another example is the wall butterfly *Lasiommata megera*, which has turned up occasionally without becoming established, and it is still too soon to know if the appearance of comma *Polygonia c-album* in 1997 (personal observation), 2003 (Goodey, 2004) and 2004 (personal observation) will result in another species becoming established in

Scilly. Certainly the presence of elm, nettle *Urtica dioica* and other of its food plants is encouraging. The comma has sometimes been mistaken for one of the fritillary butterflies, but they are totally absent from the islands and seemed unlikely ever to occur – until a queen of Spain *Issoria lathonia* turned up in August 2006 where Martin Goodey was working on St Mary's and he was able to take a photograph (Fig. 163). Although the queen of Spain fritillary is a notable migrant it is unlikely to become resident in Scilly. But there are still other possibilities for new colonists in the future.

Among the white butterflies large white *Pieris brassicae*, small white *P. rapae* and green-veined white *P. napi* all occur, although not very commonly. Green-veined white has been resident since the 1970s and has the strongest populations on St Mary's (Beavis, 2004). Both large and small white can sometimes appear in numbers on Scilly when there is a migrant influx. Many common butterflies are much less frequent on St Agnes than on the other inhabited islands. So although the tortoiseshell *Aglais urticae* and red admiral *Vanessa atalanta* are quite common, peacock *Inachis io* is less so, and they are all more abundant on St Mary's and Tresco. From May onwards pretty little small copper butterflies can be seen around the coastland fringe of the islands. They can produce two broods a year,

FIG 163. A first for Scilly: the queen of Spain fritillary photographed at Trenoweth, St Mary's, in August 2006. (Martin Goodey)

laying their eggs on *Rumex* species, especially common sorrel and possibly some of the several abundant dock species of the coastal grasslands. A blue-spotted colour variety of small copper, ab. *caeruleopunctata*, which has a row of small blue spots on the inside of the copper band on the hindwing, occurs in small numbers (Wacher *et al.*, 2003).

Historically, the common blue butterflies in the Isles of Scilly were part of a frequently quoted study of island populations (Fig. 164). In 1938 Ford and Dowdeswell commenced a 38-year study on populations of common blue and meadow brown *Maniola jurtina* on the small island of Teän (Ford, 1975). It seems the common blue butterflies were not very cooperative, only flying in sunshine and then not for very long, and none flew across the channel to St Martin's only 300 metres away. Because the Teän butterflies were distinctively different from those elsewhere Ford decided they were 'at a stage in the evolution of an independent subspecies'. More recent visits to Teän by several entomologists have not found the common blue to be significantly different from the variations found elsewhere in Scilly, so perhaps Ford's remarkable form no longer exists and the unusual female colour forms and aberrations are just occurring at greater frequency in Scilly than in mainland Britain (Penhallurick, 1996; Beavis, in Smith, 1997; Beavis, 2004).

FIG 164. Male common blue butterfly, a common species of coastal grassland. May 2005. (Rosemary Parslow)

FIG 165. Speckled wood on three-cornered leek. The Scilly form of this butterfly is slightly different from those on the mainland. (Martin Goodey)

There are consistent differences in the Scilly form of speckled wood (Fig. 165). The species was first recorded on Tresco in 1903 and again in the 1920s, but these appear to be isolated records and the butterfly does not seem to have been resident until the late 1960s (Penhallurick, 1996). The Scillonian subspecies, *Pararge aegeria insula*, was first described from specimens taken by Austin Richardson in 1970 (Howarth, 1971; Smith, 1997), by which time they had spread to all the larger islands. The deeper orange spotting compared with the mainland specimens is nearer that of the nominate southern European subspecies. Beavis (2004) found specimens from Scilly to be identical with ones from the Channel Islands, so this may have been the source of the colonisation.

The subspecies of the meadow brown found on the larger islands, *Maniola jurtina cassiteridum*, has slightly different wing spotting and brighter colour compared with specimens from the uninhabited islands (Ford, 1975; Hicks & Hale, 1998). Much has been written about the variation in the spotting on the underside of the hindwing of meadow browns on the different islands (Fig. 166). Dowdeswell and Ford showed that the female butterflies on the larger islands with more habitats, St Martin's, Tresco and St Mary's, mostly show more

FIG 166. Meadow brown also has Scilly variations. (Bryan Thomas)

variation (from no spots to just one or two on their hindwing), whereas those on Great Arthur have two spots and those on White Island have none. On Teän the spot numbers vary between none and two. There may now be some doubt about the status of the endemic subspecies, but there is clearly a tendency to show more differences in the colour and spotting than is usual on the mainland (Beavis, 2004). Other experiments by Dowdeswell and Ford included introductions or re-establishments of meadow brown to Menawethan and Great Innisvouls in the Eastern Isles, although neither was ultimately successful (Dennis & Shreeve, 1996).

The only other blue butterfly resident in Scilly is the holly blue *Celastrina argiolus* (see Fig. 137). A recent arrival in the islands, the date of the first appearance is not recorded but it was probably before 1973. Holly blue was certainly on Tresco and St Mary's by 1978, and it has now colonised St Agnes (Hicks & Hale, 1998). Although the usual food plants of the holly blue are holly *Ilex aquifolium* and ivy, only the latter is present in any quantities, so observations of the butterfly laying eggs on hedge veronica are interesting as it may prove to be an alternative food plant in Scilly (Heckford, 1987).

One of the exciting aspects of studying natural history in a small discrete area such as an island is that new arrivals are more likely to be noticed. So when ringlet butterflies turned up in Scilly very recently, the first report was from a visiting naturalist, Jeff Benn, who found them on St Martin's in 1995. Within a few years they had become widespread on St Martin's, being common along all the hedgebanks and around the cricket field and behind the dunes. They then invaded St Mary's and Tresco, spreading quickly again so that by 2001 ringlets had been seen in Hugh Town (Fig. 167). How the ringlet reached Scilly is not known, but as they do not lay their eggs on the food plant but scatter them in flight it is possible some may have been introduced with soil or horticultural material. It had been suggested the reason they were absent from Scilly was because their usual food plant, tufted hair-grass *Deschampsia cespitosa*, is absent from the islands. However several authors have commented that they will eat other species of grass such as cocksfoot *Dactylis glomerata* and false tor-grass *Brachypodium sylvaticum*, both of which are abundant in Scilly (Penhallurick, 1996; Wacher *et al.*, 2003).

Perhaps the most exciting events in autumn are not only the appearance of rare migrant birds from North America but also the occasional rare monarch (milkweed) butterfly. These butterflies are apparently carried across the Atlantic by some of the same extreme weather conditions that carry the bird migrants to Scilly. Some earlier immigrants that reached the Canary Islands, Madeira and Spain, and have become established there, are suspected of occasionally being the source of the monarchs that turn up in Scilly (Penhallurick, 1996). However, as the monarchs usually arrive at times of autumn hurricanes and westerly gales and have sometimes been seen flying in over the sea, they are accepted as originating from North America. Another immigrant butterfly frequently occurring in the Isles of Scilly is the clouded yellow (Fig. 168). Its arrivals are irregular, so that in some years none or hardly any will be seen and in other years they will arrive in dozens. In some years the first arrivals will breed, resulting in a further flush of the butterfly later in the year, followed by others which emerge early in the year from eggs or larvae that have overwintered (Hicks & Hale, 1998; Wacher *et al.*, 2003). The very pale female form *helice* also turns up and is often mistaken for the very rare pale clouded yellow *Colias hyale*. To confirm the identity it is necessary to capture a specimen, and since 1900 there has only been one record of pale clouded yellow, in 1968 (Smith, 1984). Unfortunately clouded yellow butterflies are restless and very fast, so attempting to net or photograph one is not an easy prospect!

FIG 167. Ringlet butterfly, a recent arrival in Scilly that is now spreading rapidly. (Alma Hathway)

FIG 168. Clouded yellow butterflies are regular migrants that sometimes occur in large numbers. (Bryan Thomas)

Two more common immigrants are the red admiral and painted lady *Vanessa cardui*. Both may be very common in some years; they breed on the islands and are suspected of occasionally overwintering. That both species also emigrate from Scilly has been shown by records of them flying around Round Island lighthouse on several occasions (Nicholson, 1934, in Smith, 1997; Penhallurick, 1996).

TRUE FLIES

A number of different families of true flies (Diptera) are found in the Isles of Scilly. Soldierflies are small insects with metallic colouring and a style of folding their wings neatly parallel, giving them their military name. Most soldierflies are found near water, but one species, the broad centurion *Chloromyia formosa*, is a much less aquatic species and is often found well away from water, usually on the flowers of umbellifers (Apiaceae). Robberflies are hairy flies that have very bearded faces; they are predators on other insects. Three large species found in Scilly, kite-tailed robberfly *Machinus atricapillus*, brown heath robberfly

M. cingulatus and dune robberfly *Philonicus albiceps*, are often conspicuous on sunny days sitting on the sandy paths in the dunes waiting to pounce on any passing insect prey (I. Beavis, *in litt.*). A bee-fly, the only one found in Scilly, dune villa *Villa modesta*, can often be found on sunny days in the sand dunes visiting the flowers of Portland and sea spurge, common stork's-bill and other nectar sources. Another fly that lives in the dunes is the coastal stiletto-fly *Acrosanthe annulata*, covered in beautiful silvery-white fur and very well camouflaged against the white sand (Fig. 169).

Typically small, yellow and black, or black and white, hoverflies are very familiar both on garden plants and on wild flowers, where their bright colours and hovering flight attract attention. Sometimes they are bee or wasp mimics and feed on nectar or pollen. Most hoverflies are predators in the larval stage, with many species feeding on aphids on a range of plants, while others live among fungi or as scavengers on other insects; some live in pools or tree holes as rat-tailed maggots.

Many hoverflies are superficially very similar and although they are a popular group not many have vernacular names. Comparing their colour patterns with illustrations in books can identify some of the most common or distinctive species. Others are more difficult and may need specialist attention and access to books such as Stubbs and Falk (2002).

Most records of hoverflies are from the inhabited islands; little recording seems to have taken place on the uninhabited islands. Some species rely on wetland habitats or damp places to breed, and these tend to be absent from St Martin's, where there are no large freshwater pools.

FIG 169. The coastal stiletto-fly with its silvery fur is difficult to see against the sandy background. (Ren Hathway)

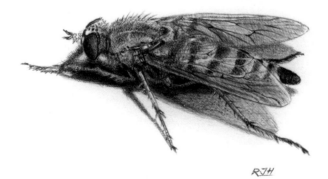

RJH

FIG 170. The hoverfly *Chrysotoxum festivum* may be a migrant, recorded from St Martin's and Tresco. (Ren Hathway)

Some species of hoverflies, *Episyrphus balteatus* and *Scaeva pyrastri* for example, are migratory and occur in large numbers at the same time as large influxes of migrant butterflies. *Chrysotoxum festivum* is also a possible migrant that has occasionally been recorded from St Martin's and the Abbey Gardens, Tresco (Fig. 170). Others such as the large, orange-bodied *Xanthandrus comtus* and one of the sun-flies, *Helophilus trivittatus*, may also be migrants as they are numerous some years and absent in others (Beavis, 2004).

Among the most widespread species in the Isles of Scilly are a number of species of the small yellow and black striped or banded hoverflies. These include several species of *Platycheirus* as well as other quite similar species. Just to complicate things, sometimes males and females may look different, and others may come in several colour forms. *Metasyrphus corollae* and *Episyrphus balteatus* are medium-sized flies that have been recorded recently from all the inhabited islands. Another well-known species is the large *Syrphus ribesii*, also yellow and black with a striped thorax, and then there is the large and impressive sun-fly *Helophilus pendulus*, which does not usually appear until the sun comes out, hence its name. Also large, but with a black abdomen with white half-moon markings, is the widespread *Scaeva pyrastri*. A slightly alarming hoverfly is *Rhingia campestris*, a large insect with long mouthparts that look like a beak. The beak is not a sting, but a device to enable it to reach deep into tubular flowers (Gilbert, 1993). A number of the drone flies *Eristalis* spp. including the well-known *E. tenax* are widespread in Scilly; like others of the genus it is a bee mimic. Similar in appearance to the drone flies are species of the genus *Eristalinus*. One, *E. aeneus*, is a large insect found on the coast, where it often basks for brief periods on the rocks.

Several species of hoverflies mimic other insects. Perhaps the largest and most obvious in Scilly is a pest in the bulb fields, the large narcissus or bulb fly *Merodon equestris* (Fig. 171), whose larvae attack narcissus and daffodil bulbs, hollowing out and destroying the bulbs from the inside (Burton, 1968). The narcissus fly is a bumblebee mimic; it has a distinctive 'buzz', is large and furry and occurs in several different colour varieties. At one time the large males were seen visiting the greenhouses where narcissus were being packed (A. Stubbs, personal communication), but this is unlikely to happen these days when the season is over before the hoverfly is on the wing (M. Goodey, personal communication). *Eumerus funeralis* and *E. strigatus* are together known as the lesser bulb fly and are found inland and in coastal areas. Another bumblebee mimic, *Eristalis intricarius*, can resembles the narcissus fly, although it is smaller and does not have the completely black abdomen. *Volucella bombylans*, as its name suggests, looks very much like a bumblebee, and its larvae are scavengers in bees' nests. The small, inconspicuous, all-black *Paragus haemorrhous*, found on the coast, resembles some solitary bees and wasps. *Xylota segnis* is a distinctive and

FIG 171. The narcissus fly is a serious pest of the narcissus crop. (Martin Goodey)

common species with a narrow orange abdomen with a black tip that mimics solitary wasps; it can most often be seen on sunlit foliage collecting pollen from leaves and other places rather than directly from flowers (Gilbert, 1993).

HYMENOPTERA

The islands' hymenopteran fauna shows a similar pattern to that of the butterflies, with species that had not been found in earlier surveys becoming established very quickly once they have arrived in the islands (Beavis, 2004). Descriptions of those species that occur in Scilly and their distribution in Scilly have been published by Ian Beavis (2003).

Ants
Fourteen different species of ants have been recorded on the Isles of Scilly, several of which are quite common. One is the yellow meadow ant *Lasius flavus*, the species responsible for anthills in old meadows, although in Scilly it does not appear to make large anthills. The garden black ant *Lasius niger* is common on all the inhabited islands, and another black ant, the long-legged negro ant *Formica fusca* is widespread in both inland and coastal habitats on all the main islands except St Agnes (Beavis, 2003). The Isles of Scilly guide books and other tourist literature all refer to the St Martin's ant *Formica rufibarbis*. 'This remarkable rarity', according to Beavis (2000), was first reported by Yarrow (1967) and appeared to be restricted to Chapel Down, St Martin's, and some of the Eastern Isles. The only place it is found in Britain outside Scilly is a site in Surrey. It is large species, one of the 'wood' ants (as is the negro ant) that usually build large obvious nests above ground. In this species the nests are difficult to find, as they are completely underground with nothing obvious on the surface. The ant usually frequents rather open heathland with plenty of bare ground, where they have been known to surprise picnickers sitting on the ground by emerging to defend their nests from attack. I accidentally found a nest on Teän in July 2002, a new site for the species: I put down a knapsack on the ground in an area of dune grassland to answer a mobile phone, and when I picked the bag up again a stream of large, angry, bicoloured ants rushed out of a small hole in the sandy ground.

Wasps
That wasps were unknown in Scilly was once the proud boast of the local guidebooks. In fact occasional wasps have been turning up in Scilly for many years. There is a watercolour in the Abbey Collection that is reproduced in Sam

Llewellyn's book (2005) of what looks like a German wasp queen, inscribed 'first seen in 1871'. German *Vespula germanica* and common wasps *V. vulgaris* have probably made repeated efforts to colonise the islands over the years. There are anecdotal accounts of what were probably one or other of these species in the Abbey Gardens some years before the recent spate of records (R. Hathway, personal commnunication). In 1996 five different individual queen German wasps were recorded on St Mary's and Tresco: they were probably migrants and appear to have been unsuccessful in establishing colonies (Beavis, 2003, 2005). Common wasp workers have been recorded by Beavis a couple of times on Tresco in 2001 and 2003 and are occasionally seen on St Mary's but no colony had been confirmed until 2004 when Martin Goodey found a colony near Trenoweth, St Mary's (Beavis, 2005), so it seems likely they will soon become established.

The tree wasp *Dolichovespula sylvestris* is the only social wasp native to the islands. It is found on all the inhabited islands (including Gugh), as well as Great Ganilly in the Eastern Isles. The wasp is often found on the flowers of balm-leaved figwort and on umbellifers. As tree wasps generally keep out of the way of humans they probably go unnoticed by the general public (I. Beavis, *in litt.*). A nest was found in the root plate of a fallen tree in Tresco Wood in 1999.

The other wasps that occur in Scilly are solitary species, including spider-hunting wasps (Pompilidae), a group of very small insects that fly close to the ground to catch spiders, which they sting to paralyse them, then drag them to their cells as food for their larvae. Digger wasps are another interesting group with an extremely narrow 'wasp-waist' and often yellow and black striped bodies; they prey on other insects, which they also paralyse before storing them in their cells to feed their grubs. Their cells are often in holes excavated in the ground or in cliffs. Like many related species, the field digger wasp *Mellinus arvensis* is found on coastal dune sites such as Appletree Banks. Males frequently visit wild carrot flowers. Two species of the little ruby-tailed wasps are found in the Isles of Scilly but only one, *Chrysis rutiliventris*, is common. This is a very distinctive insect with a deep red abdomen and shiny, metallic blue-green head and thorax. They can often be seen on sunny walls or the flowers of wild carrot and other umbellifers.

Bees

The family of bees called 'solitary bees' do not have workers or live communally, although they do congregate in places where they nest. The commonest group are the mining bees, especially conspicuous in the spring and summer when they are active around their nest holes along the 'ram' cliffs around the coasts. Some species also nest in dry banks beside footpaths, as well as inland in the earth-filled 'hedges'. Although they are 'solitary' some form large colonies with hundreds of nest holes peppering the cliff face, and they may also share a common entrance to their nests. There are a number of species of these bees in Scilly, but most of them are very similar in appearance. Two of the commonest are *Andrena nigroaenea sarnia* and the widespread *Andrena thoracica*. The former is a subspecies that also occurs in the Channel Islands; it superficially resembles and is frequently found with *A. thoracica*, and they even share nest sites (Richards, 1978; Beavis, 2000). Another of these bees that is sometimes encountered in coastal areas or gardens where heather is growing is *Andrena fuscipes*: the males appear to have distinctive blue-grey abdomens in flight. The yellow-legged mining bee *Andrena flavipes* is a recent colonist that makes nests in soft cliffs on St Mary's (Fig. 172). Two species of the leaf-cutter bees are also found in Scilly, Willughby's leaf-cutter *Megachile willughbiella* and common leaf-cutter *M. centunculus*: the females may be seen cutting neat semicircular sections out of leaves and carrying them away to their burrows.

The bumblebee most frequently encountered in the Isles of Scilly is the buff-tailed bumblebee *Bombus terrestris*, a large and conspicuous bee that has been recorded from all the main islands. It is often the first bee to appear in spring (it is also often seen on mild days in winter) and can initially be confusing as it varies considerably in size and the much smaller workers may be taken for a

FIG 172. The yellow-legged mining bee makes its nests in soft cliffs on St Mary's. (Ren Hathway)

different species. Often the bee will be seen along the coast working the open flowers of Hottentot fig. It can sometimes be seen flying between the islands and may land on boats, even on occasion on the deck of the RMV *Scillionian* crossing from the mainland.

The bumblebee most associated with the Isles of Scilly, however, is the Scilly bee *Bombus muscorum scyllonius*, a subspecies of the moss carder bee found on the mainland (Fig. 173). Queens are described as being impressively large and colourful insects (Beavis, 2000), but it is uncommon and is known more by reputation than by familiarity. Andrew Cooper coined the name 'Scilly bee' in 1980 when he made a television film about the Isles of Scilly and it has since been adopted locally (Cooper, 1992). The Scilly bee was first described as a subspecies by Yarrow (1967), who recorded it from St Agnes, Gugh and St Martin's. About the same time it was recorded from all the inhabited islands except Bryher.

FIG 173. The Scilly bee is an uncommon form of moss carder bee found in Scilly. (Martin Goodey)

Studies of the distribution of the Scilly bee by W. E. Almond over a number of years from 1960 found that it had declined in abundance over the years and disappeared from former sites. He had originally found the species on all the main islands including Annet and his map no. 9 indicates they were also found later on Samson, Teän, the Eastern Isles and Gugh (Almond, 1975).

Since 1978 most of the records of Scilly bee have been from St Agnes (Beavis, 2000). Most of the sightings have been along the coast and include Wingletang, Troy Town and Castella Down, as well as near Big Pool and on Gugh. Beavis found the bee was 'quite numerous' on Great Ganilly and Great Arthur in the Eastern Isles, and in Holy Vale, St Mary's. Recent records have also been from St Agnes, St Mary's and Tresco. The distribution is clearly associated with nectar sources: the bees feed on the flowers of bird's-foot-trefoil, red clover *Trifolium pratense* and heather (Beavis, 2003, 2004). In July 2002 I followed one of the beautiful foxy brown and buff queens along the cliff path as she flew from clump to clump of bird's-foot-trefoil for about thirty minutes before she flew out of sight.

Several other species of bumblebees are found in Scilly, including the garden bumblebee *Bombus hortorum*, which is found on the inhabited islands and appears to prefer gardens and sheltered areas. Garden bumblebees are very similar to the buff-tailed, but have a very white tail and an additional yellow band on the thorax. There is also another similar species, heath bumblebee *B. jonellus*. Unfortunately, it is not easy to distinguish several of these bumblebees from each other in the field. Just to complicate matters there are several other insects that resemble bumblebees – hoverfly bee mimics (see earlier) and cuckoo bees. Two species of cuckoo bees have been recorded in Scilly: these are nest parasites and resemble their host species but have smoky coloured wings. Only one is now found in the islands, the vestal cuckoo bee *Psithyrus vestalis*, which is a parasite on the buff-tailed bumblebee.

One common bee that is frequently encountered is not a wild species: the honeybee *Apis mellifera*. Several islanders keep a few hives and their bees stray quite far afield; honeybees have been seen on all the inhabited islands including Gugh and as far out as on the uninhabited island of Great Arthur in the Eastern Isles (Beavis, 2004).

BEETLES

Most beetles (Coleoptera) that are encountered in the Isles of Scilly do not have common names and are generally the province of the specialist coleopterist. Blair

(1931) compiled a very comprehensive list of more than 500 species of beetle from his and other entomologists' collections and publications; he also listed the species recorded on the smaller uninhabited islands. Some of the larger or more obvious beetles such as ladybirds are well known in the islands and will be encountered on a summer visit. One very distinctive beetle is the oil beetle *Meloe proscarabaeus*, a feature on the islands in spring and early summer (Fig. 174). They are flightless, large, black slow-moving insects that crawl ponderously across the concrete roads, where many get squashed by passing vehicles. Sadly some people dislike the beetles and, perhaps unaware of their extraordinary life history, kill them. The females when swollen with eggs are especially slow and vulnerable. They graze on tender leaves of roadside herbs in full view of passers-by. The eggs are laid in a hole in the ground that has been excavated by the female; they hatch a few weeks later into small, louse-like larvae called triungulins, which climb to the top of a flowering plant and hitch a ride on a visiting bee (or other large insect). If they are lucky they get carried back to a bee's nest where at first they feed on the eggs or larvae before moving on to the honey. There is a delightful account of the life history of the beetle by Gordon Simmons, who describes the emergence of the triungulins in his study when about a thousand of them were

FIG 174. Flightless oil beetles spend part of their life cycle in the nests of bees. (Rosemary Parslow)

FIG 175. The rose chafer occur in two colour forms, iridescent green and, less commonly, black. (Rosemary Parslow)

found frantically climbing up curtains and swarming around the room. On another occasion Simmons found an *Andrena* bee so covered in the larvae it had become completely grounded and unable to fly. After wintering in the bee's nest the successful larvae pupate and eventually emerge as the adult beetles (Burton, 1968; Simmons, 1976).

In the summer holiday visitors are often startled by iridescent, viridian green rose chafers that buzz across the heathland and pitch down clumsily to land. At other times the beetles may be found sitting in flowers eating the petals; they appear to favour bramble flowers but will also eat the flowers of many cultivated plants (Fig. 175). Most of the beetles are the common green version, but a black colour variety *Cetonia aurata* ab. *nigra* also occurs in small numbers. Frequently the beetles fall on the ground, where they are quite slow-moving, and where their buzzing makes them very obvious. As a result they seem vulnerable to predators, and fragmented remains of their shiny carapaces and tarsi are frequently found in kestrel *Falco tinnunculus* pellets and in hedgehog faeces. Another beetle that is predated by kestrels and hedgehogs is the minotaur beetle *Typhaeus typhoeus*. The name refers to the fanciful resemblance of the male beetle to the mythical minotaur. The male beetle has three prong-like projections on the front of the carapace, two of which are horn-like. This easily identified part of the beetle is usually found intact in the kestrel pellets. The live beetles are occasionally found on pathways on heathland; their burrows are usually under cow-pats or rabbit droppings, on which they feed. It is sometimes possible to see the beetle rolling rabbit droppings back to its burrow like a miniature scarab beetle (Fig. 176). Closely related to the minotaur are the dor beetles, *Geotrupes stercorarius* and the very similar *G. spiniger*, which also live on dung and are frequently found on heathland and coastal grassland. Dor beetles are large, heavy-bodied beetles with metallic purple undersides and usually many tiny brown mites clinging to them. When they fly they too buzz along and usually make a crash-landing; locally they are called 'dumbledors' (M. Hicks, personal communication). Keith Hyatt found one that had landed on the ground and was apparently unable to rise again due to a large burden of mites (c.370) that had apparently exhausted it (Hyatt, 1990).

Another obvious and attractive heathland and coastal grassland species, often around at the same time as the rose chafers, is the green tiger beetle. These attract attention by flying above the vegetation and dropping down onto a patch of bare ground and scuttling along very fast. Frequently the mating beetles will run along pathways with the female carrying the male 'piggy-back' style. Tiger beetles are fierce predators and eat any smaller insects that come their way. The larvae live in burrows in the sandy ground with their large jaws poking out of the top of the tunnel ready to grab a passing meal. One of the other common beetles

FIG 176. Minotaur beetle rolling a rabbit dropping back to its burrow. (Rosemary Parslow)

found in late summer, usually on the flowers of wild carrot and other umbellifers, is a bright orange soldier beetle with a dark tip to the body/wings, *Rhagonycha fulva*. The largest of the group of chrysomelid beetles, leaf-beetles, is the bloody-nosed beetle *Timarcha tenebricosa*. Most of the group are small and brightly coloured, often metallic. The bloody-nosed beetle is black and easily recognised when handled as red liquid oozes from the mouth and joints – hence its common name. Unable to fly, the beetle is sometimes found walking along pathways in early summer. Other common beetles that are frequently encountered are the violet ground beetles *Carabus violaceus* or *C. problematicus*. Turning over stones may reveal the largest of the huge family of rove (staphylinid) beetles, the devil's coach-horse *Ocypus olens*, a large black beetle with a very intimidating habit of cocking its tail over its back and opening its jaws wide to bite. One odd introduction was the wharf beetle *Nacerdes malanura*, a wood-boring beetle from North America found in timbers, boats etc. that was recorded by K. G. Blair on St Mary's (Turk & Turk, 1980).

SPIDERS

Most of what is known about spiders in the Isles of Scilly arises from two seminal papers by W. S. Bristowe (1929 & 1935) based on his visits to the islands in July 1927, 1928 and 1934. From his account it would seem that Bristowe was very lucky with the weather at the time as he was able to land on a significant number of the uninhabited islands. Very few spiders have vernacular names, but some of Bristowe's observations seem so interesting that they are referred to here. One of these was a record of the rare Red Data Book spider *Clubiona genevensis*, recorded on the shore above high water mark on five islands, a species that had only been found in Dorset at that time. Since then *Clubiona genevensis* has also been recorded from two Cornish sites (Bratton, 1991) and from Ramsey and Skokholm islands (Harvey *et al.*, 2002). Other spiders also occur in the splash zone and above, where presumably there is plenty of food and available shelter. There do not seem to be any recent records of the jumping spider *Sitticus pubescens*, a melanic form of which was found by Bristowe both on Rosevear in the Western Rocks and on Little Innisvouls in the Eastern Isles. The familiar little black and white zebra spider *Salticus scenicus* was found in similar areas among boulders on Annet, where it is still present, as well as being common on buildings and other man-made structures on the inhabited islands. Also very widespread is the common garden spider *Araneus diadematus*, which spins its classic orb webs in all manner of habitats around the islands. They are particularly abundant in stands of bracken on the uninhabited islands. *Pisaura mirabilis* is another common and distinctive spider. The females are often seen carrying the large egg sac as they run through the vegetation, and on sunny days even in winter they will bask on leaves with the legs spread in pairs in a cruciform shape (Fig. 177). *Textrix denticulata* is common on several islands, and Bristowe found that the irregular band down its abdomen is much paler than usual in the Scillonian specimens. Another spider that was found by Bristowe on coastal sites was the purse-web spider *Atypus affinis*, the female of which makes her burrows among boulders at the top of the beach. This spider has not been found recently, although searched for in 1999 on several islands without success (A. Colston, *in litt.*). Woodlouse spiders, *Dysdera crocata* and *D. erythrina*, are sluggish spiders with bright red legs that feed on woodlice, animals not usually tackled by most spiders; they are common both in coastal habitats and under rocks in gardens. Some spiders, such as *Halorates reprobus*, are associated with the nests of seabirds, especially those of shag and cormorant, where there is probably plenty of invertebrate life to feed on. This species was collected in 1993 from Piper's Hole sea cave on Tresco (Ashmole & Ashmole, 1995).

Some of the spiders found living in the open in Scilly are species usually associated with hothouses, one of which is *Achaearanea tepidariorum*. Mild

FIG 177. *Pisaura mirabilis* basks on a wall pennywort leaf in the winter sun. (Rosemary Parslow)

winters enable species such as the cobweb spiders *Tegenaria* spp. and the large *Amaurobius ferox*, usually associated with warmer climates or found inside buildings, to survive in Scilly often in quite open conditions – such as sand dunes. Another species, the Nationally Scarce *Achaearanea veruculata*, has so far been found only on Tresco, its only known European site. The spider was found on gorse bushes in 1959 and again in 1960 (Merrett & Rowe, 1961) and is said to have been present since the beginning of the 1900s (Roberts, 1995). As with many other invertebrate species from Australia and New Zealand, it is presumed to have been imported with horticultural material for the Abbey Gardens on Tresco (Harvey *et al.*, 2002). Another more widely distributed Nationally Scarce spider, *Achaearanea simulans*, has also been recorded from Tresco and St Mary's (Smithers, in Spalding, 1997).

Two common spiders, *Zygiella x-notata* and *Textrix denticulata*, were found on Rosevear in the Western Rocks by Bristowe, who suggested they may have accidentally been transported there by the workmen who lived there while building the Bishop Rock lighthouse. *Pardosa agricola*, also Nationally Scarce, is another coastal species that was recorded from the very isolated island of Melledgan in the Western Rocks (Smithers, in Spalding, 1997) but is not included in the recent atlas (Harvey *et al.*, 2002). Two more Nationally Scarce spiders have been found on Scilly: *Episinus truncatus*, a heathland species recorded from all the larger islands, and *Dipoena inornata* from Tresco. One local species is *Scytodes thoracica*, found in houses at night. Houses in Scilly, as well as sheds and barns, are home to the fragile-looking daddy-long-legs spider *Pholcus phalangioides* (Fig. 178).

The only animal recorded from the small island of Mouls in the Eastern Isles by Bristowe (1929) was the pseudoscorpion *Neobisium (Obisium) maritimum* from between tidemarks. It is still common on most islands in Scilly (Smithers, in Spalding, 1997). Another pseudoscorpion is *Chthonius orthodactylus*, a generally common species that is local in the southwest. Bristowe also recorded three species of harvestmen (Opiliones) in his first paper, and in 1934 he collected the same species again (Bristowe, 1935). Smithers lists a local harvestman, *Nelima gothica*, from Tresco and St Mary's.

A large mite fauna, 169 species, has been recorded in Scilly (Hyatt, 1993). As most mites are very tiny and are usually only found in litter, rotting seaweed, among lichens etc. they are only really studied by specialist scientists. Perhaps the species most likely to be noticed by the casual observer are those on the undersides of dung beetles or on bees. More than one species of mite is involved: seven species have been recorded associated with beetles, usually on one of the dor beetles, or in one case a minotaur beetle (Hyatt, 1990). Other mites are found

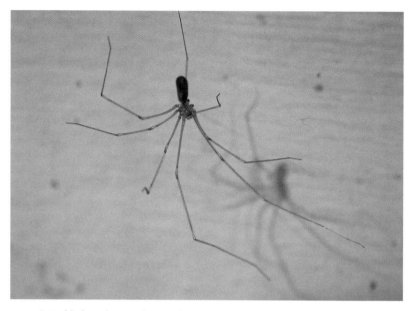

FIG 178. Daddy-long-legs spiders are found in almost every building in the Isles of Scilly. (Rosemary Parslow)

on bumblebees: large numbers found on the buff-tailed bumblebees in February 2004 were probably one of the species of *Parasitellus*, possibly *P. fucorum* (K. Hyatt, *in litt.*). Another group are those found on birds or in their nests, which may be noticed when ringing birds (Hyatt, 1993). One mite that most naturalists may get to know only too intimately is the harvest mite *Trombicula autumnalis*. This almost invisible 'bracken bug', as they are called locally, is very common in bracken and any tall vegetation in late summer. The six-legged larvae find their way onto the skin of any warm-blooded animal (including humans) and feed on areas of thin skin – armpits, waist or ankles – for a few days before dropping off to continue their life cycle in the soil. The bites become inflamed and itchy and the reaction may continue for weeks (Evans *et al.*, 1961).

CRUSTACEANS AND OTHERS

Turn over a rock or piece of wood on any of the inhabited islands in Scilly and dozens of amphipods, like black versions of the common sandhoppers, will jump away. These are woodland hoppers or New Zealand land-hoppers, a recent arrival in Scilly, first found on Tresco in 1925, since when they have spread to all the inhabited islands. Their country of origin is New Zealand and they arrived on the Isles of Scilly and mainland Cornwall in consignments of plants from Treseder's Nursery in Truro, which at the time was the main supplier of New Zealand plants to gardens in the West Country and the Abbey Gardens on Tresco, until they closed down in the 1980s (Lee, 2003).

A species of springtail new to Britain, *Onychiurus argus*, was found by the Ashmoles in Piper's Hole, the large sea cave on the north coast of Tresco (Ashmole & Ashmole, 1995). A common, blue-black coloured springtail, *Anurida maritima*, is usually found in clusters on the water surface of pools and on the upper shore. Also on the upper shore the prehistoric-looking bristletail *Petrobius maritimus*, a larger version of the common silverfish *Lepisma saccharina*, can be found under boulders and plants at the top of the beach.

MOLLUSCS

In the *Atlas of the Land and Freshwater Molluscs of Cornwall and the Isles of Scilly* (Turk *et al.*, 2001) it is said that 'the Isles of Scilly are markedly poorer in species than the Cornish mainland, as one might expect from their small size, restriction of habitat and isolation.' Even so, at the time the atlas was published there were 60 species recorded from Scilly, since when another ten species have been added (Holyoak, 2003). According to Cameron (2006) the molluscan fauna of the larger islands in Scilly is in fact as rich as that of similar-sized areas on the mainland. But many of the species found in Scilly are introduced and are now widespread, inhabiting both natural and man-made habitats; some few species are still only found in association with buildings and gardens.

The granite composition of the rocks results in a predominately acidic substrate that does not favour snails, as they require calcium to build their shells. Several of the most interesting and important species of native molluscs are those found around the coast in Scilly. The rocky granite shores of most of the islands are the habitat of a rare mollusc, a lagoon snail *Paludinella littorina* (Turk *et al.*, 2001). This is a very small snail of no more than 2mm, which is found both among pebbles and boulders on the beaches and in rock crevices at and above high tide level. Although this species may be overlooked due to its small size, it is genuinely rare elsewhere in Britain (Kerney, 1999) so the populations found on Scilly are significant. These beach habitats are also where mouse-eared snail *Ovatella myosotis* and two-toothed white snail *Leucophytia bidentata* can be found.

Another significant species is also coastal in distribution: a small green, hairy, land snail called *Ponentina subvirescens*. This species occurs only around the coasts of Cornwall, Devon, Pembrokeshire and the Atlantic coast of Europe, where it is associated with the mosaic of maritime grassland and heathland with thrift and ling that grows over thin soils and rocky outcrops. *P. subvirescens* is unusually tolerant of acidic substrates and this may account for its wide distribution on all the larger islands, where it can often be the most common land snail in suitable habitat. Other native land snails found in the same habitat include garlic snail *Oxychilus alliarius* (it smells of garlic), slippery moss snail *Cochlicopa lubrica*, pellucid glass snail *Vitrina pellucida* and rayed glass snail *Nesovitrea hammonis*. An interesting incident involving the pellucid glass snail happened when one was found attached to the flank feathers of a northern waterthrush, a vagrant from North America. As the snail has a wide distribution on both sides of the Atlantic and specimens have been found attached to birds before, we will never know whether the snail had travelled the Atlantic as a passenger or had been picked up on arrival in Scilly (Williamson *et al.*, 1959).

It is difficult not to be aware of the grove or brown-lipped snail *Cepaea nemoralis*, as this is the species most often targeted by song thrushes and whose smashed shells are found on their anvils. Grove snails are very abundant on all the inhabited islands and have also been found in subfossil remains on Nornour in the Eastern Isles (Turk, 1978). Another snail still found in Scilly that was also identified from the Nornour excavations is the rounded snail *Discus rotundatus*.

Dune and coastal grasslands appear to attract a number of different snails, perhaps because there may be more available calcium from ground-down seashells. Among common dune species are the wrinkled snail *Candidula intersecta*, striped snail *Cernuella virgata* and pointed snail *Cochlicella acuta*. The familiar garden snail *Cornu aspersum* (*Helix aspersa*) is also abundant in dunes and coastal habitats. All four of these molluscs are introduced species. Garden snails usually appear after rain, and during the day they generally hide – in gardens often under the straplike leaves of *Agapanthus* lilies (Fig. 179). On Annet this snail was found to be the most common species, despite the island being frequently saturated in salt spray (Holyoak, 2003). They were probably an early introduction to Scilly, some time after the Iron Age, but there is no evidence that it has been used commonly as a food item in the islands. According to Stella Turk those living in the dunes among white sand have paler shells than elsewhere, although this apparently had not prevented them dying in their hundreds on Samson in drought conditions in July 2006. The common large black slug *Arion ater* is also found in Scilly, including on heathland (Fig. 180). Native species also occur in these coastal habitats, for example *Ponentina subvirescens* and the associated

FIG 179. Garden snails hide under the leaves of *Agapanthus* plants. (Rosemary Parslow)

FIG 180. Large black slug, a common mollusc in the islands. (David Holyoak)

molluscs mentioned above, silky snail *Ashfordia granulata* and also common whorl snail *Vertigo pygmaea* – which is very rare on the islands.

Molluscs associated with wetland habitats are very poorly represented in Scilly due to the lack of freshwater habitats other than on the larger islands. For example, only five species of pea mussels *Pisidium* spp. have ever been recorded, and common pond snail *Lymnaea peregra*, dwarf pond snail *L. truncatula*, white-lipped ramshorn *Anisus leucostoma*, Pfeiffer's amber snail *Oxyloma pfeifferi* and hollowed glass snail *Zonitoides excavatus*, all of which are extremely common snails elsewhere in Britain, are very rare and localised on Scilly.

What is so evident in the Isles of Scilly is the small number of native species, their restricted diversity, and that they are both very localised and often sparse where they do occur. As with so many other species in Scilly, the influence of human occupation is clearly illustrated by the number and widespread occurrence of introduced species of land and freshwater molluscs. Although it is not easy to date the arrival of any individual 'alien' species on an island, it is known that both the worm slug *Boettgerilla pallens* and tree slug *Lehmannia valentiana* are relatively recent introductions to Britain (Kerney, 1999). Their arrival in Scilly is believed to have been associated with horticultural material brought in by flower farmers, or rather more likely for the Gardens on Tresco. This may also be how introduced species of slug such as jet slug *Milax gagates*, keeled slug *Tandonia sowerbyi* and Caruana's Sicilian slug *Deroceras panormitarum* first arrived in Scilly, where they are now common and widespread. For some other species, such as pointed snail and striped snail, it seems less likely that this was their route to Scilly.

PLANARIANS AND LAND NEMERTINES

Planarians (flatworms) are a group of small animals probably best known from their small, black, freshwater forms. The terrestrial planarians known from the Isles of Scilly are also small (usually only a few centimetres in length) and are generally overlooked; most are variously black, grey or brown, although some of those found in Scilly are quite colourful. One, the orange-coloured 'Australian' flatworm *Geoplana sanguinea*, was first found on Tresco in 1960 and has turned up since in other places in Britain and Northern Ireland. *Geoplana coxii*, whose body is deep blue with white iridescent lines, was also first found on Tresco. These flatworms are carnivorous: they feed on earthworms and are considered a pest in gardens (Spalding & Sargent, 2000). *Kontikia andersoni* may also originate from Australasia or New Zealand; it is a pale brown flatworm with darker markings. Two scavengers are *Microplana scharffi* and *M. terrestris*; the first is bright yellow but looks pink after feeding. Both *Microplana* species are native species, and another species that may also be native is *Rhynchodemus sylvaticus*.

Only two land nemertines are known from Scilly. These are small, terrestrial relatives of the extraordinary long marine bootlace or ribbon worms. *Argonemertes dendyi* originated from Western Australia; it is only 1–2.5cm in length, cream or pale brown in colour with darker stripes, and feeds on soil invertebrates. *Antiponemertes pantini* from New Zealand can reach 3cm; it is pinky-cream in colour, also with two brown stripes, but mottled. This species is only known in Britain from Tresco.

CHAPTER 15

Mammals, Reptiles and Amphibians

There is no Adder, or any venomous creatures of any kind to be found in these Islands.

William Borlase (1756)

THERE ARE VERY few species of vertebrate resident on the Isles of Scilly (Table 5). Many common mammals such as fox, badger *Meles meles*, stoat, weasel *Mustela nivalis*, all voles and most small mammals are totally absent, and those that are present, other than grey seal, are found mainly on the larger islands. Amphibians and reptiles are dealt with later in this chapter.

MAMMALS

Rabbit

Rabbits are believed to have been introduced from France to England in the eleventh century. The first historical record of a rabbit in Britain was from the Isles of Scilly in 1176, and later 'rabbits and birds called puffins' were said to be on Tresco in the 1470s (Sheail, 1971). After they were introduced to Scilly in the twelfth century rabbits may have been taken to the other inhabited and perhaps the larger uninhabited islands, where they would have provided a valuable additional food source for the population. When John Leland visited Scilly some time after 1533 he mentioned there being 'plenty of conyes'. Borlase, who visited the islands in 1756, comments that there were so many rabbits that the islanders did what they could to reduce the numbers: on Bryher, for example, stones taken from the barrows had been 'removed to make stands for shooting

TABLE 5. Distribution of land vertebrates (other than birds) in the Isles of Scilly.

	RABBIT Oryctolagus cuniculus	BROWN RAT Rattus norvegicus*	HOUSE MOUSE Mus musculus	WOOD MOUSE Apodemus sylvaticus	SCILLY SHREW Crocidura suaveolens cassiteridum	HEDGEHOG Erinaceus europaeus	COMMON/SOPRANO PIPISTRELLE Pipistrellus pipistrellus/P. pygmaeus**	LONG-EARED BAT Plecotus auritus	NOCTULE Nyctalus noctula	BRANDT'S/WHISKERED BAT Myotis brandtii / M. mystacinus	FROG Rana temporaria	TOAD Bufo bufo	SLOW WORM Anguis fragilis
St Mary's	P	P	P	P	P	P	P		R	R	P	?	
Tresco	P	P	P	P	P		P			R	?		
St Martins's	P	P	P		P		P						
St Agnes	P	P	P		P		P						
Gugh	P	P	?		P								
Bryher	E?	P	P		P		P						P
Samson	E?	P?			P								
White Is (Samson)			P										
St Helen's	E?				P								
Teän	E?	P	P		?								
Northwethel			P		P								
Great Arthur			P										
Middle Arthur		P											
Little Arthur		P											
Annet	P	P			P								
Great Ganilly	P	P	P		P								
Little Ganilly		P											
Great Innisvouls		P			P								
Little Innisvouls													
Great Ganinick													
Little Ganinick	P												
Gweal		P	P										

P, present   R, record, may not be resident   E, extinct
* Rat populations on the uninhabited islands are being controlled.
** Flight records of pipistrelle also over Samson, Annet and Round Island. Nathusius's pipistrelle *Pipistrellus nathusii* unconfirmed.

rabbits, with which this part of the hill abounds.' An eighteenth-century map (see Fig. 4) has an inscription that says there are 'plenty of conies'. Today there are rabbits on all the inhabited islands with the possible exception of Bryher, and on many of the larger uninhabited islands, including Great Ganilly, Little Ganinick, Annet and until recently St Helen's, Teän and Samson.

During the nineteenth century Augustus Smith introduced different coloured rabbits onto some of the smaller islands, and these may have been the origin of the populations of black rabbits on Samson and St Helen's (Grigson, 1948). The black rabbits may have died out on Samson about 2000, or at least their numbers were seriously reduced, possibly as a result of their eating bait laid for rats. Augustus Smith had also put white rabbits on White Island (Llewellyn, 2005) and on Teän, where they seem to have died out fairly quickly. There is also a record of a warren of silver-grey rabbits in Scilly in the early years of the twentieth century, but this was about the time when rabbit pelts were losing commercial value and rabbits were only being kept for meat (Sheail, 1971). A few black rabbits still occur on St Mary's, some of which have white throat patches; the main population is the normal brown colour (D. Mawer, personal communication).

During the 1960s and 1970s the number of grazing animals kept on the islands dropped substantially as farmers no longer kept working horses and the number of cattle was also reduced. This had two obvious effects: firstly, managing grasslands for hay became less important, allowing some former hayfields to revert to bracken; secondly, the vegetation on heaths and uncultivated land began to grow unchecked, with only rabbits providing any grazing. Despite this, myxomatosis was introduced to the islands, almost certainly deliberately, about 1977 (at least two attempts to introduce the disease in the 1950s having failed). This further compounded the changes by virtually eliminating the only remaining grazing animal, and many open areas soon became invaded by gorse and bracken. On St Agnes, for example, the gorse burgeoned in 1981, leading to a most dramatic display as much of Wingletang Down became a sea of gold. Sadly it was soon realised that all this beauty was at a price. Paths became impassable, and some former pastures and meadows were disappearing under advancing gorse and bracken; sites for rare plants, especially the tiny adder's-tongue ferns, were becoming swamped. As a result there were many attempts, both official and unofficial, to recover the situation by cutting and burning. The success of these trials has been variable: not all led to the desired effect; some heathland fires burned too well and burned right down into the peat; frequently the resulting regrowth was even more gorse. By 1999 it looked as though the gorse had been reduced, but the grassland was becoming rank, bracken was also expanding, and there was concern again for the rare ferns and other plants. Rabbits were not completely exterminated by myxomatosis, and in a letter to Dr F. A. Turk in 1984 Professor L. Harvey refers to them having recovered from the disease on St Mary's, Samson and possibly Tresco. Rabbits numbers slowly returned on most islands, but recovery was often followed by periodic disease outbreaks; there does not appear to have been a return to their former status for any length of time, and the rabbits are now much less effective as grazing controls.

On Bryher the introduction of myxomatosis was so successful that by 1999 there were no signs of rabbits. By 2003 it was already becoming noticeable that the vegetation was becoming taller and some of the important heathland areas were becoming rank. If there is still an extant nucleus of rabbits surviving on the island, they may eventually build up their numbers again. Meanwhile, active cutting and strimming are being using to control vegetation, and in 2001 the first group of Shetland ponies was introduced to graze some of the important heathland sites (see Figs 124 & 206).

Brown hare

There is a curious reference to brown hare *Lepus europaeus* as 'not native, but has been sparingly propagated since its introduction a few years back' (Courtney, 1845). No hares now occur on Scilly and, if they were one of the many introductions to Tresco by Augustus Smith, they may not have survived long. An alternative explanation is that that these were not hares, but a variety of domesticated rabbit, possibly one of those introduced by Augustus Smith.

Grey squirrel

There is a reference to grey squirrel *Sciurus carolinensis* being on Tresco in 1968, but when (or if) they were introduced to the island, when they died out, or any other details are still unanswered questions (Bere, 1982).

Bats

When I first stayed on St Agnes in the farmhouse at Lower Town Farm from 1958 until 1967, we saw bats frequently. These were usually assumed to be pipistrelles, but on two occasions in September 1959 larger bats were seen, once flying over the garden and on another occasion taking moths attracted to a moth trap (Parslow, 1988). At Lower Town Farm there was a large summer pipistrelle roost in the narrow space between the house and the edge of the lean-to greenhouse along the face of the building. Just before dusk we would see a stream of between 25 and 40 bats (counts recorded 42 one night in June 1961, 39 in May 1963) squeeze from a tiny aperture, with audible chittering from the other bats in the rear. On sunny days the bats would get very noisy in their roost; it was on the south side of the house and must have got very hot inside the narrow cavity. At this time, in the early 1960s, bats were seen flying up and down the lanes on St Agnes and we took them for granted (Fig. 181). John A. Burton ringed pipistrelles from this roost on several occasions during 1961 and 1962. Sadly the roost was lost when the building was renovated, although some bats may have moved to a nearby roost in the Island Hall. Other roosts in buildings on St Agnes, in the parsonage and in the church porch, also disappeared – and by 1987 it was realised there were no longer any bats on the island.

Not much is known about roosts on the other islands. Formerly there had been a large roost in the roof of Tresco Abbey that had been substantial enough to need wire over the bedroom windows to stop bats flying in. Unfortunately the Abbey was reroofed between 1972 and 1974, when there were said to have been hundreds of small bats present. There had also been a roost in the roof of the Valhalla Museum and the stable block nearby. A survey carried out by Heather and Denny Booker refers to reports of a barn at Borough Farm having several

FIG 181. Pipistrelle bat: taken for granted in the 1960s but almost wiped out by the 1980s. Numbers now appear to have recovered to some extent. (Ren Hathway)

hundredweight of bat-droppings in the loft when it was demolished in 1972; the droppings were then used as fertiliser (Booker & Booker, 1981). There was a small roost there still in 1981.

In 1988 I was commissioned by Bat Groups of Great Britain to carry out a survey of the inhabited islands to ascertain the status of bats. This revealed that islanders were justified in believing bats were now virtually extinct. The survey revealed that bats were in very low numbers, with small populations still present on Tresco and St Mary's. Rumours that bats still occurred on Bryher persisted but could not be substantiated at the time. As a result of the survey a number of anecdotal records came to light. There were several accounts of bats flying in off the sea or coming to lighthouses, suggesting there may be some immigration at times. One very curious record was of a large ginger-coloured bat, probably a noctule *Nyctalus noctula*, being shaken out of a tree by the down-draft from a helicopter (Humphrey Wakefield, personal communication).

For a while it was feared the bats in Scilly might not recover, and serious consideration was given to reintroducing pipistrelles to Scilly by releasing bats from Cornwall – possibly from a colony that had to be relocated. After consultation with many of the experts including Dr Robert Stebbings, English Nature eventually rejected the idea. It was felt that more needed to be known about the reasons for the decline in Scilly before attempting to introduce more bats. Also there was a concern that released bats would attempt to return to their former roosts on the mainland. The best outcome was felt to be to wait and see whether the remaining bats might build their numbers up again given time.

It is now thought that the decline of bats could well have been linked to the use of pesticides in the bulb fields. This is given some credence by the post mortem results on a bat that was shown to have very high levels of the pesticide aldrin. Agricultural chemicals such as aldrin, lindane and dieldrin are now no longer used. A contributory effect could have been the destruction of several large roosts, one of which at least may have been a breeding colony.

Surveys by the Cornwall Bat Group in August 1997 and October 1998 confirmed there were still small numbers of bats on Tresco, St Mary's and Bryher (Williams, 1997, 1998). There were also reports that islanders on St Agnes and St Martin's had seen bats. Most of those recorded by the Cornwall Bat Group were pipistrelles, but their bat detectors also picked up either whiskered *Myotis mystacinus* or Brandt's bats *M. brandtii* (they are not distinguishable by sound) on Tresco. Following their surveys the Cornwall Bat Group also set up bat workshops on the islands and instigated a great deal of local interest.

Since 1998 David Mawer (Isles of Scilly Wildlife Trust) has been regularly monitoring bats using a bat detector coupled to a voice-activated tape recorder and other methods (*Bat News*, 2001). Most recorded bats are still pipistrelles, the two species being recognised by their different echolocation frequencies on the bat detector, and *Pipistrellus pipistrellus* (45 kHz) and *P. pygmaeus* (55 kHz) have both been recorded on St Mary's, but larger bats including noctule have also been recorded (Mawer, 2001). Using automated recording equipment bats have been 'heard' on a number of islands including St Martin's, Tresco, Samson and Round Island. Encouragingly the bats are clearly building up their numbers and a large nursery roost and other roosts have been located. It is very likely all the pipistrelles on Scilly are part of the same extended colony, emanating from the one nursery roost on Tresco (D. Mawer, personal communication). Local interest in bats has increased, leading to a group of islanders become trained as 'bat wardens' in 2006, and continuing to monitor bat populations.

Hedgehog

Over the years there have been a number of proposed or attempted introductions to Scilly, most of which were ill-advised. Ferrets *Mustela putorius* f. *furo* were released on Gugh in 1975 or 1976 but fortunately for the local bird population did not survive (W. Hick, personal communication). Hedgehogs were introduced into Scilly about 1980, with one reported to Professor L. Harvey as being found dead on Buzza Hill, St Mary's, 'a few years ago' (letter to F. A. Turk, 1984). As Peter Marren wrote, commenting on the problems caused to ground-nesting waders on South Uist and North Ronaldsay, 'some bright spark decided to cheer things up by introducing hedgehogs to Sark in the Channel Islands and the Isles of Scilly. If the situation on North Ronaldsay is anything to go by, from hedgehogs introduced in 1970, in 1986 some 10,000 of their descendants had to be rounded up and deported to mainland Scotland' (Marren, 2002). Unfortunately, in Scilly too, without natural predators their numbers soon increased rapidly and they have now spread all around St Mary's (L. Knight, *in litt.*). Hedgehog droppings collected on heathland on St Mary's in 1999 were found to be composed of beetle remains, mainly legs, elytra and other parts of the exoskeletons of minotaur, dor, violet ground, rose chafer, tiger and oil beetles. These are the same species that are major prey items of the islands' kestrels (kestrels in Scilly are far more insect-dependent than mainland kestrels). So there is a concern that the hedgehogs may have a deleterious affect on heathland beetle populations, possibly on kestrels, and also on any ground or hedge-nesting birds (hedgehogs are surprisingly good climbers). Every effort should be made to ensure hedgehogs do not reach any other islands, especially those where there are populations of ground-nesting birds.

Scilly shrew

Although the occurrence of shrews has been known in Scilly since Victorian times (Cooper, 1992), they were not recognised as different until Hinton (1924) examined specimens sent to him, and he described them as a new species. The Scilly shrew belongs to the genus of white-toothed shrews, *Crocidura*, which are not found on the British mainland (where all shrews belong to the genus *Sorex*, with red-tipped teeth). White-toothed shrews are found on the Continent, with two species, *Crocidura suaveolens* and *C. russula*, occurring on some of the Channel Isles. The shrew found in the Isles of Scilly is now recognised as a subspecies of the lesser white-toothed shrew *C. suaveolens cassiteridum*.

When the Scilly shrew arrived in Scilly is subject to much discussion and speculation (Davies, 1958). Davies and other experts postulated that it was a genuine relict species that had been present before Scilly became isolated from the Continent. Remains of the shrew have been found in the Bronze Age midden at Porth Killier, St Agnes, from Bronze Age levels on Nornour, and also from Roman/Early Medieval remains on Teän. Whether these date from the same period as the site or represent later intrusions it is not possible to be certain. The root vole, a species that Turk (1978) considered to be contemporary with the site, was found in the same context, and it seems reasonable that the shrew was also there at the same time. Alternatively it has been suggested that the shrews were a relatively late arrival in Scilly, possibly as stowaways on boats from the Channel Isles or France (Corbet, 1961). It seems difficult to imagine that a pregnant shrew could survive a long sea crossing with very little available food, despite their greater reputed resistance to starvation than the *Sorex* shrews (Southern 1965; Pernetta & Handford, 1970) – but from the catholic tastes of the shrew that regularly visited a house on St Mary's (see below) it now seems much more feasible that they might find enough scraps to live on during such a journey.

Scilly shrews are now protected, and can only be trapped for study under licence from Natural England. Fortunately they seem to be under no major threat despite being caught by domestic cats (which do not eat them) and birds of prey (which do). Although some writers have suggested shrews do not come into buildings, there are plenty of examples of them entering houses, either voluntarily or when caught by domestic cats.

The Scilly shrew is very distinctive in appearance. The coat is pale-coloured, light beige or silvery, the ears are slightly protruding, giving the shrew a 'foxy' face, the tail is furry with scattered, individual longer hairs. Earlier writers had mainly assumed the shrews were a coastal species, perhaps because they are not often seen away from the shore. They are in fact known from most habitats in

Scilly, although they are most easily seen on pebble beaches as they dash between the stones – otherwise their high-pitched squeaks are the easiest way of finding them. During studies on St Mary's, Tresco and Samson, shrews were found in all habitats except in short grassland and the urban areas (Temple, 1996). If disturbed or moving nests they have an engaging habit of 'caravanning' (Cooper, 1992). The young form a line attached to their mother by holding onto the animal in front with their teeth and are dragged along in a train. This behaviour has apparently only been recorded from the white-toothed shrews (Bourlière, 1955). The shrews eat many kinds of insects and other invertebrates, including sandhoppers and probably woodland hoppers. The shrew that regularly visited David and Julie Mawer's kitchen during 2004 appeared to enjoy peanut butter, Marmite, toast crumbs and Cornish pasty (Fig. 182). Scilly shrews have been recorded from St Mary's, Tresco, St Martin's, Bryher, St Agnes, Teän, Samson, St Helen's, Annet, Great Ganilly and Great Innisvouls, and they may well be on all the larger uninhabited islands where there is reasonable cover.

FIG 182. The Scilly shrew that visited the Mawers' kitchen in 2004, eating Cornish pasty. (David Mawer)

Rats

As the islands were major anchorages on well-established trade routes it is very probable the black rat arrived in Scilly in sailing ships from the Mediterranean. Black rats were almost certainly on St Mary's when John Leland visited Scilly in 1547 to make an Itinerary for Henry VIII, and he found

> there is one isle of the Scylles cawled Rat Isle, yn which be so many rates that yf horse or any other livuing beast be brought thither they devore him.

He most likely would have been describing the Rat Island by the harbour. Unfortunately Leland's comments about Scilly may have been coloured by his going mad before he had compiled a proper report (Kay, 1956). The island of Samson was also known as Rat Isle for a time, and at some period between 1300 and 1478 it became overrun with rats, probably at a time when the island was uninhabited but still used for grazing. It is thought the rats could have come ashore from a wreck and eventually died out (Thomas, 1985).

Brown rats were known in Europe from the Middle Ages, but they only became established in England during the seventeenth to eighteenth centuries (Mitchell-Jones et al., 1999). In 1822 Woodley commented that 'many rats chiefly of the black kind' had been found on the off-islands, so it is possible the black rats managed to survive on the smaller islands until eventually ousted by brown rats. Until recently brown rats were found on all the inhabited and most of the uninhabited islands. Occasionally adverse conditions would have led to the rat population on the smaller islands dying out for a while, but they would soon have recovered. Rats are good swimmers and can easily move between islands.

From the early 1990s, when English Nature started a rat extermination programme, systematic baiting, now being carried out by the Wildlife Trust, successfully eradicated rats from Samson, Annet and Menawethan. Constant monitoring is essential, however, to detect when the rats return, as they may do, for they can very quickly become re-established. Rats are great opportunists and eat a great variety of different foods. They frequent the shores, where they appear to eat large amounts of seed and fruits of alexanders, bramble and presumably some other strandline plants. Fortunately, there is no evidence the rats eat *Rumex* seeds, so they cannot be blamed for the demise of the shore dock populations. Although it is too early to know what effect the removal of rats has had on seabird populations, it is expected there will be increased breeding success, particularly for those birds that nest in burrows. The rat clearance programme will be continuing on a number of the important seabird islands, with baiting usually carried out in winter (D. Mawer, *in litt.*).

Mice

Only two species of mice are found on the Isles of Scilly, house mouse *Mus musculus* and wood mouse. Very little seems to be known about the wood mice – other than that they are found on both Tresco and St Mary's. Their remains were also found on Nornour in the same Bronze Age midden as root vole and Scilly shrew, but it is also not possible to tell whether these were later intrusions or from animals living at the time (Turk, 1978; Ratcliffe & Straker, 1996). But it is thought wood mice may have been introduced by humans, probably early in the post-glacial period (Pernetta & Handford, 1970). It is additionally hypothesised that the mice co-existed with root vole, living in the more wooded areas while the vole was found in low-lying areas. Without more persuasive evidence, however, we will probably never know for certain when and how the wood mouse reached Scilly.

The house mouse is found on all the inhabited islands and probably some of the uninhabited islands as well, but wood mouse only occurs on St Mary's and Tresco. When live-trapping on St Agnes in the 1960s I found that house mice were living in habitats well away from human habitation such as close to the shore and under hedges. It seems that the house mice are able to occupy niches in Scilly that would otherwise be occupied by other small mammals. Interestingly, one of the trapping sites where I caught house mice was close to the shore above the Bronze Age midden at Porth Killier. It was at this site that skeletal remains of wood mice were found in the archaeological excavations (Ratcliffe & Straker, 1996). In 2003 David Mawer began finding droppings, chewed twigs and excavations on Bryher, White Island (St Martin's), Gweal and Teän that puzzled most of the 'experts'. Eventually these were identified as house mouse droppings, so there must be mice on these islands living in far more extreme conditions than usual. No voles are now found in Scilly, although the root vole or Pallas's vole was present during the Bronze Age (see Chapter 2). Remains of a water vole *Arvicola terrestris* found on Annet in a gull pellet must have come from outside the islands (Parslow, 2003).

Grey seal

Grey seals are the largest resident mammals found in Scilly. In 2000 there were about 350 animals, a very small percentage of the 123,000 grey seals in the UK (Lambert, 2001). Accurate numbers are difficult to estimate because of the mobility of the seals within the islands and probably further afield. In August 2006 passengers on the RMV *Scillonian* were surprised to pass a seal at sea, approximately halfway between Scilly and Land's End.

With 41 per cent of pups born in southwestern Britain occurring in Scilly, the Isles are one of the main breeding sites for the species (Duck, in Barne *et al.*, 1996). Visitors to the islands in summer will be encouraged to take one of the advertised boat trips to see 'seabirds and seals'. Seals breed among the more inaccessible uninhabited islands, mainly in the Eastern Isles, Western Rocks and Norrard Rocks, where they can easily be observed from the tripper boats (Fig. 183). Perhaps because more boat trips go to the Eastern Isles, due to their greater accessibility, the seals there seem particularly indifferent to the boatloads of camera-snapping holidaymakers. The seals' attitude to disturbance is apparently site-related, so that when they move from one group of islands to another they adopt the local character (S. Westcott, personal communication). A more recent holiday opportunity is to take to the water with the seals, so it is now possible to don a wetsuit and flippers and 'swim with the seals'. This seems to be a very popular experience and other than the occasional nibbled flipper the seals appear to be cooperative. The warnings of C. J. King (1924) 'to go and see them by all means, but take no liberties with them' do not seem to be taken seriously these days! But this warning came from a man who conducted experiments into the musical tastes of the seals by playing 'music of various kinds' to them on his gramophone and spent nights close by them inside a large wooden box.

The seal population in Scilly has at different times been exploited, hunted and tolerated. As with other marine animals such as stranded cetaceans, seals

FIG 183. Grey seals are easily seen from boat trips to the uninhabited islands. (Bryan Thomas)

were always an important commodity, providing meat, skins and blubber that could be boiled down to provide oil for lamps and candles. There are remains on St Agnes and Annet of what may have been early seal-hunting stations. When seals were no longer exploited they became instead a nuisance, considered a serious competitor by local fishermen, with a bounty on their heads (or more strictly their tails) (Lambert, 2001). Seals still raid fishing nets, but they are no longer shot (or at least not officially): their value to tourism probably now outweighs the damage they cause.

Despite the interest in the seals, for many years they attracted very little serious study in Cornwall, little additional information having until recently been added to the pioneering work of G. A. Steven, 'that intrepid naturalist and his companion, Midshipman G. P. Blake' (Steven, 1936; Westcott, 1993). In 1952 the main population of breeding seals was found to be based on the west of the archipelago, around the Western Rocks and the Norrard Rocks, the number of pups being static at 50 (Davies, 1956). Darling and Boyd (1964) stated 'there are very few left in the Isles of Scilly'. Peter MacKenzie, who was both the local vet and the Honorary Warden for the Nature Conservancy Council from 1971, also used to observe the seals and carried out counts, but unfortunately his notes do not seem to have survived.

For more than twenty years Stephen Westcott has carried out long-term monitoring of the seals, using a kayak so he is able to get closer to the animals without disturbing them. He has identified the main areas favoured by the seals (Table 6). The main pupping sites are on the Western Rocks, the Norrard Rocks and the Eastern Isles. Outside the breeding season seals haul out on the rocks in the same areas. These studies, including Anglo-French tagging, in which he was involved, have also shown that seals from other populations, in Brittany and Wales, may visit Scilly at times.

Grey seals usually breed between August and October, though exceptionally pups may be born as early as July or as late as November or December. The white-coated pups (Fig. 184) moult after two to three weeks into their sleek 'grey' coat. Although the pups can swim, they usually stay on the rocks for several weeks and are visited there by their mother to feed them. In Scilly it seems the pups swim more readily in the white-coat stage: this may be necessary where the sites are so much more exposed than elsewhere. The expenditure of more energy by swimming in their first weeks of life rather than remaining sedentary is suggested as the reason pups in Scilly tend to have lower body weights than those that are more static (Westcott, 1993). At this stage, before they are completely free-swimming, the pups are vulnerable in rough weather; they can be swept away by the sea and lost or trapped among the boulders out of reach of their

TABLE 6. Grey seal pupping and haul-out sites.

MAIN PUPPING SITES	
Western Rocks	Rosevean
	Rosevear – the main site in the Western Rocks
	Gorregan
	Melledgan – a main pupping site
	Annet
Norrard Rocks	Mincarlo – a main pupping site
	Seal Rock
	Illiswilgig – a main pupping site
	Gweal – occasional pupping site
Eastern Isles	Great Innisvouls
	Little Innisvouls
	Menawethan – reputed cave pupping site, needs confirmation

FAVOURED HAUL-OUT SITES*	
Western Rocks	Daisy
	Rosevear
	Jacky's Rock
	Great Crebawethan
	Rags
	Carn Ithen
	Melledgan
Norrard Rocks	Black Rocks
	Illiswilgig
Eastern Isles	Menawethan

* These are not the only haul-out sites, but those identified by Stephen Westcott as being their favourites.

mother. Cyril Nicholas and I rescued a pup trapped among the rocks on Rosevear in 1990. If we had not visited the island that day, the animal would not have survived; this must be quite a common occurrence. Because the pups are mobile at this early stage, they may be born on one island and swim to another, so observing a pup on a particular beach does not necessarily mean the animal was actually born there. The mother only suckles the pup for two weeks or so before she abandons it, as she is now receptive to the bull.

FIG 184. This seal pup is still at the white-coat stage. (David Mawer)

Common seal

At one time records of common seals *Phoca vitulina* were usually assumed to be misidentified young grey seals. Recently several experienced observers have seen and photographed common seals, however, suggesting that an occasional animal does visit Scilly (R. Hathway, *in litt.*).

Deer

Among the deer remains found in Scilly some from the Romano-British site on Nornour were identified as roe deer (Turk, 1978). Remains from other archaeological sites are all of red deer. The history of red deer in Scilly is contentious. It is not clear whether the deer were already wild in Scilly or whether they were transported there later, as had been common practice historically (Pernetta & Handford, 1970; Ratcliffe & Straker, 1996). Among the skeletal remains were those of young animals, so it is possible a reasonable breeding population could have been maintained on the islands. Frank Turk (1960, 1968) argued, based on measurements of their bones, that the deer were beginning the tendency towards dwarfing that happens in isolated island populations. Thomas (1985) was able to demonstrate there would have been enough land to support a population, but whether there had been a population 'established in Scilly before the post-glacial separation, or whether the first early colonists managed to introduce the nucleus of a breeding stock for their own benefit; either is possible.' So unless more evidence is found we can only continue to speculate.

There is a reference by J. W. North (1850) to deer (and goats) on St Helen's: 'goats and deer seem to claim the island as their domain. These animals watch from the highest points of rock those who land upon their territory, and are ill at ease until they see them again retiring to their boat.' Unfortunately, we do not know which species of deer they were or what happened to them (or the goats) later.

Augustus Smith introduced fallow deer to the Isles of Scilly. He turned Samson, after the islanders had left in 1855, into a deer park, building a wall around the hill in the south of the island (Grigson, 1948) that is still visible today. He is also said to have turned out deer on other islands but it is not known if this actually happened. His experiment on Samson was not successful: the deer got out of the 'park' and tried to swim away, and apparently they all drowned (Reeve, 1995) although other accounts suggest they were able to swim in the shallow waters between Samson and Tresco and escape. If it had been low spring tides they would have been able to walk across the flats to Tresco. For a while fallow deer were apparently kept on the Garrison, at a time when the promontory was more open (White, 1855).

Cetaceans

A number of different species of cetaceans have been recorded from waters around the Isles of Scilly and from occasional strandings. Being accompanied by dolphins or other small whales when crossing between the islands by boat or on the RMV *Scillonian* between Scilly and Land's End is always exciting. In recent years more sightings are being made, often by birdwatchers on 'pelagics' trips or sea-watching from vantage points on the islands. Records of live cetaceans are notoriously unreliable due to the problems of identification, usually based on a fleeting glimpse, but identification charts and binoculars have helped improve matters greatly, and this may have increased the numbers of positive sightings. Those species most frequently encountered are common dolphin *Delphinus delphis* (Fig. 185), bottle-nosed dolphin *Tursiops truncatus* and harbour porpoise. Pilot whales *Globicephala melaena* are seen occasionally around Scilly. Sadly most records of pilot whales are of animals that come ashore dead, such as one on St Mary's in 1975 that had to be blown up to get rid of it; one on Gugh was similarly disposed of in 1974, and a local farmer blew up one that was stranded on St Agnes in November 1995. Another whale sometimes seen off Scilly is the orca or killer whale *Orca orca*. They have a predominantly western distribution around Britain, including Scilly, and are generally found in groups of fewer

FIG 185. Common dolphins are frequently seen around the islands or from the RMV *Scillonian.* (Ren Hathway)

than eight animals, mostly in summer. In recent years most sightings have been in May (Weir, 2002). Risso's dolphins *Grampus griseus* are very uncommon, but are occasionally recorded, such as one seen from a pelagic boat trip off Scilly in July 2000 (Martin, 2001).

One of the best-documented sightings of striped dolphin *Stenella coeruleoalba* was in October 2000 by Tim Melling, who with several other birdwatchers watched a school of about 80 striped dolphins and some common dolphins in the area between St Agnes and St Mary's for upward of five hours (T. Melling, personal communication). Six harbour porpoises were also seen 'regularly' in October 2000, often near St Agnes, again by Tim Melling. Records of most of the rare species have unfortunately been strandings; the fin whale *Balaenoptera physalus* that came ashore on Annet in 1917 and the sperm whale *Physeter macrocephalus* on Samson in 1967 are unfortunate examples.

Stranded cetaceans are reported to the Natural History Museum, London, where records have been maintained since 1913. A summary of these records, including a few that were not reported to the Museum, was published in the *Isles of Scilly Bird Report* (Turk, 1999). This was followed by further observations on cetaceans off Scilly by Amanda Martin (2001). Records of sightings and strandings of cetaceans, turtles and basking sharks are now kept locally by Seaquest South-West, a database maintained jointly by the Cornwall and Devon Wildlife Trusts since 1998. A note of those relating to Scilly is included in the annual *Isles of Scilly Bird & Natural History Review*.

AMPHIBIANS AND REPTILES

Only common frog *Rana temporaria* is now naturally resident in the Isles of Scilly, although it is possible there may have been introductions of tadpoles or spawn from elsewhere at times. There is archaeological evidence that toads were once present, from bones found in a seventeenth-century occupation site associated with the Steval Point Battery, St Mary's (Ratcliffe & Straker, 1996). There is a rumour suggesting toads may have been introduced to St Mary's, but there is no evidence of this, or that they have become established. Troutbeck (1794) refers to frogs in his survey and their bones were also identified from a tenth- to thirteenth-century site at Lower Town, St Martin's (Locker, 1992). Frogs are currently common in areas around both Higher and Lower Moors and Porthloo Duck Pond, as well as elsewhere on St Mary's. Although frogs are only known from St Mary's and Tresco, in June 1963 giant, albino tadpoles were found in a pool near the beach on St Martin's. Identified as common frog tadpoles, they were diagnosed as suffering from a form of gigantism, possibly caused by mineral deficiency (Turk & Turk, 1977).

Until very recently it was believed there were no reptiles on Scilly, but there had long been rumours of escaped pet slow worms on Bryher (*The Scillonian*, 1981/2). Most of the reports came from the same area on Bryher, mainly centred around Great Popplestone Bay. A former schoolmaster remembers them being present in the 1960s. Then in 2003 workmen rebuilding a wall found several live slow worms (D. Mawer, personal communication). Local resident Chris Hopkin was able to photograph one before they were released (Fig. 186).

FIG 186. The introduced slow worms on Bryher are rarely seen. (Chris Hopkin)

344 · THE ISLES OF SCILLY

Unfortunately, it seems almost inevitable there will be introductions of other species, accidentally if not deliberately. The temptation to add to the fauna seems to be a common human failing, but every attempt should be made to prevent this happening, as so often it can have unforeseen and undesirable consequences – as has already happened with the hedgehog.

CHAPTER 16

Birds

Gulles and Puffines be taken in diverse of these Islettes.

John Leland (1535–43)

MANY EARLY WRITERS include lists of birds as well as other groups in their accounts of visits to Scilly. F. R. Rodd wrote to his uncle E. H. Rodd (author of *Birds of Cornwall*, 1880) from Scilly several times between 1864 and 1871, giving a vivid picture of a sportsman's approach to the birds that arrived there in winter (Rodd, 1880). The Reverend R. W. J. Smart's account of his egg-collecting expeditions (1852) and a more comprehensive paper on the birds of Scilly (1885–6) are interesting historically, with his tales of species 'obtained' and many added to the Abbey Collection. Two interesting accounts written by Scilly residents are C. J. King's *Some Notes on Wild Nature in Scillonia* (1924), illustrated with his own photographs (see Fig. 193), and Hilda Quick's *Birds of the Scilly Isles* (1964), enlivened by her own delightful, quirky woodcuts (see Figs 23 & 24). Important reference works on birds are the sections on Scilly in Penhallurick's account of the birds of Cornwall (1969), and more recently Robinson's monumental *Birds of the Isles of Scilly* (2003). Another book on Scilly birds is due to be published in 2007 (Flood *et al.*, in press). The Isles of Scilly have long been one of the exceptional places where rare vagrants are a regular occurrence, and checklists of rarities and annual bird reports enable birdwatchers to keep up to date with the status of these unusual migrants (Gantlett, 1991; Evans, 1995). The birds of Scilly have also been well served by bird reports. These include the *Isles of Scilly Bird Reports* published by the Cornwall Birdwatching and Preservation Society from 1957 to 1999, the *St Agnes Bird Observatory Reports*, 1957–64, and since 2000 the *Isles of Scilly Bird & Natural History*

Review, published by the Isles of Scilly Bird Group. Additionally there have been many scientific reports and papers about the birds of Scilly.

HISTORICAL BIRDS

From the bones found in excavations of archaeological sites and especially among the other detritus in the limpet shell middens we can surmise that birds were long exploited as an important food source by early Scillonians. The local people in the past would have harvested any birds that were easily caught or accessible, especially ground-nesting birds and colonial seabirds. They would also have collected eggs. There are many references to the rent for the islands being paid to the Crown in puffins (Fig. 187). It seems that in fact the payments were usually presented in coin rather than the alternative – dried, cured puffins. Also it is rather more probable that the species referred to was not necessarily the puffin but Manx shearwater, as the name 'puffin' was formerly attached to that species (see Chapter 3).

Most of the species of birds that have been identified from bones are ones that are or could still be found in the islands today, with just a few exceptions

FIG 187. The puffin has a long association with Scilly, and today is the one bird all visitors want to see. (Bryan Thomas)

(Table 7). A large proportion of the birds were either sea or coastal species, and the rest mainly from wetland, farmland or open country. There is a distinct lack of woodland birds in the list, reflecting the situation as it is today, when there are still no typical woodland birds such as woodpeckers or owls. The most unusual record is of great auk *Pinguinus impennis*, a flightless seabird of the North Atlantic that became extinct in 1844 and probably nested in Scotland (Fair Isle) until about 1812 (Parslow, 1973). Remains of two great auks were found among material from an archaeological excavation on Halangy Down, St Mary's. Although they could not be dated accurately, other material on the site was from somewhere between 400 BC and the third century AD (Locker, 1996; Ratcliffe & Straker, 1996). Some of the bones were from a young bird, but as young auks leave nesting ledges and go to sea at a very immature stage this does not mean they necessarily bred locally (young guillemots and razorbills can be encountered with their parents well out at sea in late summer). Another apparently unusual species whose bones have been found was black grouse *Tetrao tetrix*, a bird that used to be resident in Cornwall but was probably extinct before 1920 (Parslow, 1973).

STUDIES OF BIRDS ON SCILLY

St Agnes Bird Observatory
From 1957 to 1967 pioneer work carried out by the teams of volunteers who manned the bird observatory on St Agnes (see Chapter 4) added much to ornithological knowledge at the time, particularly of migration and of breeding seabirds. These were important years in the study of bird migration in Britain. John Parslow, a founder member and secretary of the St Agnes Bird Observatory, was one of David Lack's research team at the Edward Grey Institute in Oxford, where he was working on radar studies of bird migration. One of the most valuable aspects of this work was the linking of the radar studies with the field observations and the trapping (Durman, 1976). Unfortunately, St Agnes Bird Observatory closed in 1967 and David Lack's radar studies also came to an end, so this aspect of migration studies did not continue.

Ringing and surveys
When the observatory closed, bird-ringing in Scilly was carried out by a number of groups of ringers who spent their holidays there during migration periods. Two resident birdwatchers, Will Wagstaff and Peter Robinson, also ringed migrants and resident birds on St Mary's during the 1990s, concentrating latterly on the British Trust for Ornithology's Common Birds Census (and its

TABLE 7. Bird species from archaeological sites in Scilly. (Adapted from Ratcliffe & Straker, 1996)

SPECIES	BRONZE AGE	IRON AGE/ROMANO-BRITISH	ROMANO-BRITISH/EARLY MEDIEVAL	POST-MEDIEVAL
Great northern diver		✓		
Shearwater	✓	✓		
Gannet	✓	✓		cf.
Cormorant	✓	✓		✓
Shag		✓		✓
Grey heron	✓	✓		cf.
White stork	✓			
White stork/swan		✓		
cf. swan	✓			✓
Bean goose				
Brent goose		✓		
Goose (unspecified)		✓	✓	
Duck (unspecified)		✓		✓
Shelduck	✓	✓		✓
Teal				✓
Scaup				✓
Long-tailed duck				✓
Buzzard			✓	
Black grouse		✓		
Partridge		✓		
Pheasant/fowl		✓		
Corncrake	✓			
cf. Moorhen				✓
Coot	✓		✓	
Stone-curlew	✓	✓		
Lapwing	✓	✓		
Knot		✓		
Redshank		✓		
cf. Ruff	✓			
Godwit	✓			

PRESENT STATUS & COMMENTS

RECENT

✓	Winter visitor
✓	Summer visitor
✓	Common around islands all year, non-breeding
✓	Resident
✓	Resident
✓	Present all year (scarce in summer)
	Rare vagrant
	Stork rare vagrant/mute swan resident
✓	Other swans rare visitors
✓	Rare
	Rare
	Several spp. Rare vagrants
?	Several spp. Mallard possible as common resident
✓	Resident
✓	Small numbers visit/stay
	Occasional
	Rare in winter
	Scarce
	Unknown
	Introduced
	Introduced
	Migrant, formerly bred.
✓	Resident
✓	Resident
	Rare migrant
✓	Winter visitor, migrant
	Scarce
✓	Migrant & winter visitor
	Migrant
	Migrant

TABLE 7. – *cont.*

SPECIES	BRONZE AGE	IRON AGE/ ROMANO-BRITISH	ROMANO-BRITISH/ EARLY MEDIEVAL	POST-MEDIEVAL
Woodcock		✓	cf.	
Snipe		✓		✓
Herring/lesser black-backed gull		✓		
Great black-backed gull		✓		
Gull (unspecified)			✓	
Great auk		✓		
Guillemot	✓	✓	✓	✓
Razorbill	✓	✓	✓	✓
Puffin	✓	✓	✓	✓
Pigeon	✓	✓		
Barn owl		✓		
Skylark	✓	✓		✓
Wren	✓			✓
cf. Blackbird		✓		
Redwing	✓			
Song thrush	✓	✓		✓
cf. Mistle thrush	✓			
Thrush sp.		✓	✓	✓
Spotted flycatcher	✓			
Chough				✓
Raven	✓	✓		✓
Crow		✓		
House sparrow		✓		
Corn bunting				✓

PRESENT STATUS & COMMENTS

RECENT	
	Winter visitor
✓	Migrant & winter visitor
✓	Resident
✓	Resident
	Extinct
✓	Summer breeder
✓	Summer breeder
✓	Summer breeder
✓	Resident
	Rare
✓	Formerly bred
✓	Resident
✓	Resident
✓	Winter visitor
✓	Resident
✓	Occasional migrant or winter visitor
✓	
	Summer visitor
	Vagrant
✓	Resident
✓	Resident
✓	Resident
	Rare

FIG 188. Ringed song thrush. Ringing studies have contributed to our knowledge of the common birds of Scilly. (Rosemary Parslow)

replacement the Breeding Bird Survey, which are census methods not linked to the ringing scheme). This work, as well as other population studies, has informed much of what is known about some of the resident passerine species (Fig. 188).

Seabird studies have continued, usually commissioned by the Nature Conservancy Council or its successor body, English Nature. Robert Allen surveyed all the islands in 1974; there were repeat surveys by Harvey (1983) and by Birkin and Smith (1987). During the 1990s there were counts most years by Will Wagstaff and Peter Robinson (for Isles of Scilly Wildlife Trust – formerly Environmental Trust), and counts were carried out as part of the Joint Nature Conservancy Council (JNCC) national seabird survey, Seabird 2000. Heaney and others concentrated on studies of Manx shearwaters and storm petrels (Heaney *et al.*, 2002).

During the time of the St Agnes Bird Observatory some studies of resident birds were made, but since then land birds have not attracted as much attention as seabirds. Chown and Lock (2002) carried out a two-year breeding-bird survey that incorporated the results of the Breeding Bird Atlas (2000–2001) and Seabird 2000 (1999–2000). A repeat survey was carried out in summer 2006, coordinated by Vickie Heaney and Tamara Weeks. The project was part of the joint English Nature/RSPB Action for Birds in England Project in collaboration with IOSWT and ISBG. Wintering waders were surveyed by Will Wagstaff and other local birdwatchers over three seasons in the 1990s, and the results were written up by Lock (1999).

Birdwatching in Scilly

Scilly was already known to be a place where unusual birds could turn up long before birdwatching became a popular hobby, the fashion then being to collect the birds in a more permanent shape. The collection of stuffed birds (now in the Isles of Scilly Museum) started by Augustus Smith and continued by the Dorrien-Smith family is a very comprehensive representation of the resident and migrant birds of the islands, and contains an extraordinary number of rare vagrants.

To most birdwatchers today, the Isles of Scilly are primarily associated with rare birds, migrants and vagrant species, especially those that usually turn up in autumn. Robinson (2003) gives the number of species recorded in Scilly as a 'possible 426', and the checklist in the *Isles of Scilly Bird & Natural History Review* (IOSB&NHR) includes 430 species, but the difference hardly matters and is probably only significant to the cognoscenti. With communications now so much more sophisticated, and with widespread use of websites, pagers and mobile phones, it is easy to find out when and where rare birds have turned up, so it is not unusual to find birdwatchers flying across to Scilly just for the day to see something special. Within the islands, firstly CB radios and now mobile phones and pagers mean that there is continual monitoring of any rarity during October at least.

Perhaps more than anything else it was the expectation of extremely rare birds, vagrants from North America and eastern Europe – combined perhaps with greater accessibility than Fair Isle – that led to the rise of Scilly as a Mecca for birdwatchers in the 1980s and 1990s. In October, a motley army, bristling with telescopes and tripods, invades the islands (Fig. 189). These visitors are probably tolerated for the additional income brought to the islands and for the extension of the tourist season to the end of October. More recently a small number of 'birders' have become resident on the islands, which has resulted in much more interest being taken in birds generally, as well as in the other wildlife of the islands. In 2000 the Isles of Scilly Bird Group began publishing its own journal (IOSB&NHR), which includes notes and articles on all aspects of natural history as well as being a 'traditional' bird report.

Over the past few years there has been a revolution in birdwatching generally. With so much first-class optical and photographic equipment available it is now possible for almost all birdwatchers to have a photographic record of what they

FIG 189. Arrivals of very rare migrants will attract birdwatchers in hundreds. Porth Hellick, October 2003, waiting for the little crake *Porzana parva* to appear. (Bryan Thomas)

have seen. It is not unusual to see whole groups 'digiscoping' (photographing birds using digital cameras that can be attached to their telescopes). So not only can you get a good view of a rare bird through your 'scope, you can catch it for ever as a photographic image. At the October evening logs it is possible to see superb images of the latest migrants, captured earlier that day, and also to buy professional-quality photographs and paintings as mementos. There are also a number of websites where you can catch up with all the rarities almost as soon as the birds have arrived.

THE ORNITHOLOGICAL SIGNIFICANCE OF THE ISLES OF SCILLY

Scilly is covered by a number of designations (see Chapter 1). Those that relate specifically to birds include the SPA (Special Protection Area), which covers 4.09km², and the Ramsar site over the same area. The uninhabited islands and some areas on the inhabited islands are also protected by notification as Sites of Special Scientific Interest (SSSI), with some of the smaller uninhabited islands having been designated especially for their colonies of breeding seabirds.

BREEDING BIRDS

A paper by Tim Reed (1984) lists the numbers of breeding birds, divided into seabirds and land birds, on thirty islands in Scilly. He correlated the number of species with the number of habitats and the area of land on the islands and found that the number of bird species increased with the number of habitats present, rather than the size of the island. Exactly how many species of land birds breed in Scilly is probably debatable. Robinson says forty-five plus four that do so irregularly, but the number depends on interpretation. Thirteen seabird species breed regularly, with two terns possibly breeding occasionally (Table 8).

On visiting Scilly for the first time you cannot help but notice how unusually tame the birds are. The five commonest passerines on Scilly are song thrush, blackbird, wren, rock pipit and dunnock. Song thrushes, like the resident blackbirds, are ubiquitous, standing out by their confiding behaviour – you almost trip over them in places. In tea gardens around the islands common birds such as blackbirds and song thrushes as well as house sparrows, robins and chaffinches are very much in evidence and specialise in forays to snatch food from trays and tables – even from your lips! Wrens also seem to be more obvious

TABLE 8. Breeding birds of the Isles of Scilly.

Fulmar	*Fulmarus glacialis*	Resident. Breeds on uninhabited and inhabited islands; increasing.
Manx shearwater	*Puffinus puffinus*	Summer visitor. Breeds on Annet, with smaller numbers at five other sites.
Storm petrel	*Hydrobates pelagicus*	Summer visitor. Breeds in large numbers on eleven uninhabited islands.
Cormorant	*Phalacrocorax carbo*	Resident. Breeds in small numbers on a few uninhabited islands.
Shag	*Phalacrocorax aristotelis*	Resident. Breeds on almost all uninhabited islands.
Little egret	*Egretta garzetta*	Possibly attempted breeding 2006.
Grey heron	*Ardea cinerea*	Very rarely breeds.
Mute swan	*Cygnus olor*	A few pairs breed on Tresco, occasionally elsewhere.
Canada goose	*Branta canadensis*	Feral birds have bred on Tresco. Used to breed on White Island (Samson). Numbers declining.
Shelduck	*Tadorna tadorna*	Breeds in small numbers on several islands.
Gadwall	*Anas strepera*	Breeds in small numbers on Tresco, Porth Hellick and pools on other islands.
Teal	*Anas crecca*	Has occasionally bred. Duck with young, Porth Hellick, 1969.
Mallard	*Anas platyrhynchos*	Resident. Breeds on inhabited and some uninhabited islands but includes introduced and feral birds.
American black duck	*Anas rubripes*	Rare vagrant. May have hybridised with mallard.
Shoveler	*Anas clypeata*	Occasionally breeds on Tresco.
Pochard	*Aythya ferina*	Recorded breeding on Tresco most years.
Tufted duck	*Aythya fuligula*	Breeds occasionally on Tresco since 1983.
Marsh harrier	*Circus aeruginosus*	Probably bred 2005 & possibly 2006.
Kestrel	*Falco tinnunculus*	Resident. Small numbers breed.
Peregrine	*Falco peregrinus*	Resident. One breeding pair since 1994.
Bobwhite quail	*Colinus virginianus*	Extinct. Introduced 1964/5, last recorded c.1980.
Red-legged partridge	*Alectoris rufa*	Introduced. Breeding on several islands as a result of introductions.
Grey partridge	*Perdix perdix*	Extinct. Was sustained by releases of captive-bred birds.
Pheasant	*Phasianus colchicus*	Introduced. Tresco, St Mary's and other islands, numbers augmented by captive-reared birds.

TABLE 8. – *cont.*

Golden pheasant	*Chrysolophus pictus*	Introduced to Tresco.
Water rail	*Rallus aquaticus*	Recorded in summer but breeding not confirmed.
Moorhen	*Gallinula chloropus*	Resident. Breeds in small numbers on larger pools.
Coot	*Fulica atra*	Resident. Breeds on larger waters, especially on Tresco.
Oystercatcher	*Haematopus ostralegus*	Resident. Breed around all coasts throughout islands.
Ringed plover	*Charadrius hiaticula*	Resident. Breeds on the larger islands, including uninhabited ones.
Black-headed gull	*Larus ridibundus*	Mainly winter visitor. May have bred occasionally in the nineteenth century.
Lesser black-backed gull	*Larus fuscus*	Summer visitor. Breeds on most islands except St Mary's.
Herring gull	*Larus argentatus*	Resident. Breeds on most islands, but in Hugh Town nesting is discouraged.
Great black-backed gull	*Larus marinus*	Resident. Breeds mainly on uninhabited islands.
Kittiwake	*Rissa tridactyla*	Summer visitor. Breeds on five islands; decline in sites and numbers since 1980s.
Sandwich tern	*Sterna sandvicensis*	Migrant. Former breeding species; occasional attempts since 1998.
Roseate tern	*Sterna dougallii*	Rare summer visitor. Formerly bred in small numbers, last in 1993.
Common tern	*Sterna hirundo*	Summer visitor. Breeds colonially, frequently moving sites.
Arctic tern	*Sterna paradisaea*	Migrant. Has bred very occasionally.
Guillemot	*Uria aalge*	Summer visitor. Small numbers breed on a few remote sites.
Razorbill	*Alca torda*	Summer visitor. Breeds on *c.*14 uninhabited islands.
Puffin	*Fratercula arctica*	Summer visitor. Total of 100–200 pairs breed on some eight uninhabited islands.
Stock dove	*Columba oenas*	Resident. Breeds in small numbers mainly on Tresco and St Mary's.
Woodpigeon	*Columba palumbus*	Resident. Breeds in small numbers on inhabited islands.
Collared dove	*Streptopelia decaocto*	Resident. Breeds on all inhabited islands.
Turtle dove	*Streptopelia turtur*	Migrant. Former breeding species until *c.*1959.

TABLE 8. – *cont.*

Cuckoo	*Cuculus canorus*	Summer visitor. Breeds on inhabited and larger uninhabited islands, but marked decline.
Swift	*Apus apus*	Migrant. Possible breeding on Tresco, 2003.
Skylark	*Alauda arvensis*	Migrant. Bred on larger islands until 1980s, but no recent records.
Sand martin	*Riparia riparia*	Migrant. Formerly bred.
Swallow	*Hirundo rustica*	Summer visitor. Breeds in small numbers on inhabited islands.
House martin	*Delichon urbica*	Summer visitor. A few pairs breed on St Mary's and elsewhere.
Meadow pipit	*Anthus pratensis*	Migrant. A few pairs may breed occasionally.
Rock pipit	*Anthus petrosus*	Resident. Common, breeds on most islands.
Yellow wagtail	*Motacilla flava*	Summer visitor. Has bred (possible hybrid *flava* × *flavissima*), 1966.
Pied/white wagtail	*Motacilla alba*	Migrant. Has bred occasionally, including white wagtails *M. alba alba*.
Wren	*Troglodytes troglodytes*	Resident. Common, breeds on most islands.
Dunnock	*Prunella modularis*	Resident. Breeds on the larger islands.
Robin	*Erithacus rubecula*	Resident. Common, breeds on inhabited islands.
Stonechat	*Saxicola torquata*	Resident. Breeds in small numbers on larger islands, including at least Samson and St Helen's.
Wheatear	*Oenanthe oenanthe*	Migrant. Very rarely a few stay to breed.
Blackbird	*Turdus merula*	Resident. Common, breeds on inhabited and largest uninhabited islands.
Song thrush	*Turdus philomelos*	Resident. Common, breeds on inhabited and largest uninhabited islands.
Mistle thrush	*Turdus viscivorus*	Rare migrant. Breeding records in 1930s.
Lesser whitethroat	*Sylvia curruca*	Summer visitor. Bred in 1965.
Whitethroat	*Sylvia communis*	Summer visitor. Occasional breeding records since 1965.
Blackcap	*Sylvia atricapilla*	Mainly summer visitor (a few winter). A few pairs breed.
Sedge warbler	*Acrocephalus schoenobaenus*	Summer visitor. Breeds on Tresco and St Mary's.
Reed warbler	*Acrocephalus scirpaceus*	Summer visitor. A few breed on Tresco and St Mary's.
Chiffchaff	*Phylloscopus collybita*	Mainly summer visitor (a few winter). A few pairs breed on the larger islands.

TABLE 8. – *cont.*

Willow warbler	*Phylloscopus trochilus*	Summer visitor. A few breed on the main islands.
Goldcrest	*Regulus regulus*	Migrant. A few breed on St Mary's and Tresco.
Spotted flycatcher	*Muscicapa striata*	Summer visitor. One or two pairs breed annually.
Coal tit	*Parus ater*	Migrant. Formerly bred on Tresco.
Blue tit	*Parus caeruleus*	Resident. Breeds mainly on St Marys and Tresco.
Great tit	*Parus major*	Resident. Breeds on all inhabited islands.
Jackdaw	*Corvus monedula*	Vagrant. Pair have bred on Tresco since *c.*2000 although young have not remained in Scilly.
Carrion crow	*Corvus corone*	Resident. Breeds on larger islands. Some hybrid offspring from a mating with hooded crow C. *corone cornix* in late 1970s.
Raven	*Corvus corax*	Resident. One pair breeds.
Starling	*Sturnus vulgaris*	Resident. Breeds on all the larger islands.
House sparrow	*Passer domesticus*	Resident. Breeds on the inhabited islands.
Chaffinch	*Fringilla coelebs*	Resident. Breeds mainly on Tresco and St Mary's.
Greenfinch	*Carduelis chloris*	Mainly summer visitor. Breeds mainly on the inhabited islands.
Goldfinch	*Carduelis carduelis*	Resident. Breeds on the inhabited islands.
Linnet	*Carduelis cannabina*	Summer visitor. Breeds on the larger islands.
Bullfinch	*Pyrrhula pyrrhula*	Vagrant. Formerly bred, Tresco, 1980s.

in Scilly than they do on the mainland, and they may seem slightly more bleached and brighter in colour, as do the song thrushes. The wren's explosive song, delivered from the top of a wall or some exotic plant, also seems louder, perhaps slightly different from the usual mainland version (Fig. 190). Attempts have been made to describe the Scilly wren as a distinct island race, but they have not been found significantly different from the nominate race. Rock pipits are also abundant: they are mainly a coastal species, found everywhere including on the uninhabited islands. They are the principal host of the cuckoo in Scilly, and in summer parent rock pipits can often be seen anxiously attending their over-sized, continually begging foster-offspring. Dunnocks often seem

FIG 190. The explosive song of the wren is often heard from a wall or hedge top.
(Rosemary Parslow)

under-regarded. They are probably only noticed when their half-hidden form in
a bush is mistaken for something rare; usually they are given away by the curious
little wing-shuffling movements they make.

Two species of waders nest in the Isles of Scilly, ringed plover and oystercatcher. Ringed plovers, unfortunately, always seem to nest just where they are
most likely to be disturbed by people, on sandy beaches and footpaths, and on
the open heathland. The 'broken wing' display may be effective at drawing away
predators but unfortunately probably does not work so well with curious holidaymakers. The strident calls of oystercatchers are almost a continual background
sound in Scilly. They nest all around the coast, both on the uninhabited islands
and on many of the rocky offshore stacks.

Many common species of British birds are not at all common in Scilly. Blue
tits *Parus caeruleus* (Fig. 191) and great tits *P. major* do breed on the inhabited
islands in low numbers, but coal tits *P. ater* are uncommon (the Continental race

ater has bred on Tresco in the past). None of the other tits are resident in the islands. Some common finches and buntings are also totally absent as breeding species and may only occur as rare immigrants: yellowhammer *Emberiza citrinella* and reed bunting *E. schoeniclus* for example. Goldfinch *Carduelis carduelis* and chaffinch are resident; greenfinch *C. chloris* breeds but is mainly a summer visitor; bullfinch *Pyrrhula pyrrhula* has nested in the past but is now only an occasional visitor; linnets *Carduelis cannabina* breed on all the larger islands, collecting in big flocks that feed on the arable-field weeds at the end of the breeding season. Also to be found feeding in the arable fields are the doves that breed in the islands, woodpigeon *Columba palumbus*, collared dove *Streptopelia decaocto* and surprisingly stock dove *Columba oenas*, the last managing to find a few suitable nest holes in some of the older elm trees. A common breeding bird is the starling, which is found on all the inhabited islands: they sometimes nest in the cliffs and in holes in rock carns, on rare occasion in holes at ground level. House sparrows have also been recorded using cliff nests at times. They are still

FIG 191. Blue tits breed on the inhabited islands in Scilly. (Ren Hathway)

a common species in Scilly – and at one time frequently built 'weaver bird' type nests in the hedges. This habit seemed to have been particularly prevalent on St Agnes, where they often used tamarisk trees, but this interesting practice now seems much less common.

The corvids have never been very common in Scilly. Possibly they have always been considered a threat to any game birds and consequently not tolerated. A pair of ravens still nests on the inaccessible cliffs of Men-a-vaur. Carrion crows *Corvus corone* have increased in recent years; interestingly some of the resident birds are descended from hybrids with hooded crow *C. corone cornix*, some showing grey markings on their plumage. Jackdaws *C. monedula* breed only on Tresco, but they do not seem to build up their numbers, as the young appear to leave Scilly in winter. Among the warblers, blackcap *Sylvia atricapilla*, willow warbler and chiffchaff *Phylloscopus collybita* all still breed on the islands, as do sedge warbler and reed warbler. Whitethroat *Sylvia communis* breed occasionally and one or two pairs of spotted flycatcher *Muscicapa striata* breed each year; goldcrest have bred in pines on St Mary's and Tresco. Small numbers of house martins *Delichon urbica* nest on St Mary's and usually at least one of the other inhabited islands, and swallows *Hirundo rustica* still manage to find nesting places in sheds and outbuildings; they breed on all the inhabited islands. Both pied *Motacilla alba yarrellii* and white wagtails *M. alba alba* have also bred, including once a hybrid pair.

One bird that seems to evoke the atmosphere of the Isles of Scilly is the stonechat, with its 'chack-chack' stone-on-stone call from the top of a stone hedge, a gorse bush or other tall vegetation (Fig. 192). They are frequently encountered both on the heathland and around the coast. Wheatears are frequent early arrivals, often encountered along the coast or on the heathlands; very occasionally a pair will stay on late and breed.

Tresco's Great and Abbey Pools and Porth Hellick Pool on St Mary's are large enough to attract a number of waterbirds, although few species actually breed. Mute swans usually manage to rear a brood, as do the remaining feral Canada geese *Branta canadensis* on Tresco. Both mallard and gadwall are breeding species, although mallard numbers may be augmented by released birds; there are also some mallard hybrids on other pools on St Mary's. Shelduck *Tadorna tadorna* usually manage to hatch a few broods each year, but usually lose most of their ducklings to predatory gulls. The most common waterbird in Scilly is the moorhen, often found on the smaller pools, sometimes with coot. Coots breed on most of the larger pools. Although water rails *Rallus aquaticus* are often present in summer they have not been proved to breed. Teal *Anas crecca*, shoveler *A. clypeata* and other duck turn up on the Tresco pools or Porth Hellick Pool –

FIG 192. Stonechat on foxglove: they often perch on a high vantage point. (Bryan Thomas)

but although they breed occasionally they do not yet seem to have become
established. The occasional vagrant American black duck *A. rubripes* that have
turned up and stayed on Tresco Great Pool or on St Mary's have been seen
mating with mallard. What appeared to be a hybrid female was seen on St Mary's
in 2004.

Scilly is poorly off for birds of prey. Only two species, kestrel and peregrine,
regularly breed in the islands, although a pair of marsh harriers *Circus aeruginosus*
may have bred in 2005 and 2006. A few pairs of kestrels breed on the inhabited
islands, usually on ledges on the cliffs, sometimes in pines, although one pair
nested for two years in a rabbit burrow on Samson (P. Robinson, *in litt.*). It is
possible their low numbers may reflect the paucity of small mammals, although
numbers have been higher in the past, with at least seven pairs in the mid-1990s
(W. Wagstaff, *in litt.*). From the pellets collected from kestrel roosts on St Agnes,
it appears the main prey items in spring and summer are large beetles, including
minotaur beetle, dor beetle, rose chafer and oil beetle. At other times the pellets

consist of feathers and bones of small passerines. Peregrines were a breeding bird in Scilly until 1928 and then did not return as a breeding species until 1994, although they were usually present during summer from the mid-1970s (IOSBR; IOSB&NHR). They now breed regularly in the Eastern Isles and have become familiar enough to be pointed out by the boatmen on the 'seal and seabird' boat trips. Marsh harriers are believed to have bred in reedbeds on Tresco in 2005 and 2006 – though the excitement of the latter event was somewhat marred when the harriers appeared to have taken a little egret *Egretta garzetta* chick from the nest, as the egrets were also thought to be nesting in Scilly for the first time!

It is quite common to hear or see pheasants *Phasianus colchicus*, not only on Tresco, where they are released for shooting, but also on the other main islands, especially Bryher and St Mary's and occasionally Samson. Grey partridge *Perdix perdix* bones were found in Iron Age remains on Nornour (F. A. Turk, 1971), but there is no evidence they were still on the islands until introduced in the mid eighteenth century (Borlase, 1756) – although they were apparently soon wiped out (Troutbeck, 1794). Red-legged partridge *Alectoris rufa* were also released on Tresco from the mid nineteeth century, according to Clark and Rodd (1906), although records do not always make it clear which partridge was involved. Red-legged partridges have continued to be released on Tresco and now breed there and on the other off-islands with the exception of St Agnes. Golden pheasant *Chrysolophus pictus* may be breeding in the Tresco plantations, and hybrids with pheasant can sometimes be seen. During the 1960s, bobwhite quails *Colinus virginianus* were introduced to Tresco. According to Cramp *et al.* (1977–94) there were six in 1964, and six the following year. For a few years it was possible to see the quails feeding on the fields north of the Great Pool, but they eventually died out about 1980, as did the colony of free-flying budgerigars *Melopsittacus undulatus* that had roamed the islands until 1977.

Grey herons were believed to have bred in the islands; certainly there are rumours of them nesting on the ground on various islands, including a report from the gamekeeper of a pair nesting in the reeds on Tresco in the early 1980s (W. Wagstaff, *in litt.*), but there is no settled heronry. Only a few adult herons are usually seen; most of the birds in Scilly, usually roosting in groups, are immatures. Little egret, first recorded in 1955 when Hilda Quick saw one on St Agnes, has over the past decade become resident in Scilly and it had been speculated that they would eventually become established as a breeding bird. So it was no surprise when a pair apparently bred on Tresco in 2006 – but to the chagrin of the local birdwatchers a marsh harrier was seen carrying off what may have been a young egret (W. Wagstaff, personal communication).

SEABIRDS

'The seabirds of the Isles of Scilly are of national and international importance
... in many cases representing the most important component of the populations
of these species at the southwest edge of their ranges. The diversity of seabird
species is high, matched elsewhere in Britain only by larger island groups or
sites, such as on St Kilda' (Tasker, 1991). Some 20,000 seabirds breed on the
islands. Scilly is the sole English breeding location for storm petrel and has
internationally important numbers of lesser black-backed gull and shag (Heaney,
2006). Many of the visitors to the Isles of Scilly will take at least one of the boat
trips around the uninhabited islands to see seals and seabirds. Some may go on
the evening 'seabird special' to look out for Manx shearwaters collecting in large
rafts off Annet.

For many people the bird they most want to see is the puffin, hardly
surprising when every gift shop on the islands is festooned with puffins, from
logos on clothing and tea towels to puffin toys, ornaments and postcards. From
the puffinalia it is easy to imagine puffins are large and obvious birds, so when
eventually encountered, their small size and sudden disappearance when the
boat approaches may cause some disappointment. But perhaps not – the visitors
still seem to buy the tee shirts and maintain their love affair with puffins. Puffins
occur on about eight islands, but only in tiny numbers: the Seabird 2000 figure
put the total at between 100 and 200 pairs. When King wrote his little book about
Scilly in 1924 he stated that when they arrived at the end of March they came in
their thousands and nested on Annet in an area he called 'Puffin Town', forming
one huge colony around the bay from Carn Irish to the Haycocks (Fig. 193). Only
a hundred years ago Clark and Rodd (1906) could also describe them as breeding
in thousands on Annet, alongside Manx shearwaters, and how one could fall
through the roofs of their nests because the ground was so riddled with their
burrows. They also stated that on Scilly Rock and on Men-a-vaur puffins usually
laid their eggs on bare rock rather than in burrows.

The other two resident species of auks, razorbill (Fig. 194) and guillemot
(Fig. 195), are also popular, although not in the same league as the puffins. In
other parts of Britain guillemots nest in serried ranks along exposed cliff ledges,
but in Scilly both species nest mostly under boulders. On Gorregan, for example,
many are found in the tunnels that form there between the rocks (J. Parslow,
in litt.). Razorbills are more common than guillemots, with c.296 pairs on about
fourteen islands compared with 196 pairs on four islands for guillemot
(Seabird 2000).

FIG 193. 'Puffin Town', Annet: an old photo from King (1924).

FIG 194. Razorbills are frequently seen around the islands. (Bryan Thomas)

FIG 195. Guillemot: another of the three species of auks breeding in Scilly. (Bryan Thomas)

Shags also typically nest under large boulders and in cavities under the edge of the ram cliffs. Scilly has a large population of shags, with over a thousand nesting pairs spread over 24 islands. Most of these are concentrated on Annet, Rosevear, Gweal and Melledgan. Cormorants are much less common than shags, with a population of only 50–60 pairs; they only breed in small numbers on the more remote groups of islets in the Norrard Rocks, Western Rocks and Eastern Isles. Although the Melledgan cormorants have been faithful to the island for many years, others apparently move their nest sites around from season to season; this may be a reflection of the insalubrious state of their nests, untidy heaps of seaweed or even weeds from the freshwater pools liberally whitewashed with guano.

Fulmars are a late arrival in Scilly. Birds were recorded around the islands from the 1940s, but the first breeding record was not until 1951 (Ryves et al., 1951). Within a few years fulmars were nesting at a number of sites and are now breeding throughout the islands, 183 pairs being recorded in 1999 (Seabird 2000).

Because they are nocturnal and breed underground, Manx shearwaters and storm petrels are perhaps the least well known of the seabirds that breed in Scilly. King (1924) writes of thousands of shearwaters when he visited Annet at night. During the time of the St Agnes Bird Observatory 2,545 shearwaters were ringed, mostly on Annet (a few birds also nested on St Agnes and Gugh at the time). Parslow (1973) estimated there to be *c*.2,000 pairs on Annet, although the numbers were probably already decreasing (Fig. 196). Rafts of 2,000–6,000 were seen at the time, presumably containing large numbers of non-breeding birds. In 1974 Allen estimated there to be between 500 and 800 pairs, but also observed how difficult it was to get accurate counts. Since then the numbers of shearwaters have apparently continued to plummet, with recent counts estimating the current population at only 201 pairs (Heaney *et al.*, 2002).

Numbers of storm petrels are also difficult to estimate, as their nests are invisible below beach boulders. In the mid-1960s John Parslow estimated there were at least 1,500 pairs on Annet alone. When counts were made recently of 'responding' storm petrels (answering tape-recorded calls from their nests) there were estimated to be 1,475 nests (Heaney *et al.*, 2002). These figures are worked out by counting the birds that react to a tape-recording along each stretch of boulder beach and then multiplying by the amount of suitable beach. During the day it is possible to detect the presence of petrels either by their purring below the rocks or by their distinctive musky scent. So distinctive is the odour that it can still be recognised on some old petrel feathers I have kept in a desk drawer for more than twenty years. It is very unusual to see the petrels in daytime, as they stay well away from land, but occasionally in summer they may be seen from the boat on a 'shearwater special' or on one of the evening pelagics trips that go further offshore, or from the *Scillonian*. Although shearwaters also feed well away from the islands they gather in large rafts offshore before nightfall. Boat trips to see them and any other seabirds have become another of the popular expeditions now laid on for the tourists.

FIG 196. Shearwaters return from sea to their burrows on Annet on dark, moonless nights. (D. I. M. Wallace)

FIG 197. Lesser black-backed gulls on the deer-park wall, Samson, July 2006. (Rosemary Parslow)

Of the three large gulls, the lesser black-backed is the one seen least around the built-up areas on St Mary's; they are a more maritime species and tend to feed more at sea. They are in fact the most abundant species, with over 3,500 pairs breeding on some 26 of the islands. Most nest on Gugh, Samson, Annet and St Helen's (Fig. 197). On Annet and a few other places there are mixed colonies with herring gulls. Although the two species tend to prefer different areas to nest, with lesser black-backs usually being found among deep bracken or other vegetation away from the coastal strip preferred by herring gulls, on Gugh both species nest among vegetation as well as on carns and on the beach. Some 900 pairs of herring gulls breed on about 34 of the islands.

Some of the gull colonies, such as the one on Gugh, are in places where people frequently disturb them. This does not seem to be a real problem, as the gulls are supremely able to cope with disturbance and will dive-bomb anyone approaching too close. Generally, herring gulls give the impression of being the commonest gull in Scilly, probably because they impinge more on the human population, being virtually commensal around habitations, hotels, boats and anywhere where people may afford them a free lunch. Anyone visiting Scilly will become only too aware of the herring gulls, in the streets, following the boats and raiding picnic tables. Unfortunately, they are enough of a nuisance for attempts to be made to prevent them nesting on the roof-tops in Hugh Town, and also to try and stop people feeding them around the beaches.

The largest of the big *Larus* gulls, the great black-backed, is widespread in the Isles of Scilly, with 800 pairs in 1999 on 38 islands. The largest concentration is on Annet, but great black-backs are spread widely among the uninhabited islands, including some very small islets. Great black-backs have long been persecuted in Scilly, although there is no sound evidence that they were the direct cause of declines in seabird numbers. Great black-backs have received their unfortunate reputation due to their habit of preying on puffins, shearwaters and other birds. Kay (1956) was vituperative on the subject, claiming that great black-backed gulls killed 'hundreds of thousands of young birds' every spring, and that they were responsible for 'thousands and thousands of dead birds' on Annet after the nesting season. Because Kay had such a hatred of the great black-back it is not possible to accept all his comments as being very rational; he was fervently in favour of declaring open season on the gulls. Although King (1924) clearly admired the great black-back he too could not help describing in detail the 'crude and cruel' way the bird dispatches its victims. It is therefore surprising he does not mention the technique by which the gull turns the empty skin of its victim completely inside out like a glove, even a bird as large as a shag.

It has been a common practice in the past for the islanders to collect any gulls' eggs for eating. This appears to have taken place wholesale, eggs that were not wanted immediately being preserved in waterglass (Vyvyan, 1953). Combined egg-collecting and egg-pricking expeditions were apparently popular; some were organised by the 'Governor of Tresco to the uninhabited islands for the benefit of puffins and other weak species'. Vyvyan also describes joining in on a visit to an island where the nests of herring gull and lesser black-back were emptied of all the eggs they contained, and those in the nests of the great black-back, 'the cannibal gull', were drilled with a hat pin. Gulls' eggs were still being collected on

Gugh in the early 1960s. Continuing persecution of great black-backed gulls, both officially and unofficially, may have served only to push the gulls onto less accessible nesting sites. For a while the use of narcotic poisons (alpha-chloralose) near the nests was tried, but when drugged gulls began to appear in the open, the public outcry caused the plan to be dropped.

Other seabirds were persecuted in the past. Both cormorant and shag were considered to compete for fish and were killed by fishermen. Between 1880 and 1882 the Reverend Smart 'in the interests of the fishing, attempted some reduction of these birds'. He destroyed at least 1,308 birds and 835 eggs (it is not clear whether these were all cormorants or may have include green cormorants – i.e. shags) and claimed that the numbers of birds fishing had been appreciably reduced. Returning after being away for a year he found things were back to normal – if not worse (Smart, 1885–6). Cormorants (possibly including shags) were apparently at one time shot during Christmas cormorant-shooting parties, until the high cost of cartridges put a stop to the practice (Vyvyan, 1953). It is possible that the recent reduction in persecution is due not so much to legislation as to the realisation that seeing the birds is enjoyed by the holidaymakers

Kittiwakes always seem popular with visitors, perhaps because their dark eyes give them a more gentle expression, and because their habit of sitting in pairs 'billing and cooing' is also very appealing. The history of the kittiwake in Scilly before 1950 is unclear. Gorregan had been one of the islands where one could see kittiwakes easily from a boat. Kay (1956) describes seeing them there, and they were certainly present during the 1960s and 1970s, but the colony declined after 1983 and although a few pairs nested throughout the early 1990s the island has not yet been recolonised. This pattern has occurred elsewhere and, according to Robinson (2003), the birds move on after a site failure. He also states that most of the kittiwake breeding sites 'lack long-term stability', with the complete failure of a whole colony quite a frequent occurrence. Breakdown of the major food source is most likely to be the common reason, but kittiwakes are also vulnerable to other causes such as weather, predation, disturbance, and infestations of lice that overwinter on the nesting ledges and re-infest returning birds (W. Wagstaff). But there is a well-marked ongoing pattern of colonisation, decline and desertion in the population. In 2003 the total population in the Isles of Scilly was reported to be only c.250 pairs on five islands (*Isles of Scilly Bird & Natural History Review*, 2004).

The common tern is the only tern now breeding regularly in Scilly, and they have bred on several different islands. Usually the majority breed together, but a few pairs may nest away from the main colony. The favoured islands in recent years have been Samson, Annet and Tresco with outliers on Green Island (off Samson), and a few on St Agnes. The tern recovery programme that has been under way on Samson since 2000 is designed to encourage terns to settle on Samson, where they can be monitored and protected. If the common terns stay put on Samson, it is hoped that roseate terns might be enticed back as a breeding species (Fig. 198). There is a now rather chilling reference to roseate tern when in May 1840 a Mr Mitchell visited Scilly, 'for the purpose of investigating the ornithological resources of the islands during the nesting season'. He 'found the Roseate Tern tolerably common there, and obtained as many of the eggs as he required' (Clark & Rodd, 1906). After that the species seems to have declined, so that C. J. King (1924) describes a situation very similar to today: 'in 1920, at least two pairs of Roseate Terns were seen here among the Common Terns, but our hopes that the birds were returning to us after their long absence of 60 years, were doomed to disappointment. Even the Sandwich Terns are now comparatively rare in Scilly, and the Tern family is represented here, almost exclusively by the Common Tern'.

The history of roseate tern in Scilly seems complicated by very differing accounts of numbers, but the largest count was of twenty pairs during the 1970s (Lloyd *et al.*, 1975). The population in Scilly seems to have followed a national decline. During the 1960s a few roseate terns would be seen by the birdwatchers on St Agnes, their pale wings and distinctive call distinguishing them from other terns. On occasion, when we passed Green or Stony islands, a few roseate terns would be seen among the common terns. Later, in the 1990s a few roseate terns still bred among the common terns. From 1991 nest boxes were put out on a few of the former breeding sites and in 1993 two pairs used boxes. Since 2000 the multi-agency Isles of Scilly Roseate Tern Recovery Programme has been

FIG 198. Roseate tern, a former breeding species it is hoped can be attracted back to Scilly. (D. I. M. Wallace)

operating in the hope of encouraging roseate terns to breed in the common tern colony on North Hill, Samson. The island has been cleared of rats (although baiting has to be repeated when any return), decoy terns have been set up, and initially a solar-powered CD player was used to send out tern calls. Samson does not have the huge gull colonies that Annet does, or at least not on North Hill where the terns have nested, and there is an attempt to control visitors in the breeding season by roping off sections of the hill. Although it was encouraging to find common terns breeding on Samson in 2001, the birds proved fickle and the main population transferred to Annet in 2002. Disturbance, especially by people, has continually been a concern; despite fencing and signs these are still ignored by a considerable number of people. Tern warden Ben Lascelles identified predation by gulls and bad weather at critical times as major factors in the losses of eggs and chicks. In 2004 providing tern shelters (tyres and stone or driftwood shelters where the chicks can hide) on Annet, Samson and Tresco, and removing gull nests where they impinged on the tern colonies, enabled 46 chicks to fledge (Lascelles, 2005a, 2005b). Most nested on North Hill, Samson, after some had earlier abandoned Appletree Banks, Tresco. As before, a few pairs nested on other islands. However, the programme is still in its infancy, and it will be very interesting to see whether common terns can be encouraged to continue using Samson as their main breeding place – and also whether roseate terns can be lured back. But perhaps the terns will have the last word and nest where they want!

The history of Sandwich terns in Scilly is hardly very encouraging. Other than a few breeding attempts, usually unsuccessful, it was not until 1978 that they bred successfully on Green Island. Breeding occurred most years throughout the 1980s, with twenty pairs present in 1987 on Green Island. In 1991 fifteen pairs nested on Samson among the common and roseate terns, but failed: this was blamed on predation by brown rats. Since then, although Sandwich terns have sometimes attempted to nest, there do not seem to have been any successful breeding attempts. Sandwich terns are seen regularly and are often seen feeding young, although they probably have bred elsewhere.

WINTER VISITORS

The Isles of Scilly in winter have their own particular magic. Although it may be the time of fierce storms, gales and wild seas, there are quieter spells of balmy weather. The mean temperature rarely goes much below 10°C, there are almost no frosts, and snow is infrequent. There are some species of birds that turn up regularly in winter, although not many spend the whole time in the islands. Redwings *Turdus iliacus* and fieldfares *T. pilaris* usually overwinter on St Mary's and Tresco (W. Wagstaff, *in litt.*). A few flocks of waders frequent the beaches, redshank *Tringa totanus*, greenshank *T. nebularia*, turnstone *Arenaria interpres* and purple sandpiper *Calidris maritima* among them. Lapwing *Vanellus vanellus* and golden plover *Pluvialis apricaria* frequently turn up and can be found feeding usually on farmland or grassland. Occasionally large flocks of woodcock *Scolopax rusticola* arrive, especially if there is hard weather, and many will be shot by the islanders. Shooting woodcock seems to have long been considered a traditional winter pursuit in Scilly. Great northern divers *Gavia immer* frequent the islands in winter; it is not unusual to see them in St Mary's Harbour between November and April and on the seas between the islands. Later in the year there is often a small passage of the divers, when as many as twenty-five have been seen on one day between Samson and Annet. A few black-throated divers *G. arctica* and Slavonian grebes *Podiceps auritus* may also visit the islands in winter.

In Francis Rashleigh Rodd's account of his visits to Scilly during 1864–71, he gives a vivid picture of how he spent winter on Tresco. Most of his days there seem to have been spent shooting whatever he could find. Some of the species he mentions, woodcock, snipe, jack snipe *Lymnocryptes minimus* and long-eared owls *Asio otus* still occur in winter. The lakes on Tresco, and Porth Hellick Pool on St Mary's, attract flocks of wildfowl (although shooting still occurs in winter on Tresco). Throughout most winters flocks of passerines will visit the islands, ranging from skylark *Alauda arvensis* and meadow pipit *Anthus pratensis* to snow bunting *Plectrophenax nivalis* and occasionally bramblings *Fringilla montifringilla*. Some of these will be attracted to the feeding stations set up by the ISBG. Chiffchaffs are usually quite numerous during winter on the inhabited islands, especially where there is a bit of cover, as in the willow carr on St Mary's and in some of the sheltered corners of the bulb fields. Robin numbers increase substantially in winter, goldcrests are also quite common, and recently more firecrests *Regulus ignicapillus* winter. Starlings arrive in autumn, sometimes in large flocks, but these usually move on quite quickly, leaving just small numbers to stay until spring. Two interesting accounts by Rodd (1880) tell of large flocks of starlings on ships: one in November had a large flock of starlings come aboard some 300 miles west of Scilly, 'a large number were killed for the crew's use' and the rest stayed on board, leaving the ship when they reached the islands; later that month another 'great flock' of starlings came aboard a ship 200 miles west of Scilly, and some lasted until they left the boat in Scilly, the rest 'being made into pies by the sailors'. Rose-coloured starlings *Sturnus roseus* are one of the more unusual winter visitors. One that spent winter 2003/4 on St Agnes, alternating its days between a compost heap in one garden and handouts of currants in another garden, eventually stayed on into summer, by when it was developing its pink plumage (Wendy Hick, *in litt.*).

MIGRANTS AND VAGRANTS

Like many present-day birdwatchers, my first visits to Scilly during migration times were full of hope and expectation. We did not have any of the modern aids, so news of a rarity usually came by a sort of bush telegraph – or the sound of running feet could alert you to a possible find! As Lee Evans (1995) says, 'Scilly acts as a magnet for the leading ornithologists in Britain, and also provides the ideal holiday for those wishing to share in the excitement of rare bird phenomena.' In his introduction to *Birds of the Isles of Scilly* (2003) Peter Robinson comments, 'who among those involved, for example, will ever forget the excitement of the second week of October 1999, when the arrival of Britain's first short-toed eagle was followed over the next seven days by White's thrush, Siberian thrush and then a fine male blue rock thrush'? That week I was in Scilly and had just arrived on St Agnes as the eagle flew over my head, so I spent that week on the fringe of the excitement that ensued. That was an exceptional week, but there have been others, equally enjoyable, but where the birds that arrived were more common migrants. There are many emotional accounts in the bird reports of some of the most exciting finds, for example the cream-coloured courser *Cursorius cursor* in 2004 (Fig. 199; Fisher & Flood, 2005), and even more agonised sagas of the misses! When watching an exceptionally rare vagrant perhaps no one wants to think too much that this is likely to be a bird that is not going to make it and will almost certainly die, as happened in October 2004 both to an ovenbird *Seiurus aurocapillus* from North America and to the cream-coloured courser. Until I spent some time working in southern Israel, I had not realised the toll that migration often takes; on one occasion I saw thousands of swallows arriving in the desert and settling on everything, even people, and many birds were falling to the ground dying. Another time there were exhausted buzzards *Buteo buteo vulpinus* walking on the ground too weak to fly or feed.

Most birdwatchers hoping to see very rare vagrants arrive in the Isles of Scilly in autumn, usually October, as that is often the month, provided there are the 'right' weather systems, when big depressions over the Atlantic may divert North American birds migrating down the eastern seaboard of the United States across the Atlantic to Scilly. Spring migration time can also be very rewarding, although

FIG 199. Cream-coloured courser, a rare vagrant from North Africa and the Middle East. The first for Scilly turned up in September 2004. (Martin Goodey)

not usually the time to expect the very rare vagrants, but anything can turn up. One of the oddities of the Isles of Scilly is that when rarities arrive some may be from North America and others from eastern Europe – even sometimes all at the same time.

According to Rodd (1880) it was the wheatear that Borlase (1756) described as 'a small Bird here scarce so big as a Lark, of a cinereous and white colour, called a Hedge-chicker, thought by many equal food to an Ortolan'. Troutbeck (1794) also refers to them as 'hedge chuckar – scarce as big as a lark ashen & white, equal food to ortolan'. Wheatears are often the first spring migrants, usually from March onwards; they tend to be seen on the coastal grassland, where their upright stance and white rump as they fly usually draws attention to them (Fig. 200). Rocky parts of the coast are the place to look out for another early migrant, black redstart, a few of which regularly overwinter. April and May are the main spring migration months; alongside the black redstarts the usual arrivals include whinchat *Saxicola rubetra* and any of the common warblers. Purple herons *Ardea purpurea* sometimes turn up and hide away in the reeds around Porth Hellick or Tresco Great Pool. Everyone enjoys seeing hoopoes *Upupa epops*, and their arrival will often bring out the non-birdwatchers for a look (Fig. 201). Sometimes golden oriole *Oriolus oriolus* will arrive at the same time: one memorable day I spent watching a hoopoe prodding the ground for worms and a little later that same morning had the amazing sight of a male golden oriole sitting on top of a flowering gorse bush. Turtle doves *Streptopelia turtur* often do not arrive until May, when their crooning song announces them.

FIG 200. Wheatears are very common on migration around the coast. (Ren Hathway)

FIG 201. Hoopoe: their arrival always attracts a great deal of attention. (Bryan Thomas)

Fumitory is said to be an important item in the food of the turtle dove and has been linked with their distribution (Murton *et al.*,1964), but although several species of fumitory are widespread in some of the bulb fields, turtle doves may have ceased breeding in Scilly before 1959 and now only occur in small numbers in spring and autumn. Some curlew *Numenius arquata* arrive at the end of summer, their numbers building up in autumn and then dropping off by winter when just a few overwinter. Some non-breeding birds may stay in Scilly during the summer. Whimbrel *N. phaeopus* usually turn up before May; they are known as 'seven-whistlers' from their characteristic call. A few may also stay around in summer, as do other non-breeding waders.

Autumn brings a larger number of different species of migrants. Many of these are regular arrivals; they include many waders, from little stint *Calidris minuta* and others on the coasts, to some that are more likely to be found on grassland or around freshwater pools. The airfield, golf course and some of the meadows attract pectoral sandpiper *Calidris melanotos*, dotterel *Charadrius morinellus* and buff-breasted sandpiper *Tringites subruficollis*. Spotted crake *Porzana porzana* are not unusual: they, and pectoral sandpipers, can be found around freshwater pools. One group of passerines that frequently arrive together in October are the flycatchers, and it is not unusual to see spotted, pied *Ficedula hypoleuca* and red-breasted flycatcher *F. parva* all on the same day, even in the same field.

Tree pipit *Anthus trivialis* and meadow pipit commonly turn up, mostly in autumn but some in the spring, and meadow pipit has occasionally nested. The less common tawny pipit *A. campestris*, Richard's pipit *A. richardi*, olive-backed *A. hodgsoni* and red-throated pipits *A. cervinus* are all regular arrivals. The walls around the Garrison, St Mary's, and on Wingletang Down, St Agnes, are likely places to look out for wryneck *Jynx torquilla*, either in spring or autumn, sometimes several on the same day (Fig. 202). They can be difficult to find, their plumage is so cryptic: they are the classic 'stick' that gets up and hops away!

Yellowhammer, snow bunting, Lapland bunting *Calcarius lapponicus*, ortolan *Emberiza hortulana* and other species of bunting, and most of the warblers from barred *Sylvia nisoria* to icterine *Hippolais icterina* and melodious *H. polyglotta*, are also mainly autumn migrants. Woodchat *Lanius senator* and red-backed shrike *L. collurio* are also regulars; they usually give themselves away, like the flycatchers, by making sallies out from their perch to catch large insects. Bee-eaters *Merops apiaster* are not a common migrant, but one group that stayed for a few days in 1983 probably caused consternation to the farmer on St Agnes when they spent their visit raiding his hives. The large mixed flocks of tits and goldcrests that pour through the islands at this season are so noisy they cannot be ignored; they may also include a few firecrests or yellow-browed warblers. Like goldcrests, yellow-browed warblers will sometimes spend a while in clumps of isolated tree-mallow on the coast, combing through the leaves for aphids.

Around the pools and meadows yellow wagtails *Motacilla flava*, including different races, may be discovered feeding, and also grey wagtails *M. cinerea* at times. In spring and autumn the majority of the pied wagtails will be the white subspecies; the male birds are stunningly handsome. Many of the resident birds such as robins often have their numbers increased overnight by the arrival of

FIG 202. Cryptic colouring makes the wryneck difficult to find. (Ren Hathway)

Continental birds. Large influxes of jackdaws and rooks *Corvus frugilegus* occur occasionally. The jackdaws that are now resident on Tresco are believed to have derived from some birds that stayed on. Among the more regular migrants are redpolls *Carduelis flammea*, bluethroats *Luscinia svecica*, and some of the rare thrushes. Ring ouzels are frequent, usually given away by their distinctive calls, which is just as well, as there are some pied blackbirds resident in Scilly (Fig. 203). Red-eyed vireo *Vireo olivaceus*, Pallas's warbler and Radde's warbler *Phylloscopus schwarzi* are just some of the birds recorded most years. It is impossible to predict what will turn up, and even more satisfying to find one's 'own' rarity.

There are a number of places on the islands where migrants are more likely to be found, the 'hot spots'. Usually these are places where there is some shelter and where there is available food. The ISBG have negotiated several areas where farmers will allow birdwatchers access, and where there are crops such as quinoa *Chenopodium quinoa* that have been sown deliberately to attact birds. Places with cover, the willow woodland on Lower Moors, Holy Vale and sheltered places on

FIG 203. Ring ouzels are a regular migrant, usually seen on heathland. (D. I. M. Wallace)

the Garrison on St Mary's, as well as the trees around the parsonage on St Agnes, are often where migrants can be found. There are bird hides by the pools on the main wetland sites. The meadows such as those on St Agnes and St Martin's, the airfields on Tresco and St Mary's, and any coastal areas, can be the places to see birds. Special arrangements are usually made to view the airfield on St Mary's, as it is otherwise out of bounds. In the past the thoughtless attitude of a few birdwatchers singularly intent on seeing rarities has caused conflict with the islanders. Stone hedges were sometimes knocked down, fields trampled and islanders looked out to suddenly find their cottage gardens under siege from bristling telescopes. David Hunt and others drew up a Code of Conduct for birdwatchers that everyone is encouraged to follow. Most islanders are very tolerant, but all the farmland is private, and the possibility of transferring disease from field to field is a great concern. So if you want to enter a field, ask first.

SEA-WATCHING AND PELAGICS

One form of birdwatching that is perhaps least understood by the non-birdwatcher is sea-watching. This is probably one of the most frustrating forms of the pursuit, given the difficulty of picking up a moving dot in your telescope in all that sea and then, even more unlikely, resolving it into an identity. But at times there are huge movements of seabirds passing close inshore, and several species of shearwaters, skuas, gulls, frequently gannets *Morus bassanus* are seen. The great 'wreck' of grey phalaropes in autumn 1960 was one of the more spectacular events. A bonus can be sightings of dolphins, harbour porpoises or even basking sharks off the islands.

An even more extreme form of sea-watching is the 'pelagic'. These are sea trips sailing south of the islands down towards the Bay of Biscay. *Scillonian* usually sails in August but some of the bigger island launches also now make pelagic trips. These can last upwards of five hours and give birdwatchers a glimpse of species that are more southern in distribution – but it needs a pretty strong stomach to cope with the conditions and the use of 'chum', a stinking mess of fishy remains intended to lure petrels and other birds attracted by the smell. Besides birds there is always a chance of sighting cetaceans, basking sharks or other marine species. For the more timorous the short sail between Scilly and Penzance is usually quite testing enough. And there can be some impressive crossings when there are good numbers of birds to be seen. Manx, sooty *Puffinus griseus*, great *P. gravis*, Cory's shearwaters *Calonectris diomedea*, storm and Leach's petrel *Oceanodroma leucorhoa*, grey phalarope, Sabine's gull *Larus sabini* and many others are all possible (Fig. 204). As with much of the natural history of the Isles of Scilly, there is always the chance of something interesting or unusual to be seen.

FIG 204. Great shearwaters are one of the species that may be seen on pelagic trips. (Ren Hathway)

CHAPTER 17

The Future

Few districts in the United Kingdom can vie with Scillonia for wild, romantic,
unspoiled Nature.

C. J. King (1924)

So what is the future for the Isles of Scilly? Over the centuries the
islands have been subjected to all manner of changes, both natural and
man-made. Many of the changes may be large and inevitable, sea-level
rise for example, while other changes are quite small, although they may have
consequences that are not foreseen at the time. For example, when the heliport
was being laid out on Tresco the grassland area that was selected was reseeded,
which changed the species composition there. On St Martin's the building of
the hotel destroyed an area of marram and sand dune (as well as controversially
winning many large stones from the granite fences on the island to face the
building). When the contentious extension to the runway at the airport on
St Mary's was built in the early 1990s it removed 75 per cent of the heathland
on a headland that was part of the Heritage coast (Farr, 1992).

Sea defence work has changed many places along the coasts of Scilly;
fortunately the use of local materials, the agency of windblown sand and wind-
carried seed seem to eventually restore the areas to some degree. When the sea
defences were rebuilt at Porth Cressa on St Mary's in 1995 the grass banks were
reseeded and many of the rare clovers and other plants there were lost, but now
some of the former plants are gradually returning, presumably spreading in
from the surrounding areas. Fortunately most work is carried out with as much
mitigation as can be devised, although many of the mistakes that happen are
probably quite unconscious on the part of the perpetrators – such as the

importation of species and materials that are not of local origin. Two examples that come to mind are using turf made up of coarse grasses to make local repairs to the species-rich grass tops of Bronze Age barrows such as Bant's Carn, and the use of a soil and seed mixture along the top of part of the Garrison walls, possibly without realising the value of the naturally occurring plant community already there. The introduction, probably accidental, of the fern *Azolla* to the pools on St Mary's was another near-disaster: the fern quickly covered the water and, although extraordinary attempts were made to eliminate it, the plant spread quickly. Fortunately, although all attempts to destroy the plant with chemicals seem to have failed, it eventually became diminished to the now small amounts in pools in Lower Moors and Porth Hellick Pool, and appears to have been checked for the time being.

SEA-LEVEL RISE

The seas are becoming stormier, and the combination of sea-level rise and increased storm surges is continuing to make inroads into the coastline of the islands. An early reference to sea-level rise in Scilly was by William Borlase (1753). He realised that the remains of ancient stone walls now under the sea indicated there had been farmed land there in the past. Insidiously the sea has continued to rise, despite small local accretions – such as the 'building' sand bank on the northeast corner of Samson. The effort to save more land from being inundated has resulted in a huge and expensive programme of sea defence work. But in time the sea is expected to take back some of the present low-lying 'protected' areas. No one can say when, but it is very likely, if the trend continues, that the sea will eventually cut through and render islands of several current promon-tories. Among the most vulnerable places is Hugh Town, part of which is built on a former sand bar between Porth Cressa and the Pool (Fig. 205).

The central theme of Charles Thomas's book *Exploration of a Drowned Landscape* (1985) is that the Isles of Scilly are the remnants of a larger, inundated landmass, and one where the sea is still rising. At the time Thomas was writing the revival of interest in sea-level rise was just beginning, so his predictions were very conservative compared with those in the report of the UK Climate Impacts Programme (1998). In the 1980s sea-level rise in Scilly was the same as the sea-level fall at Malin Head, the northernmost point of Ireland, 2.4mm per year. Thomas extrapolated the predicted rise in Scilly between 1900 and 2000 as a gain of 22.5cm (a rate of 2.25mm per year based on measurements from west Cornwall). However, Thomas also suggested that the rate for Scilly could be

FIG 205. Porth Cressa is the part of Hugh Town most clearly vulnerable to sea level rise. May 2005. (Rosemary Parslow)

somewhat greater than 2.4mm per year due to differences in geography and geology, and suggested 2.6mm per year. Recent predictions (UK Climate Impacts Programme, 1998) give four possible scenarios based on global climate changes. The sea-level rise estimates for the period centred on the 2050s could be between 12cm and 67cm according to the particular scenario.

In 1997 the Council of the Isles of Scilly commissioned a Shoreline Management Plan of the coastline of Scilly. As a result a number of the major sea defence works recommended have been carried out on St Mary's, Bryher, Tresco and St Agnes to protect property and water supplies in particular. But as J. Pontin, the then Duchy of Cornwall Land Steward, commented, 'any significant rise in sea levels around the islands would necessitate a reappraisal of the study and further protection schemes where necessary.'

Over the past thirty years there has been a concentrated programme of sea defence work on the most vulnerable sections of coastline, especially those which affect human habitations. In 1993/4 the harbour wall on St Mary's was raised, widened and strengthened; several bays have also had new sea walls. Other defences have been built on all the inhabited islands and around the

Romano-British site on Nornour. Even so, it was noted in October 2000 that the spring tide had just reached the top of the defences between the massive new concrete wall and the reinforced boulder bank at Porth Killier on St Agnes. During storm surges in October 2004 the seas drove inland in many places, demonstrating the vulnerability of some of the beaches and low-lying ground.

Among many areas of very low-lying land in Scilly are places like Rushy Bay and Great Pool on Bryher, the meadow on St Agnes, the neck between Porth Askin and Wingletang Bay on St Agnes, the land behind Porth Cressa on St Mary's: all are particularly at risk from the sea. And eventually even hugely expensive sea defences may not be enough. Initially it may be a question of whether the cost of protecting some areas is prohibitive and only land in the inhabited areas like Hugh Town should be prioritised. At present the prospect of the Isles of Scilly becoming smaller and smaller until only the tops of the highest land are left seems so far off that no one can really take the prospect very seriously. But on a small local scale the incremental loss of the coastal margins of the islands has probably been the main reason for the decline of shore dock over the last century (see Chapter 9). A sea-level rise of as little as 30–50cm would inundate several of the plant's current sites, which are currently just above HWM. There is probably no other plant in quite the same predicament – as yet. Our knowledge of many of the invertebrate animals is too poor even to speculate on what we may have lost unknowingly.

CLIMATE CHANGE

Any changes in the climate could have considerable consequences for the Isles of Scilly. Changes to the weather pattern could lead to wetter winters and drier summers with consequent problems for farming, water supply and tourism. Storm surges are unusual situations caused when high spring tides coincide with a sustained period of very strong winds. These surges are more damaging and destructive than the usual gales as they push the seas to considerably higher levels and their effect can be felt above the limits of EHWS. In 1962 the quay was destroyed on St Martin's, houses were flooded on St Mary's, sea walls were washed away, boats were swept inland and great boulders were flung into bulb fields. There have been other similar surges over the years, including September 2000 and October 2004, and although those with the gales from the south cause most damage they can come from any direction. Increased storminess may be one of the features of climate change, and there is the possibility of more storm surges in future.

Situated on the edge of the Atlantic, Scilly lies in the path of storms that are generated a long way from the islands. A build-up of water forms waves far out to sea and the upward deflection of these waves when they reach the edge of the islands means they are particularly vulnerable. Low barometric pressure can cause an additional increase in wave height (as in October 2004). There are occasions when huge waves have broken over the top of the Bishop Rock lighthouse (49 metres high). These occurrences are more frequent in Scilly than elsewhere on the Southwest Peninsula because of the geographical position of the islands. Also the configuration of the island, with carns interspersed by channels and lower land, can effectively concentrate and increase the impact. One place this can be seen is on Teän, where tides at EHWS can be driven through a gap on the lower part of the shore between the granite rock platform and an offshore carn.

Any rise in temperature may initially not have serious consequences for plant life in the Isles of Scilly, as many of the species have origins in the Mediterranean and warmer climates. But if climate change results in increasingly dry summers this could lead to water shortages for the human population and for farm stock. Growing some crops, such as soft fruit and salads, would also become difficult without good supplies of water. Hot summers could also lead to the drying up of the limited numbers of natural springs and pools. It has already been seen that plants like shore dock die when the seepages that support them dry up.

Another phenomenon probably due to climate change is the apparent increase in the number of sightings of marine species of more southern distribution. A documented rise of 0.5°C in sea temperatures since 1980 has been accompanied by occurrences of a number of southern fish new to Cornish and Scillonian waters as well as an increase in sightings of ocean sunfish, grey triggerfish, Couch's seabream *Sparus pagrus* and common puffer-fish *Lagocephalus lagocephalus* (Stebbing *et al.*, 2002). Other marine animals may also be showing a similar trend.

HOUSING

There has been a necessary resistance to building more houses in Scilly, so property prices are very high. There is a real lack of affordable homes for local people wanting to live and work on the islands, and it is difficult to find lodgings for summer casual staff. Houses are often bought as second homes or as holiday lets by people living outside the islands. The housing situation ensures any job that comes up on the islands has almost automatically to go to someone already living there unless it has tied accommodation. Building more housing is not considered the answer, on account of the limited resources of the islands, especially water, which preclude much expansion. In addition, a lot more building would inevitably have a detrimental effect on the landscape.

In 1982 the Duchy of Cornwall and the Isles of Scilly Council initiated a project to look into the future of the islands, and this was published as the *Moss Report* (Graham Moss Associates, 1984). The project analysed what was desirable and important and proposed the ways forward, especially with a view to making the islands more independent and less reliant on the Duchy of Cornwall. Much of the report is still relevant today, although some specific recommendations have been overtaken by events. For example the plan to make the islands a National Nature Reserve was eventually abandoned, and so was the Marine Nature Reserve, although in the latter case there is now a Voluntary Marine Park around the islands and most of the important areas on the islands have been designated Sites of Special Scientific Interest (SSSIs), managed by the Isles of Scilly Wildlife Trust.

TOURISM AND WILDLIFE

Attempts to increase the holiday facilities in Scilly have also been suggested. At one time people have come up with ideas for turning Samson into a holiday camp or building a luxury hotel there. Fortunately, these ideas never came to anything, but there are hotels, besides those on St Mary's, on Tresco, St Martin's and Bryher. Proposals to build hotels on the smaller islands are of concern, not because a hotel per se is a problem, but because they inevitably put great stress on the already limited water supply and other resources. When the hotel on St Martin's was built it was faced with local granite; the effect was acceptable but the sourcing of it was contentious. The extension to the hotel on Bryher in 2003 was also debatable because the building and its surroundings now dominate a very small and rugged island, which some people feel is out of keeping with the scale of the landscape.

Tourism and the natural history of the Isles of Scilly are now deeply entwined, and those whose business depends on the holiday visitors ignore this at their peril. Even though not everyone who spends their holiday in Scilly is an ardent naturalist, there are many who are attracted by the beauty of the landscape, the sea and the wildlife. Many visitors, for the short time they are on Scilly, take an avid interest in the islands, their history and their natural history.

With the natural world becoming more and more a focus for tourists, people will want to go on snorkelling safaris, swim with seals, see the Bronze Age burial sites or go on boat trips to see puffins and other seabirds as well as seals (from the safety of a boat). Television has made everyone aware of wildlife and brought it into the living room; numerous films have been made about Scilly, including several about the natural history, and Samson was the setting of Michael Mulpurgo's children's book *Why the Whales Came* (1985) and the subsequent film. Every boatman has become a natural history guide and expert on wrecks and history of the island. Evening activities on St Mary's often tend to have an environmental theme: slide shows on wildlife, archaeology, marine life as well as special boat trips at dusk to see the gathering of Manx shearwaters off Annet. Every week in the tourist season specialist tours arrive to visit the Isles of Scilly in increasing numbers: groups to watch birds, paint landscapes, visit gardens or work as volunteers for the Wildlife Trust (Fig. 206). Those who return year after year are not looking for seaside entertainments but for quiet, low-key activities and safe beaches, and that indefinable magic that makes Scilly special. The Isles of Scilly are a classic case of the golden goose: it would be so easy to kill the goose.

FIG 206. Wildlife Trust volunteers cutting and clearing dense gorse that was invading heathland on Samson Hill, Bryher. June 2002. (Rosemary Parslow)

The marine environment of the Isles of Scilly leaves the islands exposed to the continual danger of pollution (see Chapter 8). With large amounts of shipping passing the islands every day there is always the risk of an accident. So far the islands have been fortunate in that they have not suffered any major oil spill – the *Torrey Canyon* slick fortunately mainly missing Scilly. But there is always the prospect of oil spills in future, and even a small amount of oil causes problems for visitors and islanders. Every day masses of plastic and other detritus washes up on beaches (Fig. 207). These concerns are not only for the local tourist board, local people and interests, but should be the province of planners and government.

Some concerns are more parochial: fears that waste water from the hotel could get into the brackish Great Pool on Bryher and affect the fragile ecosystem, for example. Or will the new gardens on Bryher parachute even more aliens into the local area to overtake the native flora – and would it really matter, with so many aliens in the flora anyway? Will increased numbers of people requiring more and more entertainment push the natural resources to their limits? In 2003 I went on two different boat trips to see the puffins off Annet. On one the launch drove into the bay very fast, flushing a group of puffins off the cliff; oh

FIG 207. Rubbish left by winter storms blows inland to litter the heathland. Wingletang, St Agnes, December 2004. (Rosemary Parslow)

yes, everyone saw them – but as they flew away. On the second boat we slid gently into the same bay and waited quietly; the puffins stayed on the cliff and others flew past, we moved slowly around so everyone got good views, and the birds apparently tolerated the disturbance. More and more visitors are tending to land on the uninhabited islands; this is certainly a very pleasant experience, but it may be putting additional pressure on fragile habitats. Disturbance to nesting terns has already been commented on (see Chapter 16) – although it is not only visitors who ignore signs and barriers, and many of the culprits appear to be locals.

But generally things are improving. Gradually awareness of the value of the 'natural heritage' of the islands is increasing, even if only because it is seen to have a commercial value. The work by the Wildlife Trust and the farmers to manage the unfarmed land for nature conservation also has benefits in terms of access and landscape. The publishing of the Countryside Agency's landscape assessment (2004) brings together the work of all the agencies involved in protection and promotion of the special qualities and features of the Isles of Scilly AONB. As it states, 'gradual erosion of the more intangible qualities of peacefulness, tranquility and isolation ... is the greatest threat to the landscape and the most potent force for change.' Two full-time officers are employed to administer the AONB and implement the AONB Management Plan. There is also a Joint Advisory Committeee representing the various interest groups in Scilly. An important part of the remit of the AONB is to administer both a system of grants – the Sustainable Development Fund – and the Planning Consultative Panel, which advises the Isles of Scilly planning department on planning applications that impact on the natural heritage of the islands.

CHANGES IN FARMING PRACTICE

In the past few years, as flower farming has declined, many farmers in Scilly have been trying to find alternative solutions. The competition faced by the flower growers from other markets has already led to considerable reduction in the production of narcissus as cut flowers and as bulbs. The Trenoweth Horticultural Centre is continuing to look for ways to improve horticulture on the islands and keep the industry viable in the face of worldwide competition. The local farmers are also proposing, if not mixed farming, more stock farming on the islands. The number of cattle has declined over the past decades due to changes in regulations over dairying and the requirement to send animals to the mainland for slaughter.

Proposals for the islands to have their own abattoir would make it worthwhile for the local farmers to keep a few cattle again. More cattle are already being kept, and more Shetland ponies arrived on Bryher in 2005. The Isles of Scilly Wildlife Trust lease almost all the unfarmed land from the Duchy of Cornwall, and most of this land is heathland or coastal habitats that were traditionally grazed. There are many hectares of this type of land that need grazing if they are to retain their nature conservation interest, and if this could happen the advantages would be tremendous: scrub could be reversed, grassland and heathland restored and with them many of the wild flowers and other species (Fig. 208). With better access to more of the open land, visitors could wander without, perhaps, causing quite so much erosion to paths. Ideally more stock should result in locally produced meat products. If these proposals turn out to be a practical possibility and not a pipe dream it could be a great boost for local farmers. A good living for the farmers and one that also benefits nature conservation would be ideal for the future of the islands.

As to the future of the bulb fields, it is hoped there will still be a viable future for flower farming, especially scented narcissus: not only because it is an attractive aspect of island life, and something that is very much associated with

FIG 208. Ruby red Devon cattle, introduced for conservation grazing on Bryher. April 2006. (David Mawer)

FIG 209. Arable weeds in a field growing both bulbs and pinks. May 2003. (Rosemary Parslow)

Scilly, but because of the hope that some of the associated rare and beautiful arable weed species will survive. Cultivating some bulb fields and other arable land in the traditional way (see Chapter 12) could ensure the survival of many of these species. Perhaps the fact that so many visitors get so much enjoyment out of the spectacle of the colourful fields, both the narcissus and the weeds, will make them worth retaining (Fig. 209). Farmers are trying many alternative crops and products, including trialling the production of plant essences from narcissus, lavender and other plants, making soap perfumed with local flowers. Other farms have gone over to more intensive summer flower production, including specialist floral products, while others are producing vegetables, salads and soft fruit, honey or other locally made commodities.

LOSSES AND INTRODUCTIONS

In the *Nature Conservation Review* (Ratcliffe, 1977), the 'gazetteer' that identified the most important nature conservation sites in Britain, the Isles of Scilly have two entries, one of which describes the islands as having

over 250 species of lichens ... including many rare southern species. The best British
population of Rumex rupestris (shore dock), Lavatera cretica (smaller tree-mallow)
and Ornithopus pinnatus (yellow vetch – now usually called orange bird's-foot) and
many established aliens occur on these cliffs and beaches. The islands are of additional
interest for the variety of marine biological life on rocky shores, breeding colonies of
seabirds (including Manx shearwaters, storm petrels, puffins and roseate terns) and the
Scilly shrew and grey seals. This is an important bird migration landfall that is of
considerable interest for North American bird vagrants which occur in the autumn.

Since that was written there have been a number of changes in Scilly. The roseate
tern is no longer a breeding species; it is rarely recorded these days. Numbers
of the shore dock have declined, several colonies having been totally lost to the
sea, washed away in storms. The mainland population of this rare plant may
now have outranked the Scilly populations, once considered the largest and most
important in northwest Europe (Lousley, 1971). Numbers of Manx shearwater
have also declined drastically.

Some other species of plants have been lost or are becoming rare. This is
probably inevitable in an island situation when the potential for recolonisation
is very limited. Sea cottonweed *Othanthus maritimus* had become extinct by 1938,
moonwort has not been seen since 1940, and purple viper's-bugloss has also
apparently become extinct more recently, as has a delightful variety of small-
flowered catchfly *Silene gallica quinquevunera* as a wild plant. Work on the shore
dock over more than twenty years has not only tracked the loss of several colonies
of this plant, but has also, given its existence on the precarious interface between
shore and land, graphically demonstrated the vulnerability of the coastline.

Besides roseate tern, a number of other birds, once quite common, no longer
breed in Scilly, or only do so irregularly, such as turtle dove and skylark. Some
of these losses reflect national trends, but others, like the loss of some arable
weeds, may have local causes.

The mild climate has enabled many introductions of plants and animals from
warmer climates to become established and although most have not apparently
had any deleterious effect on the native wildlife there have been exceptions. Some
of the most obvious examples of introductions that have gone wrong include
the New Zealand flax plants that have proliferated, especially on St Martin's,
the water fern that got into pools on St Mary's, the Hottentot fig that has
overwhelmed large areas of coastal vegetation and the arrival of japweed or
Sargasso weed, which is becoming one of the most widespread seaweeds. When
hedgehogs were brought to the islands it may not have been realised they would
soon get out and multiply. Now there is a real concern that in the long term

they are likely to have an impact on some bird species and on the populations of larger beetles. There is even an introduced liverwort, *Lophocolea semiteres*, that is spreading aggressively over native species on Chapel Down and has become ubiquitous on all the inhabited islands; similarly a moss, *Campylopus introflexus*, has overwhelmed the micro-habitats of some native bryophytes (Paton & Holyoak, 2005).

So what is the future for the Isles of Scilly? And how will it affect all the amazing and fascinating animals and plants that make up the natural history of the islands? Although we want to keep the matchless beauty of the islands and maintain their unique natural history, we cannot preserve the islands in aspic. There is still a community of people on the islands and none of them would appreciate living in a museum. The whole history of the islands has been one of change. How the islands survive the next decades and even the next centuries will be a challenge to the intelligence and integrity of the islanders themselves and those who manage the environment. Somehow a way has to be found to allow the islands to change and thrive, without losing any of their wonderful natural wealth.

Vegetation Communities

W hat is probably the first serious description of plant habitats in the Isles of Scilly was by Charterhouse biology master, Oleg Polunin, who produced a handout for use by his students on school field trips. This is referred to in the *Flora* (Lousley, 1971), and I was able to acquire a copy from a former pupil, botanist Jonathan Akeroyd.

Since then all five volumes of the National Vegetation Classification (NVC) have been published (Rodwell, 1991–2000). Some data on the vegetation communities that occur in the Isles of Scilly have been included in the volumes of the NVC. Cover of vegetation types for Scilly is patchy, so that in certain habitats there are communities that do not conform very well with published descriptions, or where some species may be missing. This may simply be due to limited data from Scilly.

Some ecologists, when describing plant communities in Scilly, have commented on differences, or on how good a 'fit' they are getting. One worker, Dargie (1990), has gone further and has produced his own vegetation classification, particularly for sand dunes.

The following pages describe some of the habitats and vegetation communities in the Isles of Scilly. This is a very incomplete account and is included in the hope it may stimulate further study of this fascinating aspect of plant biology in Scilly. The account is not intended to be used to identify NVC communities, but rather to explore those that have been recognised in the Isles of Scilly. There are some habitats we found difficult to assign to any published in NVC. Others, like the 'salt marsh' on Bryher, are almost too small to count – but it has been fun trying!

HEATHLAND

Heathland plant communities in Scilly have slightly different species compositions from those on the mainland, usually because there are far fewer species on the islands. The heath frequently forms mosaics or transitions from one community type to another, all within a small compass. Also, because of the close proximity of the sea there is a continuum from maritime cliff and coastal grassland communities to heath. The dramatic 'waved heath', where the heathland is sculptured by the winds, commonly occurs in H7 and H8. Lichens, especially *Cladonia* species, are common on heathland, and in some areas the growth is so heavy that areas appear white from a distance (see Fig. 121). Burning of heathland, either deliberate burning to remove gorse or accidental heath fires, are frequent in Scilly and cause changes in the composition of the heathland communities that may persist for decades. It is possible that fires have also affected the distribution of western gorse, as it now appears to be less common in Scilly than formerly. The most typical Scillionian heathland communities are described below.

H7 *Calluna vulgaris – Scilla verna* heath
This is one of the most common types of heathland in Scilly, found mainly near the coast often in mosaics with other communities. The *Armeria* sub-community is found closer to the sea, with the *Calluna* sub-community forming some of the more species-poor 'waved heath' away from the cliff. The constant species are ling, bell heather, Yorkshire fog, common cat's-ear, bird's-foot-trefoil, tormentil, and especially in the *Armeria* sub-community rare species including autumn lady's-tresses, western clover and occasionally Portland spurge. Spring squill is absent from much of Scilly, and sheep's fescue also has a patchy distribution.

H8 *Calluna vulgaris – Ulex gallii* heathland
Some of the best places to see this type of heathland are along the eastern side of St Mary's such as on Salakee Down. Characteristically it is dominated by three dwarf shrubs, ling, bell heather and western gorse. Other commonly associated species in this community include tormentil, heath bedstraw *Galium saxatile*, sheep's sorrel and milkworts *Polygala* spp. Between the low shrubs it is common to see the *Danthonia* sub-community, especially along pathways.

H10 *Calluna vulgaris – Erica cinerea* heathland

The constants in this community, ling, bell heather and tormentil, are all common on Scilly. Other species present include heath bedstraw, milkworts, goldenrod *Solidago vigaurea* and lousewort. This is more generally a northern and western type of heathland, but has been reported from Scilly.

H11 *Calluna vulgaris – Carex arenaria* heathland

Another common heathland community type, dominated by ling and sand sedge. In Scilly the *Erica cinerea* sub-community is typical: it is frequent as 'dune-heath' found on sandier areas and often has very interesting lichen populations. Suffocated clover and Portland spurge are often found here. H11 is often seen at the dune/heathland interface, and there are good examples on St Martin's.

MARITIME CLIFFS

MC1 *Crithmum maritimum – Spergularia rupicola* maritime rock crevice community

This is a very common community all around the exposed rocky coasts in Scilly and even on man-made habitats such as the outer wall of Cromwell's Castle, Tresco, and on the Garrison, St Mary's. Typically scattered plants grow in crevices in the granite or between the stones of the walls where there is protection from maximum exposure to wind and sea spray. Below this zone are found lichens of the splash zone. Rock samphire, red fescue, rock sea-spurrey and thrift are all constant species. Buck's-horn plantain, common and Danish scurvygrasses, wild carrot (the coastal form) and other common coastal plants also occur here. Where there is shelter in deep clefts there may be fine specimens of sea spleenwort.

MC5 *Armeria maritima – Cerastium diffusum diffusum* maritime therophyte community

This is another very characteristic community of the cliffs in Scilly and also on the tops of granite walls near the coast, such as on the Garrison. Therophytes are annuals that stay dormant in seed during adverse conditions, germinating and completing their life history in one season. MC5 is frequent on the rocky carns and other outcrops where the soils are shallow and become baked by the sun in summer, but where there is still enough moisture for the plants to survive. MC5 frequently occurs in mosaics with MC1 and heathland communities. Cushions of thrift and patches of English stonecrop, buck's-horn plantain and sea mouse-ear *Cerastium diffusum* may be interspersed with some of the rarer *Trifoliums* and smaller grasses, such as early meadow-grass and early hair-grass. Other typical species that occur here include western clover, orange bird's-foot, hairy bird's-foot-trefoil and the lichen *Heteroderma leucomela*. There are good examples at Heathy Hill, Bryher, Deep Point, St Mary's, and on Wingletang Down, St Agnes. It is not obvious which MC5 sub-communities occur on Scilly, probably several of them. It would appear that one of the commonest types should be MC5b, the kidney vetch *Anthyllus vulneraria* variation, but kidney vetch is now extinct in Scilly and it is unclear whether it was ever more than a very rare plant.

MC6 *Atriplex prostrata – Beta vulgaris maritima* seabird community
This kind of vegetation is common of the rocky islets where there is disturbance due to nesting seabirds; there are examples on the Eastern Isles. The constant species in this very variable vegetation type are red fescue, cocksfoot grass, fleshy-leaved plants of sea beet, spear-leaved orache, common scurvygrass, sea mayweed and often other species of *Atriplex*, the coastal form of curled dock and often stands of tree-mallow. On some sites clumps of tree-mallow may be significant, as on Rosevear in the Western Rocks. Outside the breeding season the vegetation recovers somewhat, but there may be a brief flurry of annual weeds taking advantage of the disturbed and well-manured ground.

MC7 *Stellaria media – Rumex acetosa* seabird cliff community
This is another seabird community dominated by a fleshy form of common chickweed, with common sorrel and several species of grasses, red fescue, Yorkshire fog and creeping bent, plus thrift, curled dock, large plants of sea mayweed and in some places sea campion. It may occur in mosaics with MC6.

MC8 *Festuca rubra – Armeria maritima* maritime grassland
This community is found all round coasts in Scilly. It has typical coastal components such as the coastal form of wild carrot, western clover and, in places where it occurs, spring squill. It is notable for the distinctive red fescue 'mattresses' found on some cliffs and islands; Hottentot fig is often found in this habitat in Scilly. On the island of Annet there are extensive areas of an extreme form of the *Armeria* sub-community that appears to be associated with shearwater and former puffin colonies. It consists of enormous thrift tussocks with a small amount of red fescue and often rock sea-spurrey on the bare ground in the gaps between the tussocks. Another sub-community represented in Scilly is the *Plantago coronopus* sub-community. This forms a close sward around the edge of the coast and is usually rabbit-grazed, although in the absence of grazing it appears to be maintained by wind-pruning. In this sub-community red fescue is

still dominant but not as mattresses. Other significant species are thrift, creeping bent, buck's-horn plantain and sea plantain *Plantago maritima* where it occurs (along the east coast of St Mary's). Other common sub-communities are also represented; the *Holcus lanatus* variation with several common grasses, common sorrel, common cat's-ear and yarrow is common. The *Anthyllus* sub-community also may be found in Scilly – but without kidney vetch.

MC9 *Festuca rubra – Holcus lanatus* maritime grassland
This grassland is a progression from MC8. It is relatively species-rich and frequent on more sheltered coasts. Generally it is a rather rough, tussocky sward dominated by red fescue and Yorkshire fog. Ribwort plantain, cocksfoot and thrift are frequent. Other species include bird's-foot-trefoil, yarrow, lady's bedstraw *Galium verum*, tormentil and western clover. The *Dactylis glomerata* sub-community is probably the most common in Scilly.

MC10 *Festuca rubra – Plantago* spp. maritime grassland
The *Armeria maritima* sub-community is the one represented in Scilly. It is composed of red fescue, buck's-horn plantain, ribwort plantain and creeping bent. Rare species include western clover and spring squill. This type of grassland appears to be close to that found as a mosaic in maritime heaths. There are grasslands in Scilly that seem to approximate to this community type. Some of the close-mown grasslands have proved difficult to categorise, but may be close to this. Many have a distinctive appearance due to the presence of chamomile. Several of the larger areas of grassland on the off-islands have been managed as cricket pitches, and a similar type of grassland is maintained around some of the ancient monument sites by close mowing. This has produced interesting and species-rich grassland that must be very like the closely grazed habitats that may have existed formerly.

MC12 *Festuca rubra – Hyacinthoides non-scripta* maritime bluebell community
Some of the slopes with grasses, bluebells, common sorrel and bracken may be attributed to this plant community. It can be confused with other bracken communities such as W25, although there is no obvious woodland component in most places in Scilly.

GRASSLAND

U1 *Festuca ovina – Agrostis capillaris – Rumex acetosella* grassland
This is one of the common 'inland' grasslands on the islands. Examples can be found as a mosaic with heathland. Typically it grows in places that become dry and parched in summer. In Scilly sheep's fescue is largely replaced by red fescue. The sward is usually maintained by rabbits; where the surface is scuffed and broken, the succulent, English stonecrop, and sometimes wall pennywort, may appear. In Scilly the *Hypocharis radicata* sub-community with early hair-grass, common cat's-ear and plantains is typical.

U4 *Festuca ovina – Agrostis capillaris – Galium saxatile* grassland
Red fescue again replaces sheep's fescue where this community occurs in Scilly. Other typical species are common bent *Agrostis capillaris*, heath bedstraw, tormentil and sweet vernal-grass. Heath-grass can be prominent in places such as along pathways in heathland/grassland mosaics. This grassland is also found in mosaics with heathland.

MG5 *Cynosurus cristatus – Centaurea nigra* grassland
This is a very rare type of grassland in Scilly, although it may have been more common when there were more hay meadows. There is an example on St Martin's of the heath-grass sub-communitiy with pignut, black knapweed and masses of the deep red form of white clover. The list for these fields includes a number of grasses: red fescue, sheep's fescue, Yorkshire fog, creeping bent, common couch *Elytrigia repens*, common bent, crested dog's-tail and rye-grass, plus characteristic forbs including daisy *Bellis perennis*, smooth hawk's-beard *Crepis capillaris*, knapweed, germander speedwell *Veronica chamaedrys*, ragwort, creeping buttercup *Ranunculus repens*, common cat's-ear, sheep's sorrel, fiddle dock, yarrow, common mouse-ear *Cerastium fontanum* as well as the pignut and clover. In places bluebell is also present, presumed to have been associated with a former bracken community, since cleared.

MG10 *Holcus lanatus – Juncus effusus* rush-pasture
This grassland occurs on permanently moist soils that are usually grazed. The constant species are creeping bent, Yorkshire fog, soft rush and creeping buttercup; the typical sub-community with white clover, sorrel and some dock species is found in some of the low-lying pasture on St Mary's. The *Iris pseudacorus* sub-community is also found on St Mary's, where there are several

fields with much yellow iris. Other plants of wet grassland include tubular water-dropwort and greater bird's-foot-trefoil. This community also seems to form mosaics with MG13 *Agrostis stolonifera – Alopecurus geniculatus* grassland. Some of these fields may formerly have been more species-rich, but the lowering of the water table has possibly eliminated some plants that formerly grew there.

MG11 *Festuca rubra – Agrostis stolonifera – Potentilla anserina* grassland

Wet grassland with both freshwater and brackish influences. Often present in small patches where there is standing water. In some places silverweed may be dominant. Where there are freshwater seepages in sand or shingle areas the sea sandwort sub-community is found. This community may also be found around some of the freshwater pools near the coast with maritime species including sea-milkwort and saltmarsh rush, as around the pools on Bryher and St Agnes.

MG13 *Agrostis stolonifera – Alopecurus geniculatus* grassland

This type of grassland is not uncommon in Scilly, although one of the constants, marsh foxtail *Alopecurus geniculatus*, is quite rare. It occurs in patches around freshwater pools and can include several species of rush, toad rush, soft rush and saltmarsh rush, and lesser spearwort can also be present. The most typical stands are found near the Pool on St Martin's, on School Green on Tresco and in fields near Porthloo Road, St Mary's.

COASTAL POOLS

A21 *Ranunculus baudotii* community

This community appears to occur in most of the brackish pools in Scilly. The dominant species are usually either one or more of brackish water-crowfoot, fennel-leaved pondweed and beaked tasselweed.

SALT MARSH

SM16 *Festuca rubra* salt-marsh community *Juncus gerardii*

A dense grassland with saltmarsh rush, red fescue, creeping bent and sometimes sea-milkwort found around brackish or slightly brackish pools. On Bryher it appears to merge into SM23.

SM23 *Spergularia marina – Puccinellia distans* **salt-marsh community**
The narrow strip of salt-marsh vegetation along the sides of the leat from
Bryher Pool and adjoining grassland is possibly close to this. It is dominated by
creeping bent, common saltmarsh-grass, sea-milkwort and discrete patches of
lesser sea-spurrey.

SAND DUNES

It is the sand dune communities that have perhaps caused most 'angst' among
botanists. When Dargie (1990) carrying out his detailed surveys of the dune
systems in Scilly he produced his own classification; this included parallels to
NVC plus additional communities not included that he considered more
appropriate to Scilly. A recent survey by Coleman and O'Reilly of dwarf pansy
sites (2004) also looked at vegetation communities. One of the interesting
comments they made was that the pansy grew in patches of one community
within a larger area of another community. These small-scale mosaics seem to
be a particular feature not only of dunes in Scilly, but also of other habitats such
as heath and maritime cliffs.

SD1 *Rumex crispus – Glaucum flavum* **shingle community**
Curled dock is a constant species in this community, although yellow horned-
poppy and sea-kale are rather local in Scilly. There are examples of this type of
vegetation at Beady Pool, St Agnes, and on some of the Eastern Isles.

SD2 *Honckenya peploides – Cakile maritima* **strandline community**
This typical strandline vegetation community is found in Scilly, but the
populations of sea rocket fluctuate greatly from year to year.

SD4 *Elytrigia juncea* **spp.** *boreoatlantica* (*Elymus farctus* **spp.** *boreoatlanticus*)
foredune community
This is the sand couch community found on the edge of the dunes just in front
of the marram area.

SD6 *Ammophila arenaria* **mobile dune community**
In Scilly this dune community is where several rare plants occur. These include
Babington's leek, balm-leaved figwort, sea spurge and Portland spurge.

SD7 *Ammophila arenaria – Festuca rubra* semi-fixed dune community

Marram is still the major component of this community but a greater range
of other species are able to become established here including grasses, of which
red fescue is the most significant. Sea spurge and Portland spurge also occur
here.

SD8 *Festuca rubra – Galium verum* fixed dune community

This community forms a closed, low turf over sand substrate. In many ways it is
the step on from SD19 with a more stable community. Red fescue is constant and
abundant, with lady's bedstraw (where it occurs), ribwort plantain, white clover
(also, in places, western clover), bird's-foot-trefoil and Yorkshire fog. One of the
few places where wild thyme grows in Scilly is in the SD8 on Gugh.

SD19 *Phleum arenarium – Arenaria serpyllifolia* dune annual community

This community is found on sandy areas on several islands, but probably the
best-known examples are found at Rushy Bay, Bryher. The community also
occurs on Teän, Gugh, Tresco and elsewhere on Bryher. Of the main protagonists
thyme-leaved sandwort *Arenaria serpyllifolia* is a very rare plant in Scilly (it has
only been recorded recently from Bryher) and the grass *Phleum arenarium* is not
known from the islands. Typically the community in Scilly consists of a range of
winter annuals and dwarf forms of common perennials, often in areas with bare
sand or mosses. Where rabbits are abundant the community is frequently found
in areas where they have been digging. But even when rabbits are absent or at
low density the sward appears to remain open due to the effect of trampling,
drought and wind. Activity by ants may also be significant, and on occasions
severe storms may open the area up again. In Scilly this community grows on
pure sand, where the annuals dry up and disappear in early summer, and where
in some years even the tiny perennials shrivel up.

The constant species for SD19 in Scilly include red fescue, lesser hawkbit,
sand sedge, bird's-foot-trefoil, buck's-horn plantain, English stonecrop, common
stork's-bill, dovesfoot cranesbill *Geranium molle* and several common mosses
including sandhill screw-moss *Syntrichia ruraliformis*. Although Dargie (1990)
and Randall (2004) considered SD8 the main community for the rare dwarf pansy,
Coleman & O'Reilly (2004) found it mainly occurred in small patches of SD19
within larger areas of SD8. SD19 does seem to be a neater fit for the more
ephemeral elements of the short turf sward.

REEDBEDS AND SWAMPS

s4 *Phragmites australis* swamp

Where the reedbeds are dominated by common reed as on Great Pool, Tresco, and Higher Moors, St Mary's, this is the typical community. On Higher Moors and especially on Lower Moors the reedbeds in places give way to areas that include sea rush. In Scilly sea rush is apparently all a form var. *atlanticus*, with very lax stems and a shorter lower bract (Lousley, 1971). The understorey of this swamp community consists of a wide range of wetland plants, with marsh bedstraw and marsh pennywort all abundant.

s21 *Bolboschoenus (Scirpus) maritimus* swamp

This is a species-poor community that in Scilly occurs around brackish and freshwater pools. On St Mary's there are areas of the community on both Higher and Lower Moors. A wide circle of this vegetation type surrounds Big Pool, St Agnes, where it includes saltmarsh rush and creeping bent. It also occurs around pools on Tresco and Bryher. There is even a small area of s21 in a seepage by the shore on Annet.

WOODLAND

There is no true semi-natural woodland on the Isles of Scilly; the plantation woods of Tresco are possibly the closest approach to woodland on the islands.

w1 *Salix cinerea – Galium palustre* woodland

There are wet copses of grey willow carr. These areas are quite distinctive, and are slowly invading the wet ground except where active management is keeping the trees in check. This type of community is similar to w1 *Salix cinerea – Galium palustre* woodland although there is no birch or oak and only occasionally suckering elm. On Scilly there is frequently a typical wetland ground flora in these copses.

Elm copses are also quite frequent on St Mary's, but are all very recently formed. They are usually based on elm suckers with an understorey of ivy, three-cornered leek, hogweed, bluebell, arum and a range of other common species. In wetter areas they may include grey sallow, lady fern and elements from the sallow copse. There are examples along the valley between Holy Vale and Longstone.

w25 *Pteridium aquilinum – Rubus fruticosus* underscrub

There are extensive areas dominated by bracken or bracken/bramble on all the main islands, including many of the larger uninhabited islands. There may have been trees associated with this community in the distant past, but there are none now. Two sub-communities, the *Hyacinthoides non-scripta* and the *Teucrium scorodonia*, occur, although the division between them is not always very distinct, especially as there are no trees associated with the community. In places tall plants such as hogweed may be prominent, and after burning other plants may be temporarily common.

OPEN HABITATS

Three published NVC plant communities are particularly associated with arable fields in Scilly. It is difficult correlating species lists with those in the NVC, possibly due to the limited samples on which the description was based, especially in OV2, which is based on only eight samples and includes some species that are now quite rare in Scilly, for example lesser canary-grass *Phalaris minor*.

OV2 *Briza minor – Silene gallica* community

This vegetation community is described as unique to the Isles of Scilly. Besides the dominant species, lesser quaking-grass and small-flowered catchfly, this community includes many of the small annuals including grasses. The other constant species include scarlet pimpernel, sheep's sorrel, and lesser trefoil *Trifolium dubium*. Rare species associated with the community include great brome, four-leaved allseed, rough-fruited buttercup, small-flowered buttercup and balm-leaved figwort. In the NVC account suffocated clover is included, but this would be very unusual, except perhaps on sandy pathways. Many of the same species occur in the OV6 *Cerastium glomeratum – Fumaria muralis boraei* community but at lower frequencies and with a strong bias towards fumitories and toad rush. There does appear to be a degree of merging between the two communities, and some fields may in fact be mosaics.

OV4 *Chrysanthemum segetum – Spergula arvensis* community

This community is dominated by corn marigold and corn spurrey. It is frequently common in patches around fields. Occasionally a whole field can be assigned to this community type. An extreme form may occur in sandy fields near the coast (see Fig. 29); here the whole field is white with corn spurrey, sometimes with scattered corn marigolds and poppies dotted about over an understorey of small annuals. Where fields have been left fallow and just topped or sown with grass, it was interesting to note that corn marigold continues to be prominent in the vegetation for several seasons.

ov6 *Cerastium glomeratum – Fumaria muralis boraei* community

This community type is found only in Scilly and a few places in southwest Cornwall. This is the plant community in which sticky mouse-ear *Cerastium glomeratum* and fumitories are particularly prominent. All the arable fumitory species that occur in Scilly are found here, as well as corn marigold, toad rush, small-flowered buttercup, lesser quaking-grass and whistling jacks. Other rarities found in this community are Babington's leek and small-flowered catchfly.

Both ov2 and ov6 are found in close association, although it is suggested that ov6 is found on slightly moister soils than ov2, according to the NVC. Also the NVC divides ov6 into three sub-communities with slightly different assemblages of species, the *Aphanes microcarpa – Ranunculus muricatus*, the *Valerianella locusta – Barbula convuluta* and the *Vicia hirsuta – Papaver dubium* sub-communities. Of these the *Valerianella – Barbula* sub-community is the most distinctive, with bare ground supporting several bryophyte species.

ov13 *Stellaria media – Capsella bursa-pastoris* community

Where fields with ov6 communities are heavily fertilised to produce vegetable or salad crops there can be a shift to this community. Among the constant species are shepherd's-purse, fat-hen, groundsel, common knotgrass *Polygonum aviculare* and common chickweed. Some fumitories occur in this community, with tall ramping-fumitory as a rarity. On Bryher the fields that probably were an ov6 community previously are now much closer to the *Fumaria officinalis – Euphorbia helioscopa* sub-community of ov13. This is still quite species-rich and often includes other species of fumitories. Other fields which are mainly growing crops other than bulbs – potatoes or beet, for example – if well fertilised, may also conform to this community, with more large and robust species such as *Atriplex*, docks, sow-thistles and nettles. Some of the fields on Peninnis appear to fit this community type. Further use of fertiliser will convert these fields to far less interesting communities.

ov35 *Lythrum portula – Ranunculus flammula* community

This community appears to be close to the unusual drawdown marginal vegetation that is found around Abbey Pool, Tresco. This is quite species-rich, ranging from marsh pennywort, bog pimpernel and shoreweed, a tiny form of lesser spearwort, water-purslane to six-stamened waterwort in deeper water. The fluctuations in water level mean that sometimes the whole water margin is submerged and at other times the exposed mud is covered in low vegetation, dominated at times by red-coloured six-stamened waterwort.

References and Further Reading

While writing this book I have compiled a large list of references. Lack of space has meant not all could be included here, so a full list has been lodged at the Isles of Scilly Museum, St Mary's.

Several journals are worth looking at for information on the Isles of Scilly. The *Isles of Scilly Bird & Natural History Review* is published annually by the Isles of Scilly Bird Group (ISBG). The Group also has a website (www.scillybirding.co.uk) which includes recent reports on birds, dragonflies etc. *British Wildlife* has Scilly records occasionally, and there are regular reports on insects in *Atropos*. The Environmental Records Centre for Cornwall and the Isles of Scilly (ERCCIS) holds records for Scilly and publishes occasional papers and books on Cornwall and the Isles of Scilly, including *Botanical Cornwall*.

Allen, R. (1974) *Gulls and Other Seabirds in the Isles of Scilly, April to August, 1974*. Report to Nature Conservancy Council's Scientific Committee for the Isles of Scilly.

Almond, W. E. (1975) The distribution of bumblebees in Cornwall and Isles of Scilly. *Cornish Studies* **3**.

Anon. (date unknown) *A Short Guide to the Geology of the Isles of Scilly*. Isles of Scilly Museum Publication 11.

Ashbee, P. (1974). *Ancient Scilly: From the First Farmers to the Early Christians*. David and Charles, Newton Abbot.

Ashmole, P. & Ashmole, M. (1995) Arthropod fauna of a cave on Tresco, Isles of Scilly, English Channel. *The Entomologist* **114**: 79–82.

Ballantine, W. J. (1961) A biologically defined exposure scale for the comparative description of rocky shores. *Field Studies* **1**(3): 1–19.

Bamber, R. N., Evans, N. J., Chimonides, P. J. & Williams, B. A. P. (2001) Investigations into the hydrology, flora and fauna of the Pool of Bryher, Isles of Scilly. Unpublished report to English Nature by NHM Consulting (Report ECM 759/01).

Barne, J. H., Robson, C. F., Kaznowska, S. S., Doody, J. P., Davidson, N. C. & Buck, A. L. (eds) (1996) *Coasts and Seas of the United Kingdom. Region 11. The Western Approaches: Falmouth Bay to Kenfig*. JNCC, Peterborough.

Barrow, G. (1906) *The Geology of the Isles of Scilly* (with petrological contributions by J. S. Flett). HMSO, London.

Beavis, I. C. (2000) Aculeate Hymenoptera on the Isles of Scilly. *Entomologist's Gazette* **5**: 59–68.

Beavis, I. C. (2003) Bees, wasps and ants of Scilly. *Isles of Scilly Bird & Natural History Review* **2002**: 168–183.

Beavis, I. C. (2004) Resident and regular migrant butterflies on the Isles of Scilly. *Entomologist's Record* **116**: 97–102.

Beavis, I. C. (2005) Bees, wasps, ants and hoverflies of Scilly: 2004 update. *Isles of Scilly Bird & Natural History Review* **2004**: 175–178.

Bere, R. (1982) *The Nature of Cornwall.* Barracuda Books, Buckingham.

Berry, R. J. (1985) *The Natural History of Orkney.* New Naturalist 70. Collins, London.

Besant, W. (1890) *Armorel of Lyonesse.* Chatto & Windus, London.

Birkin, M. & Smith, A. (1987) Breeding seabirds: Isles of Scilly. Unpublished Report to the Nature Conservancy Council.

Bishop, G. (1985) Study of *Echinus esculentus* populations in the Isles of Scilly, October 1984. Report to NCC.

Blair, K. G. (1931) The beetles of the Scilly Islands. *Proceedings of the Zoological Society of London* **4**: 1211–1258.

Booker, H. & Booker, D. (1981) Bats on Tresco. Unpublished report to NCC.

Borlase, W. (1753) Of the great alterations which the Islands of Scilly have undergone since the time of the Ancients. *Philosophical Transactions of the Royal Society* **48**: 55–67.

Borlase, W. (1756) *Observations on the Ancient and Present State of the Islands of Scilly.* W. Jackson, Oxford. Reprinted by Frank Graham, Newcastle-upon-Tyne, 1966.

Bourlière, F. (1955) *The Natural History of Mammals.* Harrap, London.

Bowley, R. L. (1990) *The Fortunate Islands: the Story of the Isles of Scilly,* 8th edn. Bowley Publications, Scilly.

Bratton, J. H. (ed.) (1991) *British Red Data Book 3: Invertebrates Other Than Insects.* JNCC, Peterborough.

Bristowe, W. S. (1929) The spiders of the Scilly Isles. *Proceedings of the Zoological Society of London,* 149–164.

Bristowe, W. S. (1935) Further notes on the spiders of the Scilly Isles. *Proceedings of the Zoological Society of London,* 219–232.

Burton, J. (1968) *The Oxford Book of Insects.* Oxford University Press, Oxford.

Butcher, S. A. (1978) Excavations at Nornour, Isles of Scilly, 1969–73. *Cornish Archaeology* **17**: 29–112.

Cameron, R. A. D. (2006) Slugs and snails on Scilly. *Isles of Scilly Bird & Natural History Review* **2005**.

Campbell, A. C. (1976) *The Hamlyn Guide to the Seashore and Shallow Seas of Britain and Europe.* Hamlyn, London.

Cheffings, C. M. & Farrell, L. (eds) (2005) *The Vascular Plant Red Data List for Great Britain.* Species Status 7. JNCC, Peterborough.

Chown, D. & Lock, L. (2002) *Breeding Birds in the Isles of Scilly, Incorporating the Results of the Breeding Bird Atlas (2000–2001) and Seabird 2000 (1999–2000).* RSPB, Sandy.

Clark, J. (1909) Notes on the Cornish Crustacea. *Zoologist* **13** (4): 281–308.

Clark, J. & Rodd, F. R. (1906) The birds of Scilly. *Zoologist* **10**: 241–246.

Coleman, C. & O'Reilly, J. (2004) [Dwarf pansy.] Unpublished report for the Isles of Scilly Wildlife Trust.

Coles, J. W. (1965) A critical review of the marine nematode genus *Euchromadora* De Mam, 1886. *Bulletin of the British Museum (Natural History): Zoology* **12** (5): 159–194.

Cook, K. J., Hinton, C. & Reid, T. J. (2001) Report on the Coral Cay Conservation Sub-Aqua Club 2000 Expedition to the Isles of Scilly. Report to English Nature.

Coombe, D. E. (1961) *Trifolium occidentale*, a new species related to *T. repens* (L). *Watsonia* **5** (2): 68–87.

Coombe, D. E. & Morisset, P. (1967) Further observations on *Trifolium occidentale*. *Watsonia* **6** (5): 271–275.

Cooper, A. (1992) *Secret Nature of the Channel Shore.* BBC Books, London.

Cooper, A. (2006) *Secret Nature of the Isles of Scilly.* Green Books, Dartington.

Corbet, G. B. (1961) Origin of the British insular races of small mammals and of the 'Lusitanian' fauna. *Nature* **191**: 1037–1040.

Countryside Agency (2004) *The Isles of Scilly Area of Outstanding Natural Beauty Management Plan 2004–2009.*

Courtney, J. S. (1845) *A Guide to Penzance and its Neighbourhood, including the Isles of Scilly.* Penzance.

Cowan, Z. (2001) *Francis Frith's The Isles of Scilly.* Frith Book Company, Salisbury.

Cramp, S. Simmonds, K. E. L. & Perrins, C. M. (1977–94) *Handbook of the Birds of Europe, the Middle East, and North Africa: the Birds of the Western Palearctic.* Vols. 1–9. Oxford University Press, Oxford.

Crisp, D. J. & Southward, A. J. (1958). The distribution of intertidal organisms along the coasts of the English Channel. *Journal of the Marine Biological Association UK* **37**: 157–208.

Dargie, T. (1990) *Isles of Scilly Dune Vegetation Survey 1990.* A report to the Nature Conservancy Council. 3 vols.

Darling, F. F. & Boyd, J. M. (1964) *The Highlands and Islands.* New Naturalist 6b. Collins, London.

Davies, J. L. (1956) The grey seal at the Isles of Scilly. *Proceedings of the Zoological Society of London* **127**: 161–166.

Davies, J. L. (1958) The problem of the Scilly shrew. *Annals & Magazine of Natural History* (13) **1**: 97–101.

Davis, R. (1999). *Species Action Plans for Plants: Shore Dock.* English Nature, Peterborough.

Dennis, R. & Shreeve, T. (1996) *Butterflies on British and Irish Offshore Islands.* Gem Publishing, Wallingford.

Dimbleby, G. W. (1977) A buried soil at Innisidgen, St Mary's, Isles of Scilly. *Cornish Studies* **415**: 5–10.

Dobson, F. S. (2000) *Lichens: an Illustrated Guide to the British and Irish Species.* Richmond Publishing, Slough.

Dorrien-Smith, T. (1954) in *The Scillonian* **29**: 64.

Durman, R. (ed.) (1976) *Bird Observatories in Britain and Ireland.* Poyser, Berkhamsted.

Edmonds, E. A., McKeown, M. C. & Williams, M. (1975) *British Regional Geology: South-west England.* HMSO, London.

Edwards, B. (2002) The current status of *Heterodermia leucomela* (L.) Poelt on the Isles of Scilly. Report 193. Plantlife/English Nature.

Evans, G. O., Sheals, J. G. & Macfarlane, D. (1961) *The Terrestrial Acari of the British Isles: an Introduction to Their Morphology, Biology and Classification.* Vol.1. British Museum (Natural History), London.

Evans, J. G. (1984) Excavations at Bar Point, St Mary's, Isles of Scilly, 1979–80. *Cornish Studies*, **11**: 28–30.

Evans, L. G. R. (1995) *Rare Birds and Scarce Migrants on the Isles of Scilly 1600–1995.* LGRE Publications.

Farnham, W. F., Fletcher, R. L. & Irvine, L. M. (1973) Attached *Sargassum muticum* found in Britain. *Nature* **243**: 231–232.

Farr, H. (1992) Tourism and the environment on the Isles of Scilly: conflict or complementarity? Unpublished MSc thesis, Rural Resources & Environmentary

Policy, Wye College, University of London.

Fisher, A. & Flood, R. (2005) Cream-coloured courser: first for Scilly, September 28, 2004. *Isles of Scilly Bird & Natural History Review* **2004**: 138–139.

Flood, B., Hudson, N. & Thomas, B. (in press) *Essential Guide to The Birds of the Isles of Scilly*. St Mary's.

Ford, E. B. (1975) *Ecological genetics*. 4th edn. Chapman & Hall, London.

Foster, I. D. L. (2006) Big Pool (SV878086). In Scourse (2006).

Fowler, S. L. (1990) Sub-littoral monitoring in the Isles of Scilly 1987 & 1988. Report to NCC from the Nature Conservation Bureau.

Fowler, S. L. (1992) Sub-littoral monitoring in the Isles of Scilly 1991. Report to NCC from the Nature Conservation Bureau.

Fowler, S. L. & Pilley, G. M. (1992) Report on the Lundy and Isles of Scilly marine monitoring programmes 1984–1991. Report to English Nature from the Nature Conservation Bureau.

Frohawk, F. W. (1904) Larvae of *Arctia caja* swarming in the Scilly Isles. *Entomologist* 58: 3–10, 38.

Gantlett, S. (1991) *The Birds of the Isles of Scilly*. S.J.M. Gantlett, Norfolk.

Gilbert, F. S. (1993) *Hoverflies*, revised edn. Naturalists' Handbooks 5. Richmond Publishing, London.

Gilbert, O. (2000) *Lichens*. New Naturalist 86. Collins, London.

Gill, C. (1975) *The Isles of Scilly*. David & Charles, Newton Abbot.

Gill, C., Booker, S. & Soper, T. (1967) *The Wreck of the Torrey Canyon*. David & Charles, Newton Abbot.

Gillham, M. E. (1956) Ecology of the Pembrokeshire islands: V. Manuring by the colonial seabirds and mammals, with a note on seed distribution by gulls. *Journal of Ecology* **44**: 429–454.

Gillham, M. E. (1970) Seed dispersal by birds. In Perring, F. (ed.) *The Flora of a Changing Britain*. BSBI/Classey, Hampton, pp. 90–98.

Godwin, H. (1975) *The History of the British Flora*, 2nd edn. Cambridge University Press, Cambridge.

Goodey, M. (2004) Arrival of the comma butterfly on Scilly. *Isles of Scilly Bird & Natural History Review* 2003.

Graham Moss Associates (1984) *The Isles of Scilly Comprehensive Land Use and Community Development Project*. Graham Moss Associates, London & Bristol.

Grigson, G. (1948) *The Scilly Isles*. Paul Elek, London.

Groves, M. (1988) *Exploring Underwater: the Isles of Scilly*. Porth Books, Goonvrea.

Gurney, J. H. (1889) Notes on the Isles of Scilly and the Manx shearwater (*Puffinus anglorum*). *Transactions of the Norfolk and Norwich Naturalists' Society* 4: 447–454.

Haes, E. C. M. (1999) *Orthopteroid Insects of Cornwall and the Isles of Scilly: a Revised Provisional Atlas (with 2 supplements)*. CISFBR Occasional Publication 1. Cornwall and the Isles of Scilly Federation of Biological Recorders, Truro.

Haes, E. C. M. (2001) Orthopteroid insects on Scilly. *Isles of Scilly Bird & Natural History Review* 2000.

Haes, E. C. M. (2003) The discovery of the large cone-head bush-cricket *Ruspolia nitidula* (Scop.) in the Isles of Scilly. *Atropus* 20.

Haes, E. C. M. (2004) *Orthopteroid Insects of Cornwall and the Isles of Scilly: an Updated Provisional Atlas*. CISFBR Occasional Publication 2. Cornwall and the Isles of Scilly Federation of Biological Recorders, Truro.

Harvey, L. A. (1964) A hermit crab new to Britain. *Nature* **203**: 99–100

Harvey, L. A. (1969) The marine flora and fauna of the Isles of Scilly: the islands and their ecology. *Journal of Natural History* **3**: 3–18

Harvey, P. (1983) Breeding seabird populations, Isles of Scilly 1983. Unpublished report to the Nature Conservancy Council.

Harvey, P. R., Nellist, D. R. & Telfer, M. G. (eds) (2002) *Provisional Atlas of British Spiders (Aranida, Aranea)*. Vols. 1 & 2. Biological Records Centre, Huntingdon.

Hathway, R., Stancliffe, P. & Goodey, M. (2003) The discovery of large conehead bush-cricket in the Isles of Scilly. *British Wildlife* **15**: 45–46.

Hayward, P., Nelson-Smith, T. & Shields, C. (1996) *Collins Pocket Guide to the Sea Shore of Britain & Northern Europe*. HarperCollins, London.

Hayward, P. J. (2004) *Seashore*. New Naturalist 94. Collins, London.

Heaney, V. (2006) *Isles of Scilly Bird Group (ISBG) Newsletter* **9** (Summer 2006).

Heaney, V., Ratcliffe, N., Brown, A., Robinson, P. & Lock, L. (2002) The status and distribution of storm petrels and Manx shearwaters on the Isles of Scilly. *Atlantic Seabirds* **4**: 1–16.

Heath, R. (1750) *A Natural History and Historical Account of the Islands of Scilly*. Manby & Cox, London. Reprinted by Frank Graham, Newcastle-upon-Tyne, 1967.

Heckford, R. J. (1987) Lepidoptera recorded in the Isles of Scilly in May, 1986. *Entomologist's Record* **99**: 268–270.

Hencken, H. O'Neill (1932) *The Archaeology of Cornwall and Scilly*. Methuen, London.

Herdson, D. (2002) Slipper lobster *Scyllarus arctus*. *Isles of Scilly Bird & Natural History Review 2001*.

Hicks, M. E. & Hale, J. W. (1998) *Lepidoptera of St Agnes, Isles of Scilly: a systematic list and analysis of the species recorded on St Agnes, 1992–1997*. Privately published.

Hiemstra, J., Evans, D. J. A., Scourse, J. D., Furze, M. F. A., McCarroll, D. & Rhodes. E. (2005) New evidence for a grounded Irish Sea glaciation of the Isles of Scilly, UK. *Quaternary Science Reviews* **25**: 299–309.

Hinton, M. A. C. (1924) On a new species of *Crocidura* from Scilly. *Annals & Magazine of Natural History* (9) **14**: 509–510.

Hiscock, K. (1984) Rocky shore surveys of the Isles of Scilly: March 27th to April 1st 1983 and July 7th to 15th 1983. Vol 1. Survey Report, Nature Conservancy Council.

Holme, N. A. (1983) Report on certain sediment shores in the Isles of Scilly. Nature Conservancy Council Technical Report. Marine Biological Association, Plymouth.

Holyoak, G. (2003) Recording land and freshwater Mollusca on the Isles of Scilly, April 2003. *Mollusc World* **3**: 20–21.

Howarth, T. G. (1971) Descriptions of a new British subspecies of *Pararge aegeria* (L.) (Lep.: Satyridae) and an aberration of *Cupido minimus* (Fuessly) (Lep.: Lycaenidae). *Entomologist's Gazette* **22**: 117–118.

Hunkin, J. W. (1947) Tresco under three reigns. *Journal of the Royal Horticultural Society* **72**: 177–191, 221–237.

Hunt, D. (1985) *Confessions of a Scilly Birdman*. Croom Helm, London.

Hyatt, K. H. (1990) Mites associated with terrestrial beetles in the British Isles. *Entomologist's Monthly Magazine* **126**: 133–148.

Hyatt. K. H. (1993) The acarine fauna of the Isles of Scilly. *Cornish Studies* **1**.

Ingle, R. (1969) *A Guide to The Seashore*. Paul Hamlyn, London.

Kay, E. (1956) *Isles of Flowers: the Story of the Isles of Scilly*. Alvin Redman, London.

Kay, E. (1963) *Isles of Flowers*, 2nd edn. Alvin Redman, London.

Kerney, M. P. (1999) *Atlas of the Land and Freshwater Molluscs of Britain and Ireland*. Harley Books, Colchester.

King, C. J. (1924) *Some Notes on Wild Nature in Scillonia: Particularly of Seabirds & Seals*. C. J. King & Son, St Mary's.

King, R. (1985) *Tresco: England's Island of Flowers*. Constable, London.

Kirby, K. (2004) Table of ancient woodland indicator plants (AWI) in Rose, F. (2006).

Lambert, R. (2001) Grey seals on Scilly. *Isles of Scilly Bird & Natural History Review* 2000.

Laney, B. (2003) Discovery of new species of stick insect for the Isles of Scilly. *Phasmid Study Group Newsletter* **97**: 5.

Larn, R. & Larn, B. (1995) *Shipwreck Index of the British Isles*. Lloyd's Registry of Shipping, London.

Lascelles, B. (2005a) Roseate tern Species Recovery Program: 2004 update. *Isles of Scilly Bird & Natural History Review* **2004**: 153–165.

Lascelles, B. (2005b) *Roseate Tern Report*. Report to English Nature.

Lee, M. (2003) The light brown apple-moth *Epiphyas postvittana* (Walk.) and the spread of alien species. *Atropos* **18**: 9–12

Leland, J. (1535–43) *The Itinerary of John Leland in or about the Years 1535–43*. First published 1710. In Kay (1963) 2nd edn. Another edn (ed. L. T. Smith), Bell, London, 1907.

Lewes, G. H. (1858) *Sea-side Studies at Ilfracombe, Tenby, the Scilly Isles and Jersey*. Blackwood, Edinburgh.

Lewes, G. H. (1860) *Sea-side Studies at Ilfracombe, Tenby, the Scilly Isles and Jersey*, 2nd edn. Blackwood, Edinburgh.

Llewellyn, S. (2005) *Emperor Smith: the Man Who Built Scilly*. Dovecote Press, Dorset.

Lloyd, C. S., Bibby,C. J. & Everett, M. J. (1975) Breeding terns in Britain and Ireland. *British Birds* **68**: 221–237.

Lock, L. (1999) *Assessment of the Importance of Winter Waterfowl/Wader Populations of the Isles of Scilly*. RSPB, Sandy.

Locker, A. (1992) The mammal, bird and fish bones from excavations at Lower Town, St Martin's, Isles of Scilly. Unpublished report to Cornwall Archaeological Unit.

Locker, A. (1996) in Ashbee, P. Halangy Down, St Mary's, Isles of Scilly: excavations 1964–1977. *Cornish Archaeology* **35**: 113–116.

Lousley, J. E. (1939) Notes on the flora of the Isles of Scilly I. *Journal of Botany* **77**: 195–203.

Lousley, J. E. (1940) Notes on the flora of the Isles of Scilly II. *Journal of Botany* **78**: 153–160.

Lousley, J. E. (1971) *The Flora of the Isles of Scilly*. David & Charles, Newton Abbot.

Lousley, J. E. & Kent, D. H. (1981) *Docks and Knotweeds of the British Isles*. BSBI Handbook 3. Botanical Society of the British Isles, London.

Magalotti, L. (1821) *Travels of Cosmo the Third, Grand Duke of Tuscany through England during the reign of King Charles the Second, 1669*. London.

Malloch, A. J. C. (1972) Salt-spray deposition on the maritime cliffs of the Lizard peninsula. *Journal of Ecology* **60**: 103–112.

Margetts, L. J. & David, R. W. (1981) *A Review of the Cornish Flora 1980*. Institute of Cornish Studies, Redruth.

Marren, P. (2002) *Nature Conservation: a Review of the Conservation of Wildlife in Britain 1950–2001*. New Naturalist 91. Collins, London.

Martin, A. (2001) Cetaceans in Scillonian waters. *Isles of Scilly Bird & Natural History Review* 2000.

Matthews, G. F. (1960) *The Isles of Scilly*. George Ronald, London.

Mawer, D. (2001) Bats on Scilly. *Isles of Scilly Bird & Natural History Review* 2000.

Maybee, R. (1883) *Sixty-Eight Years' Experience on the Scilly Islands*. [Quoted by Bowley, 1990.]

McDonnell, E. J. & King, M. P. (2006) *Rumes rupestris* Le Gall (shore dock) in SW England: review of recent surveys and assessment of current status. In Leach, S. J., Page, C. N., Peytoureau, Y. & Sanford, M. N. (eds) *Botanical Links in the Atlantic Arc*. BSBI, London.

Merrett, P. & Rowe, J. J. (1961) A New Zealand spider *Achaearanea veruculata* (Urquhart) established in Scilly and new records of other species. *Annals & Magazine of Natural History* (13) 4: 89–96.

Mitchell-Jones, A. J., Amori, G., Bogdanowicz, W. *et al.* (1999) *The Atlas of European Mammals*. Poyser, London.

Moore, N. W. (1987) *The Bird of Time: the Science and Politics of Nature Conservation*. Cambridge University Press, Cambridge.

Morpurgo, M. (1985) *Why the Whales Came*. Heinemann, London.

Mortimer, M. (1991) Memories of pre-war Scilly. *The Scillonian* 236: 140–144.

Mothersole, J. (1910) *The Isles of Scilly: Their Story, Their Folk and Their Flowers*. Religious Tract Society, London.

Mothersole, J. (1919) *The Isles of Scilly*, 2nd edn, reprinted with two additional plates. Religious Tract Society, London.

Mumford, C. T. (1987) *The Isles of Scilly*. In Gill, C. (ed.) *The Duchy of Cornwall*. David & Charles, Newton Abbot.

Murton, R. K., Isaacson, A. J. & Westwood, N. J. (1964) The feeding habits of the woodpigeon *Columba palumbus*, stock dove C. *oenas* and turtle dove *Streptopelia turtur*. *Ibis* 106: 174–188.

Neil, C. J., King, M. P., Evans, S. B.,

Parslow, R. E., Bennallick, I. B. & McDonnell, E. J. (2001) Shore dock (*Rumex rupestris*): report on fieldwork undertaken in 2000. Plantlife Report 175.

Nelhams, M. (2000) *Tresco Abbey Garden: a Personal and Pictorial History*. Dyllansow Truran, Truro.

North, J. W. (1850) *A Week in the Isles of Scilly*. Penzance. [Section on ferns by E. W. Cooke.]

Norton, T. A. & Burrows, E. M. (1969) Studies on marine algae of the British Isles. 7. *Saccorhiza polyschides* (Lightf.) Batt., *British Phycological Journal* 4: 19–53.

Ottery, J. (1996) *The Isles of Scilly Wild Flower Guide*. Julia Ottery & Amadeus Fine Arts, Scilly.

Over, L. (1987) *The Kelp Industry in Scilly*. Isles of Scilly Museum Publication 14.

Page, C. N. (1988) *Ferns: Their Habitats in the British and Irish Landscape*. New Naturalist 74. Collins, London.

Parslow, J. (1973) *Breeding Birds of Britain and Ireland: a Historical Survey*. Poyser, Berkhamsted.

Parslow, R. (1984) A survey of the shore dock *Rumex rupestris* in the Isles of Scilly 1984. Report to the British Ecological Society.

Parslow, R. (1988) *Bats on the Isles of Scilly*. Report to the Bat Groups of Britain Support Fund.

Parslow, R. (1996) Shore Dock *Rumex rupestris* Le Gall in the Isles of Scilly: Species Recovery Programme. Unpublished report to English Nature.

Parslow, R. (1999) Colour changes in the Tresco green darner *Anax junius*. *Atropos* 7: 54.

Parslow, R. (2002) Management Plan for the Isles of Scilly. Unpublished document for IOSWT.

Parslow, R. (2003) Water vole remains in gull pellet on Annet. *Isles of Scilly Bird & Natural History Review* 2002: 196.

Parslow, R. (2006) Maritime communities as habitats for *Ophioglossum* ferns in the Isles of Scilly. In Leach, S. J., Page, C. N., Peytoureau, Y. & Sanford, M. N. (eds) *Botanical Links in the Atlantic Arc.* BSBI, London.

Parslow, R. & Colston, A. (1994) The current status of *Rumex rupestris* Le Gall in the Isles of Scilly. Unpublished report, English Nature Species Recovery Programme.

Paton, J. A. & Holyoak, D. T. (2005) *The Bryophyte Flora of the Isles of Scilly.* ERCCIS Publication 2. Environmental Records Centre for Cornwall and the Isles of Scilly, Truro.

Penhallurick, R. D. (1969). *Birds of the Cornish Coast Including the Isles of Scilly.* Bradford Barton, Truro.

Penhallurick, R. D. (1978) *The Birds of Cornwall and the Isles of Scilly.* Headland Press, Penzance.

Penhallurick, R. D. (1990) *Turtles off Cornwall, the Isles of Scilly and Devonshire.* Dyllansow Pengwella, Truro.

Penhallurick, R. D. (1996) *The Butterflies of Cornwall and The Isles of Scilly.* Dyllansow Pengwella, Truro.

Pernetta, J. C. & Handford, P. T. (1970) Mammalian and avian remains from possible Bronze Age deposits on Nornour, Isles of Scilly. *Journal of Zoology* **162**: 534–540.

Polunin, O. (1953) Some plant communities of the Scilly Isles. Duplicated typescript.

Pontin, J. G. (1999) Agriculture and land use: case studies. Isles of Scilly climate: a historical view. www.ex.ac.uk/ccvc/case6_d.htm.

Potts, G. W. & Swaby, S. E. (1993) A study of the distribution, status and potential vulnerability of the giant goby *Gobius cobitus* in the British Isles. Report to JNCC.

Pounds, N. J. G. (ed.) (1984) *The Parliamentary Survey of the Duchy of Cornwall: Part 2 (Isles of Scilly).* Devon & Cornwall Record Society, Exeter.

Preston, C. D. & Finch, R. A. (2006) *Bryum valparaisense* Thér. in the Isles of Scilly. *Journal of Bryology* **28**: 118–122.

Preston, C. D., Pearman, D. A. & Dines, T. D. (eds) (2002) *New Atlas of the British and Irish Flora.* Oxford University Press, Oxford.

Quick, H. M. (1964) *Birds of the Scilly Isles.* Bradford Barton, Truro.

Raines, P., Nunney, R. & Cleator, B. (1993) Coral Cay Conservation Sub-Aqua Club 1992 expedition to the Isles of Scilly. Report to English Nature.

Randall, R. E. (2004) Biological flora of the British Isles: *Viola kitabeliana* Schlt(es). *Journal of Ecology* **92**: 361–369.

Ranwell, D. S. (1966) The lichen flora of Bryher, Isles of Scilly and its geographical components. *Lichenologist* **3** (2) 224–232.

Ratcliffe, D. A. (ed.) (1977) *A Nature Conservation Review.* Cambridge University Press, Cambridge.

Ratcliffe, J. (1992) *Scilly's Archaeological Heritage.* Cornwall Archaeological Unit, Truro.

Ratcliffe, J. & Johns, C. (2003) *Scilly's Archaeological Heritage.* Historic Environment Unit, Cornwall County Council. Twelveheads, Truro.

Ratcliffe, J. & Straker, V. (1996) *The Early Environment of Scilly.* Cornwall Archaeological Unit, Cornwall County Council, Truro.

Ratcliffe, J. & Straker, V. (1997) The changing landscape and coastline of the Isles of Scilly: recent research. *Cornish Archaeology* **36**: 64–76.

Raven, J. E. (1950) Notes on the flora of the Scilly Isles and the Lizard Head. *Watsonia* pt VI: 356–358.

Reed, T. M. (1984) The numbers of landbird species on the Isles of Scilly. *Biological Journal of the Linnean Society* **21**: 431–437.

Reeve, G. (1995) *A Sacred Place of Elder Trees: a History of Tresco in the Isles of Scilly.* Historic Occasions.

Richards, O. W. (1978) The Hymenoptera Aculeata of the Channel Islands. *Report & Transactions of La Société Guernesiaise* **20**: 389–424.

Roberts, M. J. (1995). *Spiders of Britain and Northern Europe.* Collins Field Guide. HarperCollins, London.

Robinson, P. (2003) *The Birds of the Isles of Scilly.* Christopher Helm, London.

Rodd, E. H. (1880) *The Birds of Cornwall and the Scilly Isles.* (ed. J. E. Harting). Trübner & Co., London.

Rodwell, J. S. (ed.) (1991–2000) *British Plant Communities.* Cambridge University Press, Cambridge. 5 vols.
  Vol. 1. (1991) *Woodlands and Scrub.*
  Vol. 2. (1991) *Mires and Heaths.*
  Vol. 3. (1992) *Grasslands and Montane Communities.*
  Vol. 4. (1995) *Aquatic Communities, Swamps and Tall-Herb Fens.*
  Vol. 5. (2000) *Maritime Communities and Vegetation of Open Habitats.*

Rose, F. (2006) *The Wild Flower Key.* 2nd edn, revised and expanded by C. O'Reilly. Frederick Warne, London.

Ryves, B. H., Parsons, A. G. & Quick, H. M. (eds) (1951) *Cornwall Birdwatching and Preservation Society Annual Report* **21.**

Scaife, R. G. (1984) A history of Flandrian vegetation in the Isles of Scilly: palynological investigations of Higher Moors and Lower Moors peat mires, St Mary's. *Cornish Studies* **11**: 33–47.

Scaife, R. G. (2006) Higher Moors (sv925107–921115). In Scourse (2006).

Scourse, J. D. (2005) [Notes from lecture in Isles of Scilly Museum, 13 April 2005, per K. Sawyer.]

Scourse, J. D. (ed.) (2006) *The Isles of Scilly Field Guide.* Quaternary Research Association, London.

Scourse, J. D., Austin, W. E. N., Bateman, R. M., Catt, J. A., Evans C. D. R., Robinson, J. E. & Young, J. R. (1990) Sedimentology and micropalaentology of glacimarine sediments from the central and southwestern Celtic Sea. *Special Publication of the Geological Society of London* **53**: 329–347.

Selwood, E. B., Durrance, E. M. & Bristow, C. M. (eds) (1998) *The Geology of Cornwall.* University of Exeter Press, Exeter.

Seth-Smith, D. (1910) American birds liberated on the Scilly Isles. *British Birds* **4**: 28–29.

Sheail, J. (1971) *Rabbits and Their History.* David and Charles, Newton Abbot .

Simmons, G. E. (1976) Observations on the strange life cycle of the oil-beetles (*Meloë*). *Countryside* Autumn 1976.

Smart, R. W. J. (1852) Bird-nesting on Scilly. *Penzance Natural History & Antiquarian Society.*

Smart, R. W. J. (1885–6) The birds of the Scilly Islands. *Penzance Natural History & Antiquarian Society Report & Transactions* 1885–6: 162–179.

Smart, R. W. J. & Cooke, A. H. (1885) The marine shells of Scilly. *Journal of Conchology* **4**: 185–303.

Smith, B. D. (1995) *The Emergence of Agriculture.* Scientific American Library, New York.

Smith, F. H. N. (1984) *A List of Butterflies and Moths Recorded in Cornwall, 1950–1983.* Cornwall Trust for Nature Conservation.

Smith, F. H. N. (1997) *The Moths and Butterflies of Cornwall and the Isles of Scilly.* Gem Publishing, Wallingford.

Smith, F. H. N. (2002) *A Supplement to The*

Moths and Butterflies of Cornwall and The Isles of Scilly. Gem Publishing, Wallingford.

Sneddon, P. & Randall, R. E. (1994) *Coastal Vegetated Shingle Structures of Great Britain. Appendix 3: England.* JNCC, Peterborough. [Isles of Scilly pp. 82–87.]

Southern, H. N. (1965) *The Handbook of British Mammals.* Blackwell, Oxford

Spalding, A. (ed.) (1997) *Red Data Book for Cornwall and the Isles of Scilly.* Croceago Press, Praze-an-Beeble.

Spalding, A. & Sargent, P. (2000) *Scilly's Wildlife Heritage.* Twelveheads Press, Truro.

Stace, C. (1997) *New Flora of The British Isles,* 2nd edn. Cambridge University Press, Cambridge.

Stebbing, A. R. D., Turk, S. M., Wheeler, A. & Clark, K. R. (2002) Immigration of southern fish species to south-west England linked to warming of the North Atlantic (1960–2001). *Journal of the Marine Biological Association of the United Kingdom* **82**: 177–180.

Steven, G. A. (1936) Seals (*Halichoerus grypus*) of Cornwall coasts. *Journal of the Marine Biological Association of the United Kingdom* **20**: 493–506.

Stewart, A., Pearman, D. A. & Preston, C. D. (1994) *Scarce Plants in Britain.* JNCC, Peterborough.

Stubbs, A. E. & Falk, S. J. (2002). *British Hoverflies: an Illustrated Identification Guide,* 2nd edn. British Entomological and Natural History Society, Reading.

Tarrant, M. (2000) *Cornwall's Lighthouse Heritage.* Twelveheads, Truro.

Tasker, M. L. (1991) Seabird conservation in Scilly. Unpublished report.

Tebble, N. (1976) *British Bivalve Seashells,* 2nd edn. British Museum (Natural History), London.

Temple, R. (1996) The population distribution and status of the lesser white-toothed shrew (*C. suaveolens*) on the Isles of Scilly 29/5/95–3/7/95. Unpublished report to English Nature.

Thomas, C. (1985) *Exploration of a Drowned Landscape: Archaeology and History of the Isles of Scilly.* Batsford, London.

Thomas, L. (1968) *Some Lovely Islands.* Arlington Books, London.

Thurston, M. H. (1970) The marine flora and fauna of the Isles of Scilly: Crustacea, Eucarida. *Journal of Natural History* **4**: 239–248.

Tompsett, A. (1997) Notes from Trenoweth: 30 years of research. *Scilly Up To Date* 110. www.scillyonline.co.uk/sutd/sutd110.html.

Townsend, F. (1864) Contributions to a Flora of the Scilly Isles. Reprinted from *Journal of Botany*, April 1864. [Reprint with corrections and comments by J. E. Lousley in IOS Museum archives.]

Trevithick, W. (1885) *Gardener's Chronicle.* 14 March 1885.

Troutbeck, J. (1794) *A Survey of the Ancient and Present State of the Scilly Islands.* Sherborne.

Turk, F. A. (1960) Deer on the Isles of Scilly. *Royal Cornwall Polytechnic Society* 127th Report: 42–49.

Turk, F. A. (1967) Report on the animal remains on Nor-nour, Isles of Scilly. *Journal of the Royal Institution of Cornwall.* New series, **5**: 250–265.

Turk, F. A. (1968) Notes on Cornish mammals in prehistoric and historic times, 1 (Teän, St Agnes). *Cornish Archaeology* **7**: 75–78.

Turk, F. A. (1971) Notes on Cornish mammals in prehistoric and historic times: 4. A report on the animal remains from Nornour, Isles of Scilly. *Cornish Archaeology* **10**: 79–91.

Turk, F. A. (1973) Distribution patterns of the mammalian fauna of Cornwall (with 73 maps). *Cornish Studies* **1**: 5–32.

Turk, F. A. (1978) The animal remains from Nornour: a synoptic view of the finds. In Butcher (1978).

Turk, F. A. (1984) A study of the vertebrate remains from May's Hill, St. Martin's. *Cornish Studies* **11**.

Turk, F. A. & Turk, S. M. (1977) *Cornish Biological Records* **1**. Institute of Cornish Studies.

Turk, F. A. & Turk, S. M. (1980) The occurrence in Cornwall of animals alien to the British fauna. *Cornish Biological Records* **3**. Institute of Cornish Studies.

Turk, S. M. (1971) *An Introduction to Sea-shore Life in Cornwall and the Isles of Scilly.* Bradford Barton, Truro.

Turk, S. M. (1991) *Check List of Scillonian Marine Mollusca.* Isles of Scilly Museum Publication 16.

Turk, S. M. (1999) Cetaceans stranded on Scillonian shores. *Isles of Scilly Bird Report* **1999**: 118–121.

Turk, S. M. & Seaward, D. R. (1997) The marine flora and fauna of the Isles of Scilly: Mollusca. *Journal of Natural History* **31**: 555–633.

Turk, S. M., Meredith, H. M. & Holyoak, G. A. (2001) *Atlas of the Land and Freshwater Molluscs of Cornwall and the Isles of Scilly.* ERCCIS, Cornwall.

Turner, G. (1964) Some Memorials towards a Natural History of the Sylley Islands. [Reproduction of manuscript dated c.1695.] *The Scillonian* **159**: 154–157.

UK Climate Impacts Programme (1998) *UK Climate Impacts Programme Technical Report 1, September 1998.* Climatic Research Unit, University of East Anglia, Norwich.

Vagabondo (1886) Tresco. *Gardener's Chronicle* **26**: 558.

Vyvyan, C. C. (1953) *The Scilly Isles.* Robert Hale, London.

Wacher, J., Worth J. & Spalding, A. (2003) *A Cornwall Butterfly Atlas.* NatureBureau, Newbury.

Weir, C. R. (2002) Killer whales in British waters. *British Wildlife* **14** (2): 106–108.

Westcott, S. (1993) Seal summer 1991: studying the grey seal of Devon and Cornwall. *Zoological Cornwall and The Isles of Scilly* **2**. CBRU.

Wheeler, A. (1994) Field key to the shore fishes of the British Isles. *Field Studies* **8**: 481–521.

White, W. (1855) *A Londoner's Walk to the Land's End and a Trip to the Scilly Isles.* London.

Wigginton, M. J. (ed.) (1999) *British Red Data Books 1. Vascular Plants*, 3rd edn. JNCC, Peterborough.

Williams, C. (1997) *Bats of the Isles of Scilly.* Report on behalf of Cornwall Bat Group.

Williams, C. (1998) *Bats of the Isles of Scilly: Report No. 2.* Report on behalf of Cornwall Bat Group.

Williamson, K, Parslow, J. L. F & Dance, S. P. (1959) Snails carried by birds. *Bird Migration* **1**: 91–93.

Wilson, P. & King, M. (2003) *Arable Plants: a Field Guide.* English Nature & Wildguides, Old Basing.

Woodley, G. (1822) *A View of the Present State of the Scilly Islands.* London.

Yalden, D. (1999) *The History of British Mammals.* Poyser, London.

Yarrow, I. H. H. (1967) The Aculeate Hymenoptera of the Isles of Scilly. *Entomologist's Monthly Magazine* **103**: 63–65.

Yonge, C. M. (1949) *The Sea Shore.* New Naturalist 12. Collins, London.

Species Index

brown rat 39, 184, 327, 335, 373
brown shrimp 170
brown venus 167
bryophytes 24, 57, 88–9, 184, 216, 218, 247, 278, 395
bryozoans 139, 148, 160, 161
Bryum bornholmense 218
B. torquescens 218
B. valparaisense 247, 418
buck's-horn plantain 70, 81, 187, 205, 206, 398, 399, 400, 404
budgerigar 364
buff-breasted sandpiper 379
buff-tailed bumblebee 311, 313, 320
Bufo bufo (toad) 22, 327
bugle lily 82
bugloss 260, 269
bulbous buttercup 257
bulbous rush 67, 233
bullfinch 359, 361
bulrush 85, 232
bumblebees 308, 311–13, 320, 409
Bunodactis verrucosa (gem anemone) 149–50
buoy barnacle 175
bur chervil 258, 268
burdock 43
Burhinus oedicnemus (stone-curlew) 348
bush-crickets 57, 196, 289–90
butcher's-broom 125, 128
Buteo buteo (buzzard) 348, 375
buttercups 205, 239, 246, 252, 255–6, 262
butterfish 147
butterflies 298–305
buzzard 348, 375
by-the-wind-sailor 174, 176, 189

cabbage palm tree 285, 292
caddis flies 295
cage fungus 255
Cakile maritima (sea rocket) 91, 183, 188, 190, 403
Calamagrostis epigejos (wood small-reed) 125
Calcarius lapponicus (Lapland bunting) 379

Calidris alba (sanderling) 190
C. alpina (dunlin) 190
C. canutus (knot) 348
C. maritima (purple sandpiper) 374
C. melanotos (pectoral sandpiper) 379
C. minuta (little stint) 190, 379
Callionymus lyra (dragonet) 170
Calliostoma zizphinum (painted top shell) 157
Callista chione (brown venus) 167
Callitriche spp. (starworts) 81, 86, 226, 233, 237
C. brutia (pedunculate water-starwort) 235
Calluna vulgaris (ling) 26, 397, 398
Calonectris diomedea (Cory's shearwater) 382
Caloplaca spp. 140, 185
C. marina 140
C. verruculifera 186
Calyptrochaeta apiculata 88, 186
Calystegia sepium (hedge bindweed) 237
C. soldanella (sea bindweed) 97, 99, 189, 192, 193
Camptogramma bilineata (yellow shell) 296
Campylopus introflexus 89, 395
C. pilifer 218
Canada goose 356, 362
Cancer pagurus (edible crab) 153
Candidula intersecta (wrinkled snail) 322
Caprella linearis (ghost shrimp) 152
Capreolus capreolus (roe deer) 22, 340
Capsella bursa-pastoris (shepherd's-purse) 70, 407
Carabus problematicus 317
C. violaceus (violet ground beetle) 317, 332
Carcinus maenas (shore crab) 152–3, 232
Cardamine pratensis (lady's-smock) 205, 224, 234

Carduelis cannabina (linnet) 359, 361
C. carduelis (goldfinch) 359, 361
C. chloris (greenfinch) 359, 361
C. flammea (redpoll) 380
Carex arenaria (sand sedge) 83, 111, 189, 194, 204, 216, 398, 404
C. divulsa (grey sedge) 224
C. paniculata (tussock-sedge) 75, 225, 237
C. sylvatica (wood sedge) 224
Carpinus betulus (hornbeam) 23
Carpobrotus spp. 8, 75
C. acinaciformis (sally-my-handsome) 91, 194
C. edulis (Hottentot fig) 8, 68, 118–19, 125, 129–30, 192, 194, 312, 394, 399
carragheen 144
carrion crow 359, 362
Caruana's Sicilian slug 324
Caryophyllia smithii (Devonshire cup-coral) 151
Celastrina argiolus (holly blue) 250, 303
Celtic bean 28
Centaurea nigra (knapweed) 204, 401
Centaurium erythraea (common centaury) 194, 205
Centranthus ruber (red valerian) 297
Cepaea nemoralis (grove or brown-lipped snail) 322
Cephaloziella turneri 218
Cerastium diffusum (sea mouse-ear) 398
C. fontanum (common mouse-ear) 401
C. glomeratum (sticky mouse-ear) 247, 406, 407
Cerastoderma edule (cockle) 30, 167
Ceratochloa cathartica (rescue brome) 260, 275
Cereus pedunculatus (daisy anemone) 168
Cernuella virgata (striped snail) 322, 324
Cervus elaphus (red deer) 22, 340

green tiger beetle 67, 219, 316
green-veined white 299
greenfinch 359, 361
greenshank 374
grey bush-cricket 80, 196, 290
grey field-speedwell 260, 271
grey heron 96, 147, 348, 356
grey mullet 22, 80, 139, 144, 232
grey partridge 356, 364
grey phalarope 233, 382
grey sallow 66, 75–6, 118, 127, 224, **225**, 405
grey sea slug 160
grey seal **56**, 110, 116–17, 125, **127**, 129, 326, 336–9, **337**, 339, **340**
grey sedge 224
grey squirrel 329
grey top shell 157
grey triggerfish 173, 387
grey wagtail 379
ground bug 294
groundsel 296, 407
grove snail 322
guillemot 113, 347, 350, 357, 365, **367**
Gunnera tinctori (giant rhubarb plant) 66
gutweed 141

Haematopus ostralegus (oystercatcher) **184**, 190, 357, 360
hairy bird's-foot-trefoil 65, 258, 266, 399
hairy buttercup 75, 233, 257, 258
hairy crab 153, **154**
hairy tare 407
Halichoerus grypus (grey seal) **56**, 110, 116–17, 125, **127**, 129, 326, 336–9, **337**, 339, **340**
Halichondria panicea (breadcrumb sponge) 147
Haliclystus auricula 148
Halorates reprobus 318
harbour porpoise 173, 341, 342, 382
harvest mite 320
harvestmen 319
hawk-moths 295–8
hawthorn 294

hawthorn shield bug 294
hazel 23, 25–6, 223
heath bedstraw 203, 397–8, 401
heath bumblebee 313
heath dodder 93
heath-grass 209, 397, 401
heath groundsel 296
heather 1, 64–5, 67, 81, 83, 86, 91–2, 123, 127, 194, 209–12, 216, 218–19, 221, 311, 313, 397, 398
Hebe × franciscana (hedge veronica) 249, 303
Hedera helix (ivy) 224, 229, 249, 303, 405
hedge bindweed 237
hedge veronica 249, 303
hedgehog 161, 315, 327, 332, 344, 394
Helcion pellucidum (blue-rayed limpet) 141, 157
Helix aspersa (garden snail) 322, **323**
Helophilus pendulus (sun-fly) 307
H. trivittatus (sun-fly) 307
Hemiptera 294
hemlock 118
hemlock water-dropwort 23, 66, 75, 204, 225–6, 237
henbit dead-nettle 260, 269
Heracleum sphondylium (hogweed) 118
hermit crabs 155
herring gull 102, 109–11, 113, 129, 175, 350, 357, 369, 370
Heteroderma leucomela (ciliate strap-lichen) 67, 69, 216, 399
H. japonica 216
Heteroptera 294
Hieracium pilosella (mouse-ear hawkweed) **93**
Himanthalia elongata (thongweed) 138, 142, **143**
Himantopus himantopus (black-winged stilt) 77
Hinia incrassatus (thick-lipped dog whelk) 158
H. reticulata (netted dog whelk) 158, 167
Hippocampus ramulosus (seahorse) 171

Hippolais icterina (icterine warbler) 379
H. polyglotta (melodious warbler) 379
Hirundo rustica (swallow) 358, 362, 375
hogweed 118, 123, 292, 405, 406
Holcus lanatus (Yorkshire fog) 111, **112**, 129, 181, 205, 397, 399, 400–1, 404
hollowed glass snail 324
holly 303
holly blue **250**, 303
Holothuria forskali (cotton-spinner) 166
holothurians or sea cucumbers 161
Homarus gammarus (lobster) 140, **172**
Homoeosma nimbella 295
Honckenya peploides (sea sandwort) 74, 182–3, 188, 192, 403
honeybee 313
honeysuckle 297
hooded crow 362
hoopoe 377, **378**
Hordeum vulgare (barley) 28, 29, 39
hornbeam 23
hornworts 11
hornwrack 161
Hottentot fig 8, 68, 118–19, 125, 129–30, 192, 194, 312, 394, 399
house holly-fern 73
house martin 358, 362
house mouse 327, 336
house sparrow 88, 350, 355, 359, 361
hoverflies 271, 306–8, 409
hummingbird hawk-moth 297, **298**
Hyacinthoides hispanica (Spanish bluebell) 272
H. non-scripta (bluebell) 111, 204, 224, 272, 400–1, 405–6
Hydrobates pelagicus (storm petrel) 102, 110–11, 113, 117, 120, 181, 352, 356, 365, 367–8, 382, 394, 414

SPECIES INDEX · 435

Pluvialis apricaria (golden
plover) 374
Poa infirma (early meadow-
grass) 46, 97, 99, 273, 399
pochard 356
Podiceps auritus (Slavonian
grebe) 374
Poeticus recurvus 244
pointed snail 322, 324
Polinices spp. (necklace shell)
167
Polycarpon tetraphyllum (four-
leaved allseed) 60, 254, 258,
264, 284, 406
Polycera quadrilineata **160**
polychaete worms 151
Polygala spp. (milkwort) 212,
397, 398
Polygonia c-album (comma)
298–9, 413
Polygonum (knotgrass) 29
P. aviculare (common
knotgrass) 407
P. maritimum (sea knotgrass)
182, 189
P. oxyspermum (Ray's knotgrass)
189
Polyommatus icarus (common
blue butterfly) 220, 123, **300**
Polysiphonia lanosa 144
Polystichum setiferum (soft
shield-fern) 67, 226
polyzoans 139, 148, 160, 161
Pomatoceros triqueter (keeled
worm) 151
Pomatoschistus microps
(common goby) 145
P. minutus (sand goby) 170, 232
Ponentina subvirescens 322
poplar 279
Populus × *jackii* (balm-of-Gilead
or balsam poplar) 130–1
Porcellana platycheles (broad-
clawed porcelain crab) 153
Portland spurge 60, 80, 93, 99,
123, 126, 128, 194, 216, 294,
306, 397, 398, 403, 404
Portuguese man-of-war 174
Porzana porzana (spotted crake)
379

Potamogeton pectinatus (fennel-
leaved pondweed) 81, 96, 121,
233–5, 402
P. polygonifolius (bog pondweed)
236
potato 39, 40–1, 240, 247, 280,
407
Potentilla anserina 194, 402
P. erecta (tormentil) 67
Praunus flexuosus (chameleon
prawn) 152, 232
prickly saltwort 189
prickly stick insect 292, **293**
primrose **43**, 106
Primula vulgaris (primrose) **43**,
106
privet 43, 91
Prunella modularis (dunnock)
219, 355, *358*, 359
Psammechinus miliaris (green
sea urchin) 162
Pseudocyphellaria aurata (gilt-
edged lichen) 132, 216
pseudoscorpions 128, 319
Psithyrus vestalis (vestal cuckoo
bee) 313
Pteridium aquilinum (bracken) 1,
25–6, 42, 64, 66–7, 70, 73,
91–2, 97, 99, 101–3, 106–8,
111, 118–19, 121, 123, 126–8,
130–1, 195, 204, 209–10,
212–13, 215–16, 220, 273, 318,
328, 369, 400–1, 406
Puccinellia distans 403
P. maritima (saltmarsh-grass)
232, 403
puffin 32–4, 109–10, **113**, 115,
118, 120, 326, 346, *350*, 357, 365,
366, 370, 389, 390–1, 394, 399
Puffinus gravis (great
shearwater) **382**
P. griseus (sooty shearwater) 382
P. puffinus (Manx shearwater)
32, 102, 110–11, 113, 213, 220,
346, *348*, 352, 356, 365, 367–8,
368, 382, 389, 394, 413, 414
purple heart urchin 165
purple heron 377
purple-loosestrife 226, 237
purple ramping-fumitory 258,
263

purple sandpiper 374
purple sunstar 162, 175
purple viper's-bugloss 269, 394
purse sponge 147
purse-web spider 318
Puya chilensis 88
pyramidal orchid 108
Pyronia tithonus (gatekeeper)
298
Pyrrhocorax pyrrhocorax
(chough) 350
Pyrrhosoma nymphula (large red
damselfly) 287
Pyrrhula pyrrhula (bullfinch) 359,
361

quaking-grass 254, 273
Queen of Spain **299**
Quercus (oak) 23–6, 125, 223, 279,
405

rabbit 40, 48, 73, 97, 99, 102–3,
105, 108, 111, 203, 205, 218,
234, 326, 327, 328–9, 363, 399,
401, 404
Radde's warbler 380
Radiola linoides (allseed) 234
ragworms 151, 232
ragwort 194, 296, 401
Rallus aquaticus (water rail) 357,
362
Ramalina spp. 184
R. chondrina 186
R. portuensis 226
R. siliquosa 140, 184
R. phycopsis 185
R. siliquosa 69, 140
Rana temporaria (common frog)
327, 343
Ranunculus spp. **205,** 239, 246,
252, 255–6, **262**
R. baudotii (brackish water-
crowfoot) 81, 91, 233, 236, 402
R. bulbosus (bulbous buttercup)
257
R. flammula (lesser spearwort)
67, 84, 85–6, 204, **205**, 231,
232, 233, 234, 236, 237, 402,
408
R. hederaceus (ivy-leaved
crowfoot) 229

General Index

The New Naturalist Library